PHOTOSHOP CS4

for Windows and Macintosh
Visual QuickStart Guide

Elaine Weinmann

Peter Lourekas

Peachpit Press

For Alicia

Visual QuickStart Guide
Photoshop CS4 for Windows and Macintosh
Elaine Weinmann and Peter Lourekas

Peachpit Press
1249 Eighth Street
Berkeley, CA 94710

510/524-2178
510/524-2221 (fax)

Find us on the Web at: www.peachpit.com

To report errors, please send a note to errata@peachpit.com

Peachpit Press is a division of Pearson Education

Copyright © 2009 by Elaine Weinmann and Peter Lourekas

Cover Design: Peachpit Press
Interior Design: Elaine Weinmann
Production: Elaine Weinmann and Peter Lourekas
Illustrations: Elaine Weinmann and Peter Lourekas, except as noted

ISBN-13: 978–0-321–56365–1

ISBN-10: 0-321-56365-4

9 8 7 6 5 4 3

Printed and bound in the United States of America

ACKNOWLEDGMENTS

Under Nancy Aldrich-Ruenzel's energetic leadership, Peachpit Press is a thriving and dynamic publishing house. We're grateful to her for encouraging us to redo this book in full color, and for her unwavering confidence in us.

The multitalented Victor Gavenda, longtime editor at Peachpit Press, tech edited this book in Windows with his usual keen intelligence and wit.

Susan Rimerman, our new editor at Peachpit, doesn't miss a beat. We look forward to working with her on future projects.

Production editor Lisa Brazieal does an expert job of spearheading the prepress production and sends the files off to Courier Printing.

Peachpit Press is also blessed to have Nancy Davis, editor-in-chief; Gary-Paul Prince, PTG tradeshow and conventions manager; and Keasley Jones, business manager, on staff; and a host of other terrific folks.

Elaine Soares, photo researcher, and Melinda Patelli, director, of the Image Resource Center at Pearson Education, the parent company of Peachpit Press, procured the stock images used throughout the book and responded quickly to all of our requests.

Rebecca Pepper has copy-edited so many editions of this book, she recently noted, "This book is starting to seem like an old friend!" As expected, she did a thorough and thoughtful job on this one.

Our "virtual" book packaging department for this edition also included Rebecca Plunkett, who generated the index, and Leona Benten, who did the final round of proofreading.

For creating a great product that's a pleasure to use and write about, and for helping beta testers like ourselves untangle the mysteries of Photoshop by way of the online forum, we commend John Nack, Photoshop product manager; Vishal Khandpur, senior prerelease program associate; and other members of the Photoshop CS4 product team.

Most important, our love and heartfelt appreciation to Alicia and Simona (budding Photoshoppers!), for making it all worthwhile.

Elaine Weinmann and Peter Lourekas

INSTRUCTORS! READERS!

The Adobe Creative Suite upgrades approximately every year and a half. Although that pace leaves us huffing and puffing, we also welcome the challenge and innovations that each revision cycle presents us with. At the very least, our jobs are never boring! Moreover, compulsive perfectionists that we are, each upgrade also presents us with yet another opportunity to improve, refine, and redesign our books.

Is there a topic that you would like us to cover, or cover in more depth, or clarify, or explore from a different angle? Have you discovered a special workflow or sequence of commands that you'd like to share with us — and potentially with other readers? Let us know via email, care of our publisher, Peachpit Press: www.peachpit.com/photoshopcs4vqs

Chapters at a glance

1   Color Management 1

2   Acquire, Create, Save 19

3   Bridge 33

4   Workspaces. 61

5   Panels 77

6   Pixel Basics 97

7   Layer Basics 109

8   Select. 123

9   Combine Images 145

10   History 165

11   Tonal Adjustments. 175

12   Colors & Blending Modes . .191

13   Color Adjustments 203

14   Brushes 223

15   Camera Raw 233

16   Exposure. 257

17   Refocus 265

18   Retouch 279

19   More Layers 297

20   Layer Styles. 317

21   Filters 333

22   Type 351

23   Gradients 369

24   Presentation 375

25   Preferences & Presets 387

26   Print 405

27   Export. 415

     Index 427

TABLE OF CONTENTS

★ Indicates topics in which new (Photoshop CS4) features are covered

Contents

1 Color Management

Launching Photoshop. 1
Displays, modes, and channels. 2
Introduction to color management 5
Setting a camera's color space to Adobe RGB 5
Calibrating your display ★ 7
Choosing a color space for Photoshop 10
Synchronizing color settings 12
Customizing your color policies 13
Saving custom color settings 14
Acquiring printer profiles 14
Changing color profiles 16
Proofing colors onscreen 17

2 Acquire, Create, Save

Using digital cameras. 19
16 Bits/Channel mode 21
Calculating the file resolution 22
Using a scanner. 23
Creating new, blank documents 24
Creating document presets 26
Using the Place command 27
Saving files. 28
Using the Status bar ★ 31
Ending a work session ★ 32

3 Bridge

Launching Bridge ★ 33
Downloading photos from a camera ★ 34
The Bridge window ★ 36
Choosing a workspace for Bridge ★ 38
Previewing images in Bridge ★ 40
Opening files from Bridge ★ 44
Customizing the Bridge window ★ 44
Saving custom workspaces ★ 47
Resetting the Bridge workspace ★ 47
Moving and copying files. 47
Labeling and rating thumbnails ★ 48
Choosing a sorting order ★ 49
Using the Filter panel ★ 49
Using thumbnail stacks. 50

Managing files ★ 51
Searching for files ★ 53
Creating collections ★ 54
Exporting the Bridge cache ★ 56
Assigning keywords to files ★ 57
Opening PDF and Illustrator files 58
Dealing with the "ifs". 60

4 Workspaces

Using the Application frame ★ 61
Using tabbed document windows ★ 63
Arranging document windows ★ 64
Changing the zoom level ★. 65
Rotating the view ★ 67
Changing the screen mode ★ 68
Changing the color behind the image ★ 69
Configuring the panels ★ 69
Customizing the menus ★. 72
Saving workspaces ★ 74
Restoring the default workspace ★ 75
Using the Application bar ★ 76
Using the Options bar. 76

5 Panels

The Photoshop panel icons ★ 78
The Photoshop panels illustrated ★ 79

6 Pixel Basics

Changing resolution and dimensions. 97
Changing the canvas size 102
Cropping images 103
Flipping and rotating images ★. 107
Straightening images ★ 108

7 Layer Basics

Creating layers 109
Duplicating layers 111
Converting the Background 112
Selecting layers. 113
Restacking layers 114
Working with layer groups. 114
Deleting individual layers ★ 116

Hiding and showing layers. 116
Moving layer content 117
Choosing Layers panel options. 118
Merging layers. 120
Flattening layers 122

8 Select

Creating layer-based selections 123
Using the Rectangular and Elliptical
    Marquee tools 124
Using the lasso tools 125
Using the Quick Selection tool ★. 126
Using the Magic Wand tool 128
Creating a silhouette 129
Using the Color Range command ★ 130
Refining selection edges ★. 132
Deselecting and reselecting selections 135
Deleting selected pixels 135
Moving and transforming selection marquees ★. .136
Hiding and showing the selection marquee 137
Swapping and intersecting selections 137
Creating frame-shaped selections 138
Saving and loading selections ★ 139
Using Quick Masks ★ 142
The selection methods compared 144

9 Combine Images

Moving selection contents ★ 145
Duplicating selections ★ 146
Using the Clipboard .148
Matching image dimensions. 151
Copying layers between files ★ 152
Blending imagery using layer masks 154
Using the Clone Source panel ★. 156
Stitching photos together ★. 158
Blending seams manually 160
Using the rulers, guides, and grid ★. 161
Aligning and distributing layers 164

10 History

Choosing History panel options 165
Changing history states 167
Deleting and clearing history states 168

Using snapshots 169
Creating documents from states 171
Using the History Brush tool 172
Filling an area with a history state 174

11 Tonal Adjustments

Creating adjustment layers ★ 175
Editing adjustment layer settings ★. 177
Saving adjustment presets ★ 178
Merging and deleting adjustment layers ★ 179
Adjustment layer techniques 180
Editing adjustment layer masks ★ 181
Applying a Threshold adjustment ★ 182
Applying a Posterize adjustment ★ 183
Using the Histogram panel ★ 184
Creating a Levels adjustment layer ★ 186
Adjusting brightness and contrast ★ 189
Dodging and burning 190

12 Colors & Blending Modes

Choosing colors. 191
Using the Color Picker. 192
Choosing colors from a color library 193
Using the Color panel 194
Using the Swatches panel 195
Using the Eyedropper tool ★. 197
Copying colors as hexadecimals 197
Choosing a blending mode. 198

13 Color Adjustments

Creating fill layers 204
Converting layers to grayscale ★ 206
Creating a Vibrance adjustment layer ★ 208
Creating a Color Balance adjustment layer ★ . . .211
Creating a Hue/Saturation adjustment layer ★. . .213
Applying an Auto Color Correction ★ 214
Creating a Levels adjustment layer ★ 216
Creating a Curves adjustment layer ★. 218

14 Brushes

Using the Brush tool 223
Choosing temporary brush settings ★. 224
Using the Brushes panel ★ 225

Customizing brushes. 226
Smudging colors .230
Using the Eraser tool 231
Using the Magic Eraser tool 232

15 Camera Raw

Why use Camera Raw?. 233
Choosing preferences for opening photos ★ 236
Opening photos into Camera Raw ★ 237
The Camera Raw tools ★. 239
Cropping and straightening photos. 240
Retouching photos ★. 241
Changing the Workflow options 241
Using the Basic tab 242
Using the Tone Curve tab 246
Using the HSL/Grayscale tab 248
Using the Detail tab. 250
Saving and applying Camera Raw settings 251
Using the Adjustment Brush ★ 252
Synchronizing Camera Raw settings 254
Opening and saving Camera Raw files 255
Opening and placing photos as Smart Objects . . .256

16 Exposure

Using the Shadows/Highlights command 257
Applying a Photo Filter adjustment ★. 260
Correcting exposure via the Layers panel ★ 261
Applying the Lighting Effects filter. 262

17 Refocus

Using the Lens Blur filter. 265
Using the Motion Blur filter 268
Changing the focus with a vignette. 270
Using the Lens Correction filter 272
Using the sharpening filters. 274

18 Retouch

Using the Match Color command. 280
Cloning ★ 282
Using the Replace Color command ★ 284
Using the Surface Blur filter. 287
Using the Color Replacement tool. 288
Using the Healing Brush tool ★. 290

Using the Spot Healing Brush tool 293
Using the Patch tool. 294
Using the Red Eye tool 296

19 More Layers

Changing layer opacity and fill values 297
Blending layers 298
Creating layer masks ★ 302
Editing layer masks ★ 303
Working with layer masks ★ 306
Using clipping masks 308
Linking layers ★ 309
Transforming layers ★ 310
Warping layers. 313
Using Smart Object layers 314
Filling areas with a solid color ★ 316

20 Layer Styles

Applying layer effects (general info). 317
Applying a shadow effect 320
Applying a glow effect 322
Applying a bevel or emboss effect. 324
Applying a satin effect 326
Applying the overlay effects 327
Applying a stroke effect 329
Copying, moving, and removing layer effects 330
Applying layer styles 331
Creating layer styles. 332

21 Filters

Applying filters 333
Creating and using Smart Filters ★. 336
Filter pro techniques 338
Most of the filters illustrated 341
Photos into drawings or paintings 349

22 Type

Creating editable type 352
Selecting type. 354
Converting type. 355
Importing type from Adobe Illustrator as
  a Smart Object. .355
Changing the font .356

Scaling type 356
Kerning and tracking type 357
Adjusting leading .358
Changing the type style 359
Shifting type from the baseline 359
Changing the orientation of type 360
Applying paragraph settings 361
Transforming type via its bounding box 362
Warping type. 363
Rasterizing type. 364
Filling type with imagery. 364
Making type fade ★ 366
Screening back type ★ 367
Putting type in a spot color channel 368

23 Gradients
Creating a gradient fill layer 369
Using the Gradient tool. 371
Creating and editing gradient presets 372

24 Presentation
Creating a vignette ★ 375
Adding a hand-painted border ★ 376
Adding a watermark 378
Creating a contact sheet ★ 380
Creating a PDF presentation ★ 382
Creating and using layer comps 384
Creating a PDF presentation of layer comps ★ . . .386

25 Preferences & Presets
Opening the Preferences dialogs. 387
General Preferences ★ 388
Interface Preferences ★ 390
File Handling Preferences 392
Performance Preferences ★ 393
Cursors Preferences ★ 394
Transparency & Gamut Preferences 394
Units & Rulers Preferences. 395
Guides, Grid & Slices Preferences 396
Plug-ins Preferences ★ 396
Type Preferences 397
The Bridge Preferences ★ 398

Using the Preset Manager 400
Managing presets via pickers and panels 402
Creating tool presets 404

26 Print
Choosing Properties/Page Setup settings
    for inkjet printing 406
Choosing Print dialog settings for
    inkjet printing ★ .407
Choosing Output options ★ 410
Printing the file in Windows. 411
Printing the file in the Mac OS 412
Creating a duotone. .413
Preparing a file for commercial printing. 413

27 Export
Preparing files for other applications. 415
Saving files in the TIFF format 417
Saving files in the EPS format 418
Saving files in the PDF format 420
Saving files for the Web 421
Previewing optimized files ★ 422
Optimizing files in the GIF format ★ 423
Optimizing files in the JPEG format ★ 425

Index 427

REGISTER THIS BOOK!

Purchasing this book entitles you to more than just a couple of pounds of paper. If you register the book with Peachpit Press, you're also entitled to download copies of most of the images used throughout the book, which you can use to practice with as you follow the step-by-step tutorials. To get started, follow this link: www.peachpit.com/photoshopcs4vqs. This takes you to the book's page at the Peachpit Press website. Once there, click Register your book to log in to your account at peachpit.com. If you don't already have an account, it takes just a few seconds to create one, and it's free!

After logging in, you'll need to enter the book's ISBN code, which you'll find on the back cover. Click Submit,

and you're in! You'll be taken to a list of your registered books. Find *Photoshop CS4 Visual QuickStart Guide* on the list, and click Access to protected content to get to the download page.

Please note that these images are low-resolution (not suitable for printing), and they are copyrighted by their owners, who have watermarked them to discourage unauthorized reproduction. They are for your personal use only, not for distribution.

Of course, you're not restricted to using the downloadable photos that accompany the text. For any given set of instructions, you can substitute a photo of your own or choose a different photo from the assortment offered.

Downloadable images

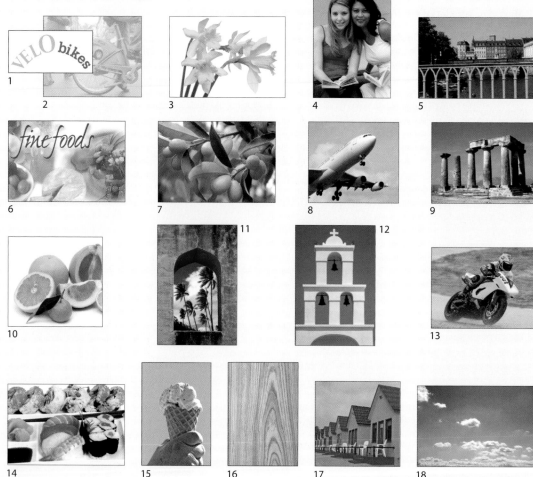

1

2

3

4

5

6

7

8

9

10

11

12

13

14

15

16

17

18

19

20

21

22a–c

23

24

25

26

27

28

29

30

31

32

33

34

35

36

37

38

39

40

41

42

43

44

45

46

47

48

49

50

51

52

53

54

55

56

57

58

59

60

61

62

63

64

65

66

67

68

69

70

Welcome to Photoshop! In this chapter, you'll launch the application, then familiarize yourself with the Photoshop color basics, such as displays, document color modes, and channels. Most important, before you start editing images—and also before outputting your file—you need to incorporate color management into your workflow. You'll accomplish this by calibrating your display, choosing color settings, and downloading the necessary printer profiles.

Launching Photoshop

To launch Photoshop in Windows:

Do one of the following:

In Windows XP or Vista, click the Start button on the taskbar, choose All Programs, then click Adobe Photoshop CS4.

Open the C:\Program Files\Adobe\Adobe Photoshop CS4 folder in My Computer, then double-click Photoshop.exe.

Double-click a Photoshop file icon.

To launch Photoshop in the Mac OS:

Do one of the following:

Click the Photoshop icon in the Dock. (If you don't have a Photoshop icon there yet, open the Adobe Photoshop CS4 folder in the Applications folder, then drag the Adobe Photoshop CS4 application icon into the Dock.)

Open the Adobe Photoshop CS4 folder in the Applications folder, then double-click the Adobe Photoshop CS4 application icon.

Double-click any Photoshop file icon.

NOT SEEING ENOUGH ONSCREEN?

If you want to open a file quickly to make the screen more "alive" as you read through this chapter, navigate to the Samples folder inside the Photoshop application folder, then double-click an image file, such as "Fish.psd." (Don't worry…you'll soon learn everything you need to know about opening photos and creating documents.)

FINDING THE NEW STUFF

This symbol ★ identifies features that are new to Photoshop CS4.

COLOR MANAGEMENT

1

IN THIS CHAPTER

Launching Photoshop 1

Displays, modes, and channels 2

Introduction to color management . . . 5

Setting a camera's color space to
    Adobe RGB 5

Calibrating your display 7

Choosing a color space for
    Photoshop. 10

Synchronizing color settings 12

Customizing your color policies 13

Saving custom color settings 14

Acquiring printer profiles. 14

Changing color profiles 16

Proofing colors onscreen 17

Displays, modes, and channels

Onscreen, your Photoshop image is a **bitmap**—a geometric arrangement (mapping) of dots on a rectangular grid. Each dot, or pixel, represents a different color or shade. Drag with a painting tool, such as the Brush, across an area of a layer, and pixels below your pointer will be recolored. With your document at a high zoom level, you can see, and even edit, individual pixels.**A** Bitmap programs like Photoshop are best suited for producing painterly, photographic, or photorealistic images that contain subtle gradations of color, called "continuous tones." The images you edit in Photoshop can originate from a digital camera or scanned photo, from a file you've saved in another application, or from scratch using painting tools and editing commands, such as filters.

To display color images, a computer display projects **red**, **green**, and **blue** (RGB) **light**. Combined in their purest form, these additive primaries produce white light. Send your Photoshop file for commercial, four-color process printing, and your print shop will render the image by using **cyan** (C), **magenta** (M), **yellow** (Y), and **black** (K) inks. Because computer displays use the RGB model, they can only simulate the CMYK inks that are used in commercial printing.

The successful translation of a digital image to a printed one isn't as simple as you might think. To begin with, the same document may look surprisingly different on different displays due to such variables as ambient lighting, the display temperature, and even the room color. Plus, many colors that you see in the natural world or that can be displayed onscreen can't be printed (have no ink equivalents), and some colors that can be printed can't be displayed onscreen. Luckily, the color management techniques that we outline in this chapter will help smooth out the kinks in the color workflow from digital input to print.

▶ In Photoshop, you can choose colors using the grayscale, RGB (red-green-blue), HSB (hue-saturation-brightness), CMYK (cyan-magenta-yellow-black), or Lab (lightness, a-component, and b-component) color model, or you can choose colors from a color matching system, such as PANTONE. If you choose a color in Photoshop that isn't within the gamut of printable colors, an exclamation point appears on the Color panel.**B** Exclamation points will also display on the Info panel if the color currently under the pointer is outside the printable gamut.**C** If you follow our steps for color management, though, you won't have to worry about converting individual colors.

Channels

Photoshop images are composed of one, three, or four **channels** (see the sidebar on the next page). In an RGB image, the three channels store the intensity of red, green, or blue at each pixel as a level of gray. Most likely you will work with images that store 256 levels of gray for each channel. Because the 256 gray levels are represented by 8 bits (short for "binary digits") of computer data, the bit depth of such an image is said to be 8 bits per channel. Files that have a higher bit depth—16 or 32 bits per channel—contain more color information (see page 21).

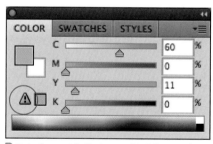

B Out-of-gamut indicator on the Color panel

A In this extreme close-up of an image, you can see individual pixels.

C Out-of-gamut indicators on the Info panel

➤ Open an RGB Color image. Click Red, Green, or Blue on the Channels panel to display only that channel, then click the topmost channel name on the Channels panel to restore the composite display. Although you can make color adjustments to individual channels, normally you'll edit all the channels at once while viewing the composite image.

In addition to the core channels just discussed, you can add two other types of channels. You can save a selection as a mask in a grayscale (alpha) channel, and you can add channels for individual spot colors.**A**

The more channels a document contains, the larger its file storage size. A document in RGB Color mode, which has three channels (Red, Green, and Blue), will be three times larger than if converted to Grayscale, a single-channel mode. Convert it to CMYK Color mode, and the file will have four channels (Cyan, Magenta, Yellow, and Black) and will be even larger.

Document color modes

A document can be converted to, displayed in, and edited in the following color modes: **Bitmap, Grayscale, Duotone, Indexed Color, RGB Color, CMYK Color, Lab Color,** or **Multichannel.** You'll use RGB and CMYK most often. To convert a document to a different mode, make a choice from the Image > **Mode** submenu.**B**

Some mode conversions can cause noticeable color shifts. For example, if you convert a file from RGB Color mode to CMYK Color mode, printable colors will be substituted for the luminous RGB colors. The fewer times you convert a file, the better, as the color data is altered with each conversion change.

Some conversions also flatten layers, such as a conversion to Indexed Color, Multichannel, or Bitmap mode. In other cases, you can click Don't Flatten in an alert dialog to preserve layers.

The availability of some commands and tool options in Photoshop will vary depending on the current document color mode.

Digital cameras and medium- to low-end scanners produce RGB images. For faster editing and in order to access all the filters in Photoshop, keep your files in RGB Color mode. In fact, most desktop color inkjet printers, especially those that use six or more ink colors, process RGB Color files directly from Photoshop.

Continued on the following page

B The Mode submenu

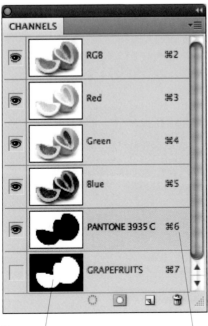

A An alpha channel   A spot color channel

DEFAULT CHANNELS PER IMAGE MODE		
One	Three	Four
Bitmap	RGB	CMYK
Grayscale	Lab	
Duotone	Multichannel	Multichannel
Indexed Color		

➤ You can use View > Proof Setup in conjunction with View > Proof Colors to preview, or "soft-proof," your RGB document in a simulation of CMYK Color mode without performing an actual mode change.

Images that are saved by high-end scanners in CMYK Color mode should be kept in that mode to preserve their color data. Photoshop can handle large scans, even those saved with a higher pixel depth of 16 bits or 32 bits per channel—although only limited edits can be made to 32-bit files.

➤ To access a mode that's dimmed on the menu, you must first convert your file to a different mode as an intermediate step. For example, for Indexed Color mode to be available, a file must be in RGB Color or Grayscale mode.

The following is a brief summary of the color modes that you can convert a document to in Photoshop:

In **Bitmap** mode, pixels are either 100% black or 100% white, and no layers, filters, or adjustment commands are available. (To convert a file to this mode, put it into Grayscale mode first.)

In **Grayscale** mode, pixels are black, white, or up to 254 shades of gray (a total of 256). If you convert a file from a color mode to Grayscale mode and then save and close it, the luminosity (light and dark) values will be preserved, but the color information will be deleted permanently.

To produce a **duotone**, two or more extra printing plates are added to a grayscale image to enhance its richness and tonal depth. This requires special preparatory steps in Photoshop and expertise on the part of your commercial printer.

Files in **Indexed Color** mode have a single channel and a color table that holds a maximum of 256 colors or shades (8-bit color). The relatively small file sizes of Indexed Color files once made this mode useful for Web output, but it's been surpassed by better methods, such as those offered in the Save for Web & Devices dialog.

RGB Color A is the most versatile mode of all and the one you'll use most often. It's the mode in which digital cameras save your photos, the only mode in which all the Photoshop tool options and filters are accessible, and the mode of choice for online output and for export to video and multimedia programs.

In Photoshop, although you can display and edit your files in **CMYK Color** mode, **B** we recommend that you edit them in RGB Color mode, then convert a copy of them to CMYK Color mode only when required for commercial printing or for export to a page layout application.

Lab Color is a three-channel mode that was developed for the purpose of achieving consistency among various devices, such as printers and displays. Lab Color files are device-independent, meaning their color definitions stay the same regardless of how a particular output device defines color. The channels represent lightness (the image details), the colors green to red, and the colors blue to yellow. The lightness and color values can be edited independently of one another. Although Photoshop uses Lab Color to produce better conversions between RGB and CMYK color modes internally, there's rarely a need for users to convert files to Lab Color mode.

Multichannel images contain multiple 256-level grayscale channels. Some Photoshop pros assemble individual channels from several images into a single composite image using this mode. If you convert an image from RGB Color to Multichannel mode, its Red, Green, and Blue channels will be converted to Cyan, Magenta, and Yellow; this may lighten the image and reduce the contrast.

With this foundation in color basics, you're ready to take the plunge into color management.

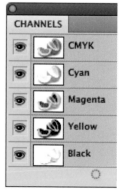

A The number of channels varies with the document color mode. This image is in RGB Color mode.

B This image is in CMYK Color mode.

Introduction to color management

Problems with color can creep up on you when the various hardware devices and software packages you use treat color differently. If you were to compare how an image looks in an assortment of imaging programs and Web browsers, the colors might look completely different in each case and may not match the picture you originally shot with your digital camera or digitized via a scanner. Print the image, and you'll probably find that your results are different yet again. In some cases, you might find these differences to be slight and unobjectionable, but in other cases such color shifts can wreak havoc with your design and turn a project into a disaster!

A color management system can solve most of these problems by acting as a color interpreter. Such a system knows how each device and program interprets color and will adjust colors if necessary to keep them as consistent as possible as you shuttle your files among various programs or devices. The applications in the Adobe Creative Suite 4 use standardized ICC (International Color Consortium) profiles, which tell your color management system how specific devices use color.

Each particular device can capture and reproduce only a limited range (gamut) of colors, which is known as the **color space** of the device. The mathematical description of the color space of each device is called the **color profile**. An input device, such as a camera, attaches its own profile to the files it produces. Photoshop uses that profile to display and edit document colors; or if the document doesn't have a profile, Photoshop uses the current **working space** (a color space you choose for Photoshop) instead.

Color management is especially important if you're going to use the same image for multiple purposes, such as for online and print output. Be sure to consult with your prepress service provider or commercial printer (if you're using one) about color management to ensure that your color management works smoothly with theirs.

The "meat" of this chapter consists of instructions for choosing color management options, which you should follow before you perform any image editing in Photoshop. Our instructions are centered around using **Adobe RGB** as the color space for your image-editing work to create color consistency throughout your workflow. We'll show you how to set the color space of your digital camera to Adobe RGB, calibrate your display, specify Adobe RGB as the color space in Photoshop, acquire the proper profiles for your printer and paper type, and use those profiles to soft-proof the image.

In the Print chapter, we'll show you how color management comes into play when outputting files from a color inkjet printer (a device that expects files to be in RGB color). In this case, the most important step is to choose the correct output profile for your printer. We'll also show you how to choose the appropriate output profiles when outputting to the Web or to a commercial press.

Setting a camera's color space to Adobe RGB

Most high-end, advanced amateur digital cameras and digital SLR cameras have an onscreen menu that lets you customize how the camera processes digital images. Although we'll use a Canon Digital Rebel as our representative model for setting a camera to the Adobe RGB color space, you'll follow a similar procedure to set the color space for your camera.

If you shoot photos in the JPEG format, you should choose Adobe RGB as the color space for your camera, regardless of which model you have. If you shoot raw files, these steps are optional, as you will assign the Adobe RGB color space when you convert your photos via the Camera Raw plug-in.

Continued on the following page

To set a camera's color space to Adobe RGB:

1. On the back of the camera, click the **Menu** button to access the menu on the LCD screen, and then, if necessary, press the **Jump** button to select the **Shooting Menu** tab.**A**

2. Press the down arrow to select the **Parameters** category (some cameras label this category as Optimize).**B** Press the **Set** button to move to the submenu on the right (on some cameras, you need to press an arrow key instead).

3. Press the up or down arrow to select **Adobe RGB** (on some cameras you have to choose a Color Mode category first to get to Adobe RGB).**C–D**

4. Press the **Set** button, then press the **Menu** button to exit the Menu screen.

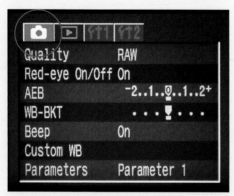

A On the Canon Menu screen, we select the Shooting Menu tab.

B We select the Parameters category next, then press Set to get to the submenu.

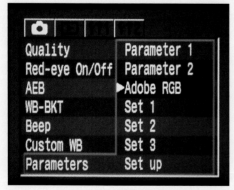

C We choose Adobe RGB from the submenu.

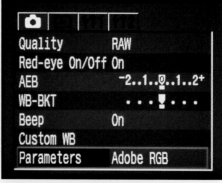

D Adobe RGB is now the color space for our camera.

Calibrating your display

Display types

There are two basic types of computer displays: CRT (cathode ray tube, as in a traditional TV set) and LCD (liquid crystal display, or flat panel). The display performance of a **CRT** fluctuates due to its analog technology and the fact that its display phosphors (which produce the glowing dots that you see onscreen) fade over time. A CRT display can be calibrated reliably for only around three years.

An **LCD** display uses a grid of fixed-sized liquid crystals that filter color coming from a back light source. Although you can adjust only the brightness on an LCD (not the contrast), the LCD digital technology offers more reliable color consistency than a CRT, without the characteristic flickering of a CRT. The newest LCD models provide good viewing angles, display accurate color, use the desired daylight temperature of 6500K for the white point (see below), and are produced under tighter manufacturing standards than CRTs. Moreover, in most cases the color profile that's provided with an LCD display (and that is installed in your system automatically) describes the display characteristics accurately.

➤ Both types of displays lose calibration gradually, and you may not notice it until the colors are way off. To maintain color consistency, try to stick to a regular monthly calibration schedule.

Understanding the calibration settings

Three basic characteristics are adjusted when a display is calibrated: The **brightness** (white level) is set to a consistent working standard; the **contrast** (dark level) is set to the maximum value; and finally, a **neutral gray** (gray level) is established using equal values of R, G, and B. To adjust these three characteristics, calibration devices evaluate the white point, black point, and gamma in the display.

➤ The **white point** data enables the display to project a pure white, which matches an industry-standard color temperature. Photographers usually use D65/6500K as the temperature setting for the white point.

➤ The **black point** is the darkest black a display can project. All other dark shades will be lighter than this darkest black, which ensures that shadow details display properly.

➤ The **gamma** defines how midtones are displayed onscreen. A gamma setting of 1.0 reproduces the linear brightness scale that is found in nature. Yet human vision responds to brightness in a nonlinear fashion, so this setting makes the screen look washed out. A higher gamma setting redistributes more of the midtones into the dark range, where our eyes are more sensitive, producing a more natural-looking image. Photography experts recommend using a gamma setting of 2.2 in both Windows and the Mac OS.

Buying a calibration device

The only way to calibrate a display properly is by using a hardware calibration device. It will produce a profile with the proper white point, black point, and gamma data settings for your display. The Adobe color management system, in turn, will use this data to display colors in your Photoshop document with greater accuracy.

If you're shopping for a calibration device, you'll notice a wide range in cost, from a colorimeter that will run between $100 and $300 to much more costly, but more precise, high-end professional gadgets, such as a spectrophotometer. A colorimeter and its step-by-step wizard tutorial will enable you to calibrate your display more accurately than a subjective "eyeball" judgment would.

Among moderately priced calibrators, our informal reading of hardware reviews and other industry publications has yielded the following as some current favorites: Spyder3Pro and Spyder3Elite by Datacolor; Eye-One Display 2 by X-Rite; and hueyPro, which was developed jointly by PANTONE and X-Rite.

Note: If, after calibrating your display, you adjust the display's brightness and contrast settings or change the room lighting, remember to recalibrate it!

For Mac OS users who don't have a calibration device, your system supplies a display calibration utility, found in System Preferences > Displays > Color. Click Calibrate and follow the instructions onscreen.

The steps outlined here will loosely apply to all three of the hardware display calibrators that are mentioned on the previous page. We happen to use Spyder3Pro.

To calibrate your display using a hardware device: ★

1. Set the room lighting to the usual level that you use for work. If you have a CRT, let it warm up for 30 minutes to allow the display to stabilize.

2. Increase the brightness of your display to its highest level. In the Mac OS, if you have an Apple-branded display, choose System Preferences > Displays and drag the Brightness slider to the far right. For a third-party display, or any display in Windows, use either an actual button on the display or a menu command in the OnScreen Display (OSD).

3. Launch the calibration application that you've installed, then follow the straightforward instructions on the step-by-step wizard screens. **A–B**

   You need to tell the application the following important information: the type of display you have (CRT or LCD); the white point you want to use (choose D65/6500K); and the gamma you want to use (choose 2.2 for both Windows and Macintosh). If you're calibrating a CRT display, you may see a few more instructional screens requesting more display setting choices.

4. After entering your display information (**A**, next page), you'll be prompted to drape the hardware calibration sensor (the colorimeter) over the monitor (**B**, next page). For an LCD, if a baffle is included with the calibration device, clip it on to prevent the suction cups from touching and potentially damaging the screen. Follow the instructions to align the sensor with the image onscreen. Click OK or Continue to initiate a series of calibration tests, which will take from 5 to 10 minutes.

5. After removing the calibration sensor, you'll be prompted to name your new display profile (**C**, next page). Include the date in the profile name for your own reference. The application will place the new profile in the correct location for use by your Windows or Macintosh operating system. The wizard will step you through one or two more screens, then you're done. Upon launching, Photoshop will automatically be aware of the new display profile.

A We launched the Sypder3Pro application, then answered questions on the Display Type screens to tell the wizard software that we have an LCD monitor and what features are present on our monitor, clicking Next to get from one screen to the next.

B On the Methods Of Attachment screen, we clicked No Suction Cup.

A The resulting settings appeared on this Current Settings screen.

B When this Measuring Display screen appeared, we draped the colorimeter over the monitor and aligned it with the onscreen image, then clicked Continue to start the actual calibration process.

C When the calibration was finished, we clicked Next, and this Specify Profile Name screen appeared. We included the monitor name and the current date in our profile name.

After clicking Next again, the SpyderProof screen appeared. We clicked Switch to compare the pre- and postcalibration results. Finally, we clicked Next, chose Quit, then clicked Next one last time to exit the software.

Choosing a color space for Photoshop

Continuing with our color management steps, you'll use the Color Settings dialog to set the color space for Photoshop. If you want to get up and running quickly in the Adobe RGB color space without wading through all the options in the Color Settings dialog, you can make one simple preset choice by following the first set of instructions below—that is, if you use Photoshop primarily to produce images for print output on a commercial or color inkjet printer and you've followed our instructions for color management so far.

To choose a color settings preset:

1. Choose Edit > **Color Settings** (Ctrl-Shift-K/ Cmd-Shift-K). The Color Settings dialog opens (**A**, next page).

2. Choose **Settings**: **North America Prepress 2** (readers outside North America, choose an equivalent for your output device and geographic location). This preset changes the RGB working space to Adobe RGB (1998) and sets the color management policies to the safe choice of Preserve Embedded Profiles (so each file you open in Photoshop keeps its own profile).

3. Click OK.

If you want to explore the Color Settings dialog in more depth, follow this set of instructions instead. Note that these instructions are generic, so you'll have to pick and choose among the options, depending on your output requirements.

To choose color settings options:

1. Choose Edit > **Color Settings** (Ctrl-Shift-K/ Cmd-Shift-K). The Color Settings dialog opens (**A**, next page).

2. Choose a preset from the **Settings** menu (we'll summarize the four basic presets):

    Monitor Color sets the RGB working space to your display profile. This is a good choice for video output, but not for print output.

    North America General Purpose 2 meets the requirements for screen and print output in North America. All profile warnings are off.

    North America Prepress 2 manages color to conform with common press conditions in North America. The default RGB color space

assigned to this setting is Adobe RGB. When CMYK documents are opened, their values are preserved.

North America Web/Internet is designed for online output. All RGB images are converted to the sRGB color space.

3. The **Working Spaces** settings control how RGB and CMYK colors will be treated in a document that lacks an embedded profile. You can either leave these settings as is or choose other options (the RGB options are discussed below). For the CMYK setting, you should ask your output service provider which working space to choose.

Choose one of these RGB color spaces:

Monitor RGB [current display profile] sets the RGB working space to your display profile, which is useful if you know that other applications you'll be using for your project don't support color management. Keep in mind, however, that if you share files that use your monitor profile (as the color space) with another user, their monitor profile will be substituted for the RGB working space. This may undermine the color consistency that you're aiming for.

ColorSync RGB (Mac OS only) matches the Photoshop RGB space to the space specified in the Apple ColorSync Utility. If you share this configuration with another user, it will utilize the ColorSync space specified in that user's system.

Adobe RGB (1998) contains a wide range of colors and is useful when converting RGB images to CMYK images. As you may have guessed by now, this is our preferred choice for print output, but it isn't a good choice for online output.

Apple RGB is useful if you need to work with older desktop publishing files for output to Macintosh displays, as it reflects the characteristics of older standard Apple 13-inch monitors.

ColorMatch RGB contains a smaller range of colors than Adobe RGB (1998), but because it matches the color space of Radius Pressview displays, it's useful for print work.

ProPhoto RGB contains a very wide range of colors and is useful for output to high-end dye sublimation and inkjet printers.

sRGB IEC61966-2.1 is a good choice for Web output, as it reflects the settings on the average computer display. Many hardware and software manufacturers are using this as the default space for scanners, low-end printers, and software. Note that for prepress work, Adobe RGB and ColorMatch RGB are better choices.

4. Click OK.

➤ The Adobe RGB color space includes more colors in the CMYK print range than the sRGB color space (which is designed for online output). For some reason, Adobe feels compelled to keep sRGB as the default RGB working space (as listed in Edit > Color Settings), but it can spell disaster for print output.

> **DOCUMENT-SPECIFIC COLOR**
>
> Photoshop supports document-specific color, meaning that each document keeps its own color profile. The profile controls how colors in the file are previewed onscreen, edited, and converted on output. For documents that lack an embedded profile, Photoshop generates previews using the current working space.

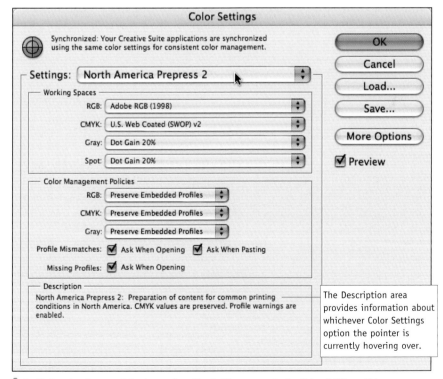

A North America Prepress 2 is chosen from the Settings menu in the Color Settings dialog.

Synchronizing color settings

If the color settings in another Adobe Creative Suite program (e.g., Illustrator or InDesign) don't match the current settings in Photoshop, an alert will display in the Color Settings dialog.**A** If you don't own the complete Adobe Creative Suite, you'll have to start up the errant application and fix its color settings by hand. If you're fortunate enough to have the whole suite, you can use the Suite Color Settings dialog in Bridge to synchronize the color settings of all of the programs in the suite that you have installed.

Before synchronizing the color settings via Bridge, make sure you've chosen the proper settings in Photoshop (see the previous two pages).

To synchronize color settings using Bridge:

1. On the Application bar in Photoshop, click the **Launch Bridge** button. In Bridge, choose Edit > **Creative Suite Color Settings** (Ctrl-Shift-K/Cmd-Shift-K). The Suite Color Settings dialog opens.**B**

MATCHING SETTINGS

The presets in the Suite Color Settings dialog will be the same as on the Settings menu in the Color Settings dialog (see page 10). Keep Show Expanded List of Color Settings Files unchecked to display just the four basic presets.

A This alert in the Color Setttings dialog in Photoshop tells us that the color settings in our Creative Suite applications aren't synchronized (don't match).

2. Click the settings preset you chose in Photoshop, then click **Apply**. Bridge will change (synchronize) the color settings of the other Adobe Creative Suite applications to match the preset you selected.

B Use the Suite Color Settings dialog to synchronize the color settings of all the applications in the Adobe Creative Suite.

Customizing your color policies

The current color management policies govern whether Photoshop honors or overrides the document settings if the color profile in a file you open or import doesn't match the current color settings in Photoshop. If you chose the North America Prepress 2 setting in the Color Settings dialog (page 10), the Ask When Opening policy (the safest one, in our opinion) is already chosen for you, and you can skip these instructions.

To customize your color management policies:

1. Choose Edit > **Color Settings** (Ctrl-Shift-K/Cmd-Shift-K). The Color Settings dialog opens.**A**

2. From the **Color Management Policies** menus, choose an option for files that you open or import into Photoshop:

   Off to prevent Photoshop from color-managing the files.

   Preserve Embedded Profiles if you expect to work with both color-managed and non-color-managed documents. Each file will keep its own profile.

Convert to Working RGB or **Convert to Working CMYK** to have all documents that you open/import into Photoshop adopt the current color working space. This is usually the best choice for Web output.

3. Do any of the following optional steps:

   For **Profile Mismatches**, if you check **Ask When Opening**, Photoshop will display an alert if the color profile in a file you're opening doesn't match the current working space. Via the alert, you will have the option to override the current color management policy for each file.

   Check **Ask When Pasting** to have Photoshop display an alert if it encounters a color profile mismatch when you paste color imagery into a document. The alert lets you override your color management policy when pasting.

   For files with **Missing Profiles**, check **Ask When Opening** to have Photoshop display an alert with an option to assign a profile.

4. Click OK.

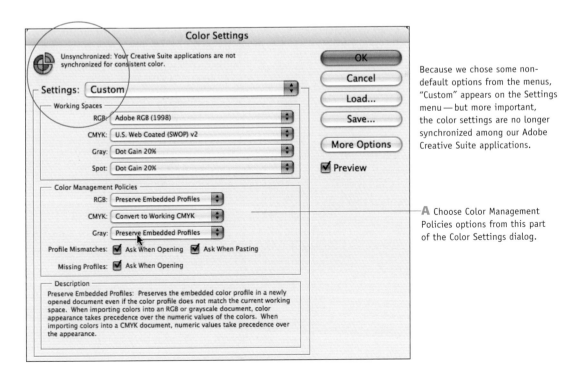

Because we chose some non-default options from the menus, "Custom" appears on the Settings menu — but more important, the color settings are no longer synchronized among our Adobe Creative Suite applications.

A Choose Color Management Policies options from this part of the Color Settings dialog.

Saving custom color settings

For desktop color printing, we recommended choosing the North American Prepress 2 color setting. For commercial printing, let the pros supply the proper color settings: Ask your print shop to send you a .csf file with all the correct Working Spaces and Color Management Policies settings for their particular press. Then all you need to do is install that custom color settings file in the proper location, as per the instructions below. Thereafter, you'll be able to access it via the Settings menu in the Color Settings dialog.

To save custom color settings as defaults for the Creative Suite:

1. In Windows, put the file in Program Files\ Common Files\Adobe\Color\Settings.

   In the Mac OS, put the file in User/[user name]/Library/Application Support/Adobe/ Color/Settings.

2. To access the newly saved settings file, relaunch Photoshop, open the Color Settings dialog, then choose the .csf file name from the Settings menu.

If your print shop gives you a list of recommended settings for the Color Settings dialog box —but not an actual .csf file—you can choose and then save that collection of settings as a .csf file, following these instructions.

To save custom color settings:

1. Choose Edit > **Color Settings** (Ctrl-Shift-K/ Cmd-Shift-K). The Color Settings dialog opens.

2. Enter the required settings by choosing and checking the appropriate options.

3. Click **Save** and enter a file name (it's a good idea to include the type of printer in the name), keep the .csf extension and default location (the Settings folder), then click Save.

4. Click OK to exit the Color Settings dialog.

Acquiring printer profiles

Thus far, we've helped you set your camera to the Adobe RGB color space, calibrate your display, and specify Adobe RGB as the color space for Photoshop. Next we'll show you how to acquire the proper printer profile(s) so you can incorporate color management into your specific printing scenario.

To download a printer profile:

Most printer manufacturers have a website from which you can download either an ICC profile for a specific printer/paper combination or a printer driver that contains a collection of specific ICC printer/paper profiles. Be sure to choose a profile that matches the particular printer/paper combination you'll be using.

1. On the following page, we step you through the websites for two manufacturers of widely used printers: **Epson** (Epson.com) (**A–C**, next page) and **Canon** (Canon.com) (**D–F**, next page).

   You can also download an ICC profile for a specific printer/paper combo from the website for a paper manufacturer, such as illford.com or crane.com/museo.

   Note: The profiles for the newest printer models may not be available yet on these sites.

2. After visiting the website, follow the installation instructions for whichever file you downloaded. In our section on proofing colors, we'll show you how to use it.

FINDING A PROFILE FOR AN EPSON INKJET PRINTER

A On the Epson home page, choose Drivers & Support > Printers.

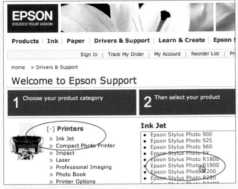

B Click Ink Jet under Printers, then click your printer model on the list of printers.

C On the page for the printer model, below Drivers & Downloads, click the link for your operating system. On the Drivers & Downloads page, click the Premium ICC Profiles for [printer name] link.

On the Premium ICC Printer Profiles page (not shown), click the profile for your chosen paper type.

FINDING A PROFILE FOR A CANON INKJET PRINTER

D On the Canon home page, choose Downloads > Consumer.

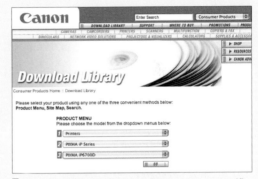

E From the menus, choose the Printers category, specific product type (printer series), and printer model, then click Go.

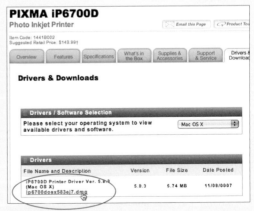

F On the Drivers & Downloads page, select your operating system, then click the appropriate printer driver. The driver will install the profiles automatically.

Changing color profiles

When a file's profile doesn't match the current working space (Adobe RGB, in our case) or the color profile is missing altogether, you can use the Assign Profile command to assign the proper profile. You may notice visible color shifts if the color data of the file is reinterpreted to match the new profile, but rest assured, the color data in the actual image is preserved. Do keep Preview checked, though, so you can see what you're getting into.

To change or delete a file's color profile:

1. Choose Edit > **Assign Profile**. The Assign Profile dialog opens.**A** Check Preview. If the file contains layers, an alert may appear, warning you that the appearance of the layers may change; click OK.

2. Click one of the following:

   To delete the color profile, click **Don't Color Manage This Document**.

   To assign your current working space to the file, click **Working** [document color mode and the name of the working space you're using]. If you followed our instructions for color management, you've already specified Adobe RGB as the Working RGB space, but you can click this option for any photo or scan that wasn't captured using the Adobe RGB color space.

   To assign a different profile, click **Profile**, then choose a profile that differs from your current working space.

3. Click OK.

The Convert to Profile command lets you preview a conversion to an assortment of output profiles and intents, then converts the color data to the chosen profile. Note! This command performs a mode conversion and changes the actual color data in your file.

To convert a file's color profile:

1. Choose Edit > **Convert to Profile**. The Convert to Profile dialog opens.**B** Check Preview.

2. From the **Destination Space: Profile** menu, choose a profile to convert the file to (it doesn't have to be the current working space).

3. Under Conversion Options, choose an **Intent** (see the sidebar on page 18).

4. Leave the default Engine as **Adobe (ACE)** and keep the **Use Black Point Compensation** and **Use Dither** options checked.

5. *Optional:* Check Flatten Image to Preserve Appearance to merge all layers and adjustment layers.

6. Click OK.

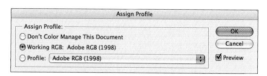

A Use the Assign Profile dialog to either delete a color profile or assign a new one.

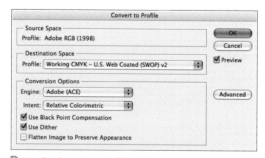

B Use the Convert to Profile dialog to convert your document to a different color profile. In this case, we're switching from the Adobe RGB profile to our working CMYK profile for a standard web press that uses coated paper.

Proofing colors onscreen

In this final step in color management, you'll create a custom proof setting for your specific inkjet printer and paper, which you'll use to view a soft proof (onscreen simulation) of your print output. Although the soft proof won't be perfectly accurate, it will give you a rough idea of how your colors will look without costing you a penny.

To proof an inkjet print onscreen:

1. From the View > Proof Setup submenu, choose **Custom.** The Customize Proof Condition dialog opens, allowing you to choose custom proofing settings for your output device.A

2. Check Preview, then from the **Device to Simulate** menu, choose the color profile for your inkjet printer and paper (this is the profile you either downloaded from a website or installed with your printer driver file).

3. Uncheck **Preserve RGB Numbers**, if available. Photoshop will simulate how the colors will look when converted to the output profile. This option is available only if the color mode of the output profile that you chose from the Device to Simulate menu matches that of the current file (e.g., if your image is in RGB Color mode and is to be output on an RGB printer).

4. Choose a **Rendering Intent** to control how colors will change as the image is shifted from one profile to another (see the sidebar on the next page). We recommend choosing either Perceptual or Relative Colorimetric, but you can evaluate each one via the preview and test prints.

Check **Black Point Compensation** to allow adjustments to be made for differences in black points among different color spaces. With this option chosen, the full dynamic range of the image color space is mapped to the full dynamic range of the output device (printer) color space. With this option off, blacks in the image may display or print as grays. We recommend checking this option if the file is to be output on an inkjet printer.

5. *Optional:* For **Display Options (On-Screen)**, check Simulate Paper Color to preview the white of the printing paper as defined in the printer profile; or if you're going to print the file on uncoated paper, check Simulate Black Ink to preview the full range of black values that the printer can produce.

6. To save your custom proof setup, click **Save**, enter a name, keep the .psf extension, keep the location as the default Proofing folder, then click OK. Saved proof setups are available on the Customize Proof Condition menu and at the bottom of the View > Proof Setup submenu. View > **Proof Colors** will be checked automatically to let you see the soft proof. Also, the Device to Simulate profile will be listed in the document title bar or tab.

Remember, the Proof Setup options control only how Photoshop simulates colors onscreen. Colors in the actual file won't be converted to the chosen profile until you convert the document color mode (e.g., from RGB to CMYK) or send your file to an inkjet printer.

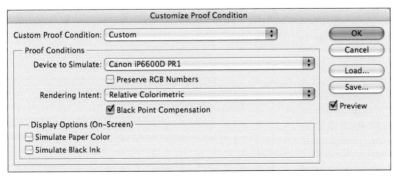

A To create a soft proof of our document, in the Customize Proof Condition dialog, we've chosen the profile for our Canon Pixma inkjet printer as the Device to Simulate.

Via one of the four presets on the Proof Setup submenu, you can soft-proof the colors in your RGB file onscreen to simulate what they'll look like when printed using CMYK inks or when viewed online on a Windows or Mac display.

To proof colors for commercial printing or online output:

1. From the View > **Proof Setup** submenu, choose the preset for the output display type that you want Photoshop to simulate:

   Working CMYK to simulate colors for whichever commercial press is currently chosen on the CMYK menu under Working Spaces in Edit > Color Settings.

   Macintosh RGB or **Windows RGB** to simulate colors for online output using the legacy Mac gamma (1.8) or the Windows gamma (2.2) as the proofing space.

   Monitor RGB to soft-proof colors using the custom display profile for your monitor.

2. View > **Proof Colors** will be checked automatically. Uncheck it to turn off soft proofing at any time (Ctrl-Y/Cmd-Y).

Moving on

Congratulations! You completed the first part of the color management workflow. You set your camera to the Adobe RGB color space, calibrated your display, specified Adobe RGB as the color space for Photoshop, acquired the profile for your inkjet printer model, assigned the Adobe RGB profile to any files that don't use that color space at the outset, and created a soft-proof setting for your particular inkjet printer and paper using those profiles.

What's left? You'll need to focus on color management again when you prepare your file for printing. In the Print chapter, we'll show you how to let Photoshop handle color conversions for an inkjet printer using the same printer profiles you used for the soft proof. The benefit of using a color management workflow is that it keeps colors more consistent from camera to display to printout. Now you can use Photoshop features to enhance images from your camera or scanner, knowing that the colors in your printout will more closely match what you're viewing onscreen. In the next chapter, you'll learn about digital cameras and creating Photoshop documents.

THE RENDERING INTENTS

➤ Perceptual changes colors in a way that seems natural to the human eye, while attempting to preserve the appearance of the overall image. It's a good choice for continuous-tone images.

➤ Saturation changes colors with the intent of preserving vivid colors, but in so doing compromises color fidelity. It's a good choice for charts and business graphics, which normally contain fewer colors than continuous-tone images.

➤ Absolute Colorimetric maintains the color accuracy only of colors that fall within the destination color gamut (i.e., the color range of your printer) but in so doing sacrifices the accuracy of colors that are out of gamut.

➤ Relative Colorimetric, the default intent for all the Adobe predefined settings in the Color Settings dialog, compares the white, or highlight, of your document's color space to the white of the destination color space (the white of the paper, in the case of print output), shifting colors where needed. This is the best Rendering Intent choice for documents in which most of the colors fall within the color range of the destination gamut, because it preserves most of the original colors.

Note: Consult your printer manual when choosing a rendering intent. For example, some inkjet printers favor Perceptual over Relative Colorimetric.

COMPENSATING FOR COLOR BLINDNESS ★

At some point you may need to design graphics, such as signage, that are fully accessible to color-blind viewers. In fact, some countries require graphics in public spaces to comply with the Color Universal Design (CUD) guidelines. To simulate how your document will look to a color-blind viewer, use the View > Proof Setup > Color Blindness – Protanopia-Type and Color Blindness – Deuteranopia-Type commands in Adobe Photoshop.

In case you're not familiar with those two terms, for a protanope, the brightness of red, orange, and yellow is dimmed, making it hard for such a person to distinguish red from black or dark gray. Protanopes also have trouble distinguishing violet, lavender, and purple from blue because the reddish components of those colors appear dimmed. Deuteranopes are unable to distinguish between colors in the green-yellow-red part of the spectrum and experience color blindness similar to that of protanopes, but without the problem of dimming.

We start this chapter off with a few basic pointers on buying a digital camera and shooting digital photos. Then you'll learn how to calculate an appropriate resolution for a file, choose scanner settings, create a new document, create document presets, use the Place command, save and copy your files, use the Status bar, and close up shop. (To learn how to download photos from a digital camera, see pages 34–35.)

Although Photoshop lets you create, open, edit, and save your files in over a dozen different formats, **A–B** on a day-to-day basis you'll probably use only a handful of those formats, such as TIFF, GIF, JPEG, EPS, Photoshop PDF, and PSD (the native Photoshop file format). The Large Document format, or PSB (nicknamed "Photoshop Big"), is used just for huge files; see the sidebar on page 25.

Because Photoshop reads so many different file formats, you can use the program to open images from many sources, such as digital cameras, scanners, drawing applications, and video captures. You can edit a single image, create a montage of imagery from multiple files, or create images entirely within Photoshop by using brushes, filters, and other commands. In the next chapter, you'll learn how to open existing files.

Using digital cameras

Digital cameras are fast becoming the primary source of imagery for Photoshop users. Pictures that are digitized by a camera can be uploaded directly to a computer, which eliminates the need for scanning.

Continued on the following page

ACQUIRE, CREATE, SAVE

2

IN THIS CHAPTER

Using digital cameras 19

16 Bits/Channel mode 21

Calculating the file resolution 22

Using a scanner 23

Creating new, blank documents 24

Creating document presets 26

Using the Place command 27

Saving files 28

Using the Status bar 31

Ending a work session 32

```
Photoshop (*.PSD;*.PDD)
BMP (*.BMP;*.RLE;*.DIB)
CompuServe GIF (*.GIF)
Dicom (*.DCM;*.DC3;*.DIC)
Photoshop EPS (*.EPS)
Photoshop DCS 1.0 (*.EPS)
Photoshop DCS 2.0 (*.EPS)
FXG (*.FXG)
IFF Format (*.IFF;*.TDI)
JPEG (*.JPG;*.JPEG;*.JPE)
Large Document Format (*.PSB)
PCX (*.PCX)
Photoshop PDF (*.PDF;*.PDP)
Photoshop Raw (*.RAW)
PICT File (*.PCT;*.PICT)
Pixar (*.PXR)
PNG (*.PNG)
Portable Bit Map (*.PBM;*.PGM;*.PPM;*.PNM;*.PFI
Scitex CT (*.SCT)
Targa (*.TGA;*.VDA;*.ICB;*.VST)
TIFF (*.TIF;*.TIFF)
```

```
✓ Photoshop
  BMP
  CompuServe GIF
  Photoshop EPS
  FXG
  IFF Format
  JPEG
  Large Document Format
  PCX
  Photoshop PDF
  Photoshop 2.0
  Photoshop Raw
  PICT File
  PICT Resource
  Pixar
  PNG
  Portable Bit Map
  Scitex CT
  Targa
  TIFF
  Photoshop DCS 1.0
  Photoshop DCS 2.0
```

A Files can be saved in any of these formats in Windows.

B Files can be saved in any of these formats in the Mac OS.

Buying a digital camera

If you're shopping for a digital camera, the first step is to figure out which model suits your output requirements and budget. Camera manufacturers usually list the resolution of a model as width and height dimensions in pixels (such as 3000 pixels x 2000 pixels). If you multiply the two values, you'll arrive at a number in the millions. That number is the camera's **megapixel value**, which is the number of pixels the camera captures. If your camera captures enough pixels, you'll be able to print high-quality closeups and enlargements of your photos. This makes the megapixel value one of the key factors to consider when deciding which model to buy.

Compact, inexpensive "point-and-shoot" cameras offer few or no manual controls and have a resolution of 6 to 10 megapixels. They capture enough detail to produce decent-quality 5" x 7" prints and acceptable Web output.

Advanced amateur camera models have a resolution of 8 to 12 megapixels. You can get high-quality 8" x 10" prints from these cameras, and they offer more manual controls.

Professional camera models (such as digital SLRs) have a resolution of 11 megapixels or higher and can produce high-quality 11" x 14" prints or larger—but they're costly. Because the digital light sensors in such cameras are larger and more sensitive than the sensors in the lesser cameras, they capture higher-quality pixel data.

The very high megapixel cameras aren't for everyone—and not just because of their high price tag. Images with a high megapixel count have larger file sizes, take longer to upload from the camera to the computer, and require a larger hard drive for storage. (See our comparison of megapixels and print size on page 25.) Unless you often print large photos (11" x 14" or larger) or tend to crop your images, a 6- to 10-megapixel camera will be better suited to your needs.

Aside from the megapixel count, look for a camera with a large digital sensor chip (a larger chip records more detail and less visual "noise"), and make sure the camera can accommodate a wide variety of lenses.

For more advice about buying a camera, you can visit the website for *PC Magazine* (pcmag.com) or *Macworld* (macworld.com); photography magazines are also good sources.

Shooting digital photographs

You've purchased or borrowed a camera (congratulations!)—now you need to know how to use it. To get the best-quality photographs, choose your camera settings wisely. Here are some basic guidelines:

➤ Medium and high-end digital cameras let you choose an **ISO** setting, which controls the sensitivity of the camera's digital sensor to light (comparable to film speed in film photography). High ISO settings tend to produce digital noise in low-light areas, so try to choose the minimum ISO setting that still enables you to get the desired exposure.

➤ Decide whether to have your camera capture the photos in the **JPEG** format or as unprocessed **raw** files.*

➤ Choose a **color space** for your camera: sRGB for onscreen or Web output, Adobe RGB for print output.

➤ For JPEGs, choose a **white balance** setting that's appropriate for the lighting conditions in which you're shooting photos; the camera will process the image data based on this setting. For raw files, ignore the white balance setting, as the images won't be processed inside the camera.

➤ If your camera has a **histogram** display (read our discussion of histograms on pages 184–185), use the histogram to verify that your shot was taken with the correct **exposure** settings. Don't deliberately over- or underexpose your photos. If you overexpose them, too much detail will be lost from the highlight areas; if you underexpose them (stop down too much), too much detail will be lost from the shadows. Remember, Photoshop can process and adjust only the details that your camera captures.

Regardless of whether you shoot JPEG or raw photos, exposure deficiencies, color casts, and other imaging problems can be corrected via the Camera Raw dialog (see Chapter 15) and then further corrected via adjustment commands in Photoshop.

*Each camera model produces its own version of a raw file. We refer to such files collectively as "raw files."

16 Bits/Channel mode

In Photoshop, you have a choice of working with your files in 8, 16, or 32 Bits/Channel mode (Image > Mode submenu). There are many advantages to working with your files in 16 Bits/Channel versus 8 Bits/Channel mode, and few advantages to working with 32-Bits/Channel files—at least for now.

The wider the dynamic color range of the input device, the finer the subtleties of color and shade it can capture. Most advanced amateur and professional digital SLR cameras capture a minimum of 12 bits of accurate data per channel. Like cameras, scanners range widely in quality. Whereas consumer-level scanners can capture 10 bits of accurate data per channel, high-end professional scanners can capture up to 16 bits of accurate data per channel.

You can't get good-quality output unless you capture a wide tonal range at the outset. Shadow areas in particular are notoriously hard to capture well. But if you start with a high-resolution scan or a photo from a digital camera that can capture 12 to 16 bits per channel, you've got a head start, because the file will contain an abundance of pixels in all levels of the tonal spectrum.

You also can't get good-quality output unless the full tonal range is preserved as you edit your file. The extra pixels in 16-bit images help mitigate the reduction in image quality caused by the editing and resampling commands in Photoshop. **A–B** The tonal adjustment commands in particular, such as Levels and Curves, remove pixel data and change the distribution of pixels across the tonal spectrum. In 8-bit images, such changes will be visible

on high-end print output, whereas 16-bit images won't show signs of pixel loss even after destructive edits because they contain an ample number of pixels in all parts of the tonal spectrum. To summarize, here are some basic facts about 16-bit files:

➤ Photoshop can open 16-bit files in CMYK or RGB mode.

➤ 16-bit files can be saved in the following widely used formats: Photoshop (.psd), Large Document (.psb), PDF (.pdf), PNG (.png), TIFF (.tif), and JPEG2000 (.jpf).

➤ With only a few restrictions, 16-bit images can be successfully edited and adjusted in Photoshop. For example, some or all of the filters on the Blur, Noise, Render, Sharpen, Stylize, and Other submenus on the Filter menu, as well as the Distort > Lens Correction filter and both filters on the Video submenu, are available, but filters on the other submenus are not.

➤ For print output, your output service provider may request that you convert your 16-bit images to 8-bit (choose Image > Mode > 8 Bits/Channel).

➤ In the Mac OS, you can print 16-bit files if your printer supports 16-bit printing.

And finally, if system or storage limitations prevent you from working with 16-bit images, we recommend this two-stage approach: Perform your initial tonal corrections (such as Levels and Curves adjustments) on the 16-bit image, then convert it to 8 bits per channel for further editing.

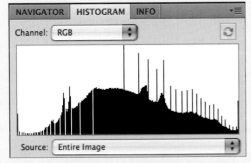

A As a result of a Levels command adjustment, this 8-bit image exhibits signs of tonal degradation (spikes and gaps)...

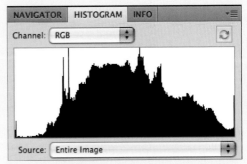

B ...whereas after the same Levels adjustment to this 16-bit version of the same image, smooth tonal transitions are preserved.

Calculating the file resolution
Resolution for print

If you shoot digital photos, your camera will pre-serve either all the pixels they capture (in raw files) or a portion of the pixels they capture (in small, medium, or large JPEG files). If you acquire images via a scanner, on the other hand, you can set the input resolution in the scanning software to control the number of pixels the device captures.

High-resolution images contain more pixels, and thus finer detail, but also have larger file sizes, take longer to render onscreen, require more processing time for edits, and take longer to print. Low-resolution images, on the other hand, look coarse and jagged and lack detail when printed. Luckily, there are methods for changing the resolution value of a digital file, because you don't want it to be larger or smaller than needed for your intended output device. Your file should have the proper resolution to obtain the desired output quality—but not much higher.

➤ When opening raw digital photos, you'll set the output resolution in the **Camera Raw** dialog (see page 241).

➤ For JPEG photos, you can set the image resolution in the **Camera Raw** dialog, or in the **Image Size** dialog (see page 98) after opening the file in Photoshop.

➤ When scanning, you'll set the image resolution via the **scanning software**.

The print resolution for digitized images (from a camera or scanner) is calculated in **pixels per inch** (ppi). **A–C** For high-end print output, before selecting a resolution for a file, ask your commercial printer what resolution and halftone screen frequency settings they're going to use for their printer or imagesetter. For a grayscale image, the proper resolution is usually in the neighborhood of one-and-a-half times the halftone screen frequency (lines per inch) of the output device, or twice the halftone screen frequency for a color image. That will amount to approximately 200 ppi for a grayscale image or 250–350 ppi for a color image. Each print shop has specific requirements for their particular output devices, so it's important to ask them for advice.

For output to an inkjet (desktop) printer, choose a resolution between 240 and 300 ppi.

A 72 ppi

B 150 ppi

C 300 ppi

Resolution for the Web

When creating an image for Web output, you need to estimate how large your user's browser window is likely to be, then calculate how much of that window you want your image to fill. Most viewers have their browser window open to around 800 x 600 pixels. Subtract the space that the menu bar, scroll bars, and other controls in the browser interface occupy, and you're left with a "live area" of approximately 740 x 460 pixels at most. The browser window for most viewers doesn't fill the entire screen, so you can count on your image filling only around **660 x 420** pixels.

➤ To quickly create a document with dimensions of 660 x 420 pixels and a resolution of 72 ppi, in File > New, choose Preset: Web, and choose the desired pixel size for your document (see the next page).

Using a scanner

Choosing settings for a desktop scanner

Using a scanning device and scanning software, you can digitize (translate into numbers) slides, flat artwork (e.g., drawings), and printed photographs so they can be read, displayed, edited, and printed by a computer. You can scan images directly into Photoshop, or you or your output service provider can scan them by using third-party scanning software, and save them in one of the file formats that Photoshop can read.

Your scanning software will have its own version of most of the options listed at right (though feature names vary from one product to another). The quality and file storage size of a scan will depend on several factors under your control, such as the mode, resolution, scale, and crop size. If you use an output service provider, they'll choose those settings for you, but if you're going to scan the photo yourself, take the time to set your scanning parameters carefully.

If you access your scanner from Photoshop, choose File > Import > [your scanner model]. If not, launch your scanning software separately.

Preview: Place your artwork in the scanner, then click Preview, PreScan, or an equivalent button.

Scan mode: Choose Black-and-White Line Art (no grays), Grayscale, or Color (choose millions of colors, if available). The file size of an image scanned in Color will be approximately three times larger than if it were scanned as Grayscale.

Resolution: Choose a resolution value that will allow you to obtain the desired quality output from your printer. For grayscale printing on a printer with a 133-line screen, enter 200 ppi as your scan resolution; for color printing, enter 300 ppi; or for line art, enter a high scanning resolution (600 ppi or higher). It's always best to scan an image at or just above the size and resolution needed for your output device.

Cropping: If you're going to use only part of the original image, you can reduce the area to be scanned by moving the handles of the bounding box in the preview area. Cropping can significantly reduce the file size of your scanned image.

Scale: Although you can enlarge the dimensions of the scan by raising the scale percentage above 100%, keep in mind that doing this may produce a blurry image, because the software will use interpolation (mathematical guesswork) to fill in the missing information.

Scan: Click Scan, and choose a location in which to save your new file. In the next chapter, you'll learn how to open files via Bridge.

➤ When scanning a print from a film-based camera, choose an image that has a wide tonal range. For professional-quality print output, take the time (and money) to have an output service provider scan your artwork on either a high-resolution CCD scanner (such as one of the Scitex scanners) or a drum scanner.

Creating new, blank documents

In these instructions, you'll create a new, blank document. Into this document, you can drag and drop or copy and paste imagery from other files, and of course you can edit it by using all the image-editing features that Photoshop has to offer, such as brushes, effects, and filters.

To create a new, blank document:

1. Choose File > **New** (Ctrl-N/Cmd-N). The New dialog opens.**A**

2. Enter a name in the **Name** field.

3. Do either of the following:

   To choose a preset size, choose from the **Preset** menu. The presets are listed in three categories: the Default Photoshop Size; paper sizes for commercial and desktop printers; and screen sizes for Web, mobile, and film and video output. Next, choose a specific size for that preset category from the **Size** menu.

   To create a custom size, choose a unit of measure from the menu next to the Width field; the same unit will be chosen automatically for the Height. Or hold down Shift while choosing a unit to change the value for that dimension only. Next, enter **Width** and **Height** values (or use the scrubby sliders).

4. Enter the **Resolution** required for your target output device—be it an imagesetter or the Web (see the previous two pages). You can use the scrubby slider here, too.

5. Choose a document **Color Mode** (we recommend RGB Color), then from the adjacent menu, choose **8 bit** or **16 bit** as the color depth. You can also convert the image to a different color mode later (see "Document color modes" on pages 3–4).

6. Note the **Image Size** listed on the right side of the dialog. If you need to reduce that storage size, you can choose smaller dimensions, a lower resolution, or a lower bit depth.

7. For the Background of the image, choose **Background Contents: White** or **Background Color**; or choose **Transparent** if you want the bottommost tier of the document to be a layer. (To choose a Background color, see Chapter 12. To learn about layers, see Chapter 7.)

8. *Optional:* Clicking the Advanced arrowhead shows (or hides) additional options, such as the Color Profile menu. You can assign a color profile here, or you can do it later via Edit > Assign Profile. The list of profiles will vary depending on which Color Mode you've chosen. To learn more about color profiles, see pages 10–11 and 16.

Continued on the following page

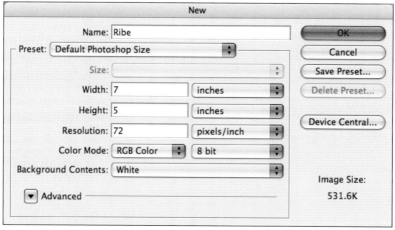

A In the New dialog, enter a Name; choose a Preset size or enter custom Width, Height, and Resolution values; and choose Color Mode and Background Contents options.

For Web or print output, leave the Pixel Aspect Ratio on the default setting of Square Pixels; or for video output, choose one of the other options. For more information about these options, see Photoshop Help.

9. Click OK. A new, blank document window appears onscreen.**A–B** To save it, see page 28.

➤ To force the New dialog settings to match those of an existing open document, open the New dialog, then from the bottom of the Preset menu, choose the name of the document that has the desired dimensions.

➤ If the Clipboard contains graphic data (say, that you copied from Adobe Photoshop or Illustrator), the New dialog will automatically display its dimensions. Choosing Clipboard from the Preset pop-up in the New dialog accomplishes the same thing. If you want to prevent the Clipboard dimensions from displaying, hold down Alt/Option as you choose File > New; the last-used file dimensions will display instead.

MEGAPIXELS, RESOLUTION, AND PRINT SIZES

Image Resolution	Megapixels in Inches (rounded off)*			
	6	8	10	12
150 ppi	13 x 20	16 x 22	17 x 24	18 x 28
300 ppi	7 x 10	8 x 11	8 x 13	9 x 14

*These print sizes are approximate. For a more exact listing, search the Web for "megapixels to print size chart."

PHOTOSHOP BIG

In Photoshop, you can create and save files as large as 300,000 x 300,000 pixels — over 2 gigabytes (GB) — and they can contain up to 56 user-created channels. These gonzo files can be saved in the Large Document (.psb) format, which is designed specifically to handle large documents. Files in this format can be opened and edited only in Photoshop versions CS through CS4.

What can you do with PSB files? If you have the disk space to store and work with them and have access to a specialty printer that can output super large images, great. Files up to 32,000 x 32,000 pixels will print fully. But in order to output PSB files on most printers, you have to lower their resolution drastically (duplicate the file first).

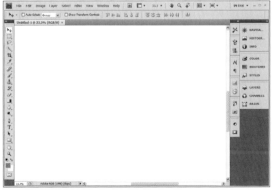

A A new document window appears in Windows (in this case, as a tabbed window).

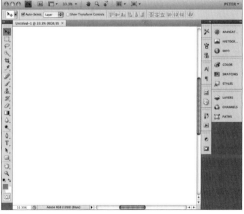

B A new document window appears in the Mac OS (in this case, as a tabbed window).

Creating document presets

If you tend to use the same document size, color mode, or other settings repeatedly in the New dialog, take the time to create a document preset for those settings. Thereafter, you'll be able to access your settings via the Preset menu, which will save you startup time when you create new files.

To create a document preset:

1. Choose File > **New** or press Ctrl-N/Cmd-N. The New dialog opens.

2. Choose settings, such as the width, height, resolution, color mode, bit depth, background contents, color profile, and pixel aspect ratio. Ignore any setting that you don't want to include in the preset; you'll exclude it from the preset in step 5.

3. Click **Save Preset**. The New Document Preset dialog opens.**A**

4. Enter a **Preset Name**.

5. Under **Include in Saved Settings**, uncheck any New dialog settings that you don't want to include in the preset.

6. Click OK. Your new preset will appear on the Preset menu in the New dialog.

➤ To delete a user-created preset, choose it from the Preset menu, click Delete Preset, then click Yes (this can't be undone).

CHOOSE YOUR DEFAULTS

In Preferences > Units & Rulers, for New Document Presets Resolutions, you can enter Print Resolution and Screen Resolution values. One or the other value will appear in the Resolution field in the File > New dialog when you choose a preset from the Preset menu. The Print Resolution value (default 300 ppi) is used for the paper and photo presets; the Screen Resolution value (default 72 ppi) is used for the Web, Mobile & Devices, and Film & Video presets.

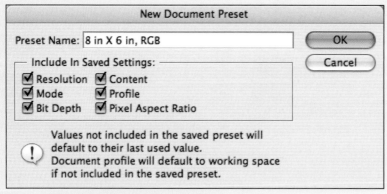

A Use the New Document Preset dialog to control which of the current settings in the New dialog will be saved in your new document preset.

Using the Place command

When you place vector art into a Photoshop document, it arrives as vector art on a new Smart Object layer; when you output the file, it's rendered in the resolution of the Photoshop image. The higher the resolution of the Photoshop image, the sharper the rendering.

To place a PDF or Adobe Illustrator file in a Photoshop image:

1. Open a Photoshop document.

2. Do either of the following:

   In Bridge, locate and click a thumbnail, then choose File > Place > **In Photoshop**.

   In Photoshop, choose File > **Place**, locate and click a file, then click Place.

3. The Place PDF dialog opens.**A** Choose a Thumbnail Size to preview the file; for a multi-page PDF file, choose the desired page; and choose a Crop To option (we recommend Bounding Box to exclude any white areas outside the artwork).

4. Click OK. A bounding box will appear in the Photoshop document, then the art will render inside it.

5. Do any of these optional steps (use the Undo command if you need to undo any of them):

   To **scale** the placed art, drag a handle on the bounding box. Shift-drag a corner handle to scale it proportionally.**B**

   To **move** the placed art, drag inside the bounding box.

   To **rotate** the placed art, position the pointer outside the bounding box (curved pointer), then drag. You can move the center point to rotate the art around a different point.

6. To accept the placed art, press Enter/Return or double-click inside the bounding box. The placed art will appear on a new Smart Object layer (see pages 314–316).**C**

➤ To delete the placed art before accepting it, press Esc.

➤ To open an Illustrator vector or PDF file as a Smart Object in a new Photoshop file, choose File > Open as Smart Object (in Photoshop). Choose settings in the Open as Smart Object dialog.

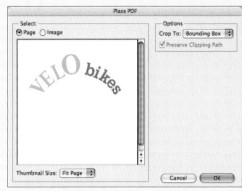

A The file previews in the Place PDF dialog.

B Move the placed object to the desired location (scale it, if desired), then press Enter/Return to accept it.

C When we accepted the object, it became an embedded Smart Object layer. If we were to edit the embedded type file using its original application, our changes would be reflected in the Photoshop file. (We added a drop shadow effect in Photoshop; see pages 320–321.)

Saving files

If you're not sure which format to use when saving a file for the first time, we strongly recommend the native Photoshop format, PSD. For one thing, PSD files are more compact than TIFF files (see also the sidebar on the following page).

To save an unsaved document:

1. If the document window contains any imagery, you can choose File > **Save** (Ctrl-S/ Cmd-S); if it's completely blank, choose File > **Save As**. The Save As dialog opens.

2. Type a name in the **File Name** field **A**/**Save As** field (**A**, next page).

3. Choose a **location** for the file.

   In Windows, if you need to navigate to a different folder or drive, use the **Save In** menu at the top of the dialog.

   In the Mac OS, click a drive or folder in the **Sidebar** panel on the left side of the window. To locate a recently used folder, use the menu below the Save As field.

4. Choose a file format from the **Format** menu. Only the native Photoshop (PSD), Large Document Format (PSB), TIFF, and Photoshop PDF formats support layers (see pages 110 and 122).

5. If you're not familiar with the features listed in the **Save** area, you can leave the settings as is. The As a Copy option is discussed on page 30.

6. If the file contains an embedded color profile and the format you're saving to supports profiles, in the **Color** area, you can check **ICC Profile/Embed Color Profile**: [profile name] to save the profile with the file. (To learn about embedded profiles, see pages 10 and 16.)

7. Click Save.

➤ In the Mac OS, to have Photoshop append a three-character extension (e.g., .tif, .psd) to the file name automatically when saving a file for the first time, in Preferences > File Handling, choose Append File Extension: Always. Extensions are required when exporting Macintosh files to the Windows platform and when posting files to a Web server.

A The Save As dialog in Windows

SAVING A FLATTENED VERSION

If you choose Maximize PSD and PSB File Compatibility: Always in Photoshop Preferences > File Handling, whenever you save a file that contains layers in the PSD or PSB format, a flattened version is saved with it (it's updated with each Save). This is helpful when exporting Photoshop images to applications that don't read layers, such as Adobe Lightroom. Or if you'd rather decide on a file-by-file basis whether to have an extra flattened version save with your file, choose Ask from the menu instead. In this case, each time you use the Save As command, an alert dialog appears, giving you the option to include the extra image.

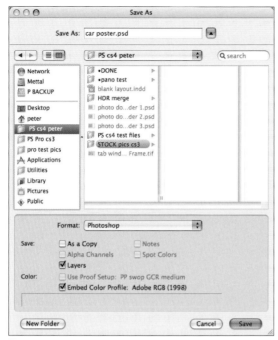

A The Save As dialog in the Mac OS

After saving a file for the first time, each subsequent use of the Save command saves over (overwrites) the last version.

To save a previously saved file:

Choose File > **Save** (Ctrl-S/Cmd-S).

The simple Revert command restores your document to the last-saved version.

Note: We know you can't learn everything at once, but keep in mind for the future that the History panel, which we cover in Chapter 10, serves as a full-service multiple undo feature. Revert does show up as a state on the History panel, so you can undo a Revert by clicking an earlier history state.

To revert to the last saved version:

Choose File > **Revert**.

► To undo the most recent modification, choose Edit > **Undo** (Ctrl-Z/Cmd-Z). Not all edits can be undone by this command.

CHOOSING THE RIGHT FORMAT

Photoshop (PSD), Large Document (PSB), TIFF, and Photoshop PDF are the only formats that preserve the following Photoshop features:

► Multiple layers and layer transparency

► Shape layers

► Smart Objects

► Adjustment layers

► Editable type layers

► Layer effects

► Alpha channels

► Grids and guides

In addition to the above-mentioned formats, the PICT, JPEG, and Photoshop EPS formats also preserve ICC color management profiles.

To prepare your document for printing from another application, or to export it to an application that doesn't read Photoshop layers, read about the EPS, PDF, and TIFF formats on pages 417–420.

For Web output, read about the GIF and JPEG formats on pages 421–426.

The Save As command lets you save a copy of your file under a new name to create a design, color mode, or adjustment variation. For example, you could save a copy of a file in CMYK Color mode while keeping the original in RGB Color mode. Another important use of this command is to save a flattened copy of a file in a different format for Web output or for export to another application (most applications can't read Photoshop layers).

To save a new version of a file:

1. Choose File > **Save As** (Ctrl-Shift-S/Cmd-Shift-S). The Save As dialog opens.**A–B**

2. Change the name in the **File Name/Save As** field. This is important!

3. Choose a **location** in which to save the new version from the Save In menu in Windows or by using the Sidebar panel and columns in the Mac OS.

4. *Optional:* Choose a different file format from the Format menu. Only formats that are available for the current document color mode and bit depth are listed.

   Beware! If the format you've chosen doesn't support layers, the Layers option will become dimmed, a yellow alert icon will display, and layers in the new version will be flattened.

5. Check any available options in the **Save** area, as desired. Check **As a Copy** to have the copy remain closed and the original stay open; or leave this option unchecked to have the original close and the copy stay open.

6. In the **Color** area, check ICC **Profile/Embed Color Profile**: [profile name], if available (see pages 10 and 16) to include the profile.

7. Click Save. Another dialog may appear. For the TIFF format, follow the instructions on page 417; for EPS, see pages 418–419; for PDF, see page 420; for GIF, see pages 423–424; or for JPEG, see pages 425–426. For other formats, see Photoshop Help.

➤ If you don't change the file name in the Save As dialog but you do click Save, an alert dialog will appear. Click Yes/Replace to save over the original file or click No/Cancel to get back to the Save As dialog.

A The Save As dialog in Windows

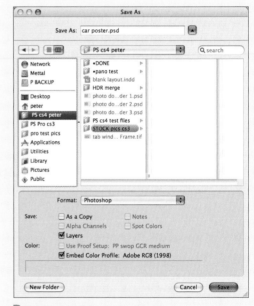

B The Save As dialog in the Mac OS

A DESIGNER'S FRIEND

Another way to create document variations — within the same file — is by using the Layer Comps panel; see pages 384–386.

Using the Status bar

Using the Status bar and menu at the bottom of the document window, you can read data about a file that's already open in Photoshop or find out how Photoshop is currently using memory.

To use the Status bar:

From the **Status** bar menu at the bottom of a floating or tabbed document window (or from the Show submenu, if Version Cue is enabled in Photoshop > Preferences > File Handling), choose one of the following:

Document Sizes to list the approximate file storage size of a flattened version of the file if it were saved in the PSD format (the value on the left) and the storage size of the file, including layers (the value on the right).**A**

Document Profile to list the embedded color profile (the words "Untagged [RGB or CMYK]" appear if a profile hasn't been assigned).

Document Dimensions to list the image dimensions (width, height, and resolution).

Scratch Sizes to list the amount of RAM Photoshop is using for all currently open files (the value on the left) and the amount of RAM currently available to Photoshop (the value on the right). If the first value is greater than the second, it means Photoshop is currently utilizing virtual memory on the scratch disk.

Efficiency to list the percentage of program operations that are currently being done in RAM as opposed to the scratch disk (see page 393). A percentage below 100 indicates the scratch disk is being used.

Current Tool to list the name of the currently chosen tool.

➤ If you don't see the Status bar, make the document window or Application frame wider, and it should appear.

To view data about a particular file, use the Metadata panel in Bridge.

To find out the storage size (and other data) for a file:

1. On the Application bar in Photoshop, click the Bridge button. In Bridge, select an image thumbnail (see page 40).

2. In the **Metadata** panel, under **File Properties**, look for the **File Size** value.**B**

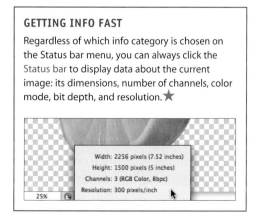

A From the Status bar menu (or Show submenu) at the bottom of your document window, choose what information you want displayed on the bar.

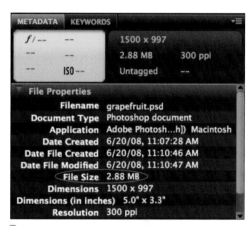

B To learn the storage size of a file, click its thumbnail in Bridge, then in the Metadata panel, File Properties category, look for the File Size listing.

GETTING INFO FAST

Regardless of which info category is chosen on the Status bar menu, you can always click the Status bar to display data about the current image: its dimensions, number of channels, color mode, bit depth, and resolution.★

Ending a work session

To close a document:

1. Do any of the following:

   Click the **Close** button in the upper right corner of a floating document window (Windows) **A**/ upper left corner of a floating document window (Mac OS).**B**

   Click the ✖ on a document tab.**C** ★

   Choose File > **Close** (Ctrl-W/Cmd-W).

2. If you attempt to close a file that was modified since it was last saved, a warning prompt will appear.**D** Click No/Don't Save to close the file without saving it; or click Yes/Save to save the file before closing it; or click Cancel to cancel the close operation.

➤ An asterisk on the title bar or tab indicates the document contains unsaved changes.

➤ In Photoshop, to close a file and launch or go to Bridge, choose File > **Close and Go To Bridge** (Ctrl-Shift-W/Cmd-Shift-W).

To exit/quit Photoshop:

1. In Windows, choose File > **Exit** (Ctrl-Q) or click the Close button for the application frame.

   In the Mac OS, choose Photoshop > **Quit Photoshop** (Cmd-Q).

2. All open Photoshop files will close. If any changes were made to any open file since it was last saved, a prompt will appear. Click No (N)/ Don't Save (D) to close the file without saving it; or click Yes (Y)/Save (S) to save it before exiting/quitting; or click Cancel to cancel the exit/quit.

A In Windows, click the Close (X) button on a floating document window.

B In the Mac OS, click the Close (red) button on a floating document window.

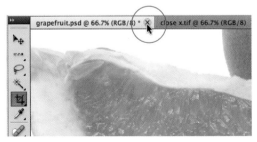

C In Windows and the Mac OS, you can close a tabbed document by clicking the ✖ on the tab.

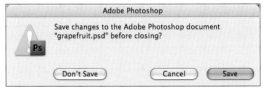

D If you try to close a file that contains unsaved changes, this prompt will appear. A similar prompt will appear if you exit/quit Photoshop and any open files contain unsaved changes.

The Bridge application ships with Photoshop and is aptly named because it serves as a bridge to all the programs in the Adobe Creative Suite. In Chapter 1, you learned how to use Bridge to synchronize the color settings for the whole Creative Suite. With its large thumbnail previews of files from Adobe Creative Suite applications, Bridge is also the best vehicle for opening files—plus it offers many other useful features. In Bridge you can preview, examine, rate, sort, and assign keywords to files; organize them into collections or collapsible stacks; use a loupe to examine minute details; and view data (metadata) about any image, such as the shooting conditions the camera recorded into a digital photo. You don't need to learn everything in this chapter at once. Master the basics in the first half of the chapter, then explore other features at your own pace. The CS4 version of Bridge contains many new features; keep an eye out for the red stars.

Launching Bridge

To launch Bridge: ★

Do one of the following:

On the Application bar in Photoshop, click the **Launch Bridge** button Br (Ctrl-Alt-O/Cmd-Option-O).**A**

In Program Files\Adobe\Adobe Bridge CS4 in Windows, Applications/Adobe Bridge CS4 in the Mac OS, double-click the **Bridge** application icon. Br

In the Mac OS, click the **Bridge** icon Br on the **Dock**. The Bridge window opens.

➤ A new feature of Bridge allows it to launch automatically at startup and stay in the background in "stealth mode." We suggest that beginning users turn this feature off by going to the Preferences dialog for Bridge (Ctrl-K/Cmd-K), Advanced panel, and unchecking Start Bridge At Login.

A On the Application bar in Photoshop, click the Launch Bridge button to launch Bridge (or to go to Bridge if it's already running).

IN THIS CHAPTER

Launching Bridge. 33
Downloading photos from a camera. . 34
The Bridge window. 36
Choosing a workspace for Bridge. . . . 38
Previewing images in Bridge 40
Opening files from Bridge 44
Customizing the Bridge window 44
Saving custom workspaces. 47
Resetting the Bridge workspace 47
Moving and copying files. 47
Labeling and rating thumbnails 48
Choosing a sorting order 49
Using the Filter panel 49
Using thumbnail stacks 50
Managing files. 51
Searching for files 53
Creating collections 54
Exporting the Bridge cache 56
Assigning keywords to files 57
Opening PDF and Illustrator files. . . . 58
Dealing with the "ifs" 60

Downloading photos from a camera

When you use a digital camera, your photos are stored in a removable memory card—most likely a CompactFlash (CF) or Secure Digital (SD) card. Rather than having to tether your camera directly to a computer, you can remove the memory card and insert it into a card reader device, then download your photos from the card reader to your computer via a USB cable or Firewire cable, depending on which connection your camera supports (Firewire is the faster of the two).

When you start downloading images from a camera, your system's default application for acquiring images launches automatically. In Windows XP, the default application is the Scanner and Camera Wizard; in Windows Vista, it's the Importing Pictures and Video Wizard. In the Mac OS, the default application will be either iPhoto or Image Capture (but note that as of this writing, in the Mac OS, only Image Capture can reliably import raw files). Not to be outdone, Adobe now includes the Photo Downloader application with Bridge.

To download photos via a card reader and the Photo Downloader:

1. Take the card out of your camera and insert it into the appropriate slot in the card reader.

2. Plug the card reader into your computer. If the default system application for acquiring photos launches, exit/quit it.

3. Launch **Bridge**, then click the **Get Photos from Camera** button ![icon] at the top of the Bridge window. ★ The Photo Downloader dialog opens. **A** If an alert dialog appears and you want to make Photo Downloader the default capture application, click Yes; otherwise, click No.

4. From the **Get Photos From** menu in the Source area, select your card reader.

5. In the **Import Settings** area, do the following:

   To change the save location, click **Browse/Choose**, then navigate to the desired folder. Click OK/Choose again to select that folder and return to the Downloader dialog.

   To create a new subfolder within the folder you just selected: choose a naming convention from the **Create Subfolder(s)** menu; or choose Custom Name and enter your own folder name (or choose None for no new subfolder).

A This is the Standard dialog of the Photo Downloader.

Optional: To assign your digital images recognizable names and shorter sequential numbers instead of the long default number, choose Custom Name from the Rename Files menu, then enter a name and a starting number. A sample of your entries will display in the Example field.

Check **Open Adobe Bridge** to have the photos display in Bridge when the download is completed.

We strongly recommend that you check **Save Copies To** and click **Browse/Choose** to send copies of your photos to a designated folder on an external hard drive.

6. If you want to download only some of the photos from your memory card, click **Advanced Dialog** to switch to the larger Advanced

dialog. **A** Below the thumbnail window, click **UnCheck All**, then check the box below each photo you want to download. Or click, then Shift-click a sequence of photos, then check the box for one of them; a check mark will appear below each selected photo.

Optional: In the Apply Metadata area, enter Creator and Copyright info to be added to the metadata of all downloaded photos (this metadata info will display in Bridge).

➤ To redisplay the smaller, Standard dialog at any time, click Standard Dialog.

7. Click **Get Photos** to start the download process. When the downloading is finished, the Photo Downloader dialog is dismissed automatically. If you checked the Open Adobe Bridge option, your photos will now display in a new window in Bridge. Don't worry about previewing or opening your photos just yet. We'll step you through that process later.

8. Now that you're done using the Photo Downloader, you should insert a blank DVD disk and burn the copies of your photo files to the DVD as a permanent backup copy. In the Mac OS, you can do this via drag-and-drop right in the Finder. If you need to learn how to copy files to a DVD, see your system Help files.

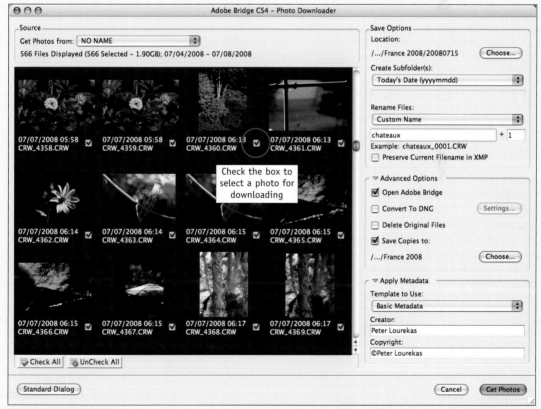

A This Advanced dialog of the Photo Downloader contains many of the same options as the Standard dialog, plus metadata features and the option to select the photos to be downloaded.

The Bridge window

Panels and panes

The Bridge window contains a toolbar at the top ★ and three panes: one in the center and a vertical pane on each side (**A**, next page). Each pane contains one or more panels, which are accessed via tabs: **Favorites**, **Folders**, **Filter**, **Collections**, **Content**, **Preview**, **Metadata**, and **Keywords**. You can hide/show or resize any of the panels or move any panel into another pane.

We'll explore the toolbar features and most of the panels in depth later in this chapter, but for now, here's a brief summary of the panels:

The **Favorites** panel displays a list of folders that you've designated as favorites, for quick access. Via check boxes in the Favorite Items area of Bridge Preferences > General, you can control which folders appear in the panel. To add a folder to the panel, drag the folder icon from the Content panel (the center pane) or the Explorer/Finder into the Favorites panel (plus sign pointer); or right-click/Control-click the folder and choose Add to Favorites. To remove a Favorites folder from the list, click it, then choose File > Remove from Favorites.

The **Folders** panel contains a scrolling window with a hierarchical listing of all the top-level and nested folders on your hard drive.

The **Filter** panel is dynamic, meaning the categories listed (e.g., Ratings, Keywords, Exposure Time) change depending on what data is available for files in the currently selected folder and what categories are checked on the Filter panel menu. ★ For example, if you haven't applied ratings to any files in the current folder, you won't see a Ratings category; should you apply a rating to a thumbnail, the Ratings category will magically appear. Click an arrowhead to expand or collapse a category. Click a listing within a category, and only image thumbnails matching that listing will display in the Content panel; click again to uncheck the listing to display the thumbnails that were filtered out. This is a fast way to control the display of image thumbnails.

The **Collections** panel displays the names (and cute folder icons) for collections, which are user-created groups of image thumbnails. ★

The **Content** panel displays image thumbnails (and optional thumbnails for nested folders) within the currently selected folder. In the lower right corner of the Bridge window, you can click a View Content button to control what displays in the Content panel. ★ For any view type, you can change the thumbnail size via the Thumbnails slider.

The **Preview** panel displays a large preview of the currently selected image (or folder) thumbnail. If you select a video or PDF file, the Preview will display a controller for playing the video or for viewing the pages. You can also preview two or more selected image thumbnails in this panel for quick comparison, and magnify details of an image with a loupe.

The **Metadata** panel lists information about the currently selected image thumbnail: a quick summary in the "placard" at the top and detailed listings in categories below. The File Properties category, for example, lists the file name, format, date created, date modified, etc.

You can use the IPTC Core category in the Metadata panel to attach creator, description, copyright, and other information to the currently selected file. (IPTC is an information standard for transferring and publishing text and images.) Click the field next to a listing, enter or modify the file description information, press Tab to cycle through and edit other data, then click the green Apply button ☑ in the lower right corner.

If a digital photo is selected, the Camera Data (EXIF) category displays the camera settings that were used to capture the photo. If the photo was edited in Camera Raw, those settings will be listed in a category called Camera Raw (like the Filter panel, this panel is dynamic). To learn more about the Metadata panel, see Bridge Help.

Use the **Keywords** panel to assign descriptive keywords to images, such as an event, name, location, or other criteria. You can run a search to find image thumbnails via keywords, or display images based on keywords using the Filter panel.

Browse Quickly
by Preferring
Embedded Images

Thumbnail
Quality and
Preview menu

Filter Items
by Rating
menu

Sort By
menu

Rotate
selected
thumbnails

Open
Recent
File menu

Create
a New
Folder

Descending Order/
Ascending Order

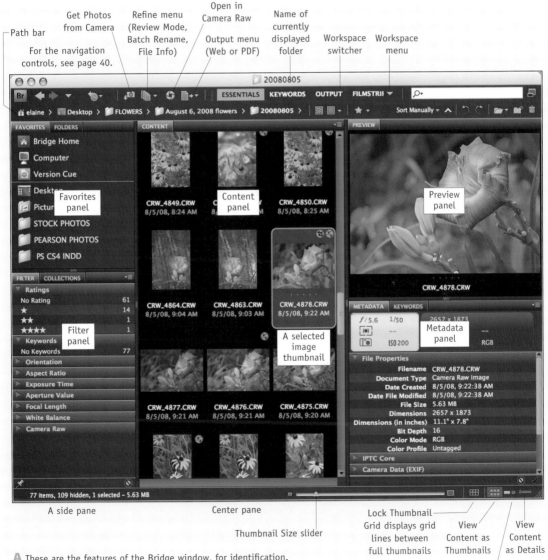

Path bar

Get Photos
from Camera

Refine menu
(Review Mode,
Batch Rename,
File Info)

Open in
Camera Raw

Output menu
(Web or PDF)

Name of
currently
displayed
folder

Workspace
switcher

Workspace
menu

For the navigation
controls, see page 40.

Favorites
panel

Content
panel

Preview
panel

Filter
panel

A selected
image
thumbnail

Metadata
panel

A side pane

Center pane

Thumbnail Size slider

Lock Thumbnail
Grid displays grid
lines between
full thumbnails

View
Content as
Thumbnails

View
Content
as Details

View Content as List

A These are the features of the Bridge window, for identification.
You'll learn about their function throughout this chapter.

Choosing a workspace for Bridge

To reconfigure the Bridge window quickly, choose one of the predefined workspaces. (To create and save custom workspaces, see pages 44–47.)

To choose a workspace for Bridge: ★

Do one of the following:

On the upper toolbar, click **Essentials**, **Filmstrip**, **Metadata** (List View for the thumbnails), **Output**, **Keywords**, **Preview**, **Light Table**, **Folders**, or a custom workspace. **A** (To display more workspace names, pull the vertical bar to the left. **B**)

From the **Workspace** menu on the workspace switcher, choose a workspace **C** (and **A–C**, next page).

Press the **shortcut** for one of the first six workspaces on the switcher (as listed on the Workspace menu): Ctrl-1/Cmd-F1 through Ctrl-6/Cmd-F6. The shortcuts are assigned automatically to the first six workspaces on the switcher, based on their current left-to-right order.

To change the order of workspaces on the switcher: ★

Drag a workspace name to the left or right.

Right-click/Control-click a workspace name and choose a different name from the context menu.

A Click a workspace on the workspace switcher.

Workspace menu

B To reveal more workspace names, drag the vertical bar to the left.

C In the Filmstrip workspace, you can click a thumbnail, then keep pressing the left or right arrow key to cycle through the thumbnails in the current folder. This workspace also features a large preview of the currently selected thumbnail.

A In the Essentials workspace, all the panels are showing, and the Center pane is wider than the side panes.

B In the Preview workspace, the Metadata and Keywords panels are hidden to allow for a large preview, and the thumbnails are displayed vertically (rather than horizontally, as in the Filmstrip workspace).

C In the Light Table workspace, the Content panel takes up the entire Bridge window so you can view a lot of images in the current folder.

► To resize the thumbnails for any workspace, drag the Thumbnail Size slider at the bottom of the Bridge window.

Previewing images in Bridge

Bridge CS4 offers new, streamlined controls on the toolbar for navigating to and opening folders, 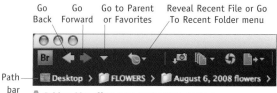 in addition to the existing controls in the Folders and Favorites panels that you may already be familiar with.

Go Back Go Forward Go to Parent or Favorites Reveal Recent File or Go To Recent Folder menu

Path bar

A Bridge CS4 offers new navigation controls.

To display and select images in Bridge: ★

1. Do any of the following:

   In the **Folders** panel, navigate to the folder you want to open. Scroll upward or downward, or expand or collapse any folder by clicking the arrowhead.

   Display the contents of a folder by clicking its icon in the **Folders** panel or by double-clicking its thumbnail in the **Content** panel. Note: If folder icons aren't displaying, check View > Show Folders.

   Click the **Go Back** button ◄ at the top of the Bridge window to step back through the last folders viewed, or the **Go Forward** button ► to show more recently viewed folders.

   Click a folder that you've placed in the **Favorites** panel.

   Choose from a list of Favorites or Recent Folders on the **Go to Parent or Favorites** menu ◄ at the top of the Bridge window.

   Click a folder name on the Path bar (Window > Path Bar).

   From one of the menus ▌ on the Path bar, choose a folder. If another submenu displays,

   click yet another folder; repeat until you get to the desired folder.

   ➤ To display thumbnails for images in all the nested subfolders inside the current folder, choose Show Items from Subfolders from its menu.▌ Click the Cancel button ◙ at any time to go back to the last display.

2. In the **Content** panel, do either of the following:

   Click an image thumbnail. A colored border will appear around it, and data about the file will be listed in the Metadata panel. An enlarged preview of the image will also display in the Preview panel, if that panel is showing.

   To select multiple images, Ctrl-click/Cmd-click nonconsecutive thumbnails (**A**, next page); or click the first thumbnail in a series of consecutive thumbnails, then Shift-click the last one.

   ➤ If an image has a number in the upper left corner, it's part of a group of thumbnails, called a stack. To display all the images in a stack, click the number; to collapse the stack, click the number again (see page 50).

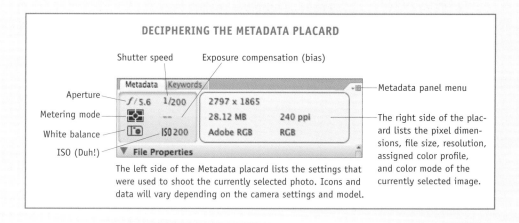

DECIPHERING THE METADATA PLACARD

Shutter speed   Exposure compensation (bias)

Aperture

Metering mode

White balance

ISO (Duh!)

Metadata panel menu

The right side of the placard lists the pixel dimensions, file size, resolution, assigned color profile, and color mode of the currently selected image.

The left side of the Metadata placard lists the settings that were used to shoot the currently selected photo. Icons and data will vary depending on the camera settings and model.

You can control whether thumbnails and the preview are rendered quickly but at low resolution, or slower but at high resolution.

To choose preview quality options: ★

From the **Options for Thumbnail Quality** menu ▦ on the Bridge toolbar, choose a preference for the thumbnail quality:

Always High Quality, the default setting, displays high-resolution thumbnails and previews, whether the thumbnails are selected or not, and renders the slowest.

Prefer Embedded (Faster) displays low-resolution thumbnails and previews, and is useful when you need to display many images quickly.

High Quality on Demand displays high-resolution thumbnails and previews for selected thumbnails only (a good compromise between the two previous options).

➤ For lower quality but faster previewing, click the Browse Quickly by Preferring Embedded Images button ▦ on the Bridge Path bar; this enables the Prefer Embedded (Faster) option. Click the button again to return to the current setting on the Options for Thumbnail Quality menu.

➤ The Generate 100% Previews option saves actual-size JPEG versions of thumbnails to disk for better previews when using the loupe or when using 100% view in Slideshow mode. Since this option consumes a considerable amount of disk space, we recommend leaving it unchecked.

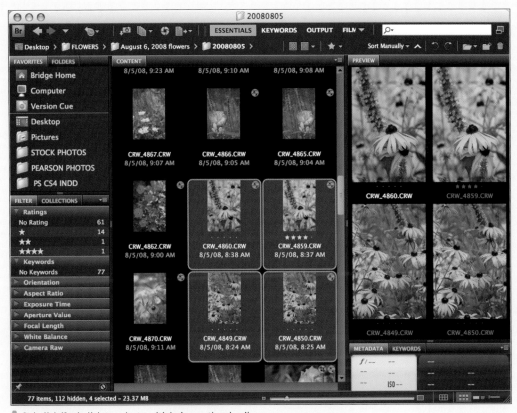

A Ctrl-click/Cmd-click to select multiple image thumbnails.

To compare image previews:

1. In Bridge, click or choose the **Filmstrip** or **Preview** workspace.

2. In the **Content** panel, Ctrl-click/Cmd-click two or more thumbnails.

3. Large versions of the selected thumbnails will display in the **Preview** panel.

4. *Optional:* Ctrl-click/Cmd-click to add more thumbnails to the panel; Ctrl-click/Cmd-click a selected thumbnail to deselect it and remove it from the Preview panel.

To display a full-screen preview of an image thumbnail: ★

Press **Spacebar** to display a full-screen preview of the currently selected thumbnail and hide the Bridge window temporarily. Press Spacebar again to return to the Bridge window.

➤ Click the full-screen preview to display it at 100% view; click it again to restore the preview to the full screen size.

To examine picture details with a loupe:

1. To make the loupe appear, click an image in the Preview panel or click the frontmost image in Review mode (see the following page).**B** Note: If the loupe doesn't appear, it's because Ctrl-click/Cmd-click Opens the Loupe When Previewing or Reviewing is checked in Preferences > General for Bridge. If this is the case, Ctrl-click/Cmd-click the image to make the loupe appear. ★

2. Click the area that you want to examine. By default, pixels display in the loupe at 100% view (the zoom level is listed below the preview image). Press + to zoom in on the loupe display or – to zoom out. Click another area or drag the loupe to examine another area.

3. *Optional:* If you're previewing two images using two loupes, you can Ctrl-drag/Cmd-drag either loupe to move them in unison.

4. Click the loupe to remove it.

B You can examine fine details by using the loupe.

A We Ctrl/Cmd clicked two image thumbnails to compare them in the Preview panel, then we clicked one of the previews to examine it with an onscreen loupe.

In Review Mode, multiple large image previews display on a black background, partially overlapping—as if on a carousel.A You can cycle through the images, as well as remove them to narrow down the selection for grouping as a stack (see pages 50–51) or as a collection (see pages 54–55).

To view images in Review mode: ★

1. Open a folder of images; or click a thumbnail stack; or select five or more image thumbnails (Ctrl-click/Cmd-click or Shift-click).

2. From the **Refine** menu at the top of the Bridge window, choose **Review Mode** (Ctrl-B/Cmd-B). The selected images will appear as large previews, and the Bridge window will be hidden temporarily.

3. To rotate the carousel, do any of the following:

   Drag any image preview to the left or right.

   Click an image preview behind the large one to bring it to the forefront.

Click (and keep clicking) the Go Forward or Go Backward button in the lower left corner, or press the left or right arrow key.

4. To examine the frontmost (enlarged) image with a loupe, click it. Drag the loupe to move it. Click the loupe again to remove it.

5. To take the front image out of the carousel, click the down-pointing arrow in the lower left corner, or drag the image to the bottom of your screen. This doesn't delete the actual file.

6. To exit Review mode, press Esc, or click the in the lower right corner.

7. After exiting Review mode, click any image thumbnail to deselect the rest.

A We Ctrl/Cmd clicked seven image thumbnails, then pressed Ctrl-B/Cmd-B to view them in Review mode.

Opening files from Bridge

You can open as many files in Photoshop as currently available RAM and scratch disk space allow. (Note: To open a raw, JPEG, or TIFF digital photo into Camera Raw, see Chapter 15.)

To open files from Bridge into Photoshop:

1. In the Content panel, display the thumbnail for the image(s) you want to open.

2. Do either of the following:

   Double-click an image thumbnail.

   Click an image thumbnail or select multiple thumbnails, then click one of them or press Ctrl-O/Cmd-O.

   Photoshop will launch, if it isn't already running, and the image(s) will appear onscreen.

   See also page 60.

➤ By default, the Bridge window stays open after you use it to open a file. To minimize/close the Bridge window as you open a file, hold down Alt/Option as you double-click a thumbnail.

➤ If a photo has been opened and settings applied to it in Camera Raw, it will have this icon ⊜ in the top right corner of its thumbnail.

Customizing the Bridge window

To choose colors for the Bridge interface:

1. Choose Edit/Adobe Bridge CS4 > **Preferences** (Ctrl-K/Cmd-K). The Preferences dialog opens.

2. On the left side, click **General**, and in the **Appearance** area A do any of the following:

   Move the **User Interface Brightness** slider to set the gray value for the side panes.

   Move the **Image Backdrop** slider to set a gray value for the center pane and the Preview panel.

   Choose an **Accent Color** for the border that surrounds selected folders, thumbnails, and stacks.

➤ To learn more about Bridge Preferences, see pages 398–399 and Bridge > Help.

REOPENING FILES

To reopen a file that was opened recently and then closed, choose that file name from the new Open Recent Files menu ◼◼ on the right side of the Path bar in Bridge, ★ or in Photoshop, choose it from the File > Open Recent submenu.

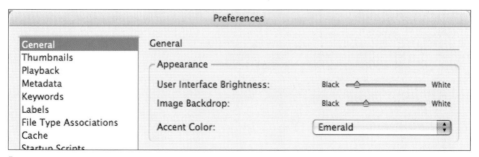

A By using the Appearance options in Bridge Preferences > General, you can customize the colors of the Bridge interface.

To control how metadata is displayed in the Content panel: ★

1. In the lower right corner of the Bridge window, click a View Content button: **A View Content as Thumbnails** (minimal file data), **View Content as Details** (more file data), **B** or **View Content as List** (small icons and columns of data). With View Content as List chosen, you can change the column order by dragging any column header to the left or right.

2. To choose which categories of metadata display below or next to the image thumbnails, go to Edit/Adobe Bridge CS4 > Preferences > Thumbnails, then select from any or all of the **Details: Show** menus. For example, if you want to display exposure settings, choose Exposure.

➤ When viewing content as thumbnails, you can toggle the display of metadata on and off by pressing Ctrl-T/Cmd-T.

METADATA IN TOOL TIPS

If Show Tooltips is checked in Preferences > Thumbnails and you rest the pointer on an image thumbnail, the tool tip will display the full metadata for that image (keep this feature off if the tool tips are more annoying than helpful).

View Content as Thumbnails   View Content as List   View Content as Details

A The View Content buttons control the format in which metadata displays in the Content panel.

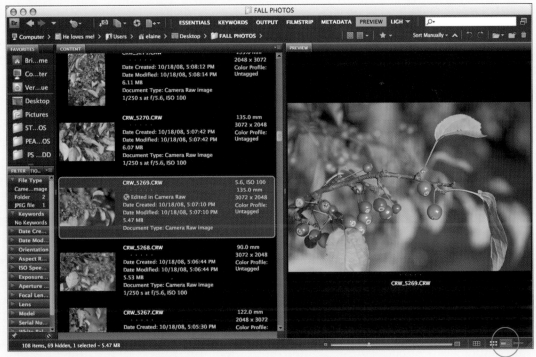

B We clicked the View Content as Details button to display metadata next to the file thumbnails.

To further customize the Bridge workspace, you can resize, move, or hide any of the panels.

To customize the Bridge panes and panels:

Do any of the following:

To make a panel or panel group **taller** or **shorter**, drag its horizontal bar upward or downward.**A**

To make a whole pane **wider** or **narrower**, drag its vertical bar sideways;**B** the adjacent pane will resize accordingly.

To **minimize** any panel except Content to just a tab, double-click its tab; double-click the tab again to maximize the panel.

To move a panel into a different **group**, drag the panel tab (name), and release the mouse when the blue drop zone border appears around the desired group.

To display a panel in its **own group**, drag its tab between two panels, and release the mouse when the horizontal blue drop zone line appears.

To resize the image thumbnails, drag the **Thumbnail Size** slider **C** or click the **Smaller Thumbnail Size** button ▢ or **Larger Thumbnail Size** button.▢

➤ To hide (and then show) the side panes, press Tab or double-click the vertical bar between the panes. To display only the Content pane in a compact window, click the Compact Mode button ▢ in the upper right corner of the Bridge window; click it again to restore the full window.

➤ Click the Lock Thumbnail Grid button ▦ (to the left of the View Content buttons) to display full thumbnails only, with grid lines between them.★ With this option on, no shuffling of thumbnails will occur if you resize the Content panel.

A Moving the horizontal bar upward shortens the Favorites and Folder panels and lengthens the Filter and Collections panels.

B Moving the vertical bar for the right pane to the left widens the Preview, Metadata, and Keywords panels.

C Use the Thumbnail Size slider at the bottom of the Bridge window to resize the image thumbnails.

Saving custom workspaces

If you save your customized workspaces, you'll be able to access them again quickly at any time and avoid having to set up your workspace each time you launch Bridge.

To save a custom workspace for Bridge: ★

1. Choose a size and location for the overall Bridge window, arrange the panel sizes and groups as desired, choose a thumbnail size for the Content panel, choose a sort order from the Sort By menu at the top of the Bridge window (see page 49), and click the desired View Content button.

2. From the **Workspace** menu on the workspace switcher, choose **New Workspace**. The New Workspace dialog opens.**A**

3. Enter a Name for the workspace, check Save Window Location as Part of Workspace and/or Save Sort Order as Part of Workspace (both are optional), then click Save.

   Note: Your new workspace will be listed first on the workspace switcher, and will be assigned the first shortcut (Ctrl-1/Cmd-F1). To change the order of workspaces on the bar, drag any workspace name sideways to a different slot. When you do this, the shortcuts will be reassigned based on the new order.

Resetting the Bridge workspace

When you make a manual change to a saved workspace, the change sticks with the workspace even when you switch back and forth between workspaces. For example, if you were to change the thumbnail size for the Filmstrip workspace, click the Essentials workspace, then click back on the Filmstrip workspace, it would still display the new thumbnail size. Via the commands for resetting workspaces, you can restore the default settings to a predefined or user-saved workspace or to all the predefined (standard Adobe) workspaces.

To reset the Bridge workspace: ★

Do either of the following:

To restore the default settings to one workspace, display that workspace, then choose **Reset Workspace** from the Workspace menu.

To restore the default settings to all the predefined (Adobe) workspaces, choose **Reset Standard Workspaces** from the Workspace menu.

Moving and copying files

You can move files to a different folder by dragging them or by using a command.

To move or copy files to other folders:
Method 1 (dragging)

1. Click the **Folders** panel tab. Display the subfolder that you want to move files to, and expand any folders, if necessary.

2. Select one or more thumbnails in the **Content** panel, then drag them over a folder name in the Folders panel to move them, or hold down Ctrl/Option and drag them over a folder name to copy them.

Method 2 (context menu)

1. Select one or more thumbnails in the **Content** panel.

2. Right-click/Ctrl-click one of the selected thumbnails, then from the **Move To** or **Copy To** submenu on the context menu, do either of the following:

   Select a folder name under **Recent Folders**.

   Select **Choose Folder**. Locate a folder in the Choose a Folder dialog, then click OK/Choose.

FINDING THE "ACTUAL" FILE

To locate a file in Explorer/Finder, click its thumbnail in Bridge, then right-click/Ctrl-click and choose Reveal in Explorer/Reveal in Finder. The folder that the file resides in will open in a window in Explorer/Finder and the file icon will be selected.

A Use the New Workspace dialog to name your workspace and choose options.

Labeling and rating thumbnails

If you assign thumbnails a star rating and/or color label, you'll be able to display them based on the presence or absence of that rating or label and find them easily via the Filter panel and Find command. You can also apply a Reject rating to image thumbnails that you want to hide from the Content panel but aren't quite ready to delete from your hard drive.

To label and rate thumbnails:

1. Select one or more image thumbnails in the **Content** panel.

2. Do any of the following:

   From the **Label** menu, choose a **Rating** (number of stars) and/or a **Label** (color-coded strip below the image).

   Right-click/Control–click a thumbnail in the **Content** panel and from the **Label** submenu on the context menu, choose a category. (You can rename the categories in Preferences > Labels.)

   Right-click/Control–click in the **Preview** panel and choose a star rating and/or label.

   Click a thumbnail, then click any one of the five **dots** below it; stars will appear. To **remove** a star, click the star to its left. To remove all the stars from a thumbnail, click to the left of the first star. (If you don't see the dots or stars, enlarge the thumbnails.)

   Press one of the keyboard **shortcuts** listed on the Label menu or context menu.

   To label the losers with a red "Reject" label, choose Label > **Reject** (Alt-Del/Option-Delete). If Show Reject Files is unchecked on the View menu, all rejected thumbnails will be hidden.

➤ If tool tips get in the way of your adding or removing stars, go to Preferences > Thumbnails and uncheck Show Tooltips.

➤ To remove the ratings from a selected thumbnail or thumbnails, choose Label > No Rating (Ctrl-0/Cmd-0).

To redisplay all rejected thumbnails:

Choose View > **Show Reject Files**. All thumbnails with a Reject rating will redisplay.

A This thumbnail has an Approved (green) rating.

B We clicked the third dot on this thumbnail to assign a 3-star rating...

C ...but then we changed our minds, so we clicked to the left of the stars to remove them.

D This poor thumbnail has a Reject rating.

RATING THUMBNAILS IN REVIEW MODE ★

To rate or label images in Review mode, right-click/Control-click the large, frontmost image and choose from the context menu.

Choosing a sorting order

The sorting order you choose from the Sort By menu controls the order in which thumbnails display in the Content panel. The sorting order of thumbnails is also important for batch and automate operations, which process files based on the current sequence of thumbnails. The current sorting order applies to all folders and thumbnails, not just to one folder in particular. By choosing a sorting order and by using the Filter panel (see below), you'll be able to locate the files you need more quickly and efficiently.

To choose a sorting order:

From the **Sort By** menu on the Path bar, ★ choose a sorting order (such as By Date Created).**A** Thumbnails will be rearranged in the Content panel (thumbnails in stacks are exempt).

➤ Click the Ascending Order ▲ or Descending Order ▼ arrowhead to switch the sorting order.

Using the Filter panel

The Filter panel lists data specific to files in the current folder, such as the label, star rating, file type, date created, date modified, etc. By checking specific criteria in the panel, you can control which thumbnails display in the current folder. A thumbnail must match all checked criteria in order to display.

To filter out which thumbnails display:

Do either of the following:

From the **Filter Items by Rating** menu on the Bridge toolbar,**B** check the desired criteria. ★ (To remove the filtering at any time, choose Clear Filter or press Ctrl-Alt-A/Cmd-Option-A.)

On the Filter panel, check a listing within any category, such as Labels or Ratings, to display thumbnails that match that criterion;**C** to display thumbnails matching additional criteria, check other listings in the **same** category. To display even fewer thumbnails, check listings in **other** categories. (To redisplay hidden thumbnails, remove the check mark by clicking the listing again.) To display only files with a Reject rating, check Reject in the Ratings category.

➤ To apply the current check marks as you display other folders, click the Keep Filter When Browsing ✿ button at the bottom of the panel.

➤ To remove all check marks from the Filter panel, click the Clear Filter ◯ button at the bottom of the panel (Ctrl-Alt-A/Cmd-Option-A).

A Choose a sorting order for your Bridge thumbnails from the Sort By menu on the Path bar.

B Filter the display of thumbnails via the Filter Items by Rating menu.

C Because we checked the two-star option under Ratings in the Filter panel, only thumbnails matching that criterion (that have two stars) will display in the Content panel.

NEW FILTER PANEL OPTIONS ★

➤ Via the Filter panel menu, you can control which categories are listed.

➤ New categories in the Filter panel are Exposure Time, Aperture Value, Focal Length, Lens, Camera Model, White Balance, and Camera Raw.

➤ Folders are now listed under File Type category in the Filter panel.

Using thumbnail stacks

Before getting into stacks, start with the simple technique of dragging thumbnails to change their location in the Content panel.

To rearrange thumbnails manually:

Drag a thumbnail (or select, then drag multiple thumbnails) to a new location. The Sort By menu header switches to "Sort Manually." Thumbnails remain where you place them unless you change the sorting order or perform a stacking operation.

An easy way to limit how many thumbnails display at a given time is to organize them into stacks. Try to create logical categories, such as all landscapes or portraits, multiple shots of the same subject, or shots taken with a particular camera setting.

To group thumbnails into a stack:

1. Shift-click or Ctrl-click/Cmd-click to select multiple thumbnails.**A** The thumbnail listed first in your selection will become the "stack thumbnail" (will display on top of the stack).

2. Choose Stacks > **Group as Stack** (Ctrl-G/Cmd-G) or right-click/Control-click and choose Stack > **Group as Stack**.**B** The stack will look like two playing cards in a pile, and instead of all the individual thumbnails, you'll see just the stack thumbnail on top. The number in the upper left corner (the "stack number") indicates how many thumbnails the stack contains.

To select thumbnails in a stack:

To **select and display** all the thumbnails in a stack, click the stack number. Click the number again to collapse the stack. The stack remains selected.

To **select** all the thumbnails in a stack while keeping the stack **collapsed**, click the stack border (bottom "card") or Alt-click/Option-click the stack thumbnail (top image in the stack).

To rearrange thumbnails in a stack:

To **rearrange** a thumbnail in an expanded stack, click it to deselect the other selected thumbnails, then drag it to a new location (as shown by the vertical drop zone line).

To move a whole stack:

1. Collapse the stack, then Alt-click/Option-click the stack thumbnail.

A Select the thumbnails to be grouped into a stack.

B A stack is created. The number in the upper left corner indicates how many thumbnails the stack contains.

2. Drag the image thumbnail (not the border).

➤ If you drag the top thumbnail of an unselected stack, you'll move just that thumbnail, not the whole stack.

To add a thumbnail to a stack:
Drag a thumbnail over a stack thumbnail (you'll see a drop zone border) or into an open stack.

To remove a thumbnail from a stack:
1. Click the stack number to expand the stack.
2. Click the thumbnail to be removed (to deselect the other thumbnails), then drag it out of the stack.

To ungroup a whole stack:
1. Click the stack number to expand and select all the thumbnails in the stack.
2. Choose Stacks > **Ungroup from Stack** (Control-Shift-G/Cmd-Shift-G) or right-click/Control-click and choose Stack > **Ungroup from Stack**. The stack number and border disappear.

Managing files

To create a new folder:
1. Via the Folders panel or the Path bar, navigate to the folder that you want to place the new folder in.
2. Click the **New Folder** button 📁 at the right end of the Bridge toolbar, type a name in the highlighted field below the new folder, then press Enter/Return.

To delete files:
1. Click a thumbnail (or Ctrl-click/Cmd-click multiple thumbnails or Shift-click a series of thumbnails).
2. Press Ctrl-Backspace/Cmd-Delete, then click OK in the alert dialog. Beware! You can also delete a whole folder full of files. To retrieve a deleted file or folder, double-click the Recycle Bin/Trash icon for the operating system, then drag the item into the Content panel in Bridge.

To rename a file:
1. Click a thumbnail, then click the file name. The name will become highlighted.
2. Type a new name **A–C** (don't try to delete the extension), then press Enter/Return or click outside the name field.

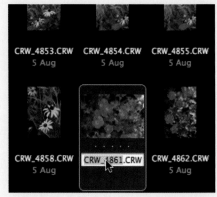

A To rename a file in Bridge, click the existing file name...

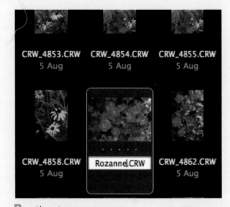

B ...then type a new name.

C Because our chosen current sort order is Sort by Filename, the image thumbnail reshuffled automatically to a different spot based on its new name.

When you download digital photos from your camera to your computer, they keep the sequential numerical labels (e.g., "CRW_0016") that your camera assigned to them. Via the Batch Rename command, you can assign more recognizable names to your photos (e.g., "Dancer" or "Dog") in a few quick steps, to help you identify them.

To batch-rename files:

1. Don't bother selecting any thumbnails if you want to rename all the files in a particular folder, or select just the thumbnails for the files you want to rename.

2. From the **Refine** menu ![icon] at the top of the Bridge toolbar, choose Tools > **Batch Rename** (Ctrl-Shift-R/Cmd-Shift-R). The Batch Rename dialog opens.**A**

3. For the **Destination Folder**, choose:

   Rename in Same Folder to rename the files and leave them in their current location.

   Move to Other Folder to rename the files and move them to a new location.

   Copy to Other Folder to leave the original files unchanged but rename the copies and move them to a new location—a quick way to duplicate your photos. We recommend this option, especially if you didn't duplicate your files when you downloaded them.

For the Move or Copy option, click **Browse**, choose or create a new folder location, then click OK/Choose.

4. For **New Filenames**, choose an option from one of the menus in the left-hand column. Text lets you enter text for the new file names (probably the best choice); Current Filename preserves the existing name; and Sequence Number and Sequence Letter let you include a number or letter that increments from file name to file name (enter a starting number or letter).

   To add another row of criteria fields, click the ⊕ button; to remove a row of fields, click the ⊖ button.

   The current and new file names will be listed in the **Preview** area in the dialog.

5. Under **Options**, you can leave Preserve Current Filename in XMP Metadata unchecked, but for **Compatibility**, do check any other operating system that you want your renamed files to be compatible with.

6. *Optional:* To save the current dialog settings, click Save, enter a name, keep the .settings extension and the default folder location, then click Save again. (Click Load to load in a saved settings file.) ★

7. Click **Rename**.

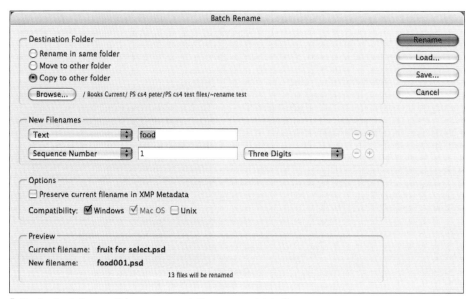

A Via the Batch Rename dialog, you can quickly rename multiple files.

Searching for files

To find files via Bridge: ★

1. In Bridge, choose Edit > **Find** (Ctrl-F/Cmd-F). The Find dialog opens.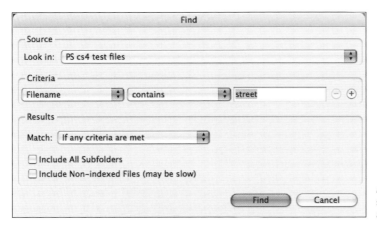A

2. From the **Look In** menu in the Source area, choose the folder to be searched (the default listing is the current folder). To select a folder that's not on the list, choose Look In: Browse, locate the desired folder, then click OK/Choose.

3. From the menus in the **Criteria** area, choose search criteria (e.g., file name, date created, label, rating, particular camera settings), choose a parameter from the adjoining menu, and enter data in the field. To include additional criteria in the search, click the ⊕, then choose and enter more search criteria.

4. From the **Match** menu, choose "If any criteria are met" to find files based on one or more criteria, or choose "If all criteria are met" to narrow the selection to files that meet all the chosen criteria.

5. Check **Include All Subfolders** to also search through any subfolders within the folder you chose in step 2.

6. *Optional:* Check Include Non-indexed Files to search through files that Bridge hasn't yet indexed (any folder Bridge has yet to display). This will slow down the search.

7. Click **Find**. The search results will display in the Content panel and also in a temporary folder called Search Results: [name of source folder].B It will be listed on both the Path bar and on the Reveal Recent File or Go to Recent Folder menu 🔲 on the Bridge toolbar.

8. To save a copy of the search results to a permanent file group, see the following page, or to cancel the search results, click the ⊠.

► To discard the current search results and perform a new search, click New Search.

A Use the Find dialog to search for and locate files according to various criteria.

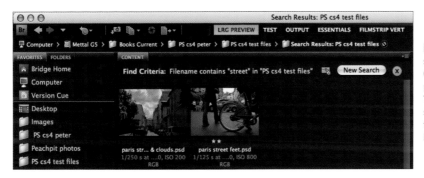

B After you click Find, the search results display in the Content panel of the temporary Search Results folder. The parameters used for the search and the name of the folder that was searched will be listed as the Find Criteria.

Creating collections ★

The collection features in Bridge give you a useful way to group and access files (without actually relocating them). There are two kinds of collections: a Smart Collection created from the results of a Find search, and a collection created by dragging thumbnails manually into a collection folder.

To create a Smart Collection:

1. Click the tab for the Collections panel (if you don't see this panel, choose Window > Collections Panel).

2. Perform a search by using the Edit > **Find** command (see the previous page). When the search is completed, click the **Save as Smart Collection** button ![icon] at the top of the Content panel or the bottom of the Collections panel.**A**

3. A New Smart Collection folder appears in the top part of the Collections panel.**B** Type a name in the highlighted field, then press Enter/Return.

To display a collection:

Click its icon in the Collections panel.

The smart thing about Smart Collections is that you can run a new search for a collection based on either new criteria or a new search folder, and the collection contents will update automatically.

To edit a Smart Collection:

1. In the **Collections** panel, click the icon for an existing Smart Collection.

2. Click the **Edit Smart Collection** button ![icon] at the top of the Content panel or in the lower left corner of the Collections panel.**C**

3. The Edit Smart Collection dialog opens. Enter a new folder to be searched and/or new search criteria, then click Save.

4. The results of the new search will display in the Content panel, and new thumbnails, if any, will replace the old in the same collection. Note: If you move a thumbnail out of a Smart Collection folder or move the actual file from the folder that was used in the search, it is removed from the collection. If you delete a thumbnail from a Smart Collection, the actual file is deleted from your hard drive!

A Click the Save as Smart Collection button to create a Smart Collection.

B The new Smart Collection displays on the Collections panel. Enter a new name in the already high-lighted field.

C To edit a Smart Collection, click a Smart Collection folder on the Collections panel, then click the Edit Smart Collection button at the bottom of the panel.

Bridge also lets you create a nonsmart collection without running a search, and lets you add to the collection by dragging thumbnails into it.

To create a nonsmart collection:

1. Do either of the following:

On the **Content** panel, select image thumbnails to be placed into a collection. On the **Collections** panel, click the **New Collection** button, 🖼 then click Yes in the alert dialog.

When viewing files in **Review mode** (Ctrl-B/Cmd-B), drag any files you don't want in the collection out of the carousel, then click the **New Collection** button. 🖼

2. On the panel, type a name for the collection, **A** then press Enter/Return.

To add files to a nonsmart collection:

1. Display the **Collections** panel.

2. Drag thumbnails to an existing collection folder. **B**

A Click the New Collection button to create a new collection, then type a name for the collection in the highlighted field.

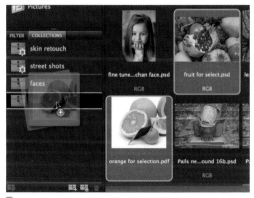

B Drag thumbnails to a collection folder to add them to that collection.

To remove a thumbnail from a collection:

1. On the **Collections** panel, click a collection folder to display its contents.

2. Select the thumbnails to be removed, then click the **Remove from Collection** button at the top of the Content panel (or right-click/Control-click a thumbnail and choose Remove from Collection). **C**

➤ Don't delete a thumbnail from a collection unless you want to delete the actual file from your hard drive!

If you rename a file or move it from its original location, Bridge will automatically update the link to any nonsmart collections that contain the file. If Bridge is unable to do so, do as follows.

To relink a missing file to a collection:

1. On the **Collections** panel, click a folder to which you want to relink a file or files.

2. Next to the Missing File Detected alert at the top of the Content panel, click **Fix. D**

3. In the **Find Missing Files** dialog, click Browse, locate and select the missing file, then click Open (Skip ignores the current missing file and proceeds to the next one). Click OK.

C Click Remove from Collection to take a selected thumbnail out of the currently selected collection.

D Click Fix to relink a file that's missing from a collection.

Exporting the Bridge cache

Each time a folder is displayed in the Content panel in Bridge, the program automatically creates a cache file, which contains information about the files in the folder, such as the data for displaying ratings, labels, and high-quality thumbnails. Having the cache helps speed up the display of thumbnails when you choose that folder again. If you want to include this display information with files you copy to a removable disk or to a shared folder on a network, you'll need to copy the cache files—but before you can do so, you have to build the cache files and export them to the current folder.

To export the cache to the current folder: ★

1. Choose Edit (Bridge, in the Mac OS) > Preferences > Cache. In the Cache area, check **Automatically Export Cache to Folders When Possible**, then click OK.

2. Choose Tools > Cache > **Build and Export Cache**. In the alert dialog, check **Export Cache to Folders**, then click OK.

3. Two hidden cache files—named .BridgeCache (metadata cache) and .BridgeCacheT (thumbnail cache)—will be placed in the currently displayed folder.

   If you use the File > Move To (or Copy To) command in Bridge to move (or copy) selected thumbnails, the folder cache you just created will also move or copy, thanks to the export option that you turned on in Preferences > Cache.

   ➤ To display the generic cache file icons in the Content panel, choose View > Show Hidden Files.

Thumbnail cache files sometimes cause display problems, in which case purging them may resolve the issue. The purge will cause Bridge to regenerate the thumbnail previews for the current folder.

To purge cache files:

To purge the cache files from the current folder, choose Tools > Cache > **Purge Cache for Folder** "[current folder name]." Two new (hidden) cache files will be generated.

To purge the cache files from multiple selected thumbnails, right-click/Control-click and choose **Purge Cache for Selection**. ★

ALAS, THE POOR OPEN COMMAND

➤ With Bridge now the best vehicle for opening files, the Open command is relegated to this puny sidebar. To use the Open command in Photoshop, choose File > Open (Ctrl-O/Cmd-O). In Windows, choose All Formats from the Files of Type menu; in the Mac OS, choose All Readable Documents from the Enable menu. Click the desired file name, then click Open.

➤ Another way to open a file is by double-clicking its file icon in Explorer/Finder; this will also launch Photoshop if it's not already running.

Assigning keywords to files

Keywords (identifying text) are used by search utilities to locate files and by file management programs to organize them. In Bridge, you can create main-level keyword categories (such as events, people, places, things, themes, etc.), and nested subkeywords within those categories, and then assign them to your files. You can also locate files in Bridge by using the Find command with Keywords as a search criterion or by checking specific keywords in the Keywords category in the Filter panel.

To create keywords:

1. To create a new main-level keyword category, in the Keywords panel, click the **New Keyword** button, then type a keyword.**A** ★

2. To create a nested subkeyword, click a main-level keyword, click the **New Sub Keyword** button, type a word, then press Enter/Return. You can also create sub-subkeywords. ★

► You can move (drag) any subkeyword into a different main-level keyword category.

► To learn about the Keywords Preferences, see page 399.

To assign keywords:

1. Select one or more image thumbnails. If the image has been assigned keywords already, they will be listed at the top of the panel; you can assign more.

2. Check the box for one or more subkeywords.**B** (Although you can assign a main-level keyword, we don't see much use for doing so.)

► The keywords for an image are also listed under Keywords in the Filter panel and in File > File Info.

► If you import a file that already contains keywords into Bridge and you want to add them as permanent subkeywords, right-click/Control-click each subkeyword under Other Keywords in the Keywords panel and choose Make Persistent from the context menu.

► You can also assign keywords via the File Info dialog. Select one or more thumbnails, then from the Refine menu on the Bridge toolbar, choose File Info. In the Description tab of the dialog, enter the desired keywords, separated by semicolons or commas (watch for typing errors!). ★

A We created a new main-level keyword called "Females," kept the category selected, then by using the New Sub Keyword button, added new subkeywords to it.

B We clicked an image thumbnail, then checked the subkeywords that we wanted to assign to it.

USING THE KEYWORDS PANEL

Rename a main-level keyword or subkeyword	Click the word, choose Rename from the Keywords panel menu, then type a name (this doesn't change already embedded data).
Delete a main-level keyword or subkeyword	Click the word, then click the Delete Keyword button (if that keyword is assigned to any files, it will be in italics).
Find a keyword or subkeyword on the list	Type the word in the search field at the bottom of the panel.

Opening PDF and Illustrator files

When you open Adobe Illustrator (AI) or PDF files in Photoshop, they're rasterized automatically, meaning they're converted from their native vector format into the Photoshop pixel format. For a PDF, you can open one or more PDF pages or extract raster images from the file. Follow these instructions to open a PDF or Adobe Illustrator file as a new rasterized document, or follow the instructions on page 27 to place a PDF or Illustrator file as a Smart Object into an existing Photoshop file.

Note: When opened in Photoshop CS4, Adobe Illustrator files that are saved with the Create PDF Compatible file option open in the Photoshop PDF format, not the EPS format.

To open a PDF or Adobe Illustrator file as a new document:

1. In Bridge, locate the PDF or AI file you want to open, then choose File > Open With > **Adobe Photoshop CS4** or right-click/Control-click the image thumbnail and choose Open With > Adobe Photoshop CS4 from the context menu. The Import PDF dialog opens in Photoshop.

2. For **Select**, do the following:

   Click **Pages** to view the whole PDF pages **A** or click **Images** to view just the images in the PDF file. **B** If you clicked Images, click the image (or select multiple images) you want to open, then click OK—you're done.

   If you clicked Pages, follow the remaining steps.

   Note: If the PDF you're opening contains multiple pages, click the thumbnail for the desired page, or Shift-click or Cmd-click to select multiple pages. Each page you select is going to open as a separate Photoshop file.

   ► From the Thumbnail Size menu, choose a size for the thumbnails.

3. Under **Page Options**, do the following:

   Optional: Type a **Name** for the new document.

   Choose a **Crop To** option. We suggest choosing Bounding Box (the default) to exclude any white areas outside the artwork.

   Check **Anti-aliased** to reduce jaggies and soften the edge transitions.

4. For **Image Size**, do the following:

   For a whole PDF page, you can enter the desired maximum **Width** and **Height** for the

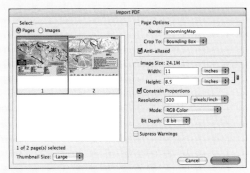

A To open a PDF as a whole page, in the Import PDF dialog, click Pages, click a page, then choose options for the new Photoshop file.

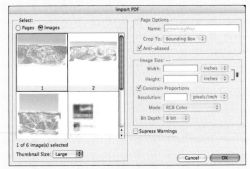

B Or to open just an image from a PDF file instead, click Images, click an image, then click OK.

ILLUSTRATOR FILES INTO PHOTOSHOP

To get Adobe Illustrator files into Photoshop, use one of these methods:

Open command	Opens the file as a new document; converts paths into pixels
Place command *(To place type, see page 355.)*	Opens the file as a Smart Object layer in an existing Photoshop document
Drag path from Illustrator into a Photoshop document	Appears as a new Smart Object layer
Copy object in Illustrator, Paste into a Photoshop document	Via the Paste dialog, choose to paste as a Smart Object, pixels, path, or shape layer; the latter two options preserve the shapes as vector objects

Photoshop document (or documents) or keep the current dimensions. You can also check **Constrain Proportions** to preserve the aspect ratio of the original PDF, to prevent distortion.

Enter the **Resolution** required for your output device. Entering the correct resolution for the image now, before it's rasterized, will produce a higher-quality image.

From the **Mode** menu, choose a document color mode. If the document contains a profile, that profile will also be listed. Adobe RGB is the color space in our color management workflow, so we recommend choosing either a document profile or RGB Color.

Choose a **Bit Depth** of 8 Bit or 16 Bit.

Leave **Suppress Warnings** unchecked to allow an alert to display should a color profile conflict arise.

5. Click OK.

► For an Adobe Illustrator file, if you didn't check PDF Compatible in the save dialog in Illustrator, the thumbnail in the Import PDF dialog will display only a text message. Reopen the file in Illustrator, choose File > Save As, rename or replace the file, then click Save. In the Illustrator Options dialog, check Create PDF Compatible File, then click OK. Now go ahead and open the file in Photoshop.

► To create a solid Background for an imported PDF in Photoshop, create a new layer, fill it with white via Edit > Fill, then choose Layer > New > Background from Layer.

To paste Adobe Illustrator art into Photoshop:

1. In Illustrator, in Preferences > File Handling & Clipboard, check **Copy As: PDF** and **AICB**, and click **Preserve Appearance and Overprints**. Copy an object via Edit > **Copy** (Ctrl-C/Cmd-C).

2. In a Photoshop document, choose Edit > **Paste** (Ctrl-V/Cmd-V). The Paste dialog opens.

3. Click **Paste As: Smart Object** (to keep the vector object editable) or **Pixels** (to rasterize the object). Click the Commit Transform button ✔ on the Options bar or press Enter/Return. To learn about Smart Object layers, see pages 314–316.

BRINGING EPS FILES INTO PHOTOSHOP

You have different options for bringing EPS files into Photoshop than for AI or PDF files:

► If you open an EPS file into Photoshop via File > Open in Photoshop or via File > Open With in Bridge, the Rasterize EPS Format dialog displays. Make Image Size, Resolution, and Mode choices, then click OK.

► If you use the File > Place command in Photoshop or File > Place > In Photoshop in Bridge, the EPS file will open directly into Photoshop without an import dialog opening. The file will appear in a bounding box at first (to allow for scaling, rotating, and moving), and will become a Smart Object layer when you press Enter/Return.

► The Rasterize EPS Format dialog also displays if you use the File > Open as Smart Object command in Photoshop. Click OK, and the file will import as a Smart Object layer.

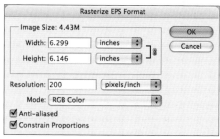

The Rasterize EPS Format dialog displays when you use the Open or Open as Smart Object command to open an EPS file in Photoshop.

AUTO SCALING

If Resize Image During Paste/Place is checked in Preferences > General in Photoshop and you paste or place a pixel or vector image into Photoshop, the image will be scaled automatically to fit the current canvas area.

CMYK COLORS FROM ILLUSTRATOR

When importing an Illustrator file containing CMYK colors, in Photoshop, use File > Place. It will arrive as a Smart Object (see page 27). This way, the file can stay in RGB Color mode for your work in Photoshop but the CMYK colors in the Smart Object will be preserved. You can convert the whole file to CMYK Color mode for output.

Dealing with the "ifs"

➤ If you open a file in Photoshop that's using a **missing font** (the font isn't available or installed), an alert dialog will appear **A** and an alert triangle will appear in the thumbnail for the offending layer on the Layers panel.**B** If you try to edit the layer, yet another alert dialog will appear.**C** You have two choices: Click OK to have Photoshop change the font to a generic one; or click Cancel, close the Photoshop document, install the required font, then reopen the document.

➤ If the **Embedded Profile Mismatch** alert dialog appears, it means the file's color profile doesn't match the current working space. See page 13.

➤ If the file you want to open simply won't open, it may be because the required **plug-in module** for that format (e.g., Scitex CT or JPEG 2000) isn't in the Photoshop Plug-Ins folder. Install the correct plug-in, then try opening the file again.

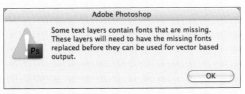

A This alert dialog will appear if the file you're opening uses a font that's missing.

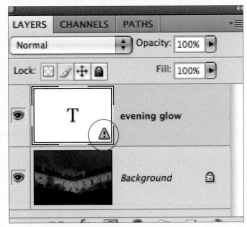

B This editable type layer has a missing fonts alert icon.

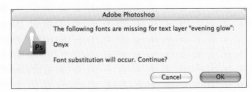

C This alert dialog will appear if you try to edit an editable type layer that's using a missing font.

Now that you know how to create and open documents, you're ready to customize your workspace. In this chapter, you'll learn about new interface options, such as the Application bar and document tabs. You'll also learn how to arrange multiple document windows, change zoom levels, rotate the canvas view, change screen modes, configure panels, customize the menus, create and save custom workspaces, and use the Options bar.

Using the Application frame ★

Photoshop CS4 lets you configure your workspace in various ways. Document windows can be docked as tabs inside one window (new) or left to float freely as in previous versions. In the Mac OS, if you opt for tabs, you can keep the document windows separate from the Application and Options bars or ensconce all the Photoshop features and your open documents neatly inside the Application frame. In Windows, the Application frame can't be hidden.

To hide the application frame (Mac OS only):

To set up your interface so it looks similar to Photoshop CS3, uncheck **Application Frame** on the **Window** menu. **A** ★ A new feature of the interface that you can display at any time, whether the Application frame is displayed or not, is the **Application bar** (choose Window > Application Bar to display it). It's illustrated on page 76.

WORKSPACES

4

IN THIS CHAPTER

Using the Application frame......61

Using tabbed document windows ..63

Arranging document windows.....64

Changing the zoom level 65

Rotating the view.............67

Changing the screen mode.......68

Changing the color behind the
    image.................69

Configuring the panels 69

Customizing the menus.........72

Saving workspaces 74

Restoring the default workspace...75

Using the Application bar 76

Using the Options bar..........76

Menu bar   Application bar   Options bar

A In this interface, Window > Application Frame is unchecked, so document windows and panels are separate from the menu, Application, and Options bars.

Next, we'll introduce you to the new interface options in Photoshop CS4.**A** After reviewing them, you'll be ready to configure your workspace to best suit your workflow.

For Mac OS users, the most dramatic new feature is the movable Application frame, which houses the Application bar, Options bar, panels, and tabbed document windows. This gives the Mac OS a sort of—well, Microsoft Windows "feel." Windows users: We will also refer to the Windows application window as the "Application frame."

The Application frame conveniently blocks out the Desktop and displays the image against a neutral gray background, which is essential when performing color correction work. Without the frame, if your Desktop is cluttered (and whose isn't?) or brightly colored, you'll have to spend time enlarging your document windows to hide the visual noise. Another advantage to using the Application frame is that in Standard screen mode, the viewing area for your document resizes dynamically as you hide or show the panels or make the panel docks wider or narrower.

➤ To minimize the Application frame in Windows, click the Minimize button; in the Mac OS, double-click the Application bar.

To show the Application frame (Mac OS only): ★

To display the Application frame, check **Window > Application Frame**. (To resize the frame, drag an edge or corner.)

Each document tab (or title bar) lists the file name, format, zoom level, current layer or Background, color mode, and bit depth. An asterisk indicates unsaved changes. Click the X to close the document.

Application bar (see page 76)

Use the Options bar to choose settings for the current tool (see page 76).

The Standard version of Photoshop has 21 movable panels, which are used for image editing. On most panels, you can enter values or move sliders; a few panels, such as Info and Histogram, only provide information.

A This is the Application frame in the Mac OS.

Using tabbed document windows ★

Whether you're a Windows or Mac OS user (with the Application frame showing or not), you can dock multiple open document windows as a tabbed group and display any document by clicking its tab. This will help keep them neatly organized and, best of all, readily accessible. If you become accustomed to working with the Application frame, you'll naturally want to dock your documents as tabs anyway.

To dock document windows as tabs:

Do any of the following:

To dock a document window **manually**, drag its title bar to the tab area (or to the bottom of the Application or Options bar) of the Application frame or just below the title bar of another floating document window, and release when the blue drop zone bar appears.**A** (If this doesn't seem to work, go to Preference > Interface, and check Enable Floating Document Window Docking, then try again.)

If one or more documents are already docked as tabs and you want to dock all floating document windows into the Application frame or into the currently active document window, right-click/Control-click a tab and choose **Consolidate All to Here** from the context menu.**B–C**

To set a preference so all future documents that you open dock as tabs automatically, go to Preferences > Interface and check **Open Documents as Tabs**.

► To override the automatic docking function as you drag a panel, hold down Control.

► To cycle among open documents, press Ctrl-Tab/ Control-Tab.

► In both platforms (in the Mac OS, whether the Application frame is displayed or not), you can float individual document windows (either right-click/Control-click a document tab and choose Move to New Window or drag the tab downward off the tab bar). We don't recommend doing this when the Application frame is displayed, because every time you click in the frame, the floating windows will be obscured behind it. Use the Consolidate All to Here command to bring stray floaters back into the frame.

To float all open document windows:

On the **Arrange Documents** menu ▦ on the Application bar, click **Float All in Windows**.

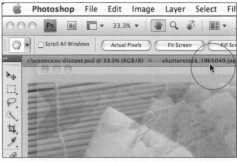

A To dock a floating document window as a tab manually, drag its title bar to the tab area of the Application frame (or just below the title bar of another document window), and release when the blue drop zone bar appears.

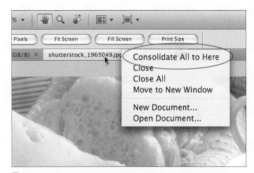

B To dock floating windows, right-click/Ctrl-click an existing document tab and choose Consolidate All to Here.

C Here, documents are docked as tabs in a floating document window; in the figure on the previous page, documents are docked in the Application frame.

Arranging document windows ★

Via icons and commands on the Arrange Documents menu on the Application bar, you can quickly display multiple tabbed or floating documents in various layouts, such as two documents side by side or top to bottom, or four or six documents in a grid formation.

To arrange your document windows:

Click the **Arrange Documents** menu icon on the Application bar to open the menu, release the mouse, then click one of the icons (the availability of the icons depends on how many documents you have open).**A**

You can just as effortlessly go back to displaying one document at a time.

To restore all windows to tabs:

On the **Arrange Documents** menu on the Application bar, click the **Consolidate All** icon (the first icon on the menu).

> **ESSENTIALS WORKSPACE**
>
> For the instructions in this chapter, we suggest you choose Essentials from the Workspace menu in the upper right corner of the Application bar or from the Window > Workspace submenu.

A We clicked the 4-Up button on the Arrange Documents menu on the Application bar to arrange these tabbed windows in quadrants.

Changing the zoom level

You can display the whole image in the document window or magnify part of it to work on a small detail. The current zoom level percentage is listed in four locations: on the Application bar, on the document title bar or tab, in the lower left corner of the tabbed or floating document window, and on the Navigator panel.

To change the zoom level using the Zoom tool: ★

1. Choose the **Zoom** tool 🔍 from the Toolbox or Application bar, or hold down **Z** for a temporary Zoom tool.

2. *Optional:* To allow a floating document window to resize as you zoom, check Resize Windows to Fit on the Options bar. It can enlarge only to the edge of the first panel dock on the right side of your screen.

3. Do any of the following:

   To **zoom in**, click in the document window, **A** or drag a marquee across an area to magnify that area.

   To **zoom out**, Alt-click/Option-click in the document window. **B**

   Click the **Zoom Level** field (to the left of the Zoom Level menu) on the Application bar or at the bottom of the document window, type the desired zoom percentage, then press Enter/Return.

   Right-click/Control-click in the document window and choose a zoom option from the **context** menu.

SHORTCUTS FOR ZOOMING IN AND OUT		
	Windows	Mac OS
Zoom in incrementally	Ctrl- + (plus)	Cmd- + (plus)
Zoom out incrementally	Ctrl- – (minus)	Cmd- – (minus)
Zoom in*	Ctrl-Spacebar click or drag	Cmd-Spacebar click or drag
Zoom out*	Alt-Spacebar click	Option-Spacebar click
Actual pixels/ 100% view	Ctrl-Alt-0 (zero)	Cmd-Option-0 (zero)
Fit on Screen	Ctrl-0 (zero)	Cmd-0 (zero)

Notes: These shortcuts work when some dialogs are open.

*To override the current Resize Windows to Fit setting on the Options bar, add Shift to the shortcut.

To set the zoom level to 100%, click **Actual Pixels** on the Options bar.

To display the entire image at the largest size that fits between the Tools panel (left) and panel docks (right)—and also inside the Application frame, if displayed—click **Fit Screen** on the Options bar.

Click **Print Size** on the Options bar to display the image at an approximation of its print size.

➤ Read about the Zoom Preferences on page 388.

A With the Zoom tool, click in the document window to zoom in (plus sign pointer)...

B ...or Alt-click/Option-click in the document window with the tool to zoom out (minus sign pointer).

By using the Navigator panel, you can change the zoom level of an image. When the zoom level is higher than 100%, you can also use the panel to move the image in the document window, to bring an area you want to edit or examine into view.

To change the zoom level or move the image in its window by using the Navigator panel:

1. Display the **Navigator** panel. ✳

2. Panel features are shown below in Figure **A**.

Ctrl-drag/Cmd-drag across part of the thumbnail to marquee that area for magnification. To move a magnified image in its window, either click outside, or drag, the view box (as shown here).

Type the desired zoom percentage, then press Enter/Return. To zoom to a percentage but keep the field highlighted, press Shift-Enter/Shift-Return.

Move the Zoom slider.

Click the Zoom Out button to zoom out.

Click the Zoom In button to zoom in.

A Use the Navigator panel to change the zoom level of your document and, when the image is magnified, to move it in the window.

MATCHING THE ZOOM OR LOCATION

If you have multiple documents open, from the Arrange Documents menu ▦ on the Application bar you can choose Match Zoom to match the zoom level of all the windows to that of the currently active image; or Match Location to synchronize the position of all the images in their windows; or Match Zoom and Location to perform both functions.

Another way to move a magnified image in the document window is by using the Hand tool.

To move a magnified image in its window by using the Hand tool: ★

Choose the **Hand** tool 🖑 from the Tools panel or the Application bar or hold down H for a temporary Hand tool, then drag in the document window.**B**

Note: If the document is in a tabbed window in the Application frame and is magnified, you can overscroll it—that is, drag it further off to the side than you can in a floating window.

➤ You can also move a magnified image in the document window by clicking the up or down scroll arrow in the lower right corner of the document window or, to move the image more quickly, by dragging the horizontal or vertical scroll bar.

➤ If you're working on an OpenGL system (you lucky devil), do a quick little drag, then release, on a magnified image. The document will float across the screen; click again to stop the motion. For this to work, Enable OpenGL Drawing must be checked in Preferences > Performance and Enable Flick Panning must be checked in Preferences > General.

B Drag the image in its window with the Hand tool.

If you have multiple documents open (say, in a 2-Up or 3-Up layout), you can save time by scrolling or zooming all of them simultaneously.

To scroll or zoom in multiple windows:

1. Open two or more documents, then on the Arrange Documents menu,▉ click a 2-Up, 3-Up, 4-Up, 5-Up, or 6-Up button. ★

2. Do either of the following:

   To scroll or zoom all the open Photoshop document windows, hold down Shift while dragging with the **Hand** tool or while zooming with the **Zoom** tool (or via a keyboard shortcut).

   Check **Scroll All Windows** on the Options bar before using the **Hand** tool or check **Zoom All Windows** on the Options bar before using the **Zoom** tool.

A With the Rotate View tool, drag to rotate the canvas area temporarily.

Rotating the view ★

OpenGL is a cross-platform API (application programming interface), or language, for 2D and 3D computer graphics applications. It was developed by Silicon Graphics. To use the OpenGL features in Photoshop, such as animated zoom (see the sidebar below), flick panning (see the second tip on the previous page), or the Rotate View tool (discussed below), your system must contain a video driver or card that provides OpenGL acceleration. To enable OpenGL drawing in Photoshop, go to Preferences > Performance, and under GPU Settings, check Enable OpenGL Drawing.

The Rotate View tool rotates the canvas view temporarily, to, say, facilitate drawing or painting at a particular angle, without permanently rotating the image, as the Image > Image Rotation commands do.

To rotate the canvas by using the Rotate View tool: ★

1. Choose the **Rotate View** tool 🔄 (R), or hold down **R** for a temporary Rotate View tool.

2. Do either of the following:

   Drag in the image.**A**

   On the Options bar, enter a **Rotation Angle** value, use the scrubby slider, or move the dial.

To reset the canvas to the default angle: ★

1. Choose the **Rotate View** tool 🔄 (R).

2. Click **Reset View** on the Options bar.

ANIMATING THE ZOOM FUNCTION ★

To zoom in or out on the image smoothly and continuously, make sure Animated Zoom is checked in Preferences > General and OpenGL Drawing is checked in Preferences > Performance. Press and hold with the Zoom tool or when using any of the zoom shortcuts.

Changing the screen mode

The screen modes control which Photoshop interface features are displayed.

To change screen modes: ★

Press **F** to cycle through the screen modes, or from the **Screen Mode** menu 🔲 on the Application bar,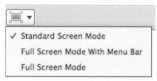 choose one of the following:

Standard Screen Mode (the default mode) to display the Application frame (if turned on) document windows, menu bar, Application bar, Options bar, and the panels, with the Desktop visible behind everything. This is the only mode in which a tabbed document window resizes dynamically as you hide or show the panels or resize the panel docks.**B–C**

Full Screen Mode with Menu Bar to display the image on a large gray (default color) background, obscuring the Desktop, with the Application bar, menu bar, Options bar, and panels visible.

Full Screen Mode to display the image on a black (default color) background, with the Options bar, Application bar, menu bar, and taskbar/dock hidden, and with the panels visible only on rollover (see the last set of instructions on the next page).

A Choose from the Screen Mode menu on the Application bar.

B This is Standard screen mode.

C In Standard screen mode, when we hid all the panels, the tabbed document window enlarged automatically to fill the entire display. If we were to redisplay the panels, the window would shrink down to its former size.

Changing the color behind the image

When color accuracy is important to us (which, come to think of it, is all the time!), we keep the area around the image gray.

To change the color of the area surrounding the image:

Do either of the following:

To change the color around the image for just the current screen mode, right-click/Ctrl-click that area and choose **Gray**, **Black**, or **Custom** (the last chosen custom color) from the context menu, or choose **Select Custom Color** and choose a color from the picker.

To change the color around the image for any or all of the three screen modes, go to Preferences > Interface, then from the Color menu for **Standard Screen Mode, Full Screen with Menus**, or **Full Screen**, ★ choose (**Gray**, **Black**, or **Custom** (the last chosen custom color) or choose **Select Custom Color** and choose a color from the picker.*

Configuring the panels

Most edits made in Photoshop require the use of one panel or another. Clever design features make the panels easy to store, expand, and collapse so they don't intrude on document space when you're not using them. Although such a flexible system may seem a bit complex at first, in no time the mechanics will become second nature to you. Note: To learn the function of the individual panels, see the next chapter.

Hide or show all the panels: Press Tab to hide or show all open panels, including the Tools panel, or press Shift-Tab to hide or show all the panels except the Tools panel. To fully maximize your screen space, hide the currently open panels, then show them only when you need to use them. If you hide the panels when Photoshop is in Standard screen mode (and if the Application frame is displayed), the tabbed document window enlarges to fill the frame. Redisplay the panels, and the window shrinks back down. ★

Make hidden, docked panels reappear: ★ With the panels hidden as per the instructions above, move the pointer to the very edge of the Application frame or your monitor, depending on the screen mode. The panel docks (but not free-standing panels) will redisplay temporarily. **A–B**

A When the panels are hidden you can position the pointer at the very edge of the monitor or Application frame...

B ...and the panel docks will reappear temporarily. Move the pointer away from the panels, and they'll disappear again. Easy come, easy go.

*The Border options apply only when OpenGL drawing is enabled (see page 393).

Move the pointer away from the panels, and they'll disappear again. (If this mechanism doesn't work, go to Preferences > Interface and check Auto-Show Hidden Panels.)

In the predefined workspaces (which are accessed from the Workspace menu on the far right end of the Application bar), panels are arranged in docks on the right side of your screen **A**—except for the Tools panel, which is on the left side. Each dock can hold as many or as few panels or panel groups as you like. We'll show you how to reconfigure the panel groups and docks to suit your working style.

Show or hide an individual panel: To show a panel, choose the panel name from the Window menu. The panel will display either in its default group and dock or in its last location. To bring a panel to the front of its group, click the tab (panel name). A few of the panels can also be shown or hidden via keyboard shortcuts, which are listed on the Window menu.

Show or hide an individual panel (icon): Click the icon or panel name. If Auto-Collapse Iconic Panels is checked in Preferences > Interface and you open a panel from an icon, it collapses back to the icon when you click elsewhere. With this preference unchecked, the panel stays expanded. To collapse a panel, click the Collapse to Icons button  on the panel bar, or click the panel icon or tab.

Maximize or minimize a panel (non-icon) **or group** (toggle the full panel to just a panel tab, or vice versa): Double-click the panel tab; or click the title bar (medium-gray bar next to the panel tabs).

Use a panel menu: Click the ⬛ icon to open a menu for whichever panel is in the front in a particular group.

Close a panel or group: ★ To close (but not collapse) a panel, choose Close from the bottom of the panel menu. To close a panel group, choose Close Tab Group from the panel menu. Both commands can also be accessed from a context menu by right-clicking/Control-clicking the panel tab. To close a group that's an icon, expand the dock first by clicking the Expand Panels button. ⬛ (To reopen a closed panel, use the Window menu.)

Collapse a whole dock into icons or icons with names: Click the Collapse to Icons button ⬛ or the dark gray bar at the top of the dock. **B** To further collapse the dock to just icons (no names), drag the vertical edge of the dock inward

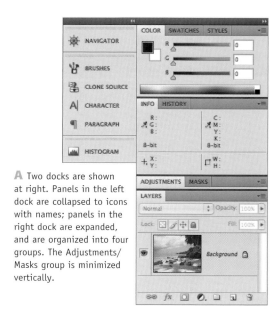

A Two docks are shown at right. Panels in the left dock are collapsed to icons with names; panels in the right dock are expanded, and are organized into four groups. The Adjustments/ Masks group is minimized vertically.

B We clicked the Collapse to Icons button to collapse the whole right dock to icons. The panel groups were preserved.

C We dragged the edge of the left dock inward to shrink it to just icons (no names).

horizontally (**C**, previous page); to expand the dock, click the dark gray bar again.

Widen or **narrow a dock and panels**: Position the mouse over the vertical edge of the dock (↔ cursor), then drag sideways. To widen or narrow the Adjustments panel, click the Expanded View button.⬚★ (Not all panels are resizable.)

Lengthen or shorten a panel, **group, or dock** (in the Mac OS, when the Application frame is hidden): Position the mouse over the dark gray line at the bottom of the panel or dock (⬍ cursor), then drag upward or downward. Other panels and groups in the same group or dock will scale accordingly. (Not all panels can be lengthened or shortened.)

Move a panel to a different slot, same group: Drag the panel tab (name) horizontally.

Move a panel to a different group: Drag the panel tab over the title bar of the desired group, and release when the blue drop zone border appears.**A**

Move a panel group upward or downward in a dock: Drag the title bar, and release the mouse when the horizontal blue drop zone bar appears in the desired location.**B**

Create a new dock: Drag a panel tab or title bar sideways over the vertical edge of the dock,**C** and release when you see the blue vertical drop zone bar.

Make a panel or group free-floating: Drag the panel tab, icon, or title bar out of the dock. You can stack free-floating panels and groups top to bottom.

Reconfigure a dock (icon): Use similar methods as for an expanded group. Drag the group title bar over the edge of a dock to create a new dock; or drag the title bar between groups to restack it (look for a horizontal drop zone line); or drag the title bar into another group to combine it with that group (look for a blue drop zone border).

➤ To reset the panels to their default locations and visibility states, choose Essentials from the Workspace menu on the Application bar.

➤ For any tool that uses a brush, you can click the Toggle Panel button ▤ on the Options bar to show or hide the Brushes panel. For the Type tool, this button opens the Character panel.

➤ To redock floating panels into the Application frame, drag the dark gray bar at the top of the panel group to the right edge of the Application frame, and release the mouse when you see the vertical blue drop zone line.

A A blue drop zone border appears as we drag a panel into a different group.

B A blue horizontal drop zone bar appears as we move a panel group upward within the same dock.

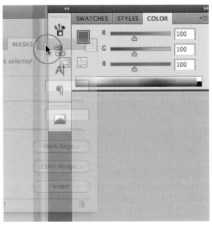

C A blue vertical drop zone bar appears as we drag a panel out of a dock and create a new dock for it.

Customizing the menus

If you find the huge number of commands in Photoshop to be intimidating, you'll be happy to know there's a way to streamline the menu listings to make them more user friendly. By using the Keyboard Shortcuts and Menus dialog, you can assign color labels to menu bar and panel menu commands to make them easier to locate, and you can also hide the commands you don't use.

To see what the labels look like, from either the Workspace menu on the Application bar or the Window > Workspace submenu, **A** choose What's New in CS4. Click Yes/OK if an alert dialog appears, then take a few minutes to browse through the menu bar and a few panel menus. Note: If you don't see any color labels, go to Preferences > Interface and check Show Menu Colors.

To assign color labels to, or hide or show, menu commands:

1. To open the **Keyboard Shortcuts and Menus** dialog (**A**, next page) do either of the following:

   Choose Edit > **Menus** (Ctrl-Alt-Shift-M/ Cmd-Option-Shift-M).

   Choose Window > Workspace > **Keyboard Shortcuts and Menus**, then click the Menus tab.

2. If you've already created a custom menu set that you want to edit, choose it from the **Set** menu; if you haven't, choose Photoshop Defaults.

3. From the **Menu For** menu, choose Application Menus or Panel Menus.

4. Expand the listing for any menu header or panel name by clicking the arrowhead, then:

   To **hide** a command from its menu, click the visibility (eye) icon; click again to redisplay it.

   To assign a **color label** to a command, click in the Color column and choose a color from the menu; or to remove a color label, choose None.

5. To create a new menu set based on all the current settings, click the **Create New Set** button. In the Save dialog, enter a new name or change the name (keep the default location, which is the Menu Customization folder, and keep the .mnu extension), then click Save. User-created sets are listed on the Set menu.

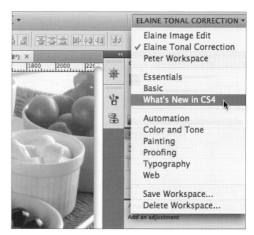

A To see what the color labels look like, from the Workspace menu on the Application bar, choose What's New in CS4, then look at a few menus.

To save your edits to the **current** (modified) **set**, click the **Save Changes to Current Set** button. Don't save changes to the Photoshop Defaults, Basic, or What's New in CS4 set; create a new set instead.

6. Click OK.

   Note: By default, each predefined workspace has a menu set assigned to it, which accounts for its unique layout. Essentials uses the Photoshop Default menu set; Basic uses the Basic menu set; and What's New in CS4 uses the What's New in CS4 menu set. On the next two pages, you'll learn how to create and save custom workspaces, which include panel locations and menu labels. We recommend that you create a custom menu set before proceeding with those instructions.

➤ To delete a user menu set, choose it from the Set menu in the Keyboard Shortcuts and Menus dialog, then click the Delete Current Set button.

➤ If you're using a workspace in which some menu items are hidden, and you want to show all the listings for a particular menu temporarily, either choose Show All Menu Items from the menu or Ctrl-click/Cmd-click the menu name. ★

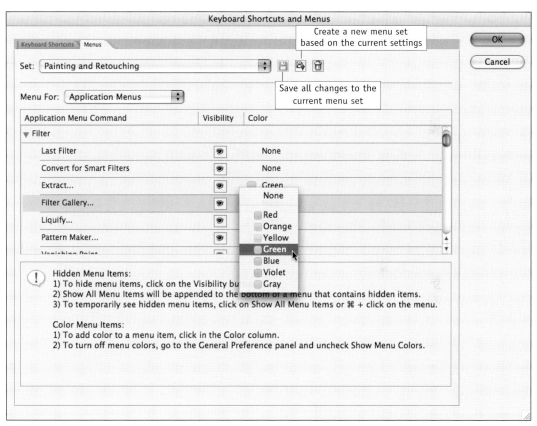

A Via the Menus pane of the Keyboard Shortcuts and Menus dialog, you can hide or show, or assign a color tint to, menu and panel menu commands.

Saving workspaces

Our goal in writing this chapter is to teach you not only how to customize your working environment in Photoshop, but also how to save yourself setup time as you start each new work session. A first step in this endeavor is to go to Preferences (Ctrl-K/Cmd-K) > Interface and check **Remember Panel Locations** under Panels & Documents. This will ensure that all the panels that are open when you exit/quit Photoshop will reappear in the same location when you relaunch the program.

To save yourself even more time, set up and save workspaces for different kinds of tasks, **A** as in the instructions below. Workspace settings can include panel locations; custom keyboard shortcuts; and menu sets, which control the color label and visibility settings for menu commands.

Your custom workspaces should reflect your normal work habits (and we don't mean working late and sleeping late). For example, to set up a text-intensive workspace, you would open the Character and Paragraph panels and assign color labels to commands that you normally use when creating text. Or to create a personal painting workspace, open the Brushes, Color, and Swatches panels, assign color labels to the brush preset commands, and maybe hide some unrelated commands.

To create a custom workspace:

1. Do any or all of the following:

   Open and **position** all the **panels** where you want them, in the desired panel groups and docks.

   Collapse the panels you use occasionally to **icons** and **close** the ones you rarely use.

   Resize any of the panels, and resize any of the pickers that open from the Options bar.

   Choose a thumbnail, swatch size, or other **panel options** from any of the panel menus, or from any of the preset menus that open from the Options bar.

   Choose Edit > **Menus** and use the dialog to assign color labels and/or visibility settings to menu commands. Be sure to save your changes to a new menu set (see page 72).

2. From the Workspace menu on the Application bar, ★ choose Save Workspace; or choose

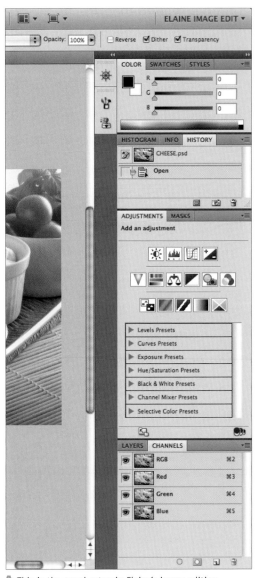

A This is the panel setup in Elaine's image-editing workspace.

Window > Workspace > **Save Workspace**. The
Save Workspace dialog opens.**A**

3. Enter a descriptive **Name** (include your name, if
you like) for the new workspace.

4. In the **Capture** area, check which current interface features you want saved in the workspace.
If you changed any of the menu settings, be sure
to check Menus.

5. Click Save. Your workspace will be listed on, and
can be chosen from, the upper portion of the
Workspace menu on the Application bar **B** (or
for a slower trek, on the Window > Workspace
submenu).

Note: To edit a workspace, choose the workspace
you want to edit, make the desired changes to
the interface, then save the workspace under the
same name (click Yes in the alert dialog).

➤ On a computer with dual displays, you can
distribute free-floating panel groups or stacks
between the two displays and save that arrangement as part of a workspace.

➤ If Remember Panel Locations is checked in
Preferences > Interface, panels that are open
when you exit/quit Photoshop will reopen in
their last location upon relaunch, as opposed
to the location specified in the workspace last
chosen under Window > Workspace.

To delete a custom workspace:

1. Choose any workspace except the one you want
to delete.

2. From the Workspace menu on the Application
bar,★ choose **Delete Workspace**. The Delete
Workspace dialog opens.**C**

3. Choose the name of the user workspace you
want to get rid of, click Delete, then click Yes in
the alert dialog.

Restoring the default workspace

At any time, you can go back to square one and
restore the factory-default panel locations, shortcuts,
menu visibility settings, and labels.

To restore the default workspace:

From the Workspace menu on the Application
bar,★ choose **Essentials**.

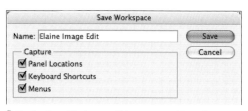

A In the Save Workspace dialog, enter a Name for your
workspace and check which features of the Photoshop
interface you want it to capture.

B Choose a predefined or user-created workspace
from the Workspace menu on the Application bar.

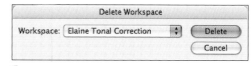

C In the Delete Workspace dialog, choose the user-
created workspace you want to get rid of.

Using the Application bar ★

Use the controls on the Application bar to manage your document windows. **A** In Windows, the main Photoshop menus also display on the Application bar. In the Mac OS, the Application bar is docked in the Application frame. When the Application frame is hidden, the Application bar is docked below the main menu bar; if you don't see the bar, choose Window > Application Bar.

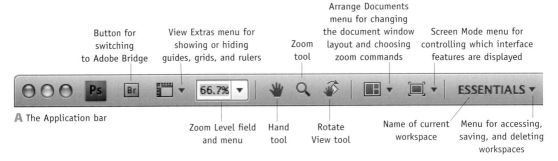

Button for switching to Adobe Bridge

View Extras menu for showing or hiding guides, grids, and rulers

Zoom tool

Arrange Documents menu for changing the document window layout and choosing zoom commands

Screen Mode menu for controlling which interface features are displayed

A The Application bar

Zoom Level field and menu

Hand tool

Rotate View tool

Name of current workspace

Menu for accessing, saving, and deleting workspaces

Using the Options bar

You'll use the Options bar (Window > Options) to choose settings every time you switch tools—and sometimes to change settings even while using the same tool. **B** Options bar features change dynamically depending on which tool is selected, but your choices remain in effect for each tool until you change them. You can move the bar anywhere onscreen by dragging its left edge. To learn about presets, see pages 400–404.

Tool Preset picker for choosing pre-defined tool settings

A preset picker (click the icon or arrowhead to open it)

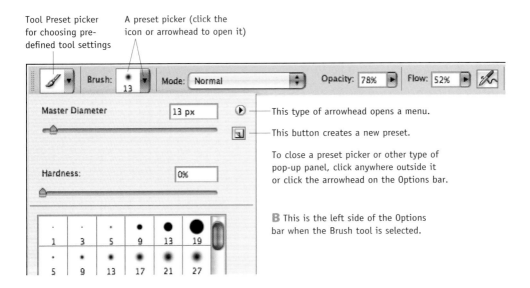

This type of arrowhead opens a menu.

This button creates a new preset.

To close a preset picker or other type of pop-up panel, click anywhere outside it or click the arrowhead on the Options bar.

B This is the left side of the Options bar when the Brush tool is selected.

This chapter will help you become more intimately acquainted with a part of the Photoshop interface that you will be using constantly as you work: the panels. In the previous chapter, you learned how to arrange them onscreen. Here, you'll be introduced to the specific function of each one—from choosing color swatches (Swatches panel), to accessing and editing masks (Masks panel), to styling type (Character and Paragraph panels), to editing layers (the all-important Layers panel—keep it open!). Note: In-depth instructions for using specific panels are amply provided throughout this book (such as creating and editing different kinds of adjustment layers by using the Adjustments panel).

You can read through this chapter with or without glancing at or fiddling with the panels onscreen, and also use it as a reference guide as you work. The panel icons are illustrated on the next page to help you identify them quickly. After that, you'll find instructions for using the Tools panel and an illustration of the tools, followed by illustrations of the other panels, in alphabetical order, with descriptions of their function.

PANELS

5

IN THIS CHAPTER

The Photoshop panel icons 78

The Photoshop panels illustrated . . . 79

CHOOSING VALUES QUICKLY

➤ You can change the numerical values in most panels and dialogs by using the scrubby sliders: drag slightly to the left or right over the option name or icon. Examples include many values on the Options bar, the Opacity and Fill controls on the Layers panel, settings in the Filter Gallery, and controls on the Adjustments, Masks, Character, and Paragraph panels.

A scrubby slider

➤ To access a pop-up slider (e.g., to choose an Opacity percentage) click the arrowhead. To close a slider, click anywhere outside it or press Enter/Return. If you click an arrowhead to open a slider, you can press Esc to close it and restore the last chosen setting.

➤ To change a value incrementally, click in a field in a panel or dialog, then press the up or down arrow key.

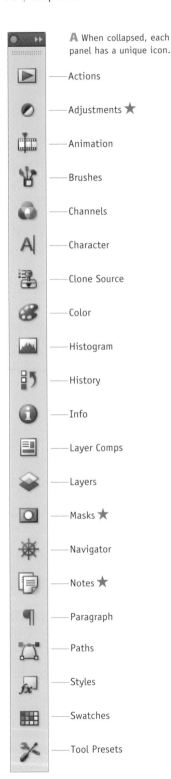

A When collapsed, each panel has a unique icon.

—— Actions

—— Adjustments ★

—— Animation

—— Brushes

—— Channels

—— Character

—— Clone Source

—— Color

—— Histogram

—— History

—— Info

—— Layer Comps

—— Layers

—— Masks ★

—— Navigator

—— Notes ★

—— Paragraph

—— Paths

—— Styles

—— Swatches

—— Tool Presets

The Photoshop panel icons

Identifying the panel icons

Each panel in Photoshop has been assigned a unique icon. **A** Try to memorize the icons for the panels—at least for the ones you use most often—so you'll be able to identify them quickly as you work.

USING CONTEXT MENUS

When you right-click/Control-click in the document window—depending on where you click and which tool happens to be selected—a menu of context-sensitive commands pops up onscreen. Many panel thumbnails, names, and features also have related context menus. If a command is available on a context menu (or can be executed quickly via a keyboard shortcut), we'll let you know, so we can spare you from having to trudge to the main menu bar.

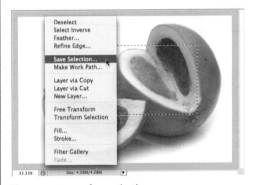

The context menu for a selection

The context menu for the color bar on the Color panel

The Photoshop panels illustrated

Using the Tools panel

The Tools panel, which is illustrated on pages 80–82, contains 60 tools and a handful of buttons. Believe it or not, by the end of this book, you'll be intimately—or at least marginally—familiar with most of them! To display the Tools panel, choose Window > **Tools**.

To **choose a tool**, do one of the following:

➤ If the desired tool is visible on the Tools panel, click the **icon**.

➤ To cycle through related tools in the same slot, **Alt-click/Option-click** the one that's visible.

➤ To choose a related tool from a **menu**, press and hold on the tiny arrowhead next to the tool icon.

➤ For fast access with your cursor anywhere (except if you're creating type), press the designated **letter shortcut**. The shortcuts are shown in the screen captures on the next three pages and in the tool tips onscreen. If Use Shift Key for Tool Switch is unchecked in Preferences > General, simply press the designated letter to cycle through related tools in the same slot (for example, press L to cycle through the three Lasso tools). With the Use Shift Key for Tool Switch option checked, you would have to press Shift plus the designated letter.

➤ To use a tool **temporarily** while another tool is selected, press and hold down its assigned letter shortcut key (see the sidebar below). ★

To learn about the function of a tool as you're using it, read the brief description (tool hints) at the bottom of the **Info** panel. If you don't see this, choose Panel Options from the Info panel menu, ▼☰ then check Show Tool Hints (see page 89).

Before using a tool that you've selected, you need to choose settings for it from the **Options** bar at the top of your screen. For example, for the Brush tool, you would choose a brush tip, diameter, hardness setting, blending mode, opacity percentage, and other settings. If the Options bar is hidden, display it by choosing Window > Options (see page 76).

Options bar settings remain in effect for each tool until you change them, reset the tool, or reset all tools. To restore the default settings to a tool, right-click/Control-click the thumbnail on the Tool Preset picker on the Options bar and choose **Reset Tool** from the context menu.**A** Or to reset all tools, choose **Reset All Tools** from the menu.

In Preferences > Cursors, you can specify whether **tool pointers** are crosshairs, or look like their icon (as on the Tools panel) or, for some tools, a circle either the size or half the size of the current brush diameter, with or without crosshairs (see page 394).

SPRING-LOADING TOOLS ★

If you want to quickly access a tool and its Options bar settings temporarily without having to actually click the tool on the Tools panel, hold down the default letter that is assigned to that tool.

For example, say you happen to have the Brush tool selected but you want to move a layer with the Move tool. You would hold down the V key, drag in the document window, then release V. Or to access the Zoom tool temporarily, you would hold down the Z key. This process is a little less efficient if you want to access a tool that shares a slot with other tools (as most tools do). In this case, the letter shortcut accesses whichever tool happens to be visible on the Tools panel, so you would have to plan ahead and select the two tools that you want to switch back and forth between first.

A To access these commands, right-click/Control-click the Tool Preset picker thumbnail at the far left end of the Options bar.

The Tools panel

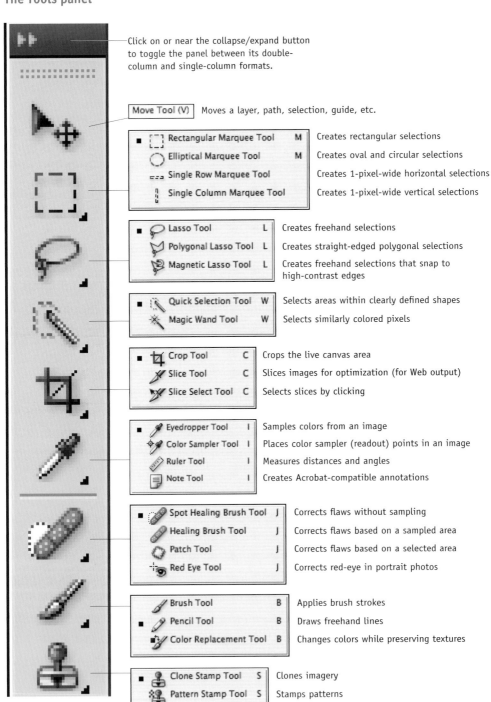

Click on or near the collapse/expand button to toggle the panel between its double-column and single-column formats.

Move Tool (V)   Moves a layer, path, selection, guide, etc.

■ □□ Rectangular Marquee Tool   M   Creates rectangular selections
   ○ Elliptical Marquee Tool   M   Creates oval and circular selections
   ⊏⊐ Single Row Marquee Tool   Creates 1-pixel-wide horizontal selections
   ⁚ Single Column Marquee Tool   Creates 1-pixel-wide vertical selections

■ ○ Lasso Tool   L   Creates freehand selections
   ▷ Polygonal Lasso Tool   L   Creates straight-edged polygonal selections
   ▷ Magnetic Lasso Tool   L   Creates freehand selections that snap to high-contrast edges

■ ⊙ Quick Selection Tool   W   Selects areas within clearly defined shapes
   ✳ Magic Wand Tool   W   Selects similarly colored pixels

■ ⊥ Crop Tool   C   Crops the live canvas area
   ✗ Slice Tool   C   Slices images for optimization (for Web output)
   ✗ Slice Select Tool   C   Selects slices by clicking

■ ⚲ Eyedropper Tool   I   Samples colors from an image
   ⊹⚲ Color Sampler Tool   I   Places color sampler (readout) points in an image
   ⚲ Ruler Tool   I   Measures distances and angles
   ▤ Note Tool   I   Creates Acrobat-compatible annotations

■ ⬮ Spot Healing Brush Tool   J   Corrects flaws without sampling
   ⬮ Healing Brush Tool   J   Corrects flaws based on a sampled area
   ⬭ Patch Tool   J   Corrects flaws based on a selected area
   ⁙⬮ Red Eye Tool   J   Corrects red-eye in portrait photos

   ✏ Brush Tool   B   Applies brush strokes
■ ✏ Pencil Tool   B   Draws freehand lines
   ✏ Color Replacement Tool   B   Changes colors while preserving textures

■ ⚱ Clone Stamp Tool   S   Clones imagery
   ⚱ Pattern Stamp Tool   S   Stamps patterns

A The upper part of the Tools panel

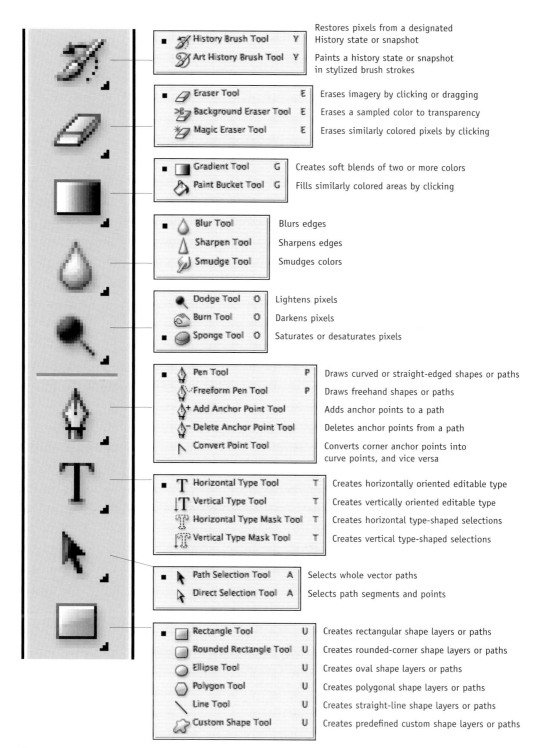

History Brush Tool	Y	Restores pixels from a designated History state or snapshot	
Art History Brush Tool	Y	Paints a history state or snapshot in stylized brush strokes	
Eraser Tool	E	Erases imagery by clicking or dragging	
Background Eraser Tool	E	Erases a sampled color to transparency	
Magic Eraser Tool	E	Erases similarly colored pixels by clicking	
Gradient Tool	G	Creates soft blends of two or more colors	
Paint Bucket Tool	G	Fills similarly colored areas by clicking	
Blur Tool		Blurs edges	
Sharpen Tool		Sharpens edges	
Smudge Tool		Smudges colors	
Dodge Tool	O	Lightens pixels	
Burn Tool	O	Darkens pixels	
Sponge Tool	O	Saturates or desaturates pixels	
Pen Tool	P	Draws curved or straight-edged shapes or paths	
Freeform Pen Tool	P	Draws freehand shapes or paths	
Add Anchor Point Tool		Adds anchor points to a path	
Delete Anchor Point Tool		Deletes anchor points from a path	
Convert Point Tool		Converts corner anchor points into curve points, and vice versa	
Horizontal Type Tool	T	Creates horizontally oriented editable type	
Vertical Type Tool	T	Creates vertically oriented editable type	
Horizontal Type Mask Tool	T	Creates horizontal type-shaped selections	
Vertical Type Mask Tool	T	Creates vertical type-shaped selections	
Path Selection Tool	A	Selects whole vector paths	
Direct Selection Tool	A	Selects path segments and points	
Rectangle Tool	U	Creates rectangular shape layers or paths	
Rounded Rectangle Tool	U	Creates rounded-corner shape layers or paths	
Ellipse Tool	U	Creates oval shape layers or paths	
Polygon Tool	U	Creates polygonal shape layers or paths	
Line Tool	U	Creates straight-line shape layers or paths	
Custom Shape Tool	U	Creates predefined custom shape layers or paths	

A The midsection of the Tools panel

Continued on the following page

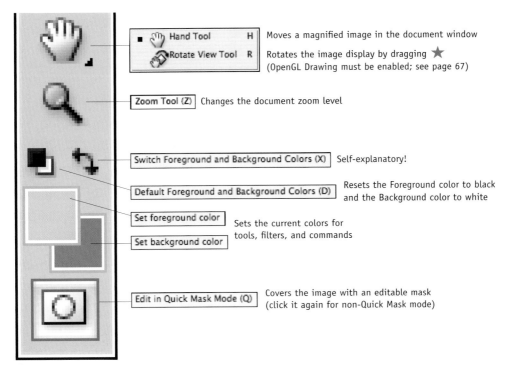

Hand Tool   H   Moves a magnified image in the document window

Rotate View Tool   R   Rotates the image display by dragging ★ (OpenGL Drawing must be enabled; see page 67)

Zoom Tool (Z)   Changes the document zoom level

Switch Foreground and Background Colors (X)   Self-explanatory!

Default Foreground and Background Colors (D)   Resets the Foreground color to black and the Background color to white

Set foreground color   Sets the current colors for tools, filters, and commands

Set background color

Edit in Quick Mask Mode (Q)   Covers the image with an editable mask (click it again for non-Quick Mask mode)

A The lower part of the Tools panel

USING THE AVAILABLE INFO

► Are you unsure what an icon means or a panel or dialog option does? If Show Tool Tips is checked in Photoshop > Preferences > Interface and you rest the pointer on a tool icon without clicking the mouse button, the tool name and short-cut pop up onscreen. You can also use the tool tips to learn the function or name of most panel, Options bar, and dialog features.

► Some dialogs (such as Select > Refine Edge) have a Description area that contains information about the option your pointer is currently hovering over.

► Keep an eye on the Info panel for color breakdowns, docu-ment data (e.g. file size, color profile, dimensions, resolution), and tool hints (ways to use the currently selected tool). See page 89.

► Use the Histogram panel to monitor changes to the tonal ranges in an image as you apply color and tonal adjustments. See pages 184–185.

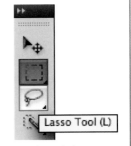

Lasso Tool (L)

Use the tool tip to refresh your memory of a tool name or shortcut.

Adjustments panel ◐ ★

Unlike commands applied via the Image > Adjustments submenu, adjustment layers don't alter image pixels until you merge them with their underlying layers. They are a great mechanism for trying out color and tonal adjustments, because you can edit their settings and delete them at any time. Plus, adjustment layers automatically have a layer mask. By editing the mask, you can hide or reveal the adjustment effect in specific areas of the image.

Using the new Adjustments panel, you can even more easily create and edit the settings for adjustment layers. The panel also lets you restore the default settings to an adjustment; hide and show the adjustment effect; view the previous adjustment state; or, in a multilayered document, clip (limit) the adjustment effect to just the underlying layer.

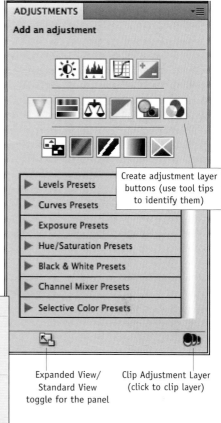

Create adjustment layer buttons (use tool tips to identify them)

Expanded View/ Standard View toggle for the panel

Clip Adjustment Layer (click to clip layer)

Panel menu

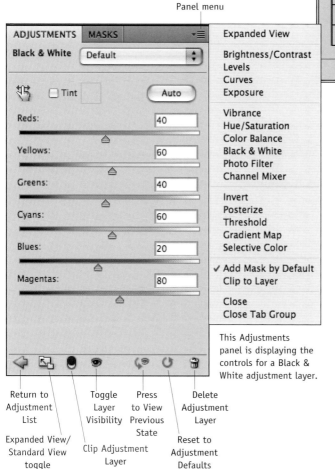

This Adjustments panel is displaying the controls for a Black & White adjustment layer.

Return to Adjustment List

Expanded View/ Standard View toggle

Clip Adjustment Layer

Toggle Layer Visibility

Press to View Previous State

Reset to Adjustment Defaults

Delete Adjustment Layer

Note: The Actions, Animation, and Notes panels aren't illustrated in this chapter because they aren't featured in this book.

Brushes panel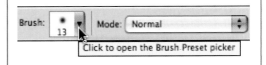

You'll use the Brushes panel to choose and customize brush tips for many tools, such as the Brush, Pencil, Clone Stamp, Pattern Stamp, History Brush, Art History Brush, Eraser, Blur, Sharpen, Smudge, Dodge, and Burn tools. You can also use it to choose options for a graphics tablet and stylus. Click an options set on the left side of the panel to display options on the right. The preview at the bottom of the panel shows an example of the current brush tip and settings.

PICKER OR PANEL?

You can choose brush tips for the painting and editing tools from either the Brushes panel or the Brush Preset picker, a pop-up panel that you open from the Options bar (click the arrowhead, as shown below). To close the Brush Preset picker, click outside it or click the Brush arrowhead again. Commands that let you load, append, and save brushes and brush libraries are available on both the Brushes panel menu and the Brush Preset picker menu.

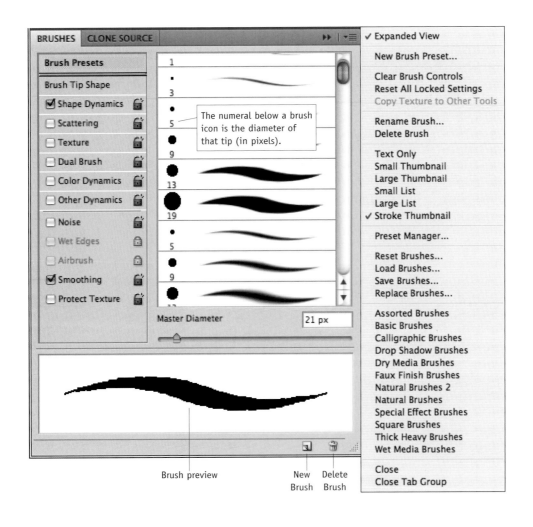

Brush preview

New Brush   Delete Brush

Channels panel

The Channels panel displays a list of the color channels in an image. To show an individual channel in the document window, click the channel name or use the keystroke listed on the panel. To redisplay the composite image (all the channels), such as RGB or CMYK, click the topmost channel on the panel, or press Ctrl-2/Cmd-2. ★

You can also use this panel to save and load alpha channels (saved selections), and to create and store spot color channels, which commercial print shops use to produce individual color plates for premixed inks, such as PANTONE inks.

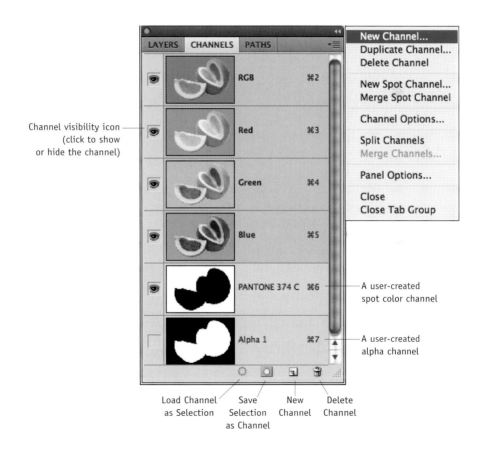

Channel visibility icon (click to show or hide the channel)

A user-created spot color channel

A user-created alpha channel

Load Channel as Selection   Save Selection as Channel   New Channel   Delete Channel

Character panel

You can choose attributes for the type tools from either the Character panel, illustrated below, or the Options bar. Open this panel from the Window menu, or by clicking the Toggle Panel button 📧 on the right side of the Options bar when a type tool is selected.

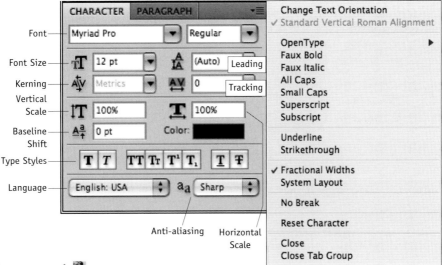

Clone Source panel 🖾

The Clone Source panel lets you keep track of up to five different sources when cloning (represented by a row of source buttons at top of the panel); reassign new sources; hide, show, and control the opacity and mode of the clone overlay; clone repeatedly from the same source; and scale, rotate, and reposition source pixels before or as you clone them.

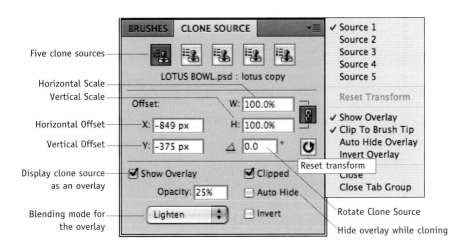

Color panel

The Color panel is but one of the vehicles that Photoshop provides for mixing colors. Choose a color model for the sliders or color bar from the panel menu, then mix a color using the sliders or quick-select a color by clicking the color bar. To open the Color Picker or Color Libraries dialog, from which you can also choose colors, click once on the Foreground or Background color square if it's already selected (has a black border), or double-click the square if it's not selected. Colors are applied via painting and editing tools and via some commands, such as Edit > Fill.

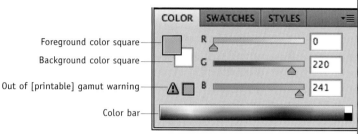

Foreground color square
Background color square
Out of [printable] gamut warning
Color bar

Grayscale Slider
RGB Sliders
HSB Sliders
✓ CMYK Sliders
Lab Sliders
Web Color Sliders

Copy Color as HTML

RGB Spectrum
✓ CMYK Spectrum
Grayscale Ramp
Current Colors

Make Ramp Web Safe

Close
Close Tab Group

COLOR | SWATCHES | STYLES

R 0
G 220
B 241

Histogram panel

While a file is being edited or while an adjustment layer is being created or edited, the Histogram panel diagrams either just the current light and dark (tonal) values of the image or both its current and modified tonal values. This panel is provided for reference only, but the feedback it provides is useful.

Via the Channel menu, you can choose to have the panel display data about the composite channel (combined channels) or about just one channel. You can also display a separate histogram for each channel by expanding the panel.

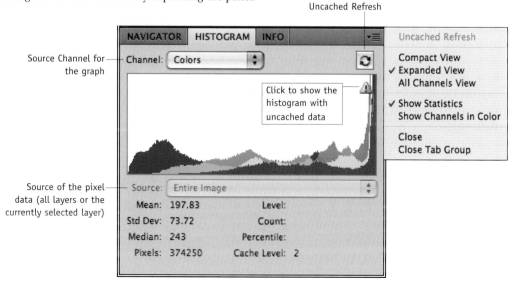

Uncached Refresh

Source Channel for the graph

Click to show the histogram with uncached data

Source of the pixel data (all layers or the currently selected layer)

NAVIGATOR | HISTOGRAM | INFO

Uncached Refresh

Compact View
✓ Expanded View
All Channels View

✓ Show Statistics
Show Channels in Color

Close
Close Tab Group

Channel: Colors

Source: Entire Image

Mean: 197.83   Level:
Std Dev: 73.72   Count:
Median: 243   Percentile:
Pixels: 374250   Cache Level: 2

History panel

By using the History panel, you can reverse your editing steps in the current work session. Each brush stroke, filter application, or other image-editing command is listed as a separate state on the panel, with the bottommost state being the most recent. If you click a prior state, the document reverts to that stage of the editing process. In linear mode, the default mode for the panel, if you click an earlier state and then resume image editing from that state (or delete that state), all subsequent (dimmed) states are discarded.

History states are deleted from the palette as new edits are made (when the maximum number of history states is reached, as specified in Preferences > Interface), whereas the New Snapshot command creates states that stay on the panel. States and snapshots are discarded when you close the image.

The History panel has two related tools. When you drag with the History Brush tool, the areas under your strokes are restored to the state that you've designated as the source. The Art History Brush does the same thing, but in stylized (sorta tacky) strokes.

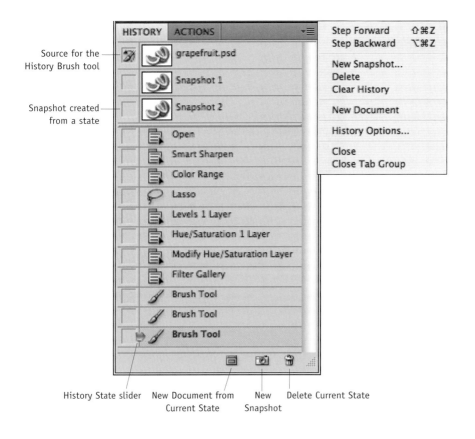

Info panel

The Info panel displays a color breakdown of the pixel under the pointer at its current location in the document window. While any color adjustment dialog is open or the Adjustments panel is being used, the panel displays before and after color readouts. The Info panel also lists the current location of the pointer on the x/y axes.

Other information may display on the panel, depending on which tool is being used, such as the distance between points when you move a selection, draw a shape, or use the Ruler tool; the dimensions of a selection or crop marquee; or the width (W), height (H), angle (A), and horizontal skew (H) or vertical skew (V) of a layer, selection, or vector object as you transform it. The panel

also displays readouts for up to four color samplers that you can place in a document.

Press one of the tiny arrowheads to choose a color model for that readout (this model can differ from the current document color mode). Or to do this via a dialog, choose Panel Options from the panel menu, then in the Info Panel Options dialog (shown below), change the Mode for the First Color Readout and Second Color Readout. In the same dialog, you can also change the Ruler Units for the panel (Mouse Coordinates); check which Status Information you want displayed in the lower part of the panel; and check Show Tool Hints to display dynamic information about the current tool or edit.

➤ To choose a different unit of measurement for the Info panel and for the rulers in the document window, click the arrowhead on the panel for the X/Y readout.

Color breakdown for the pixel currently under the pointer.

Click an arrowhead to choose a different color model for that particular readout.

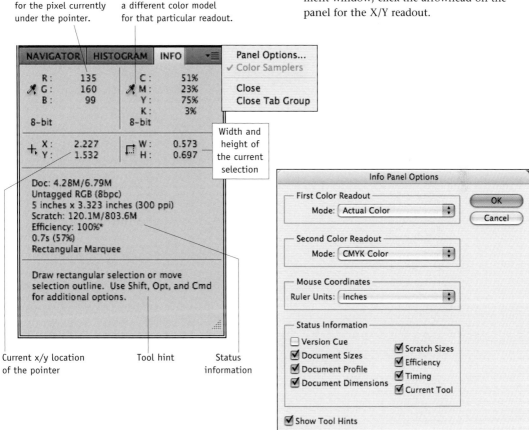

Width and height of the current selection

Current x/y location of the pointer

Tool hint

Status information

Use the Info Panel Options dialog to choose display preferences for the panel.

Layer Comps panel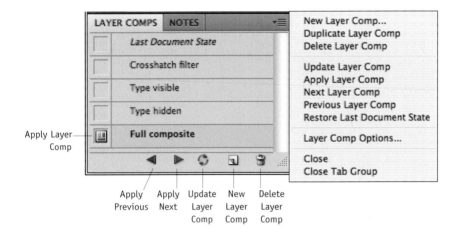

When you create a layer comp (short for "composition"), it includes, collectively, any of the following current document characteristics: the layer Visibility (which layers are showing or hidden), its Position (the location of imagery on each layer), and its Appearance (layer styles, including the layer blending mode and opacity, plus any layer effects). As shown in the dialog below, you can decide which document attributes will be included in the comp, as well as add comments.

Layer comps might come in handy if you need to decide between multiple versions of a document or present document variations to a client. For example, say you've created a few versions of a book cover. You would make each version into a layer comp, say, with or without lettering, or with the lettering or background image in two different colors. When presenting the design to your client, instead of opening and closing separate files, you would simply display each version sequentially within the same file by clicking the Apply Layer Comp icon on and off for each comp on the panel.

Layer comps save with the document in which they're created. Whereas histories affect all editing done to an image but can't be saved, layer comps can be saved but let you display only layer options and settings.

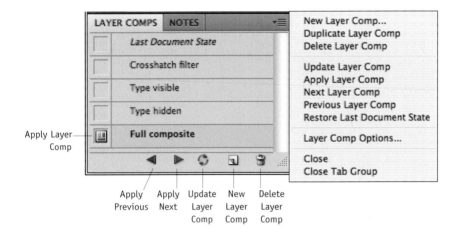

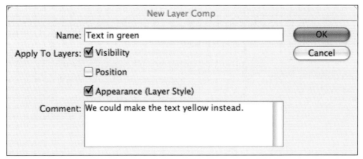

Use the New Layer Comp dialog to name the comp and to specify which attributes it will contain.

Layers panel

Every new image contains either a solid-color Background or a transparent layer, on top of which you can add layers of many types. Using the Layers panel, you can create, hide, show, duplicate, group, link, merge, flatten, delete, and restack layers; change the layer blending mode, opacity, and fill opacity; attach masks; and apply layer effects.

Only the currently selected layer can be edited. To select a layer, click the thumbnail or click next to the layer name. The panel looks complex (Egads!*), but you'll soon be using it all the time!

These are the kinds of layers that either you create or Photoshop creates automatically:

➤ **Image** layers.

➤ **Editable type** layers, which are created by the Horizontal Type or Vertical Type tool.

➤ **Fill** and **adjustment** layers for applying temporary color or tonal adjustments to underlying layers.

➤ **Smart Object** layers, which are created manually when you convert one or more layers in a Photoshop image into a Smart Object, or automatically when you place an Illustrator or PDF file, another Photoshop file, or a Camera Raw file into a Photoshop document. Double-click a Smart Object layer and the object reopens in its original application for editing; save and close it and the object updates in Photoshop. Apply a filter to a Smart Object layer and it becomes an editable and removable Smart Filter.

➤ **Shape** layers, which contain vector shapes.

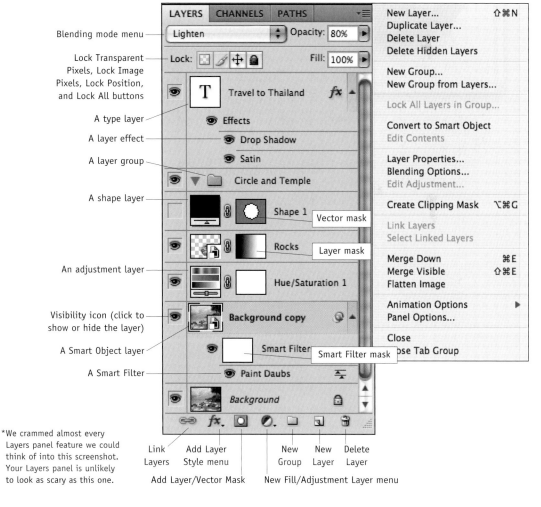

*We crammed almost every Layers panel feature we could think of into this screenshot. Your Layers panel is unlikely to look as scary as this one.

Masks panel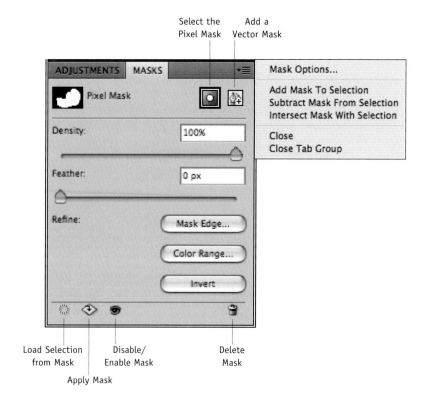

The new Masks panel gives you quicker access to many preexisting controls and also offers some new controls. In addition to letting you add a pixel, vector, or filter mask to a layer, the panel lets you disable or enable a mask, load it as a selection, and when you're done using it, either apply its effect to your document or delete it.

New controls include a Density slider for adjusting the opacity of a mask and a Feather slider for adjusting the sharpness of the edges between white and black areas in the mask. The settings for those controls can be readjusted at any time without permanently altering the original mask. The Mask Edge button opens a Refine Mask dialog that offers the same controls for a mask as the Refine Edge dialog does for a selection; the Color Range button gives you quick access to the Color Range dialog for reshaping a mask; and the Invert button swaps the black and white areas in the mask.

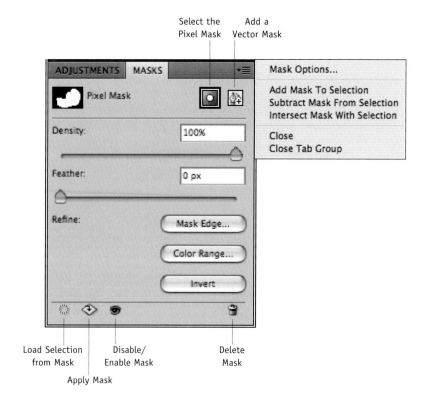

Select the Pixel Mask   Add a Vector Mask

ADJUSTMENTS   MASKS

Pixel Mask

Density: 100%

Feather: 0 px

Refine:

Mask Edge....

Color Range....

Invert

Mask Options...

Add Mask To Selection
Subtract Mask From Selection
Intersect Mask With Selection

Close
Close Tab Group

Load Selection from Mask   Disable/Enable Mask   Delete Mask

Apply Mask

Navigator panel

You can use the Navigator panel to move a magnified image in the document window or change the document zoom level—or if you prefer, you can accomplish the same tasks by using tools or keyboard shortcuts.

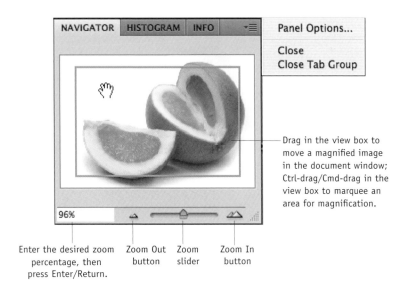

Drag in the view box to move a magnified image in the document window; Ctrl-drag/Cmd-drag in the view box to marquee an area for magnification.

Enter the desired zoom percentage, then press Enter/Return.

Zoom Out button

Zoom slider

Zoom In button

Paragraph panel

After creating paragraph type, you can use the Paragraph panel to apply attributes such as horizontal alignment, indentation, space before, space after, and auto hyphenation. Additional type formatting commands and dialogs are accessed from the panel menu.

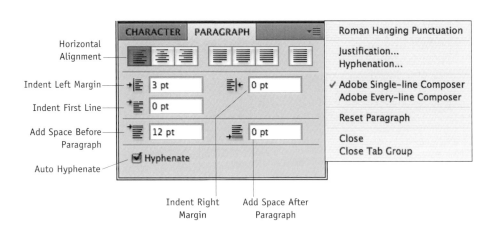

Horizontal Alignment

Indent Left Margin

Indent First Line

Add Space Before Paragraph

Auto Hyphenate

Indent Right Margin

Add Space After Paragraph

Paths panel

To the bitmap image that serves as the foundation of every Photoshop document, you can add vector shapes, called paths, which consist of curved and straight-line segments connected by anchor points. The Paths panel lets you save, activate, duplicate, and apply a fill or stroke color to any path, and load a path as a selection.

You can draw a path directly with a shape tool or the Pen tool, or you can create a selection and then convert the selection to a path. Conversely, to create a precisely drawn selection, you can draw a path and then convert it to a selection. You can reshape a path by using the Pen tool or any of its relatives, the Add Anchor Point, Delete Anchor Point, and Convert Point tools.

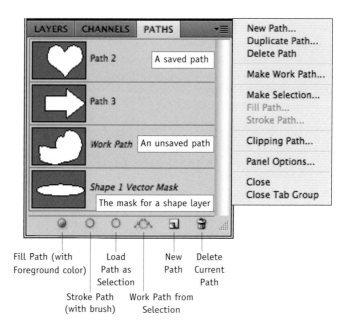

Styles panel

Each style is a unique collection of layer settings that is saved to and stored in the Styles panel. A style can include the settings for one or more layer effects and/or blending options (layer visibility, opacity, and blending mode, etc.). Like swatches on the Swatches panel, the styles on this panel are available for use in any document. Commands on the Styles panel menu let you save, load, and append style libraries, which are collections of styles.

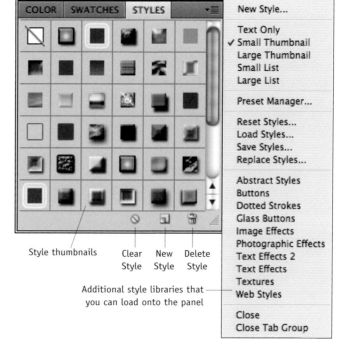

Swatches panel

The Swatches panel stores predefined and user-saved color swatches, to be applied by various tools, filters, and commands. A large assortment of predefined swatch libraries can be saved, loaded, and appended via commands on the panel menu.

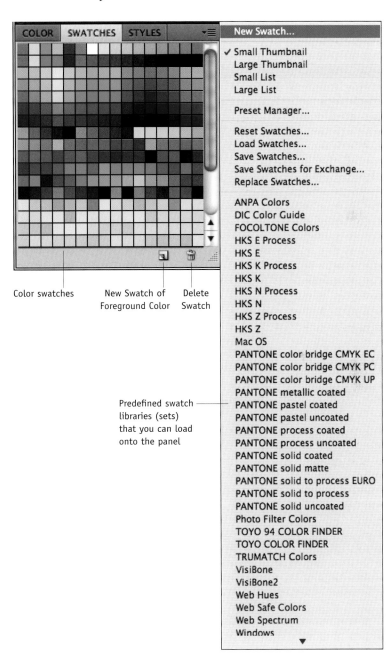

Color swatches   New Swatch of   Delete
                  Foreground Color Swatch

Predefined swatch libraries (sets) that you can load onto the panel

Tool Presets panel

You can save and reuse settings for tools as you would create and use other types of presets, and they are available for all Photoshop files. This is a great way to customize and personalize the Photoshop interface. Say, for example, you frequently resize and crop images to a particular set of dimensions with the Crop tool. By saving a preset for the tool with those width, height, and resolution parameters, the next time you use the tool, instead of having to tediously choose the same settings, all you would have to do is click the preset on either the Tool Presets panel or the Tool Preset picker (both of which are shown below). To open the picker, click the Tool Preset picker thumbnail on the far left end of the Options bar.

By using the Tool Presets panel or picker, you can create, save, load, sort, rename, reset, and delete presets for any tool. To have the panel or picker list the presets for just the current tool (for a streamlined approach), check Current Tool Only, or uncheck this option to display the presets for all tools.

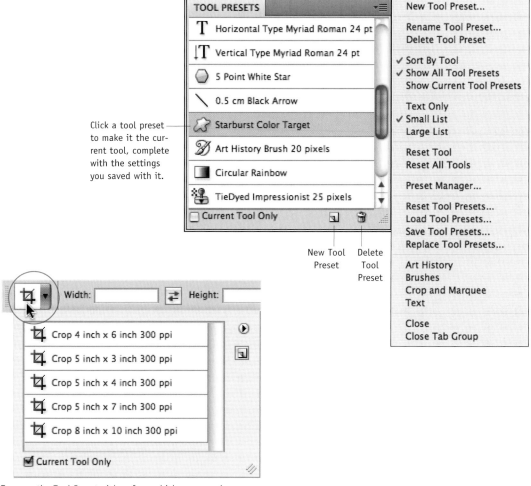

Click a tool preset to make it the current tool, complete with the settings you saved with it.

New Tool Preset   Delete Tool Preset

To open the Tool Preset picker, from which you can also choose presets for tools, click the tool thumbnail or arrowhead at the far left end of the Options bar.

Before applying adjustment or image-editing commands, you need to make sure your document is the proper size and orientation and is cropped to your liking. In this chapter, you'll learn how to change the resolution and dimensions of an image; change its canvas size; and crop, flip, rotate, and straighten it.

Changing resolution and dimensions

In this section, you'll encounter three terms:

➤ The number of pixels a file contains is its **pixel count**, or pixel dimensions (as in 3000 x 2000 pixels).

➤ The **resolution** ("res," for short) of a file is measured in pixels per inch (as in 250 or 300 ppi). The higher the resolution, the finer the detail.

➤ The process of changing the pixel count of a file is called **resampling**.

Some input devices (such as digital cameras that capture 8 megapixels of data or more and high-end scanners) produce files with a higher pixel count than is needed for most standard printing devices. In Photoshop, you can take advantage of a high pixel count to increase the print size or print resolution for your output device. You can keep the pixel count constant as you increase the print size (and thereby lower the resolution) or increase the resolution (and thereby lower the print size). No resampling occurs in either case, so the image quality isn't diminished.

You will need to resample a file if it contains too few or too many pixels to meet the resolution requirement of your target output device. If you resample a file as you increase its resolution, pixels will be added to the file and its storage size will increase accordingly. Resample a file as you decrease its resolution (downsample it), and pixels will be deleted. The only way to get those pixels back is by clicking a prior state on the History panel before closing the file. Even more important, resampling reduces the image sharpness. This can be a problem for print output (but not Web output), depending on the output resolution and how drastically the file is resampled, although it can be remedied somewhat by applying a sharpening filter afterward (see pages 274–278).

We'll show you how to resize three common types of files for print output—low res/large dimensions, high res/small dimensions, and medium res/small dimensions—and show you how to resize files for Web output.

PIXEL BASICS

IN THIS CHAPTER

Changing resolution and dimensions. . 97

Changing the canvas size 102

Cropping images 103

Flipping and rotating images 107

Straightening images 108

PIXELS

Pixels, short for "picture elements," are the building blocks that make up a digital image — the tiny individual dots that a digital camera uses to capture a scene or that a computer uses to display images onscreen. When working in Photoshop and for Web output, you'll need to be aware of the pixel dimensions, or pixel count, of an image. For print output, you'll need to be aware of the resolution of your image — the number of pixels per unit of measure (usually per inch, or "ppi").

By default, photographs from a digital SLR camera have a low resolution (72 to 180 ppi) and very large width and height dimensions. They contain a sufficient number of pixels for high-quality output (prints as large as 8" x 10"), provided you increase their resolution to the proper value. You can do this via the Image Size command in Photoshop.

To change the resolution of a digital photo (low res/large dimensions) for print output:

1. Choose Image > **Image Size** (Ctrl-Alt-I/Cmd-Option-I). The Image Size dialog opens.**A**

2. Because you need to increase the image resolution, uncheck **Resample Image**. When you lower the Width and Height in step 4, the resolution will increase automatically.

3. In the **Document Size** area, choose a unit of measure from the menu next to the Width field (we chose inches); the same unit will be chosen automatically for the Height.

4. Enter the **Width** or **Height** for the desired printout size; the Resolution value increases.

5. If the resolution falls between 240 and 300 pixels per inch, you've achieved your goal—just click OK.**B** The pixel dimensions didn't change, so resharpening won't be necessary (**A–B**, next page).

   If the resolution is higher than 300 ppi, check **Resample Image**, then enter a **Resolution** of 300. Also, from the menu at the bottom of the dialog, choose a resampling method. The **Bicubic (best for smooth gradients)**, **Bicubic Smoother (best for enlargement)**, and **Bicubic Sharper (best for reduction)** options cause the least reduction in image quality. Because you resampled the image, the pixel dimensions changed. You'll need to resharpen the image after clicking OK (see pages 274–278).

6. *Optional:* Check or uncheck **Scale Styles** to control whether any applied layer styles in the image will be scaled to fit the new size (see Chapter 20).

7. Click OK.

   ➤ To restore the settings that were in place when you opened the Image Size dialog, Alt-click/Option-click Reset (the Cancel button becomes a Reset button).

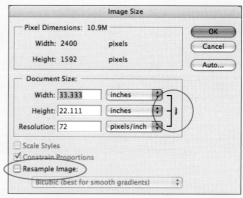

A In the Image Size dialog, uncheck Resample Image to make the Width, Height, and Resolution interdependent (as shown by the link icon).

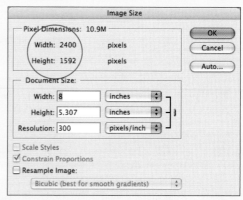

B When we changed the Width value to 8, the Height value readjusted automatically and the Resolution value increased to 300, but the Pixel Dimensions remained the same.

JPEGS FROM BRIDGE TO CAMERA RAW

From Bridge, you can open JPEG files into Photoshop by way of the Camera Raw dialog. By default, Camera Raw assigns a resolution of 240 ppi to all files it opens into Photoshop. To achieve that 240 ppi resolution, Camera Raw preserves the pixel count but alters the Width and Height (Document Size). To raise the resolution of a JPEG file (say, to 300 ppi) or to reduce its Document Size dimensions, follow the instructions on this page.

A The original photo has dimensions of 33" x 22" (much too large for our printer) and a resolution of 72 ppi.

B When we reduced the photo size to 8" x 5" via the Image Size dialog, the resolution increased automatically to 300 ppi. Because the pixel count didn't change, the image size and quality were preserved.

In many cases, scanned images have a high resolution and small dimensions and contain a sufficient number of pixels for large printouts.

To resize a scanned image (high res/small dimensions) for print output:

1. Choose Image > **Image Size** (Ctrl-Alt-I/Cmd-Option-I). The Image Size dialog opens.

2. Make sure **Resample Image** is unchecked.

3. Increase the **Width** or **Height** to the size needed for your printout. The Resolution will decrease.

    If the Resolution falls between 240 and 300 ppi, you're done; click OK. Because no resampling occurred, no resharpening is necessary.

    If the Resolution is still higher than 300 ppi, check **Resample Image,C** then lower the **Resolution** to 300. From the menu at the bottom of the dialog, choose **Bicubic Smoother (best for enlargement)** as the interpolation method. You've just resampled the image, so you'll need to resharpen it after clicking OK (see pages 274–278).

4. *Optional:* Check or uncheck **Scale Styles** to control whether layer effects in the image will be scaled to fit the new size (see Chapter 20).

5. Click OK.

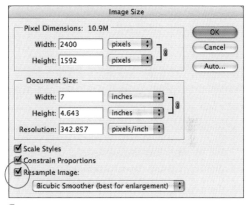

C Our first attempt at resizing our photo left us with too high a resolution, so here we've checked Resample Image and will lower just the Resolution (not the Width and Height).

Small files (with a resolution of, say, 180 to 200 ppi) don't contain enough pixels to be enlarged without resampling, so they must be resampled to achieve the dimensions needed for print output. This is not an ideal scenario, as it reduces the image sharpness, and you'll need to apply a sharpening filter afterward.

To resize a scanned image (medium res/ small dimensions) for print output:

1. Choose Image > **Image Size** (Ctrl-Alt-I/Cmd-Option-I). The Image Size dialog opens.

2. Check both **Resample Image** and **Constrain Proportions**.

3. Enter the desired **Width** for your printout. The Height value will change proportionately and the file storage size and pixel dimensions will increase.

4. Click OK. Since the image was resampled, you should now use a sharpening filter to resharpen it (see pages 274–278).

For Web output, your images must have a lower pixel count than for print output, because your viewers will see them on computer displays, which are low-resolution devices. In most cases, you will need to downsample your files (discard image pixels) to achieve the desired output size.

To change the pixel dimensions of an image for Web output:

1. Using File > Save As, copy your file, then choose Image > **Image Size** (Ctrl-Alt-I/Cmd-Option-I). The Image Size dialog opens. **A**

2. Make sure **Resample Image** is checked.

3. From the menu at the bottom of the dialog, choose the **Bicubic Sharper (best for reduction)** resampling method, which will degrade the image the least.

4. To preserve the width-to-height ratio of the image, check **Constrain Proportions**.

5. Enter a **Resolution** of 72 ppi.

6. In the **Pixel Dimensions** area, choose pixels from the menu (the default unit), then enter the exact Width and/or Height dimensions needed. **B**

7. Click OK.

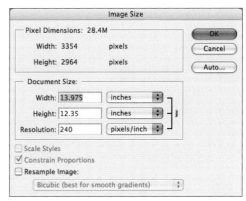

A These are initial Image Size values of a typical digital photo. To prepare this photo for Web output, we will need to lower the pixel count.

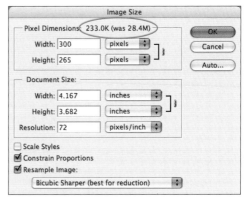

B We checked Resample Image, changed the Resolution to 72, and set the Width (in the Pixel Dimensions area) to 300. The file size, which is listed at the top, is now smaller because we lowered the pixel count. The image is now an appropriate size for online viewing.

COPYCAT

In some dialogs that have Width and Height fields, if you choose a unit of measure from the menu for the Width, the same unit is chosen automatically for the Height, and vice versa. If you want to prevent this from happening, hold down Shift as you choose a unit; the unit will change just for that dimension.

PIXEL COUNTS, RESOLUTION, AND IMAGE SIZE COMPARED

The four images below will help you grasp the concept of resolution and how it affects image size. Figures **A–B** compare the same image at two different resolutions; figures **C–D** compare the print sizes for those resolutions.

The moral here: Don't judge the size of an image or its output quality based solely on its onscreen size. Instead, compare these two factors: the current zoom level of the image in the document window and the image resolution.

A This original image has a resolution of 300 ppi (as listed in the Status bar when Document Dimensions is chosen).

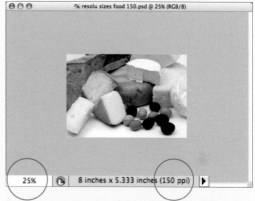

B This is the same image with the same dimensions, but here the resolution is 150 ppi, which is half that of the original. When viewed at the same zoom level (25%), the low-resolution image displays at only half its original size because it now contains fewer pixels (has a lower pixel count).

C For this 300 ppi image, we chose View > Print Size, which zoomed the image to an onscreen approximation of the printout size (that is, the Document Dimensions, as listed on the Status bar). Note the zoom level is 24%.

D We also chose View > Print Size for this low-res (150 ppi) version of the same image; the zoom level here is 48%. Although this image and the image shown at left will print at the same size, the print quality will be different because this one has a lower pixel count. Moral: Don't use Print Size view to evaluate the potential print quality of your image.

Changing the canvas size

By using the Canvas Size command, you can enlarge or shrink the live, editable image area. Pixels can be added to or removed from one, two, three, or all four sides of the image. This may come in handy, say, if you want to add room for type, as in the example on this page, or to accommodate imagery from other documents, as we show you in Chapter 9.

To change the canvas size:

1. Choose Image > **Canvas Size** (Ctrl-Alt-C/Cmd-Option-C). The Canvas Size dialog opens.

2. *Optional:* Choose a different unit of measure from the Width menu.

3. Do either of the following:

   Enter new **Width** and/or **Height** values. The dimensions are independent of one another; changing one won't affect the other.**A–B**

   Check **Relative**, then in the **Width** and **Height** fields, enter positive values to increase those dimensions or negative values to decrease them.

4. *Optional:* The small square in the center of the Anchor arrows represents the existing image area. Click a square to reposition the image relative to the canvas. The arrows indicate where the new canvas area will be added.

5. From the **Canvas Extension Color** menu, choose a color for the added pixels. Or to choose a custom color, choose Other or click the color square next to the menu, then click a color in the Color Picker (see page 192) or in the document window. If the image doesn't have a Background (take a peek at the Layers panel), this menu won't be available.

6. Click OK.**C** Any added canvas area will automatically be filled with the color you chose in the previous step, unless the image contains layers but not a Background, in which case the added canvas area will be transparent.

➤ You can also enlarge the canvas area manually by dragging a marquee with the Crop tool (see page 105).

A This is the original image.

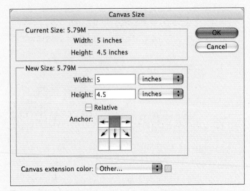

B Compare the Current Size to the New Size as you change the Width and Height values. For our image, we increased the Height value, then clicked the top Anchor square to have the extra canvas area be added to the bottom of the image.

C After adding pixels to the bottom of the canvas area, we created editable type on its own layer.

Cropping images

You can crop an image by using the Crop tool, the Crop command, or the Trim command. We'll show you how to use the Crop tool first.

To crop an image using a marquee:

1. Choose the **Crop** tool ⌷ (C or Shift-C).

2. Drag a marquee over the part of the image you want to keep.**A**

3. On the Options bar, do the following:

    If you're cropping an image that contains layers, you can either click **Cropped Area: Delete** to delete the cropped-out areas or click **Hide** to have them save with the file but extend beyond the visible canvas area. (You can use the Move tool later to move hidden pixels into view.) Imagery from the Background will be deleted, not hidden.

    Check **Shield** to darken the area outside the crop marquee with a crop shield (to help you see what will remain after cropping). You can change the shield color by clicking the Color

swatch, or change the Opacity percentage of the shield.

For the **Perspective** option, see Photoshop Help. We prefer to use the Lens Correction filter to correct perspective problems (see pages 272–273).

4. Do any of these optional steps:

    To **resize** the marquee, drag any handle (double-arrow pointer). Shift-drag a corner handle to preserve the proportions of the marquee; or hold down Alt/Option to resize the marquee from its center.

    To **reposition** the marquee, drag inside it.

    To **rotate** the marquee, position the cursor just outside it (⟳ pointer), then drag in a circular direction. (This is a quick way to both crop and straighten a photo.) To change the axis point around which the marquee rotates, drag the circle away from the center of the marquee before rotating it. The image orientation will change after the next step.

5. Do one of the following:

    Press Enter/Return.**B**

    Double-click inside the marquee.

    Right-click/Control-click the image and choose Crop.

➤ To cancel a crop marquee, press Esc, or right-click/Control-click and choose Cancel.

A With the Crop tool, drag a marquee over the area you want to keep. The crop shield will appear if that option is checked on the Options bar.

B We cropped this image to focus attention to the women's faces.

Next, we'll show you how you can crop away unwanted portions of an image with the Crop tool and wind up with a standard photo size.

To crop an image to a specific size:

1. Open an image, and choose the **Crop** tool ⛏ (C or Shift-C).

2. Do either of the following:

   On the Options bar, enter specific **Width** and **Height** values for the final image. (You can click the Swap Width and Height button ⇄ to switch the current values.)

   To crop using the Width, Height, and Resolution values from another open image, click in that other document window or click its tab, and make sure its resolution is comparable to that of the image you're cropping. Click **Front Image** on the Options bar, then click back on the window or tab for the document to be cropped.

3. Drag a crop marquee on the image (without holding down any modifier keys).**A** You can drag inside the marquee to reposition it.

4. To accept the crop,**B** do one of the following:

   Double-click inside the marquee.

   Right-click/Control-click and choose Crop.

   Press Enter/Return.

5. Apply a sharpening filter; see pages 274–278.

➤ To empty the Width, Height, and Resolution fields on the Options bar for the Crop tool, click Clear.

➤ To crop a larger image to fit inside a smaller one, see page 151.

➤ To create tool presets for the Crop tool, follow our general guidelines on page 404.

A We entered a Width of 6" and a Height of 4" on the Options bar for the Crop tool, then dragged to create a marquee. (The marquee preserved our chosen 6-to-4 ratio.)

B The image is cropped to a standard photo size of 6 x 4 inches, which you can see by looking at the rulers.

When you crop with a marquee that's larger than the image, you effectively increase the canvas size. Unlike the Canvas Size command, this technique gives you manual control over how much canvas area is added and where. Another use for this technique is to reveal imagery that extends beyond the live canvas area.

To enlarge the canvas area using the Crop tool:

1. Choose a Background color (see Chapter 12).

2. To reveal more of the work canvas (gray area) around the image, either enlarge the document window or Application frame by dragging a side or corner, or lower the zoom level.

3. Choose the **Crop** tool 🔲 (C or Shift-C).

4. Drag a crop marquee within the image.

5. Drag any of the handles of the marquee into the work canvas (outside the live canvas area).  You can drag any midpoint handle to add more canvas area to just that edge of the image.

6. Do one of the following: B

   Double-click inside the marquee.

   Press Enter/Return.

   Right-click/Control-click the image and choose Crop.

   If the image has a Background (look on the Layers panel), the added canvas area will fill with the current Background color. If the image contains layers but no Background, the added canvas area will fill with transparent pixels.

   Note: Pixels on any layer that were formerly hidden outside the live canvas area may now fall within it, and will become visible.

A Drag any of the crop marquee handles outside the canvas area, into the work canvas. Here, we're dragging the bottom center handle downward to add more canvas area to the bottom of the image.

B When we accepted the crop, the added canvas pixels filled automatically with white, our chosen Background color.

OVERRIDING THE SNAP

Normally, if you resize a crop marquee near the edge of the canvas area and View > Snap To > Document Bounds is on, the crop edges will snap to the edge of the canvas area. To override this snap function (say you want to crop slightly inside or outside the edge of the image), do either of the following: turn the Snap To > Document Bounds feature off; or start dragging a marquee handle, then hold down Ctrl/Control as you drag the handle near the edge of the canvas area.

Although the Crop command, discussed below, is simple and straightforward, it doesn't offer an image resolution option like the Crop tool does.

To crop an image using the Crop command:

1. Choose the **Rectangular Marquee** tool [⬚] (M or Shift-M).

2. Do either of the following:

   Draw a **marquee** over the part of the image you want to keep. **A**

   To constrain the proportions of the marquee to a width-to-height ratio or size (such as a standard size for a photo print), on the Options bar, choose **Style: Fixed Ratio** or **Fixed Size**, enter the desired **Width** to **Height** ratio or values, then drag in the document window.

3. *Optional:* To scale the marquee, right-click/ Control-click and choose Transform Selection, Shift-drag a corner handle, then double-click inside the marquee to accept the edit.

4. Choose Image > **Crop**, then deselect (Ctrl-D/ Cmd-D). **B**

➤ Reset the default behavior of the Rectangular Marquee tool by choosing Style: Normal from the Options bar.

A With the Rectangular Marquee tool, draw a marquee over the area of the image you want to keep.

The Trim command trims away any excess transparent or solid-color areas from around the entire image—be it a frame, border, or solid-colored background. You still wind up with a rectangular image.

To crop an image closely using the Trim command:

1. Choose Image > **Trim**. The Trim dialog opens.

2. Click a **Based On** option:

   Transparent Pixels trims away transparency from the edges of the image. If the image doesn't contain transparent pixels, this option won't be available.

   Top Left Pixel Color removes any border areas that match the color of the left uppermost pixel in the image.

   Bottom Right Pixel Color removes any border areas that match the color of the bottommost right pixel in the image.

3. Check which areas of the image you want the command to **Trim Away: Top, Bottom, Left,** and/or **Right**.

4. Click OK.

B This is the result after we chose Image > Crop.

Follow these instructions if you want to preserve the existing width to height ratio of an image as you crop it.

To crop an image according to its existing aspect ratio:

1. With an image open, choose the **Crop tool** 🔲 (C or Shift-C).

2. Drag a **marquee** diagonally across the entire image, from one corner to the opposite corner.

3. Shift-drag a **corner** handle on the crop marquee to resize the marquee proportionately to the desired crop size.

4. *Optional:* Drag within the marquee to reposition it over the portion of the image you want to keep.**A**

5. Double-click inside the marquee; or right-click/ Control-click and choose Crop; or press Enter/ Return.**B**

A After dragging a marquee across the entire image with the Crop tool, we Shift-dragged a handle, then moved the marquee over the area we want to keep.

Flipping and rotating images

You can flip all the layers in an image to create a mirror image, or flip just one layer at a time. (You'll learn about layers in the next chapter.)

To flip an image or a layer:

Do either of the following:

To flip all the layers, choose Image > Image Rotation ★ > **Flip Horizontal/Flip Canvas Horizontal** or **Flip Vertical/Flip Canvas Vertical.C–D**

To flip one layer at a time, choose Edit > Transform > **Flip Horizontal** or **Flip Vertical**. You can use this command to "unflip" a type layer (to make it readable again) after you've flipped a whole image (don't flip out!).

B We accepted the crop. The original width to height ratio of the image was preserved.

C We want to flip this original image.

D Flip Canvas > Horizontal is chosen.

The Image Rotation commands rotate all the layers in an image. (To rotate just one layer at a time, use a rotate command on the Edit > Transform submenu instead.)

To rotate an image:

Do either of the following:

Choose Image > Image Rotation ★ > **180°**, **90° CW** (clockwise), or **90° CCW** (counterclockwise).

Choose Image > Image Rotation > **Arbitrary**. Enter an **Angle** value, click **°CW** (clockwise) or **°CCW** (counterclockwise), then click OK.

Straightening images

You didn't use a tripod for that unforgettable moment? Did a sloppy job of scanning? You can use the Ruler tool to square it off.

To straighten a crooked image:

1. Choose the **Ruler** tool ✎ (I or Shift-I).

2. Drag along a feature of the image that you want to orient horizontally or vertically,**A** noting the angle (A: value) on the Options bar as you do so.

3. Choose Image > Image Rotation ★ > **Arbitrary**. The angle you dragged will appear in the Angle field. Click OK.**B**

4. Use a cropping method to remove any background color areas that the rotation produced.**C**

IT CROPS! IT STRAIGHTENS!

The File > Automate > Crop and Straighten Photos command is an action (automated script) that searches for straight edges and rectangular areas in an image, copies a rectangular section that it detects into a new document window, and rotates the image, if necessary, to square it off. You can scan multiple images at a time and let the command sort them into individual documents, or you can use the command to unrotate a Photoshop document that you've already rotated.

If you think the Crop and Straighten Photos command sounds too good to be true, you're partially correct. For one thing, it's not as smart as you are, so it can be fooled. For example, it may mistake a shadow that the scanner detected around the actual photo for the edge of the image. Also, your images may wind up being slightly off square. To help the command do its job properly, don't overlap pictures in the scanner or let them hang off the side.

A This image is slightly askew. We dragged the Ruler tool from left to right along the crooked railing.

B We used the Image Rotation > Arbitrary command to rotate the image along the angle we drew with the Ruler tool.

C We used the Crop tool to remove the white areas. Now the image looks level.

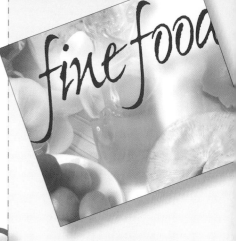

The beauty of assigning various parts of a document to layers is that you can edit them individually—maybe some text on one layer, a silhouetted shape on another, and an overall background image behind. An image can contain only one Background (note the uppercase "B"), which is always fully opaque, but you can add as many layers as you like. Unlike the Background, a layer can contain partially or fully transparent areas. By default, transparent areas on a layer are represented by a checkerboard pattern. **A–B**

Creating layers

If you choose Background Contents: White or Background Color in the File > New dialog when creating a new document, the bottommost tier of the image will be the Background; if you choose Background Contents: Transparent, the first tier will be a layer with no Background.

Layers are controlled via the **Layers** panel (Window > Layers). The Background, if present, is always listed at the bottom. This panel is so indispensable for image editing, it's the star player in two other chapters and plays an important supporting role in many others. In this chapter you'll learn basic techniques, such as how to create, duplicate, select, restack, group, delete, hide, show, move, merge, and flatten image layers. In other chapters, you'll learn about adjustment, editable type, Smart Object, and shape layers; layer masks; blending options—and more!

LAYER BASICS

7

IN THIS CHAPTER

Creating layers 109
Duplicating layers 111
Converting the Background 112
Selecting layers 113
Restacking layers 114
Working with layer groups 114
Deleting individual layers 116
Hiding and showing layers 116
Moving layer content 117
Choosing Layers panel options 118
Merging layers 120
Flattening layers 122

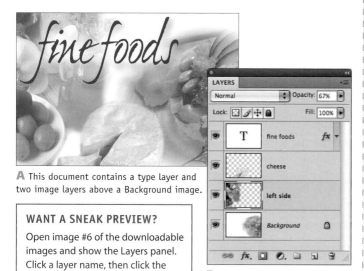

A This document contains a type layer and two image layers above a Background image.

WANT A SNEAK PREVIEW?

Open image #6 of the downloadable images and show the Layers panel. Click a layer name, then click the visibility (eye) icon on and off.

B This is the Layers panel for the image shown at left.

A new layer is created automatically when you perform some kinds of edits, such as paste a selection,
create type with the Horizontal or Vertical Type
tool, or create a shape. In these instructions, you
will learn how to create new, blank image layers.
You may add as many layers to a file as available
memory and storage allow.

To create a layer:

1. If the document already contains layers, click
   a layer.**A** (The layer you create in step 3 will
   appear above the currently selected one.)

2. Show the **Layers** panel.

3. Click the **New Layer** button ▣ at the bottom of
   the panel. The new layer will have both Opacity
   and Fill percentages of 100% and a blending
   mode of Normal.**B**

4. *Optional:* To rename the layer, double-click the
   existing layer name, type the desired name,
   then press Enter/Return.

➤ To choose options for a new layer as you
   create it, Alt-click/Option-click the New Layer
   button ▣ on the Layers panel (Ctrl-Shift-N/
   Cmd-Shift-N). In the New Layer dialog, you can
   change the layer Name or choose a nonprinting
   Color for the area on the Layers panel behind
   the visibility icon 👁 (see the tip on page 119).
   You can easily change the layer blending mode
   and opacity at any time right on the panel; see
   page 118.

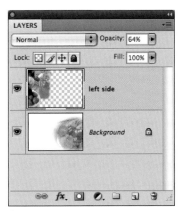

A Click the layer above which you want
the new one to appear.

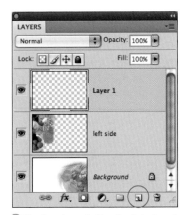

B The New Layer button is clicked, and
a new layer appears on the panel.

PRESERVING OR FLATTENING LAYERS

➤ Layers make your Photoshop files considerably
larger, so when you're completely done editing your
document, consider using a merge or flatten command to shrink it back down (see pages 120–122).

➤ If you need to preserve layers, when saving your
file, check Layers in the File > Save As dialog, and as
the file Format, choose Photoshop, Photoshop PDF,
Large Document Format (see the sidebar on page 25),
or TIFF. The formats that don't preserve layers flatten
them automatically and convert any transparency
in the bottommost layer to opaque white.

➤ If you want to preserve layers when switching
document color modes (e.g., from RGB to CMYK),
click Don't Flatten or Don't Merge in the alert dialog.

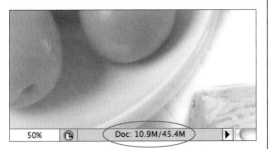

After adding layers to your file, from the Status bar menu,
choose Document Sizes. The first value is the size of the
document without layers; the second value is its approximate size with layers. This file contains three image layers
in addition to the Background, which explains why the
second value is more than four times larger than the first.

Another method for creating a layer is to copy or cut imagery from an existing layer or the Background and put it on its own layer. This can be done easily by using a simple command.

To turn selected pixels into a layer:

1. On the Layers panel, click an image layer or the Background, then create a selection in the document window.

2. To create a new layer containing the selected pixels, do either of the following:

   To place a copy of the selected pixels on a new layer and leave the **original** layer intact, right-click/Control-click in the document window and choose **Layer via Copy** (Ctrl-J/Cmd-J). **B**

   To place the selected pixels on a new layer and **remove** them from the original layer, right-click/Control-click in the document window and choose **Layer via Cut** (Ctrl-Shift-J/Cmd-Shift-J). The exposed area on the original layer will be filled with transparency; or if you cut pixels from the Background, the area will be filled with the current Background color (see page 191).

A An area of the Background is selected (the plate on the right).

Duplicating layers

Follow these instructions to duplicate a layer or layer group or to turn a copy of the Background into a layer. (To learn about layer groups, see pages 114–116.)

To duplicate a layer or layer group:

Do one of the following:

Click a layer, then press **Ctrl-J/Cmd-J.**

Drag a layer, layer group, or the Background over the **New Layer** button 🔲 at the bottom of the Layers panel. The duplicate will appear above the one you dragged.

To name the layer as you create it, right-click/Control-click a layer, layer group, or the Background and choose **Duplicate Layer** or **Duplicate Group**. In the dialog, change the name in the "As" field, then click OK. **C**

➤ When you duplicate a layer, any layer mask and/or effects on that layer are also duplicated. Similarly, when you duplicate a Smart Object layer, any Smart Filters on that layer are also duplicated (see pages 336–337).

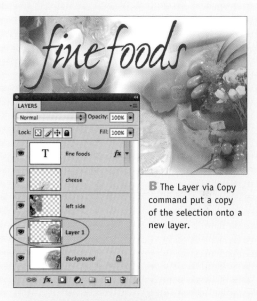

B The Layer via Copy command put a copy of the selection onto a new layer.

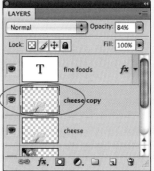

C The duplicate layer appears on the panel.

Converting the Background

There are many things you can do to a layer that you can't do to the Background. For example, you can't move the Background upward in the layer stack; change its blending mode, opacity percentage, or fill percentage; attach a mask to it; or embellish it with layer effects—all of which you can do to a normal layer. You can, however, convert the Background into a layer, at which time it will adopt all the normal layer functions.

To convert the Background into a layer:

Do either of the following:

Alt-double-click/Option-double-click the Background on the Layers panel to turn it into a layer without choosing options.

Double-click the Background on the Layers panel A to open the New Layer dialog. B Type a new Name, choose a Color for the area behind the visibility icon 👁 on the panel, if desired, choose a Mode and an Opacity percentage, then click OK. C

If you need to create a Background for a file that doesn't have one, you can **convert** any existing **layer** into the **Background**—the reverse of the previous instructions.

To convert a layer into the Background:

1. Click a layer.

2. Choose Layer > New > **Background from Layer**. The new Background will appear at the bottom of the stack on the Layers panel.

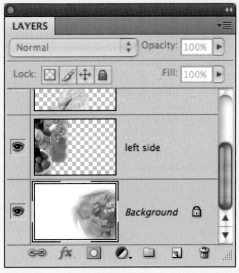

A Double-click the Background.

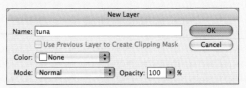

B Enter a Name and choose options for the layer-to-be.

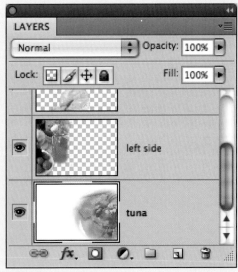

C The former Background is now a fully functional, normal layer.

Selecting layers

Always remember to select the layer or layers you want to work on before editing your document. This signals to Photoshop which part of your document you want to change. When a layer or layer group is selected, it has a highlight color (the default color is blue), **A** and the layer or group name is listed in the title bar of the document window. (To learn about layer groups, see pages 114–116.)

To select layers via the Layers panel:

Do one of the following:

To select a **layer** or **layer group**, click either the layer thumbnail or the area to the right of the layer or group name.

To select **multiple layers**, click a layer, then Shift-click the last in a series of consecutively listed layers, or Ctrl-click/Cmd-click individual layers (Ctrl-click/Cmd-click if you need to deselect individual layers).

To select **all** the layers in your document (but not the Background), choose Select > All Layers (Ctrl-Alt-A/Cmd-Option-A).

To select **all layers** of a **similar kind**, such as all image layers, shape layers, or adjustment layers, right-click/Control-click one of those layers and choose Select Similar Layers.

To select a layer or layer group with the Move tool:

1. Choose the **Move** tool ⊹ (V).
2. Do either of the following:

   Right-click/Control-click in the document window and choose a **layer** or **layer group** name from the context menu. **B** (Ctrl-right-click/Cmd-Control-click with any other tool selected.) Only layers containing nontransparent pixels under the pointer will be listed on the context menu.

   Check **Auto-Select** on the Options bar, choose **Group** or **Layer**, then click any visible pixels in the document window. You can't select the Background using this technique.

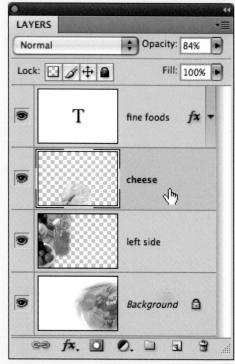

A Simply click a layer to select it.

B On the context menu, choose the name of the layer you want to select.

Restacking layers

When you restack a layer upward or downward, the content of that layer shifts forward or backward.

To restack layers:

Drag a layer or group name upward or downward on the panel, and release the mouse when a dark horizontal line appears in the desired location.A–B

➤ To move the Background upward on the list, you must convert it into a layer first (see page 112). Layers can't be stacked below the Background.

➤ You can also restack a selected layer via the commands (or via the shortcuts listed) on the Layer > Arrange submenu.

Working with layer groups

To organize the layers in a document, you can collect them into labeled groups.C Layer groups help make the panel more tidy, make the list of names on the panel shorter (less of a need to scroll up and down), and best of all, enable you to move, rotate, scale, duplicate, restack, lock, unlock, change the blending mode or opacity for, or hide or show multiple layers simultaneously.

Groups can be nested inside other groups, up to five levels deep. Furthermore, you can add a layer mask to a layer group, and it will apply to all the layers within it (see page 302).

To create a layer group:

Method 1 (from existing layers)

1. Click a layer, then Shift-click or Ctrl-click/Cmd-click two or more layers. They don't have to be listed consecutively.

2. Do either of the following:

   Press **Ctrl-G/Cmd-G**.

   From the Layers panel menu, choose **New Group from Layers**. In the dialog, change the Name, if desired, then click OK.

3. *Optional:* To add more layers to the group, drag them over the group listing, and release the mouse when the dark drop zone border appears.

➤ The default blending mode for a group is Pass Through, which we suggest you don't change.

A The "left side" layer is moved upward.

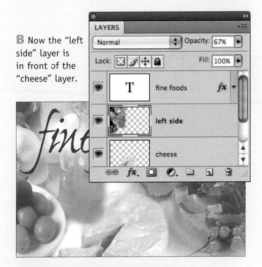

B Now the "left side" layer is in front of the "cheese" layer.

C The type ("fine foods") and "cheese" layers are in a group.

Method 2 (create a group, then add layers)

1. Do either of the following:

   To create a group without choosing settings for it, click the layer above which you want the group to appear, then click the **New Group** button ⬜ at the bottom of the Layers panel.

   To choose settings for a group as you create it, **Alt-click/Option-click** the New Group button or choose **New Group** from the panel menu. In the dialog, change the Name, Color, or Opacity setting for the group, if desired; then click OK.

2. Drag layers into the new group listing; release the mouse when the dark drop zone border appears around the group listing.

➤ Click the arrowhead to expand or collapse a group list.

➤ To group layers into a Smart Object, see page 314.

To rename a layer or layer group:

1. Double-click a layer or layer group name on the Layers panel.

2. Type a new name.**A**

3. Press Enter/Return or click outside the name.

MOVING LAYERS OUT OF A GROUP

➤ To move a layer out of a group, drag the layer above or below any layer that resides outside the group.

➤ To move a layer from one group to another, drag it over the group name or icon.

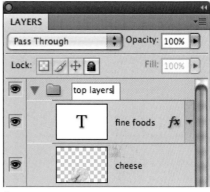

A A layer group is renamed.

**USING THE CONTEXT MENU
WITH THE LAYERS PANEL**

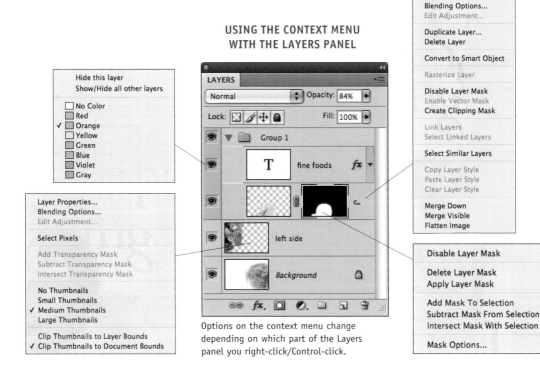

Options on the context menu change depending on which part of the Layers panel you right-click/Control-click.

You can delete a layer group and its layers or merely disband the group while preserving the layers.

To delete or disband a layer group:

Do one of the following:

On the Layers panel, click a group. Click the **Delete Layer** button, 🗑 then in the alert dialog, click **Group Only** or **Group and Contents;** or to bypass the prompt and delete both the group and its contents, Alt-click/Option-click the Delete Layer button.

Right-click/Control-click a group and choose **Delete Group** from the context menu, then click **Group Only** or **Group and Contents**.

To disband a layer group without deleting the layers it contains, click the group, then press **Ctrl-Shift-G/Cmd-Shift-G**. The group icon disappears.

Deleting individual layers

To delete a layer:

Do either of the following:

On the Layers panel, click a layer. Click the **Delete Layer** button, 🗑 then click Yes if an alert dialog appears; or to bypass the alert, Alt-click/ Option-click the Delete Layer button.

Click the layer you want to delete, then press **Backspace/Delete**. ★

➤ Change your mind? Choose Edit > Undo or click the prior state on the History panel.

Hiding and showing layers

By hiding the layers you're not currently working on, you remove them as a visual distraction. Hidden layers don't print. The instructions below apply to layers and the Background.

To hide or show layers:

On the Layers panel, do one of the following:

To hide or show a **layer** or **layer group**, click in the visibility column 👁.**A–B**

To hide or show **multiple layers**, drag upward or downward in the visibility column.

To hide or show **all layers** and **layer groups** except the **one** you click on, Alt-click/Option-click in the visibility column; or right-click/ Control-click in the visibility column and choose Show/Hide All Other Layers.

A Click in the visibility column to show or hide a layer.

B Now the type layer is hidden.

Moving layer content

Follow these instructions to move a selected layer or group of layers by dragging them with the Move tool. (To move linked layers, see page 309; to align layers via buttons on the Options bar, see page 164.)

To move layers manually:

1. On the Layers panel, do one of the following:

   Click a layer.

   Shift-click or Ctrl-click/Cmd-click multiple layers.

   Click a layer group.

2. Choose the **Move** tool ⊕ or hold down V for a temporary Move tool. ★

3. If you're going to move a whole group, check **Auto-Select** on the Options bar and choose **Group** from the menu. Or to move an individual layer in a group, check **Auto-Select** and choose **Layer** from the menu.

4. Drag in the document window.**A–B** If you move part of the layer or layers outside the canvas area, don't worry—it will save with the document and you can move it back into view at any time.

➤ To nudge a selected layer by one pixel at a time, choose the Move tool, then press an arrow key. Press Shift-arrow to move a layer by 10 screen pixels at a time. Don't press Alt-arrow/Option-arrow—unless your intention is to duplicate the layer.

A The type layer is being moved with the Move tool.

B The type layer was moved downward.

MOVING SMART

You can use smart guides to align the edge of a layer you're moving with the edge or center of other layers. Turn on View > Show > Smart Guides. As you move a layer or layer group with the Move tool, temporary guide lines will appear onscreen when the edge of the layer imagery you're moving encounters the edge or center of nontransparent pixels, type, or a shape on another layer (see page 162).

FLIPPING OUT

On the Layers panel, click a layer or layer group, then choose Edit > Transform > Flip Horizontal or Flip Vertical. Any layers that are linked to the selected layer or layers will also flip.

Choosing Layers panel options

You can change the appearance of a layer and the layers below it dramatically by using the blending mode and/or opacity controls.**A** The layer opacity control makes the layer content (e.g., imagery, brush strokes, type, shape, Smart Object, adjustments, layer effects) more or less opaque, whereas the blending mode affects how the layer content blends with underlying layers.

Note: The following is a brief introduction to these two features. The blending modes are illustrated fully on pages 198–202 and discussed on pages 298–299; the Opacity and Fill options are explored in more depth on page 297.

To change the blending mode and/or opacity of a layer or layer group:

1. Click a layer or layer group that overlaps imagery on a layer below it so you'll be able to see the results.

2. On the Layers panel, do either or both of the following:

   Choose a **blending mode** from the menu at the top of the panel.

   Change the **Opacity** percentage (use the scrubby slider).

The Lock Transparent Pixels button on the Layers panel prevents or allows the editing of transparent pixels by any command or tool. In the following instructions you'll see how this option affects strokes that you'll apply with the Brush tool, but remember that this button also affects other edits. By default, transparent pixels on a layer are represented by a gray and white checkerboard pattern.

To limit edits by locking transparent pixels:

1. Click a layer (not an editable type layer).

2. Choose the **Brush** tool ✎ (B or Shift-B). To change the brush diameter, press [or].

3. On the Layers panel, click the **Lock Transparent Pixels** button,▦ then draw brush strokes on the layer.**B** Only nontransparent pixels can be recolored.

4. Show the **Swatches** panel, then click a color.

5. Click the **Lock Transparent Pixels** button again (or press /) to toggle it off.

6. Paint on the layer again. Now all layer pixels can be edited, whether transparent or not.**C**

A We chose Color Burn mode for the type layer and lowered the Opacity of the "cheese" layer to 40% (compare this image with the one on the previous page).

B With the Lock Transparent Pixels option on, we can apply brush strokes only to nontransparent pixels.

C With the Lock Transparent Pixels option off, we can apply brush strokes anywhere on the layer.

CUSTOMIZING THE CHECKERBOARD

In the Transparency Settings area of Preferences > Transparency & Gamut, you can change the size or color of the checkerboard pattern that represents transparent pixels (or hide it from view by choosing None from the Grid Size menu).

Use the lock options for layers to prevent inadvertent edits while working on other layers.

To lock a layer or layer group:

1. Click a layer or layer group.
2. Do any of the following:

   Click the **Lock Image Pixels** button ✐ to prevent layer pixels from being edited. You can still move the layer, as well as choose options for it, such as layer effects, blending mode, opacity percentage, etc.

   Click the **Lock Position** button ✛ to lock only the location of the layer. The layer content (e.g., pixels, type characters or attributes) can still be edited.

   Click the **Lock All** button 🔒 to prevent the layer from being moved or edited (both of the above). This button is also available for layer groups.

   When any lock button is pressed, a lock icon **A** appears on the panel.

To choose thumbnail options for the Layers panel:

Right-click/Control-click a layer thumbnail and choose any of the following:

A different **thumbnail size**, or No Thumbnails (turning off thumbnails boosts the program's performance but frankly, we find it impossible to work without them).

Clip Thumbnails to Layer Bounds to show, in the panel thumbnails, only the area that encompasses the opaque pixels on the layer (you may find this useful if most of your layers contain silhouetted shapes);**B** or **Clip Thumbnails to Document Bounds** to include surrounding transparent pixels in the thumbnails.

➤ To assign a different color to the area behind the visibility icon 👁 on a layer, click the layer, then right-click/Control-click in the visibility column and choose a color.**C** You can use the color labels to categorize your layers, such as all the type layers, all the adjustment layers, etc. They make the panel look pretty, too.

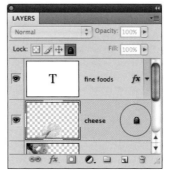

A The dark padlock indicates that this layer is fully locked; it can't be moved or edited.

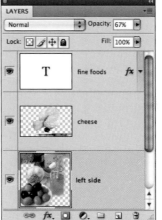

B We chose Clip Thumbnails to Layer Bounds and a large Thumbnail Size for this Layers panel.

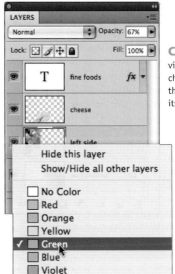

C Click a layer, then via the context menu, choose a new color for the area behind its visibility icon.

Merging layers

The merge commands—Merge Down, Merge Layers, and Merge Visible—merge two or more selected layers into one layer (the bottommost of the selected layers). You can apply any of these commands periodically during the editing process to reduce the file size of your document and to reduce clutter on the Layers panel. (The Flatten Image command, discussed on page 122, is normally applied to a copy of a file as a final step before output.)

To merge layers:

1. Do one of the following:

   Click the **upper** layer of two layers you want to merge.**A** The bottom one must be an image layer or the Background (not a group).

   Ctrl-click/Cmd-click **nonconsecutive** layers. The layers can be solo, in a group, or a combination thereof.

   Click a **group**. (All the layers in the group will be merged—but only with one another.)

   Notes: You can merge an adjustment layer, shape layer, or editable type layer downward into an image layer. Adjustment layers can't be merged together. When a type or shape layer is merged, it becomes rasterized.

2. Do either of the following:

   Right-click/Control-click the selected layer and choose **Merge Down**; or choose **Merge Layers** if multiple layers are selected; or choose **Merge Group** if you selected a group.

   Press **Ctrl-E/Cmd-E.B**

   If the underlying layer contains a layer mask, an alert dialog will appear; click Preserve or Apply, as you wish.

   If you merged the layers in a group, the group icon will disappear from the panel.

➤ If you want to merge layers while preserving access to a copy of the original, separate layers, follow the second set of instructions on the next page.

➤ The Merge Down command won't be accessible if the Lock All button is enabled for the currently selected layer.

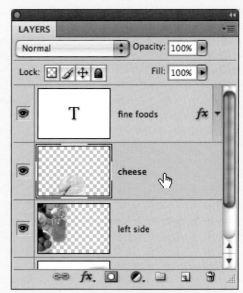

A We clicked the "cheese" layer.

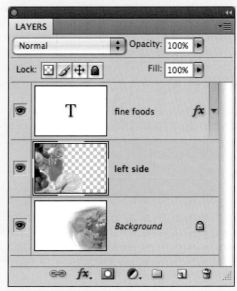

B The Merge Down command merged the "cheese" layer into the "left side" layer.

The Merge Visible command merges all the currently visible layers while preserving any hidden layers as separate layers. By hiding the layers you don't want to merge before choosing this command, you can control which ones will merge.

To merge only visible layers:

1. Make sure only the layers you want to merge are visible (have eye icons), and hide any layers (including the Background, if desired) that you don't want merged.

2. Right-click/Control-click one of the visible layers and choose **Merge Visible** (Ctrl-Shift-E/ Cmd-Shift-E).**A–B**

    Note: If you merge an editable type layer, shape layer, or adjustment layer, the specific features of that kind of layer (e.g., adjustment settings from an adjustment layer) will no longer be editable.

The commands in the following instructions copy and merge ("stamp") two or more selected layers into one new layer in one easy step, while preserving the original, separate layers. If you want to test out some edits (e.g., filters, transformations) on multiple layers instead of just one layer, you might want to use one of these commands first, then apply your edits to the merged layer.

To copy and merge layers:

Do either of the following:

Ctrl-click/Cmd-click the layers you want to copy and merge, then hold down Alt/Option as you choose **Merge Layers** from the panel menu. The new layer name will contain the word "(merged)," and the latest state on the History panel will be listed as "Stamp Layers."

To copy and merge just the currently visible layers, hold down Alt/Option as you choose **Merge Visible** from the panel menu.

➤ Instead of merging or flattening layers, consider grouping them into a Smart Object layer. You'll achieve the same reduction of layers, plus you'll gain the ability to edit the original layers individually by double-clicking the Smart Object layer thumbnail (see pages 314–316).

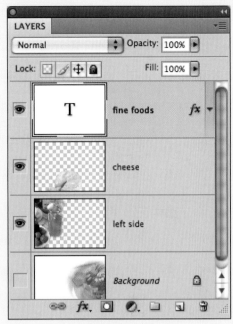

A In this document, we hid the Background because we don't want the layers to merge into it.

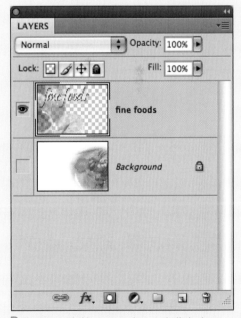

B The Merge Visible command merged all the layers except the Background, which remains hidden.

Flattening layers

The two main reasons for flattening all the layers in a file are to conserve storage space and to prepare it for output or export. At the present time, the only formats that support multiple layers are Photoshop PDF, Photoshop, Large Document Format, and TIFF. If the application you intend to export your file to can't read or accept layered files, you'll have to either flatten it or save a flattened copy of it by using File > Save As. The latter method (which we normally use) preserves the layered version so you can overwork it to death at a later time.

To save a flattened copy of a file:

1. Choose File > **Save As** (Ctrl-Shift-S/Cmd-Shift-S). The Save As dialog opens.

2. Do all of the following:

   Change the file **name**.

   Choose a **location**.

   Uncheck **Layers** (**As a Copy** becomes checked automatically; keep it that way).

   Choose a file format from the **Format** menu.

   Click **Save**.

   Note: The layered version remains open; the flattened version is saved to disk.

► The File > Scripts > Export Layers to Files script saves each layer in a document to a separate file.

If you're confident your image is totally complete, *finis,* you can use the Flatten Image command instead of saving a flattened copy. This command merges the currently visible layers into the bottom-most visible layer—and also discards hidden layers!

To flatten layers:

1. Make sure all the layers and layer groups you want to flatten are visible (have eye icons). It doesn't matter which layer is selected.

2. Right-click/Control-click any layer name and choose **Flatten Image**. If the file contains any hidden layers, an alert dialog will appear; click OK. Any formerly transparent areas in the bottommost layer will now be white.

   The Layers panel shown in figure **A** contains a type layer, layer styles, image layers, layer masks, and an adjustment layer. The Flatten Image command will rasterize all of the above, apply the masks, and flatten all the layers.**B**

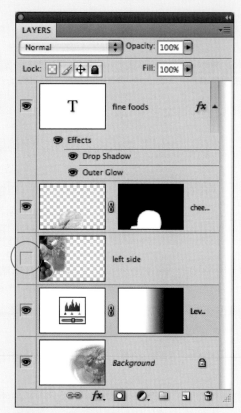

A When you choose the Flatten Image command, it doesn't matter which layer is selected. Here, the "left side" layer is hidden.

B All the visible layers were flattened into the Background and the hidden layer ("left side") was discarded.

When you select part of a layer, only that area can be edited, and the rest of the layer is protected. Apply a filter, for example, and it will affect only pixels within the selection area on the currently selected layer. Although the purpose of all selection methods is to isolate part of an image for editing, each method represents that mechanism differently: a selection uses a marquee of "marching ants," a channel uses black and white areas, and a Quick Mask uses red and clear areas. Regardless of the selection method used, you should make a habit of clicking a layer before editing your document.

In this chapter, you'll learn how to create selections using the Marquee, Lasso, Quick Selection, and Magic Wand tools, as well as the Color Range command. You'll also learn how to refine selection edges; modify, move, hide, and transform selection marquees; save selections to the Channels panel; and paint a mask in Quick Mask mode, which converts to a selection. For helping in sorting through the many selection methods, see the chart on page 144.

Creating layer-based selections

To select a whole layer:

On the Layers panel,  do either of the following:

Click a layer or the Background, then choose Select > **All** (Ctrl-A/Cmd-A). A marquee of "marching ants" will surround the entire layer.

To select only the nontransparent areas on a layer, Ctrl-click/Cmd-click the **layer thumbnail, A–B** or right-click/Control-click the layer thumbnail and choose **Select Pixels**.

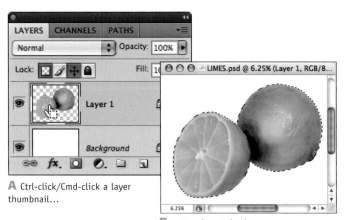

A Ctrl-click/Cmd-click a layer thumbnail...

B ...to select only the nontransparent pixels on that layer.

IN THIS CHAPTER

Creating layer-based selections 123

Using the Rectangular and Elliptical
  Marquee tools 124

Using the lasso tools 125

Using the Quick Selection tool 126

Using the Magic Wand tool 128

Creating a silhouette 129

Using the Color Range command. . . .130

Refining selection edges 132

Deselecting and reselecting
  selections. 135

Deleting selected pixels 135

Moving and transforming selection
  marquees 136

Hiding and showing the selection
  marquee. 137

Swapping and intersecting
  selections. 137

Creating frame-shaped selections . . .138

Saving and loading selections 139

Using Quick Masks 142

The selection methods compared . . . 144

Using the Rectangular and Elliptical Marquee tools

To create a rectangular or elliptical selection:

1. Click a layer.

2. Choose the **Rectangular Marquee** ⬚ or **Elliptical Marquee** ○ tool (M or Shift-M).

3. *Optional:* To soften the selection edges, choose a Feather value greater than zero on the Options bar. For a smoother edge on an elliptical selection, check Anti-alias on the Options bar.

4. Drag diagonally, **A** or Shift-drag to create a perfectly square or round selection. A marquee will appear.

5. *Optional:* To add to the selection, Shift-drag again; to subtract from it, Alt-drag/Option-drag.

➤ To move the marquee while drawing it, keep the mouse button down, then hold down Spacebar and drag. To move the marquee after releasing the mouse, drag inside it with any selection tool.

➤ As you draw a marquee, its dimensions are listed in the W and H areas on the Info panel.

➤ To create the thinnest possible selection, choose the Single Row Marquee or Single Column Marquee tool, then click on the image.

To create a selection using a fixed ratio:

1. Choose the **Rectangular Marquee** ⬚ or **Elliptical Marquee** ○ tool (M or Shift-M).

2. On the Options bar, from the **Style** menu, choose **Fixed Ratio**, then enter **Width** and **Height** values for the desired width to height ratio of the selection (e.g., 5 to 7).**B**

   ➤ Click the ⇄ button to swap the current Width and Height values.

3. Drag a marquee diagonally on the image.**C**

To create a selection of specific dimensions:

1. Choose the **Rectangular Marquee** ⬚ or **Elliptical Marquee** ○ tool (M or Shift-M).

2. From the **Style** menu on the Options bar, choose **Fixed Size**, then enter exact **Width** and **Height** values.

3. Click on the image.**D**

➤ To change the unit for the Width or Height field, right-click/Control-click the field and choose a unit from the context menu.

A Drag diagonally with the Rectangular Marquee tool.

B We chose Fixed Ratio for the Rectangular Marquee tool and entered a Width to Height ratio of 5 to 7.

C With the Fixed Ratio option chosen, any size selection marquee you draw will maintain that ratio.

D Enter Fixed Size values, then click on the image to make the marquee appear. You can drag the marquee to reposition it, as is shown here.

Using the lasso tools

We like to use the Lasso tool to select an area loosely, say, to limit subtle color adjustments to a general area. We also use this tool to clean up selections made with other tools, such as the Magic Wand or Magnetic Lasso.

To create a free-form selection:

1. Click a layer.

2. Choose the **Lasso** tool 🔾 (L or Shift-L).

3. **Drag** around an area on the layer.**A** This initial selection doesn't have to be precise, as you will be able to refine it easily in the next step. When you release the mouse, the open ends of the selection will be joined automatically.

4. *Optional:* To add to the selection, Shift-drag around the area to be added.**B** To subtract from the selection, Alt-drag/Option-drag around the area to be removed.**C–D** We get the best results by starting with our pointer positioned inside an existing selection when adding, or outside the selection when subtracting.

➤ To make a straight side with the Lasso tool, with the mouse button still down, Alt-click/Option-click to create corners. To resume creating a free-form selection, drag, release Alt/Option, then continue to drag.

To create a straight-edged selection:

1. Click a layer.

2. Choose the **Polygonal Lasso** tool 🔾 (L or Shift-L).

3. Click to create points.**E** To create a straight selection edge on the horizontal or vertical axis, hold down Shift as you click.

4. To **join** the open ends of the selection, do either of the following:

   Click the starting point (make sure you see a small circle next to the pointer).

   Ctrl-click/Cmd-click or double-click anywhere in the document window.

➤ To make a free-form segment when creating a polygonal selection, Alt-drag/Option-drag. Release Alt/Option to resume creating straight sides.

➤ To erase the last corner while using the Polygonal Lasso tool, press Backspace/Delete.

A With the Lasso tool, we select the top and side of the ice cream first.

B Then, using Shift, we add to the existing selection, to complete the shape.

C We want to remove the pistachio nut from the selection...

D ...so we Alt-drag/Option-drag with the Lasso tool.

E We created this straight-edged selection with the Polygonal Lasso tool.

Using the Quick Selection tool

The features we're going to discuss next—the Quick Selection tool, Magic Wand tool, and Color Range command—create selections more automatically than the tools we discussed previously. Because Photoshop does the work of detecting the color boundaries for you, the resulting selections tend to be very precise.

If the area you want to select has well defined borders, instead of using a lasso tool, try using the Quick Selection tool. Rather than tediously tracing a precise contour, with this tool you merely drag across a shape and watch as it detects and selects that shape's color boundary. You can enlarge a selection to include an adjacent color boundary or push a selection back to select a smaller area.

To use the Quick Selection tool:

1. Choose the **Quick Selection** tool 🖌 (W or Shift-W).

2. On the Options bar:

    Click the **New Selection** button 🖌 to deselect any existing selections (or press Ctrl-D/Cmd-D).

    Check **Auto-Enhance** for improved edge detection.

    From the Brush Preset picker, choose a **Diameter** for the area you want to select. Or to change the brush diameter via the keyboard, press] or [or Alt-right-click-drag/Control-Option-drag to the left or right. ★

3. Drag within the area of the image you want to select.**A** The selection will expand to the first significant color or shade boundary that the tool detects. The selection will preview as you drag and become more precise when you release the mouse.

4. Do any of the following optional steps:

    To **enlarge** the selection, click or drag in an adjacent area; the selection will enlarge to include it.**B–C**

    To **subtract** from the selection, Alt-drag/Option-drag across the area to be subtracted (**A–B**, next page). Alt-drag/Option-drag along the edge of the selection to contract it inward (or click the Subtract From button 🖌 on the Options bar, then drag without holding down Alt/Option).

    ➤ To block an adjacent area from becoming selected as you enlarge the selection, Alt-click/

A We selected the kumquat in the center of this image by dragging the Quick Selection tool across it.

B After enlarging the brush diameter, we clicked the kumquat on the right to add it to the selection.

C Next, we dragged across the green leaf above the kumquats. The selection spread beyond the edge of the leaf to include some of the background area.

Option-click or drag in that area, release Alt/ Option, then drag to enlarge the selection area. The block will remain in effect until you click that area again with the Quick Selection tool.**C–E**

To undo the last click or drag of the Quick Selection tool, press Ctrl-Z/Cmd-Z.

➤ To save a selection to an alpha channel, see page 139.

➤ To modify a Quick Selection, you can use any other selection tool, such as the Lasso.

➤ Via the Sample All Layers check box on the Options bar, you can control whether the Quick Selection tool samples data from just the current layer or all layers.

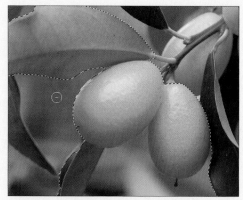

A We Alt-dragged/Option-dragged below the leaf to subtract that area from the selection...

B ...and did the same thing to subtract the area below the kumquats.

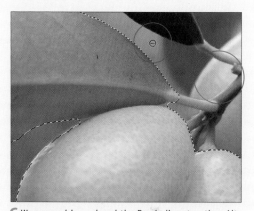

C We zoomed in, reduced the Brush diameter, then Alt-clicked/Option-clicked areas around the stems to block them from becoming selected.

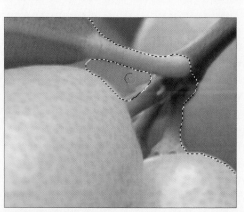

D We dragged along the stems to select them, then Alt-clicked/Option-clicked the background areas between the stems to remove them from the selection.

E Finally, we cleaned up the selection of the stems and included the kumquat tip to complete the selection.

Using the Magic Wand tool

With the Magic Wand tool, you simply click a color in the image and the tool selects all adjacent pixels of the same (or a similar) shade or color. Like the Color Range command, which is discussed on page 130, the Magic Wand lets you control the range of pixels the tool selects, but unlike Color Range, this tool lets you add nonsimilar colors to the selection.

To select color areas with the Magic Wand tool:

1. Click a layer.

2. Choose the **Magic Wand** tool ✎ (W or Shift-W).

3. On the Options bar:

   Check **Anti-alias** to allow the tool to add semi-transparent pixels along the edges of the color areas it detects. This will produce smoother edge transitions for your image edits.

   Check **Contiguous** to limit the selection to areas that are connected to the first pixel you click, or uncheck this option to allow the tool to select noncontiguous (unconnected) areas of a similar color throughout the image with the same click.

   Choose a **Tolerance** value (use the scrubby slider) to control the range of colors the tool selects (as a starting value, try 30–40).

   To select possible occurrences of a similar color on all visible layers, check **Sample All Layers**, or uncheck this option to select colors on only the current layer.

4. Click a color in the image. **A**

5. Unless your image contains nothing but totally flat color areas (which is unlikely), you'll have to do some extra work to refine the selection. Do any of the following:

   To **add** to the selection, Shift-click any unselected areas. **B** To **subtract** any areas from the selection, Alt/Option-click them. You could also perform either task using the Lasso tool with Shift or Alt/Option held down. **C**

   To select additional, noncontiguous areas of a similar color or shade based on the current Tolerance value, right-click/Control-click in the document window and choose **Similar**. (This command works the same whether Contiguous is checked or not.)

A To select the sky in this image, with the Magic Wand tool (Tolerance 25; Contiguous checked), we clicked the upper left corner, then Shift-clicked a couple of stray unselected areas in the lower right.

B Next, we Shift-clicked the area shown in the circle above. Part of the airplane became selected, so we used the Undo command, lowered the Tolerance to 15, then Shift-clicked it again.

C Finally, we used the Lasso tool with Alt/Option held down to remove sections of the airplane from the selection.

If you want to turn the selection into a silhouette, follow the next set of instructions.

➤ You can change the Tolerance value for the Magic Wand tool between clicks. For example, for better control when adding unselected shades or colors along the edges of a selection, try lowering the Tolerance value incrementally: Click with a Tolerance of 30–40 first, lower the value to 15–20 and click again, then finally lower it to 5–10 and click once more to further refine the selection edge. To select just one color or shade, use a Tolerance of 0 or 1.

➤ To undo the last click made with the Magic Wand tool or to undo the Similar command, press Ctrl-Z/Cmd-Z.

Creating a silhouette

To turn a selection into a silhouette:

1. On the Layers panel, 🟦 click an image layer. Or click the Background, press Ctrl-J/Cmd-J to copy it, and keep the copy selected.

2. Use any method (Magic Wand tool or other) to select the background area behind an object.

3. Press Backspace/Delete,**A** then choose Select > **Deselect** (Ctrl-D/Cmd-D).

4. *Optional:* Copy and paste (see page 149) or drag and drop (see pages 152–153) a new image into the layer below the silhouette layer **B–C**, or create a new, blank layer below the silhouette layer and fill it with a color or gradient.

➤ To turn a selected object or shape into a silhouette, switch the selected and unselected areas by choosing Select > Inverse (Ctrl-Shift-I/Cmd-Shift-I), then press Backspace/Delete.

A We pressed Delete to get rid of the selected pixels.

B To create a dramatic background, we drag-copied a cloud layer from another file (#34 of the downloadable images, the skier) and stacked it below the silhouetted plane layer.

TO ANTI-ALIAS OR NOT?

Before using a selection tool, check Anti-alias (if available) on the Options bar to fade the edge of the selection to transparency, or uncheck this option to produce a crisp, hard-edged selection. The effect of anti-aliasing won't be visible until you edit the selected pixels.

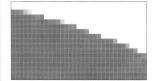

The Anti-alias option was on when this selection was created.

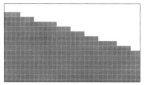

The Anti-alias option was off when this selection was created.

C This is the Layers panel for the image shown above.

Using the Color Range command

With the Color Range dialog open, you can click a color area in either the preview or the document window, and the command will select all occurrences of either just that color or a range of related colors. The dialog also gives you controls for widening or narrowing the range. After closing the dialog, you can further refine the selection with any selection tool.

To create a selection using the Color Range command:

1. Click a layer. **A** (The more flat the color areas in an image, the more effectively the Color Range command works.) The command samples colors from all the currently visible layers, but of course, only the current layer can be edited.

2. *Optional:* Select an area of the layer to confine the selection.

3. Choose Select > **Color Range**, or if you have a selection tool chosen, right-click/Control-click in the document window and choose Color Range. The Color Range dialog opens. **B**

4. Choose from the **Select** menu to limit the selection to Sampled Colors (shades or colors you'll click on with the Color Range eyedropper); to a specific preset color range (e.g., Reds, Yellows); or to a luminosity range (Highlights, Midtones, or Shadows).

5. If you chose Sampled Colors in the previous step, click with the **eyedropper** in either the dialog preview or the document window to sample a color in the image.

   To **add** more **colors** or shades to the selection, Shift-click in the document window or in the preview; **C** or Alt-click/Option-click to remove colors or shades from the selection.

   To expand the range of selected colors, move the **Fuzziness** slider to the right. If too many color areas became selected, move the slider to the left to narrow the range.

6. Choose a **Selection Preview** option for the selection in the document: None for no preview, Grayscale to see a larger version of the dialog preview, Black Matte to see the selection against a black background, or White Matte to see the selection against a white background. The latter two options are helpful for showing whether edges are selected successfully.

A We chose the Color Range command, then with the eyedropper, clicked the blue sky at the top of the image.

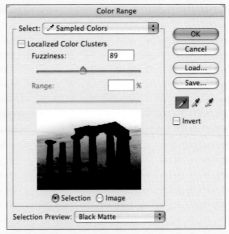

B The white in the preview represents the area of sky that became selected, gray represents partially selected pixels, and black represents unselected pixels.

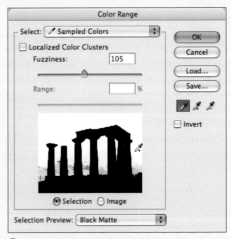

C By Shift-clicking a lower section of the sky in the preview and raising the Fuzziness value to 105, we were able to select the entire sky and background.

7. Click OK.**A.** If you chose a preset color range and the image contains only low levels of that color, an alert dialog will inform you that the selection marquee will be in effect but invisible.

A In the final Color Range selection, the entire blue sky and distant background are selected, including the noncontiguous areas between the columns.

The Localized Color Clusters option in the Color Range dialog limits the selection to similar colors that are contiguous to the area you clicked initially.

To use the Localized Color Clusters option in the Color Range dialog: ★

1. Click a layer. Choose Select > **Color Range**.

2. In the Color Range dialog, choose Select: **Sampled Colors,** then click with the eyedropper in the document window to sample a color.**B**

3. Check **Localized Color Clusters,** then adjust the **Range** value to control the number of similar color areas in the selection.**C**

4. Shift-drag to select more color areas within the current range,**D** or Alt-drag/Option-drag to remove color areas.**E**

5. Click OK. Selections produced by the Localized Color Clusters option have soft edges.

B We chose the Color Range command, then with the eyedropper, clicked the grapefruit in the image.

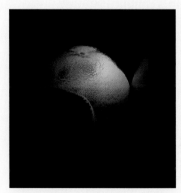

C We checked Localized Color Clusters and lowered the Range value to 15 to reduce the number of selected colors near where we clicked.

D Next, we Shift-dragged to select more of the grapefruit colors within the current range.

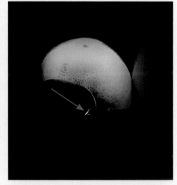

E Finally, we dragged with Alt/Option down to remove some color areas from within the current range.

Refining selection edges

By using the Refine Edge command, you can fine-tune your selection edges to remove unwanted background pixels or change the Feather value—with five dynamic preview options.

To refine the edge of a selection:

1. Create a selection and choose a selection tool, then click **Refine Edge** on the Options bar, or press Ctrl-Alt-R/Cmd-Option-R, ★ or right-click/Control-click and choose Refine Edge from the context menu. The Refine Edge dialog opens.**A**

2. Check Preview (P). If necessary, zoom (Ctrl-click/Cmd-click the image)—up to 300%—so you'll be able to see the selection edges clearly.

3. To change how the selection previews in the document window, click a preview button (use the tool tips and Description info to learn more):

   Standard for a normal marquee display.

   Quick Mask to view the selection as a Quick Mask (useful for judging whether the selection includes all the desired areas).

   On Black to view the selection in color against a black background (useful if you're going to copy the selection to a dark background or if the unselected areas are light in color).

   On White to view the selection in color against a white background (useful if you're going to copy the selection to a light background).

   Mask to view the selection as a grayscale mask.

   ➤ We usually use On Black or On White.

4. We suggest adjusting these Refine Edge options in the following order (use the scrubby sliders):

   To smooth out small bumps or jagged edges, raise the **Smooth** value.

   To soften the transition between pixels located just inside and outside the selection edge, raise the **Feather** value.

   To shrink the selection inward or expand it outward by a few pixels from the edge, change the **Contract/Expand** value.

   To increase the width of the selection border to incorporate small details (pixels just outside the current edge), raise the **Radius** value slightly.

   To heighten the contrast between pixels only within the selection border to produce a crisper edge, raise the **Contrast** value.

5. Click OK.

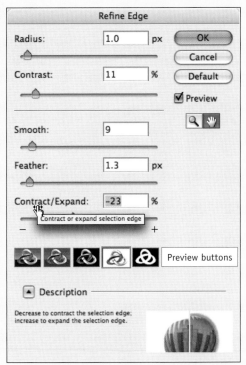

A You can switch among the preview options in the Refine Edge dialog as you refine your selection edges.

SHORTCUTS FOR REFINE EDGE

With the Refine Edge dialog open, you can use any of these shortcuts:

Toggle preview on/off	P
Toggle current preview/normal image	X
Cycle through the five preview modes	F
Zoom in	Ctrl-click/Cmd-click in document window
Zoom out	Alt-click/Option-click in document window
Open the Quick Mask Options dialog	Alt-click/Option-click the Quick Mask button
Restore the default dialog settings	Click Default
Restore settings from when the dialog was opened	Alt-click/Option-click Reset (Cancel becomes Reset)

REFINE A SELECTION EDGE TO INCLUDE A MINIMUM OF BACKGROUND PIXELS

A Download and open this image if you want to follow our steps. We will refine the kumquats and leaf selection that we created on pages 126–127. In the Refine Edge dialog, click Default, then click the On White preview button. Zoom to between 200% and 300%.

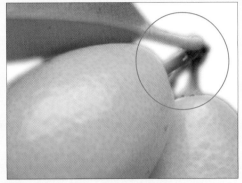

B Raise the Smooth value to 15 to remove jagged bumps from the selection edge; edges along the stems will become smoother. Raise the Feather value to 3 px, note the soft transition into unselected areas (as shown here), then reset Feather to 1 px.

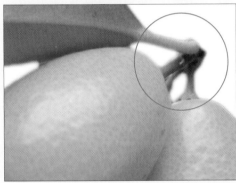

C Lower the Contrast/Expand value to –35% to shrink the selection edge inward, thereby removing background pixels from the selection (the change is subtle).

D Raise the Radius value to 7 px to include more edge pixels (shown here). At this value, because the selection edge is too soft, some background pixels are selected. Lower the Radius to 1.5 px to eliminate them.

E Raise the Contrast value to 40% to sharpen the edge. The contrast along the edge is now too strong (as shown here), and there's a hard, noticeable color outline.

F Lower the Contrast to 16% to soften the hard edge. Now the object is selected accurately. To save your selection to the Channels panel, see page 139.

REFINING SMALL, SOFT-EDGED SELECTIONS

We can't offer exact guidelines for choosing settings in the Refine Edge dialog, because it depends on what kind of shapes you selected. Large, well-defined shapes, such as those shown on the previous page, require different settings than small, soft-edged shapes, such as foliage in the landscape below.

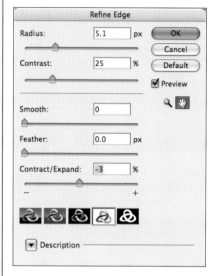

We selected these small, soft leaf shapes, then refined the selection by using the Refine Edge dialog: moderately low Radius and Contrast values to include as few background pixels as possible; a value of 0 for Smooth and Feather to preserve the naturally rough edges while excluding background pixels; and a Contract/Expand value of –3 to prevent narrow shapes from becoming deselected.

To expand a selection via a command:

Choose Select > **Grow** or **Similar.A–B** These commands use the current Tolerance setting of the Magic Wand tool (on the Options bar). You can repeat either command to further expand the selection. If the Magic Wand tool is selected, you can access these commands via a context menu.

WHY WORK HARDER THAN YOU HAVE TO?

Although you have every right to use the Smooth, Expand, Contract, and Feather commands on the Select > Modify submenu to modify selection edges, we recommend using the all-inclusive Refine Edge command instead. Not only does it offer slider equivalents of the above-mentioned commands, it also lets you monitor the changes via a dynamic preview.

A We clicked the blue sky area with the Magic Wand tool (Tolerance of 35), Shift-clicked once on the clouds...

B ...then chose Select > Similar. The Tolerance setting controlled the pixel range that was added to the selection.

Deselecting and reselecting selections

If you don't like having to retrace your steps (we sure don't), deselect your selections only when you're sure you're done using them. Selections register as states on the History panel, but the history is short-lived. To preserve a selection for future use, save it in an alpha channel (see page 139) or even better, convert it to a layer mask (see page 302).

To deselect a selection:

Do one of the following:

Choose any **selection** tool (except the Quick Selection tool), then click **inside** the selection.

Press **Ctrl-D/Cmd-D**.

Right-click/Control-click and choose **Deselect**.

To reselect the last selection:

Do one of the following:

Press **Ctrl-Shift-D/Cmd-Shift-D**.

With any selection tool except the Magic Wand chosen, right-click/Control-click and choose **Reselect**.

On the **History** panel, click the state that bears the name of the tool or command that was used to create the selection.

Deleting selected pixels

When you delete a selection of pixels from a layer, that area is filled automatically with transparent pixels. When you delete a selection of pixels from the Background, that area is filled with the current Background color.

To delete selected pixels:

1. On the Layers panel, click a layer or the Background. If you click the Background, also choose a Background color (see Chapter 12).

2. Do one of the following:

Press **Backspace/Delete**.

Choose Edit > **Cut** (Ctrl-X/Cmd-X) to place the selection on the Clipboard.

Choose Edit > **Clear**.

A Click inside a selection to deselect it.

B We selected the blue sky, then pressed Backspace/ Delete.

C Because the deleted pixels were on a selected layer, they were replaced by transparent pixels.

D Here, we deleted pixels from the Background (not a layer). They were replaced with the current Background color (which in this case is red).

Moving and transforming selection marquees

In the next chapter, you'll learn how to move and copy the contents of a selection. Here, you'll learn how to move a selection marquee without moving its contents.

To move a selection marquee:

1. *Optional:* To help you position the marquee at a particular location, choose View > Show > Smart Guides; or drag a guide from the horizontal or vertical ruler and turn on View > Snap To > Guides.

2. Choose any selection tool (except Quick Selection) or hold down M, L, or W for a temporary selection tool.

3. Do either of the following:

   Drag inside an existing selection. Let it snap to a Smart Guide or a ruler guide, if you're using either of those features. To constrain the movement to a multiple of 45°, hold down Shift after you start dragging.

   Press any **arrow** key to nudge the marquee by one pixel at a time.

➤ With a selection tool, you can drag a selection marquee from one document window into another, or drag the marquee over a document window tab to display that document, then release the mouse when the selection is in the desired location. ★

The Transform Selection command affects only the selection marquee—not its pixel contents.

To transform a selection marquee:

1. Choose any selection tool (except the Magic Wand), then right-click/Control-click the image and choose **Transform Selection**.**A**

2. Drag a handle on the transform box to scale, rotate, skew, or distort the selection (see page 312).**B–C**

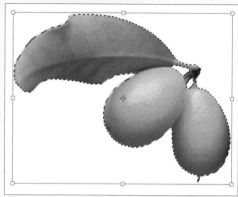

A We selected a silhouetted image, then chose Transform Selection to display the transform controls (bounding box and handles).

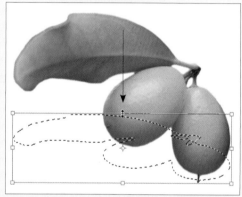

B Next, we pulled the top middle control handle downward to make the selection shorter, then double-clicked to accept the change.

C We created a new layer below the image layer, filled the selection with a gray, deselected, then applied Filter > Blur > Gaussian Blur.

Hiding and showing the selection marquee

If your selection edges (those "marching ants") become distracting or annoying, you can hide them temporarily. If you do so, remember that the selection remains in effect even when you can't see it!

To hide or show a selection marquee:

Press **Ctrl-H/Cmd-H** or choose View > Extras. If this command doesn't work, make sure View > Show > **Selection Edges** has a check mark.**A–B**

Note: The Ctrl-H/Cmd-H shortcut hides or shows all the options that are currently checked on the Show submenu.

➤ If an option is unchecked in the View > Show > Show Extras Options dialog, you can turn it on or off only via the Show submenu, not by using the Ctrl-H/Cmd-H shortcut.

➤ To verify that a selection is present in your document, click the Select menu. If most of the commands on the menu are available, a selection is present.

➤ You can hide or show selection edges (via the shortcut) while using the Adjustments panel and while some Image > Adjustments dialogs are open.

Swapping and intersecting selections

To swap the selected and unselected areas:

Do either of the following:

With any selection tool chosen, right-click/ Control-click the image and choose **Select Inverse.C–D**

With any tool chosen, press **Ctrl-Shift-I/Cmd-Shift-I** (or choose Select > Inverse).

➤ Choose the same inverse command or shortcut again to switch back to the original selection.

A We applied the Texture > Grain filter (Speckle option) to the inverse of the selection.

B Then we hid the selection edges to help us gauge the results.

C This is the original selection.

D And this is the inverse of the same selection.

The intersection of two selections is the area where they overlap.

To select the intersection of two selections:

1. With a selection present, choose a selection tool.

2. Do either of the following:

   Click the **Intersect with Selection** button 🔳 on the Options bar, then create a new selection that overlaps the current one.

   With the New Selection (default) button 🔳 selected on the Options bar, Alt-Shift-drag/ Option-Shift-drag.**A–B**

Creating frame-shaped selections

With the Rectangular Marquee or Elliptical Marquee tool, you can create a selection in the shape of a frame, either at the edge of the canvas area or floating somewhere within it. You can then apply filters or adjustment settings to the frame-shaped selection or turn it into an adjustment layer mask (don't worry, we'll teach you those tricks later in the book).

To create a selection in the shape of a frame:

Method 1 (at the edge of the canvas area)

1. Click a layer on the Layers panel.

2. Choose the **Rectangular Marquee** ▱ or **Elliptical Marquee** ○ tool (M or Shift-M).

3. In the document window, drag a marquee to define the inner edge of the frame selection.

4. *Optional:* To soften the edges of the selection, click Refine Edge on the Options bar, click Default, adjust the Feather value to achieve the desired degree of softness, then click OK.

5. Right-click/Control-click in the document window and choose **Select Inverse.C–D**

Method 2 (within the image)

1. Click a layer on the Layers panel.

2. Choose the **Rectangular Marquee** or **Elliptical Marquee** tool (M or Shift-M), then drag to define the outer edge of the selection.

3. Alt-drag/Option-drag inside the first selection to create the inner edge of the frame selection (**A**, next page).

   Now your edits will affect only pixels within the frame-shaped border.

A Alt-Shift-drag/Option-Shift-drag from inside an existing selection...

B ...to select only the intersection of the existing selection and the new one.

C For this 300 ppi image, we created an inner selection with the Rectangular Marquee tool, applied a Feather value of 25 px, then chose Select > Inverse.

D We created a Levels adjustment layer to lighten the area within the frame selection (see pages 186–187), then added an editable type layer. The type is easier to read on the lighter background.

A Alt-drag/Option-drag to create one rectangular selection inside another.

Saving and loading selections

One trademark characteristic of Photoshop pros is that they use the minimum number of steps to accomplish their tasks without redoubling their efforts. Among the most tedious of tasks, even considering the large number of tools and commands at your disposal, is creating selections. You'll be reassured to know that that intricate selection you created with the Magic Wand tool or Color Range command—and then painstakingly refined—can be saved and stored for future use. Once saved in an alpha channel, a selection can be loaded onto your document at any time, and can be copied to other files. Any selection that would be time-consuming to re-create is a logical candidate for this procedure.

After learning how to save and load an alpha channel selection, you'll learn how to delete and duplicate an alpha channel and reshape the alpha channel mask. (For an alternative to using alpha channels, see the sidebar on this page.)

To save a selection to a channel:

1. Create a selection.**B**

2. Display the **Channels** panel, ⬙ then click the **Save Selection as Channel** button ▣ at the bottom of the panel. A new alpha channel appears on the panel.**C**

▶ You can save alpha channels with a document in most formats, such as Photoshop, BMP, JPEG 2000, Large Document, Photoshop PDF, PICT, and TIFF. To do this, check the Alpha Channels option in the File > Save As dialog.

▶ To rename an alpha channel for easy reference, double-click the name on the panel, type the desired name, then press Enter/Return.

B Create a selection, then click the Save Selection as Channel button on the Channels panel.

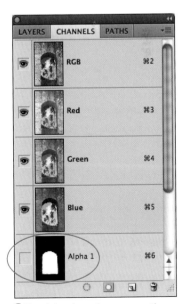

C The alpha channel appears on the Channels panel.

You can display an alpha channel in the document window without loading it as a selection, just to see what it looks like.

To display a channel selection:

1. On the Channels panel, click an **alpha channel** name. The selected area will be white, the protected area black.

2. To restore the normal document display, click the topmost (composite) channel name on the panel (not the visibility icon) or press Ctrl-2/Cmd-2. ★

To load an alpha channel onto an image as a selection:

On the Channels panel, do either of the following:

Ctrl-click/Cmd-click the alpha channel you want to load. Your selection will reappear in the document window.

Drag the channel name over the **Load Channel as Selection** button.

To combine an alpha channel with a selection:

1. Create a selection in the document to combine with the existing channel.**A**

2. Choose Select > **Load Selection**. The Load Selection dialog opens.

3. From the **Channel** menu, choose the alpha channel to be combined with the active selection.

4. Click **Operation: Add to Selection.**

5. Click OK.**B**

To duplicate an alpha channel:

Do either of the following:

Drag the name of the channel you want to duplicate over the **New Channel** button.

Right-click/Control-click an alpha channel name, then choose **Duplicate Channel** from the context menu. The Duplicate Channel dialog opens. Change the channel name in the As field, if desired, then click OK.

INVERTING AN ALPHA CHANNEL

To reverse the masked and unmasked areas in an alpha channel, click an alpha channel on the Channels panel, then press Ctrl-I/Cmd-I or choose Image > Adjustments > Invert.

A We want to combine this selection with an existing alpha channel selection.

B We combined the alpha channel selection (palm trees and sky) with our original selection (the top of the arch).

You can superimpose an alpha channel selection as a colored mask (or rubylith, for folks with traditional design training) over an image and then reshape the mask with the Pencil or Brush tool.

To reshape an alpha channel mask:

1. Make sure nothing is selected in your document.

2. Display the Channels panel. 🔖

3. Click in the **visibility** column for the alpha channel to make the visibility (eye) icon appear. **A** A colored mask will cover the whole image except where the white areas are in the alpha channel.

4. Click the alpha channel.

5. Choose the **Brush** tool 🖌 (B or Shift-B).

6. On the Options bar, do the following:

   Click the **Brush Preset** picker arrowhead, then click a brush in the picker.

   Choose **Mode**: Normal.

   Set the **Opacity** and **Flow** to 100% to create a full mask; choose a lower Opacity for a partial mask.

7. Do either or both of the following:

   To enlarge the **masked** (protected) area, draw brush strokes with black.**B–C**

   To enlarge the **unmasked** area, press X to swap the Foreground and Background colors, then draw brush strokes with white.**D**

8. To hide the mask, click the visibility icon for the alpha channel. To edit the image (not the alpha channel), click the topmost channel on the Channels panel.

➤ If a selection that you save as an alpha channel has a Feather value greater than zero, the feathered area will be gray and will be only partially affected by editing.

To delete an alpha channel:

Do either of the following:

Right-click/Control-click a channel name and choose **Delete Channel**.

On the Channels panel, drag the channel you want to delete over the **Delete Channel** button. 🗑

A On the Channels panel, both the alpha channel and the composite RGB channel should have a visbility icon, and the alpha channel should be selected.

B This is our original alpha channel mask.

C Paint with black to enlarge the masked area.

D Paint with white to enlarge the unmasked area. We're touching up areas that we overzealously masked (as shown in the previous figure).

Using Quick Masks

With your document in Quick Mask mode, you can paint a mask onto the parts of your image that need protection, and you can reshape (add to or remove areas from) the mask with the Brush or Pencil tool. If you create a selection first, the mask will cover just the unselected areas. By default, the mask is semitransparent red, as in a traditional rubylith. The Quick Mask itself can't be saved, but when you put your document back into Standard (non-Quick Mask) mode, the mask will turn into a selection automatically and can either be saved as an alpha channel or turned into a layer mask.

To reshape a selection by using a Quick Mask:

1. Select an area of a layer. **A**

2. Click the **Edit in Quick Mask Mode** button ◌ at the bottom of the Tools panel (Q) or choose Select > **Edit in Quick Mask Mode**. ★ A mask will cover the unselected areas of the image. **B** (If it doesn't, double-click the same button, click Color Indicates: Masked Areas, then click OK.) Also, "Quick Mask" will become a temporary listing on the Channels panel and will be listed in the title bar of the document.

3. Choose the **Brush** tool 🖌 (B or Shift-B).

4. On the Options bar, do the following:

   Click the **Brush Preset** picker arrowhead, then click a brush on the picker.

   Choose **Mode:** Normal.

   Set the **Opacity** and **Flow** to 100%.

5. Do any of the following:

   Draw strokes with **black** as the Foreground color to enlarge the masked (protected) area.

   Press X to swap the Foreground and Background colors, then draw strokes on the mask with **white** as the Foreground color to enlarge the unmasked area. **C**

   Draw strokes with your brush **Opacity** below 100% (Options bar) to create a partial mask. When you edit pixels within the selection, that area will be only partially affected by the edits.

6. Click the **Standard Mode** button ◌ on the Tools panel (Q) when you're done working in Quick Mask mode. The unmasked areas will become a selection. (If you want to preserve the selection, save it as an alpha channel.)

A Select an area of a layer.

B The unselected area is covered with a red Quick Mask.

C With our document in Quick Mask mode, we're unmasking the helmet by using the Brush tool.

In these instructions, you'll paint the mask directly in a document without creating a selection first. You can use this technique to select areas for retouching, such as eyes or teeth in a portrait photo.

To paint a Quick Mask:

1. Choose the **Brush** tool, 🖌 and choose tool options (see step 4 on the previous page).

2. Double-click the **Edit in Quick Mask Mode** button 🔲 on the Tools panel.

3. Click Color Indicates: **Selected Areas**, then click OK.

4. Paint on the image with **black**.  (The mask you're creating will become a selection when the document is restored to Standard mode.) Paint with white if you need to remove any areas of the mask.

5. Press **Q** to put the document back into Standard mode. **B**

➤ To store the selection as a mask on the current layer, see page 302. **C**

Via the Quick Mask Options dialog, you can control whether your mask covers the protected or unprotected areas, and also change the mask color and opacity.

To choose Quick Mask options:

1. Double-click the **Edit in Quick Mask Mode** button 🔲 on the Tools panel. The Quick Mask Options dialog opens.

2. Do any of the following:

   Click Color Indicates: **Masked Areas** or **Selected Areas**.

   Click the **Color** swatch, then choose a new color for the Quick Mask.

   Change the **Opacity** of the mask color.

3. Click OK.

➤ To switch the mask color so that it covers the selected areas instead of the masked areas or vice versa, without opening the Quick Mask Options dialog, Alt-click/Option-click the Edit in Quick Mask Mode button.

A We painted a mask on this image in Quick Mask mode to protect the critical areas — the eyes, nostrils, and mouth — from further edits.

B When we put the image back into Standard mode, the mask turned into a selection. (We'll Feather the selection slightly via the Refine Edge dialog to soften the edges before applying image edits.)

C We are storing the selection shown in the previous figure as a layer mask.

The selection methods compared

Now that you're acquainted with a wide array of selection methods, you can use this list to help you decide which ones to use.

SELECT BY DRAGGING	TOOL OR COMMAND	WHAT IT'S GOOD FOR SELECTING
	Rectangular and Elliptical Marquee tools	Rectangular and round shapes; you can specify a width to height ratio or dimensions
	Lasso tool	Irregular areas; indispensible for cleaning up selections created with other tools or commands
	Add or subtract with a selection tool	Shift to add; Alt/Option to remove; Alt-Shift/Option-Shift to select the intersection of the existing and new selections
	Polygonal Lasso tool	Straight-edged shapes

SELECT BASED ON CONTRAST/COLOR	TOOL OR COMMAND	WHAT IT'S GOOD FOR SELECTING
	Magnetic Lasso tool*	Objects or figures that are clearly delineated from their background in tonality or color
	Quick Selection tool	Well-defined shapes, including irregular areas; creates selections automatically by detecting color boundaries
	Magic Wand tool	Color areas based on a Tolerance range; good for selecting backgrounds such as sky or water; use the Lasso tool afterward to add areas or remove stray areas from the selection
	Color Range command	Discrete color areas; via a dialog, lets you select all occurrences of one color or a specific tonal range

MODIFY SELECTIONS	TOOL OR COMMAND	WHAT IT'S GOOD FOR SELECTING
	Refine Edge command	Refine the smoothness, sharpness, and precision of a selection edge; preview the selection on different backgrounds
	Grow, Similar commands	Enlarge selections based on the current Tolerance setting of the Magic Wand tool; the Similar command is good for selecting noncontiguous but similar areas
	Convert a selection to a path*	Reshape the former selection by manipulating its anchor points; convert it back to a selection after reshaping or store it as a path for later conversion

OTHER RELATED TECHNIQUES	TOOL OR COMMAND	WHAT IT'S GOOD FOR SELECTING
	Trace a shape with the Pen tool*	Create a smooth, precise path, then convert it to a selection
	Quick Mask mode	Paint a mask onto an image "by hand" in Quick Mask mode (and remove areas of the mask where necessary); it converts to a selection automatically upon return to Standard mode
	Store a selection as a layer mask; load the mask as a selection	To store a selection as a layer mask, see page 302; to load a layer mask as a selection, see page 306
	Save and load selections	Save selections as alpha channels to preserve for later use; an alpha channel selection can be combined with an existing selection

*This technique is covered in our *Visual QuickPro Guide* to Photoshop.

If we had to pick one chapter that represents the heart and soul of Photoshop, this would be it. Here you'll learn how to copy selections and layers within the same document and between documents and use layer masks to blend images together. You'll also learn about the Photomerge command and features for positioning and aligning layers. You'll be amazed at how easy (and how much fun) it is to create composite images!

Moving selection contents

In the instructions on this page, you'll move a selection of pixels in the same file. (To move a selection marquee but not its contents, see page 136.)

To move the contents of a selection:

1. Create a selection. *Optional:* To help position the selection, choose View > Show > Smart Guides to display alignment guides; or display the rulers (Ctrl-R/Cmd-R), then drag a guide or guides from the rulers. Also turn on View > Snap To > Guides.

2. Do either of the following:

   On the Layers panel, click the **Background**, then choose a Background color (see Chapter 12). The area you expose (in step 4) will fill with this color.

   Click a **layer**. The area you expose (in step 4) will fill with transparent pixels.

3. Choose the **Move** tool (or hold down V for a temporary Move tool). ★

4. Position the pointer over the selection, then drag. Imagery within the selected area will move. **A–B** When you deselect (Ctrl-D/Cmd-D), the contents will drop back into the original layer (in the new location), regardless of which layer is selected.

➤ With the Move tool chosen, press an arrow key to nudge a selection in 1-pixel increments, or press Shift-arrow to nudge a selection in 10-pixel increments.

IN THIS CHAPTER

Moving selection contents 145

Duplicating selections 146

Using the Clipboard 148

Matching image dimensions. 151

Copying layers between files 152

Blending imagery using layer masks . .154

Using the Clone Source panel. 156

Stitching photos together 158

Blending seams manually 160

Using the rulers, guides, and grid . . .161

Aligning and distributing layers 164

A A selection is moved on a layer.

B A selection is moved on the Background.

Duplicating selections

To drag-copy a selection in the same document:

1. Click a layer and create a selection.

2. Do either of the following:

   Choose the **Move** tool ▸⊕ (V), then Alt-drag/ Option-drag the selection.**A** The duplicate pixels will remain selected.**B**

   With a tool other than the Move tool chosen, Ctrl-Alt-drag/Cmd-Option-drag the selection.

➤ Include Shift with either shortcut listed above to move the selection at increments of 45°.

➤ Press Alt-arrow/Option-arrow to duplicate a selection and offset it by 1 pixel, or press Alt-Shift-arrow/Option-Shift-arrow to duplicate and offset a selection by 10 pixels.

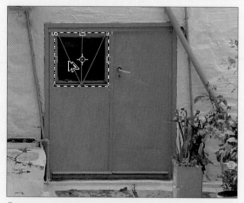

A Create a selection on a layer or the Background (we selected the window with the Rectangular Marquee tool), then Alt-drag/Option-drag it with the Move tool.

B A copy of the window is made.

REFINE EDGE IN ACTION

The Feather option in the Refine Edge dialog fades a selection edge by a specified number of pixels. With a selection tool chosen and a selection active, right-click/Control-click in the document window and choose Refine Edge, or click Refine Edge on the Options bar. Click Default, then choose a Feather value. The higher the document resolution, the higher the Feather value needed. The feather will preview while the dialog is open, disappear when you click OK, then become evident again in the document when you move, drag-copy, copy and paste, or apply edits (e.g., brush strokes, filters) to the selection.

A selection is created.

A Feather value is applied via the Refine Edge dialog.

The feather softens the selection that we drag-copied.

When you drag and drop a selection of pixels from one document to another, presto, a duplicate of those pixels appears on a new layer in the target document (without using the Clipboard).

To drag and drop a selection between documents: ★

1. Open the source and target documents. If they're floating (not tabbed), arrange them so they're both visible.

2. Click in the source document, then create a selection on a layer or the Background.

3. Choose the **Move** tool ➤⊕ (or hold down V).

4. If your document windows are **floating**, drag the selection into another document window, **A–B** then release the mouse where you want the pixels to be dropped.

   If your document windows are **tabbed**, drag the selection over the tab of the target window, **C** hold until the target document displays, then drag into it. **D**

5. The duplicate imagery will appear on a new layer; you can reposition it with the Move tool. If the imagery looks too small or too large, see the the first part of the sidebar on the next page.

➤ Hold down Shift while dragging to have the selection appear in the exact center of the target document, regardless of where you release the mouse.

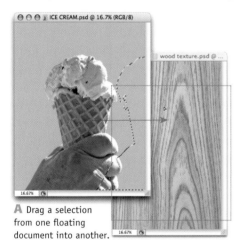

A Drag a selection from one floating document into another.

B When you release the mouse, a copy of the selected pixels appears in the target document; the source document is unchanged.

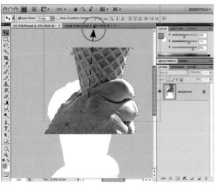

C Drag a selection from inside a tabbed window over the tab of another document.

D When the target image displays, drag the gray rectangle (not shown) into the image and release.

Using the Clipboard

You can use the Edit > **Cut**, **Copy**, or **Copy Merged** command to put a selection in a temporary storage area in memory, called the Clipboard, then use Edit > **Paste** or **Paste Into** to paste the Clipboard pixels into another layer in the same document or in another document. These commands are available only while a selection is active in your document.

If you cut a selection from the Background, the exposed area will fill with the current Background color automatically. If you cut a selection from a layer, the area left behind will be replaced with transparency. (The same thing happens when you move pixels on a layer.) To learn about the Foreground and Background colors, see Chapter 12.

The Edit > Paste command automatically pastes the Clipboard contents into a new layer. If you paste into a document of smaller pixel dimensions, any pasted pixels that extend beyond the canvas area will be preserved (and will save with the document). They can be moved into view with the Move tool.

You can paste the same Clipboard contents as many times as needed. Only one selection can be stored on the Clipboard at a time, however, and it will be replaced by new contents each time you use the Cut, Copy, or Copy Merged command. With Export Clipboard checked in Preferences > General, the Clipboard contents stay in temporary system memory even if you exit/quit Photoshop (but only until you shut down your computer).

➤ The dimensions in the File > New dialog automatically match the dimensions of the current contents of the Clipboard, if any.

HEY, MY PICTURE SHRANK!

When you paste or drag and drop a selection between documents, the copy is rendered in the resolution of the target document. If the resolution of the target document is higher than that of the source imagery, the copy will look smaller relative to imagery on other layers; if the resolution of the target document is lower than that of the source document, the copy will look larger. To prevent this size discrepancy when copying to another file, before creating the copy, change the resolution of the source document (Image > Image Size) to match that of the target document.

➤ A good way to judge the relative sizes of the source and target imagery is to set both document windows to the same zoom level, and compare them side by side.

REFINING SELECTION EDGES

You can shrink or soften the edges of a selection before you move, drag-copy, or paste it, and you can also clean up the edges afterward:

➤ To remove edge pixels from a selection before pasting it, shrink it by using the Contract/Expand slider in the Refine Edge dialog. To soften the edge of the selection, use the Feather slider in the same dialog.

➤ After pasting a selection, you can remove unwanted remnants of a black background by choosing Layer > Matting > Remove Black Matte or remove remnants of a white background by choosing Layer > Matting > Remove White Matte.

To copy and paste a selection:

1. Click a layer or the Background, then create a selection. *Optional:* To refine the selection edge, use the Refine Edge dialog (see pages 132–134).

2. Choose one of the following commands:

   Edit > **Copy** A (Ctrl-C/Cmd-C) to copy pixels from the current layer within the selection area.

   Edit > **Copy Merged** (Ctrl-Shift-C/Cmd-Shift-C) to copy pixels from all the currently visible layers in the document, within the selection area.

   Edit > **Cut** (Ctrl-X/Cmd-X) to cut the selection out of the layer.

3. Click in any document window.

4. Choose Edit > **Paste** (Ctrl-V/Cmd-V). The pasted pixels will appear on a new layer. B You can restack the layer or drag it with the Move tool.

➤ If the dimensions of the selection you pasted are larger than those of the target document, some pixels will be hidden from view outside the canvas area. To bring them back into view, move the layer with the Move tool (see also the sidebar below).

➤ Unlike the Cut command, the Edit > Clear command empties a selection area without using the Clipboard.

PIXELS OUTSIDE THE CANVAS AREA

➤ If you apply an image-editing command, such as a filter, to a layer, it will alter the entire layer, including any pixels outside the live canvas area.

➤ To enlarge the canvas area to include hidden pixels, choose Image > Reveal All.

➤ To select all nontransparent pixels on a layer, including any pixels outside the live canvas area or that are hidden by a layer mask, Ctrl-click/Cmd-click the layer thumbnail on the Layers panel. (Don't use Select > All, which selects only pixels within the canvas area.)

➤ To remove pixels that extend outside the live canvas area, click the layer in question, choose Select > All, then choose Image > Crop. This will help reduce the file size.

➤ If a layer contains pixels outside the live canvas area and you merge it with the Background (not with another layer), the hidden pixels will be deleted.

NEW LAYER VIA COPY OR CUT

As an alternative to copying and pasting, you can get imagery onto a new layer in the same file by using an easy one-step command. Create a selection, then right-click/Control-click in the document window and choose either of the following:

Command	Shortcut	What It Does
Layer via Copy	Ctrl-J/Cmd-J	Puts a copy of the selected pixels on a new layer
Layer via Cut	Ctrl-Shift-J/ Cmd-Shift-J	Removes selected pixels from the original layer and puts them on a new layer

A We created a selection, then pressed Ctrl-C/Cmd-C to execute the Copy command.

B In a new document, we pressed Ctrl-V/Cmd-V (the Paste command). The Clipboard contents appeared on a new layer.

When you use the Paste Into command to paste the Clipboard contents inside a selection, a new layer is created automatically and the active marquee becomes a layer mask. The pasted imagery can be repositioned within the layer mask, and the mask can be reshaped or modified via the Masks panel to reveal more or less of the imagery.

To paste into a selection:

1. Select an area of a layer.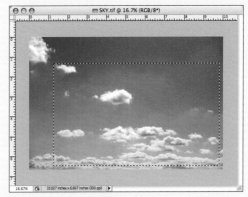

2. Choose Edit > **Copy** (Ctrl-C/Cmd-C) to copy pixels from only the currently selected layer, or choose Edit > **Copy Merged** (Ctrl-Shift-C/Cmd-Shift-C) to copy pixels within the selection area from all the currently visible layers.

3. Click a layer in the same document or in another document.

4. Select the area (or areas) that you want to paste the Clipboard contents into.**B** (Click Refine Edge and adjust the selection edge, if desired.)

5. Choose Edit > **Paste Into** (Ctrl-Shift-V/Cmd-Shift-V).**C** A new layer and layer mask appear on the Layers panel.

6. Related options to explore:

   Although the entire contents of the Clipboard were pasted onto the layer, the layer mask may be hiding some of it. To move the **layer contents** within the mask, click the layer thumbnail (on the left), then drag in the document window with the Move tool ▶♦ (V). Or to move just the **layer mask**, click the layer mask thumbnail (on the right), then drag in the document window with the Move tool.

   To **reshape** the **mask**, click the mask thumbnail, then with the Brush tool ✏ (B or Shift-B) and white as the Foreground color, paint on the layer mask in the document window to expose more of the pasted image, or paint with black to hide more of the pasted image.

   To move the layer and layer mask as a unit, click between the layer and layer mask thumbnails to make the **Link** icon appear (if it's not already present),▯ choose the Move tool (or hold down V), then drag in the document window. (Click the Link icon to unlink.)

   ➤ Having a large selection on the Clipboard usurps program memory. To empty the Clipboard at any time to reclaim memory, choose Edit > Purge > Clipboard, then click OK.

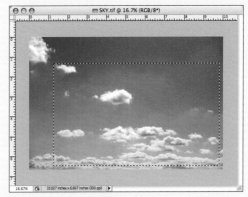

A Select an area of an image. In this image, we used the Rectangular Marquee tool.

B Select an area in another image. We used the Quick Selection tool to select the sky.

C We pasted the contents of the Clipboard into the selection via the Paste Into command.

Matching image dimensions

To prevent a size discrepancy when copying a larger image into a smaller one, make sure the two documents have the same dimensions first with the Crop tool.

To match the dimensions of two files as you copy a layer:

1. Open the source and target documents, then click in the target document window (if it's floating) to bring it to the front, or click the target document tab. (In the figures on this page, the source document is larger than the target document.)

2. Choose the **Crop** tool ⊐ (C).

3. On the Options bar, click **Front Image.A** The dimensions of the smaller document will display on the Options bar.

4. Click in the source document or click its tab, marquee as much of the larger image as you can,**B** then double-click inside the marquee to accept the crop. The source and target images now have the same resolution and dimensions.

5. Choose the **Move** tool ⊕ (or hold down V). For floating windows, Shift-drag and drop the source layer from the Layers panel into the target document window,**C** or for tabbed windows, follow the instructions in the captions on page 153. The image should fit neatly.**D**

6. *Optional:* If you need to scale the new layer slightly, see step 4 on the next page.

7. Close the source document without saving it, but do save the target document.

A Choose the Crop tool, then click Front Image on the Options bar to record the dimensions of the smaller document.

B With the Crop tool, drag a marquee to crop the larger image to the dimensions that were recorded on the Options bar.

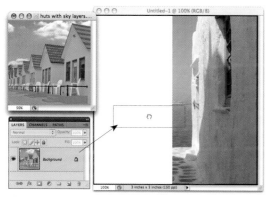

C Finally, Shift-drag the layer from the Layers panel in the source document into the target document window.

D The source imagery fits neatly in the target document window (we will reposition it).

Copying layers between files

When you drag a layer, multiple layers, or a layer group from the Layers panel in one document into the window of another document, a copy is created automatically. In addition to being quick and easy, unlike using the Copy and Paste commands, this method includes pixels outside the live canvas area. Copying between floating windows is discussed on this page, tabbed windows on the next page.

To drag and drop a layer between floating windows:

1. Open the source and target floating document windows, and arrange them so you can see at least some of each one.

2. Click in the **source** document window, then on the **Layers** panel, click the layer, Background, or layer group that you want to duplicate, or Ctrl-click/Cmd-click multiple layers.

3. Shift-drag the layer or group from the Layers panel of the source document into the target document window.**A** The new layer(s) will be centered in the target document (thanks to the Shift key) and will be stacked above the previously selected layer in the target document.

   Note: An alert dialog will appear if you try to copy a layer from an 8-bits-per-channel document to a 16-bits-per-channel document. Click Yes to accept a reduction in image quality, or click No to cancel the duplication.

4. *Optional:* To scale the imagery in the target document, choose the Move tool ⊹ (V), click Show Transform Controls on the Options bar, and if necessary, press Ctrl-0/Cmd-0 to enlarge the document window. Shift-drag a corner handle on the bounding box to scale the layer to the desired size, then press Enter/Return.**B**

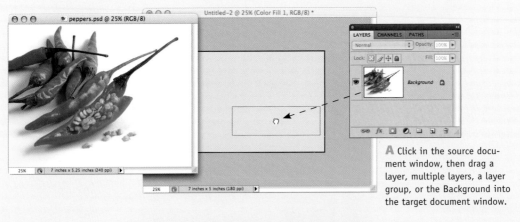

A Click in the source document window, then drag a layer, multiple layers, a layer group, or the Background into the target document window.

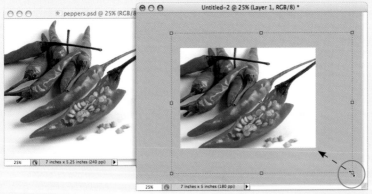

B If necessary, press Ctrl-0/Cmd-0 to enlarge the target document window, then Shift-drag a corner handle to scale the layer to the desired size.

DRAG AND DROP A LAYER BETWEEN TABBED WINDOWS ★

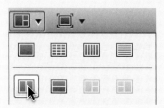

A On the Arrange Documents menu on the Application bar, click a 2 Up button. Click in the source document window, then drag a layer from the Layers panel into the target image. (If an alert dialog appears, see the note on the previous page.)

B When you release the mouse, the duplicate imagery appears inside the target document window (now active), and a new layer appears on the Layers panel.

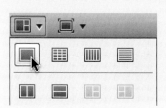

C On the Arrange Documents menu, click the Consolidate All button to make the target window the sole visible window. With the Move tool, reposition the new layer.

Blending imagery using layer masks

One very effective approach to compositing is to drag and drop image layers into a target file that contains a white or solid-color Background or a faint, low-contrast image. In the target file, the image layers can be scaled or moved individually to create a pleasing composition, and by using layer masks, you can fade the edge of each new image layer softly into the Background or into underlying layers—it's like magic!

To blend images using layer masks:

1. Open several images, one of which will be used as a background (target) image for the whole composition. **A–B** The target image should be the largest of the bunch. (To prevent any scale discrepancies, make sure all the images have the same resolution; see the first part of the sidebar on page 148.)

2. Follow the instructions on page 152 or page 153 to drag and drop the source imagery into the target image, including scaling the new image layers with the Move tool (V), if needed (**A**, next page).

3. When you're done, save the target image and close the others.

4. Click one of the new image layers, then click the **Add Layer Mask** button ◙ at the bottom of the Layers panel.

5. Keep the layer mask thumbnail selected, and choose the **Gradient** tool ▣ (G or Shift-G).

Click the Gradient picker arrowhead on the Options bar, then click the "Black, White" gradient (it's in the default library). Also click the Linear Gradient button ▣ on the Options bar.

6. In the document window, start dragging horizontally or diagonally from where you want the complete fadeout to be, and stop dragging where you want the image to remain fully opaque (hold down Shift to constrain the angle to an increment of 45°). The gradient will fill the layer mask, and the imagery on that layer will fade to transparency. Black areas in a layer mask hide layer pixels (**B**, next page).

   ► To redo the fade effect, make sure the layer mask thumbnail is still selected, then drag again with the Gradient tool.

7. Repeat steps 4–6 for the other layers (**C**, next page). Note: To touch up any obvious seams, see page 160.

A We started by opening some theme-related images, just to see how they would look together and to get our creative juices flowing. We're going to create a banner to advertise vacation travel to Thailand.

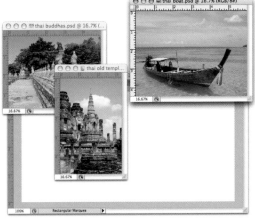

B Next, we narrowed our choices down to three images and created a larger, blank image to serve as the background for the duplicate layers.

A Drag a layer from each source image onto the target image. You can resize and reposition the new image layers, as needed.

B Create a layer mask for each new layer and fill each mask with the "Black, White" gradient to partially hide the edge of the layer imagery.

C Type adds a finishing touch to our composite image.

Using the Clone Source panel

With the Clone Stamp tool, you can clone parts of an image from one layer to another within the same document or between documents. It's useful for retouching (see pages 282–283), collaging, and video editing.

The Clone Source panel lets you keep track of up to five different clone sources (represented by a row of source buttons at the top of the panel); reassign new sources; clone repeatedly from the same source; and scale, rotate, or reposition the source pixels before or as you clone them.

To use the Clone Stamp tool and the Clone Source panel:

1. Open one or more RGB documents to use as source imagery, and create or open a document to clone to.**A** (You can also clone within the same document.)

2. Choose the **Clone Stamp** tool 📇 (S or Shift-S), then from the Options bar, choose a Soft Round brush, a Mode, an Opacity of 100% (to start with), and a Flow percentage, and check Aligned.

3. Display the **Clone Source** panel.📇 **B** By default, the first clone source button is selected.

4. Check **Show Overlay** and **Auto Hide**, then set the **Opacity** to 35–40% (use the scrubby slider), so you can preview the source as you clone. You can also check **Clipped** to display the overlay only within the brush tip. ★

5. In the document you're going to clone to, create a new layer.

6. Click in the document you want to clone from, then from the **Sample** menu on the Options bar, choose which part of the document is to be cloned: **Current Layer**, **Current & Below**, or **All Layers**. If you chose the first or second option, click a layer.

7. Alt-click/Option-click an area to set the source point for cloning. The file and layer name will be assigned to, and listed below, the first clone source button on the Clone Source panel.

8. *Optional:* If you're cloning to another document, click that document window or tab now.

9. To position the clone, move the pointer over the image without clicking (a faint overlay of the source will appear below the pointer), then drag to start cloning. The overlay will disappear

A Open the images you want to clone from, and create or open an image to clone to.

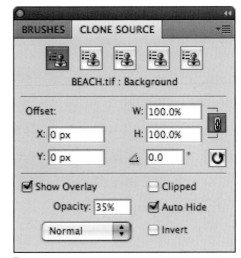

B Use the Clone Source panel to assign, keep track of, and transform imagery from multiple clone sources.

temporarily (because you checked Auto Hide), then will reappear when you release the mouse.

For other ways to transform the overlay, see the next set of instructions.

10. To clone from a new source, click the second source button, create a new layer in the target document if desired, then in any document, Alt-click/Option-click another source area. Drag to clone. Repeat to clone from more sources.

Note! The Clone Source panel keeps the links active only while the source documents are open. If you close a source document, its link to the Clone Source panel is broken!

You can scale, flip, or rotate the clone source overlay by changing values on the Clone Source panel or by using keyboard shortcuts. The new values will apply only to the currently selected source.

To reposition, scale, flip, or rotate the clone source overlay:

With the Clone Stamp tool 🔳 chosen and an overlay displaying in your document, do any of the following (if you use the Clone Source panel, you can use the scrubby sliders):

When you start cloning, the position of the source overlay becomes fixed. To reposition it, change the **Offset X** and/or **Y** values on the panel; or Alt-Shift-drag/Option-Shift-drag the overlay, then release.

To scale the overlay, change the **W** or **H** values on the panel; **A–B** or hold down

Alt-Shift/Option-Shift and press (and keep pressing) [or]. Activate the Maintain Aspect Ratio button 🔳 to preserve the current aspect ratio as you change the W or H value. To flip the source, choose negative W and/or H values. We suggest you don't scale more than 150 or –150%.

To rotate the overlay, change the **Rotate** value 🔳; or hold down Alt-Shift/Option-Shift and press < or >. Drag to clone at the chosen angle.

➤ To restore the default scale and rotation values, click the Reset Transform button.🔳

To switch to a new clone source when using the Clone Stamp tool:

Click a different **source** button at the top of the **Clone Source** panel. The new source will display as the overlay in the document window.

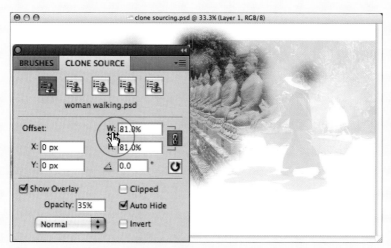

A We're using one of the scaling controls (W) on the Clone Source panel to shrink the overlay image (the woman) so it will be more in keeping with the scale of the statues.

B We created this composite image by cloning from three different source files. For the Clone Stamp tool, we chose an Opacity of 70%, a Flow of 90%, and turned on the Airbrush option.

➤ A panoramic format worked well for this composition, but you can clone to an image of any shape, and you can clone onto a blank background or right on top of existing imagery.

Stitching photos together

The Photomerge command combines two or more photos of the same scene into a single panoramic image. Each photo becomes an individual layer automatically, and layer masks create smooth, seamless edges between the photos. New layout choices and correction options make creating a panorama easier and more automatic.

To merge photos via the Photomerge command:

1. In Bridge, arrange the photos in the correct sequence for the panorama (this will enable Photomerge to work faster), then multiple-select them. All the files must be 8 bits per channel, but they can be in different file formats. PSD files work faster than raw files.

2. Choose Tools > Photoshop > **Photomerge**. The Photomerge dialog opens. **A**

3. Click a **Layout** area option: **Auto** (Photoshop determines the best layout option), **Perspective**, **Cylindrical**, **Spherical** (best for a 360° panorama), **Collage** (photos are combined by stretching and rotating), or **Reposition** (no stretching or rotating) (**A–C**, next page). ★ Unfortunately, the layout can't be previewed.

4. Check any of these correction options, if available, for a more seamless panorama or to correct deficiencies in the photos: ★

   Blend Images Together uses color matching and layer masks to create seamless transitions between the photos.

   Vignette Removal lightens any darkened areas along the edges of the photos.

   Geometric Distortion Correction corrects lens distortion, such as pincushioning (pinch), barreling (bulge), or extreme wide angles.

5. Click OK, then let Photoshop do the work for you. It will open the source files, align and blend them into a panorama, and open the panorama onscreen. You can use the **Crop** tool to crop away any unwanted transparent areas from the edges. Save the file in the PSD format.

➤ The Tools > Photoshop > Process Collections in Photoshop ★ command (from Bridge) locates a series of photos within the current folder that contain similar exposure and time creation settings, creates a panorama in the PSD format, saves it to the current folder, and closes the file.

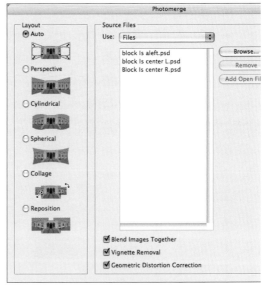

A The new, improved Photomerge command has more alignment and blending power.

SOME OF THE LAYOUT OPTIONS IN PHOTOMERGE

We chose these three source photos for our panorama.

A The Perspective Layout option in Photomerge shrank the images in the center to add depth but produced distortion on the left side (the natural curve of the road is flattened out). This option would be better suited to a narrower panorama made from just two photos that don't contain any obvious lens distortion.

B The Cylindrical option made the images in the center larger. This option is good for wide panoramas like this, which are produced from three or more photos.

C The Reposition Only option simply places the images in a row without transforming them. For our photos, this option produced results similar to those from the Cylindrical option, except here the horizon is slightly arched in the center.

Blending seams manually

An easy way to soften the seams between imagery on different layers is to apply brush strokes to a layer mask. We like this method because you have to edit only the mask—not the actual image layers. Note: Before following these instructions, read about an even simpler solution in the sidebar at right. It might just do the trick!

To blend seams on a layer mask with the Brush tool:

1. Open a document that contains multiple layers. At least one layer should contain a layer mask (see page 154).**A**

2. Choose the **Brush** tool 🖌 (B or Shift-B).

3. On the Options bar, choose a large, Soft Round brush, and also choose Opacity and Flow percentages. For partial (subtle) masking, choose an Opacity of 40% or less.

4. On the Layers panel, click the thumbnail for the layer mask you want to edit. Press X, if necessary, to make the Foreground color white.

5. Apply strokes to areas you want to unmask.**B–C** You can change the brush opacity and diameter between strokes. To restore part of the mask, press X, then apply strokes with black.

6. When you're done editing the mask, click any layer thumbnail to resume normal image editing.

MOVING THE GRADIENT IN A LAYER MASK

If your layer mask contains a gradient, you can move the mask to adjust the location where the blending effect occurs. On the Layers panel, click the thumbnail for the layer mask, then click the link icon 🔗 to unlink the mask from the layer. Hold down V (for a temporary Move tool) and drag in the document window; by moving the gradient, you change the location where the imagery begins to fade. When you're done, click the space between the mask thumbnail and the layer thumbnail to make the link icon reappear.

A Although we used layer masks successfully to connect the imagery in this composite image (see pages 154–155), the left side could still use some hand blending.

B We clicked a layer mask thumbnail, chose a large, Soft Round brush and an Opacity of 40% for the Brush tool, and are painting with white to soften the edge of the mask.

C Now the seams look smoother.

Using the rulers, guides, and grid

Sometimes successful composite images come together in a serendipitous way without a lot of fore-thought or careful alignment. At other times, you may need to plan ahead—or position objects more precisely, say, if your Photoshop image needs to fit perfectly into a larger Web or print page layout. This is when such layout features as grids, rulers, and guides come in handy.

Start by showing and hiding the rulers, which are useful for positioning objects and for creating guides.

To show the rulers:

To show the rulers if they're hidden, choose **Show Rulers** from the **View Extras** menu ▣ ▾ on the Application bar ★ or choose View > **Rulers** (Ctrl-R/Cmd-R).

The rulers will appear on the top and left sides of the document window and the current location of the pointer on the image will be indicated by a dotted marker on each ruler.**A** Move the pointer, and you'll see what we mean. (Repeat the command when you need to hide the rulers.)

If you created a composite image, try moving a layer to a specific location (with the Move tool) according to the markers on the rulers.**B**

➤ To change the units for both rulers quickly, right-click/Control-click either ruler and choose a unit from the context menu. Or to get to the Units & Rulers panel in the Preferences dialog quickly, where you can also change the units, double-click either ruler.

➤ To change the ruler origin (to measure distances from a specific location), from the upper left corner where the two rulers meet, drag diagonally into the image.**C** To restore the default origin, double-click in the upper left corner.

A The current location of the pointer is indicated by a dotted marker on each ruler.

B As we move a type layer, the current location of the pointer is indicated on each ruler.

C You can drag the ruler origin to a new location.

CHOOSE YOUR EXTRAS

The View > Extras command (Ctrl-H/Cmd-H) shows or hides whichever document features are currently enabled on the View > Show submenu. Among the Show submenu features that you can show and hide are Layer Edges, Selection Edges, the Grid, (ruler) Guides, and Smart Guides. These choices affect the current document window as well as any documents you subsequently open.

If the Smart Guides feature is on and you move an item (selection border, layer, path, type, or shape), temporary guide lines will appear onscreen, designating the top, middle, or bottom of another layer.

To use smart guides while moving a layer:

1. Make sure View > Show > **Smart Guides** has a check mark.

2. Click a layer in a document that contains two or more layers.

3. With the **Move** tool ⊹ (V), drag the layer. Magenta (the default color) lines will appear, designating the top, middle, or bottom of imagery or type on other layers.**A–B** Snap the item to a guide or to a pair of intersecting guides.

➤ In the Guides, Grid & Slices panel of the Preferences dialog, you can change the color of guides, smart guides, and the grid, and choose other related options.

The grid is a nonprinting framework that you can snap image elements to. It can be displayed or hidden as needed.

To show or hide the grid: ★

To show or hide the grid,**C** choose **Show Grids** from the **View Extras** menu ▦ ▾ on the Application bar (Ctrl-'/Cmd-'). This option can be turned on or off for individual files. With View > Snap To > Grid on, a selection, layer, path, or shape will snap to a grid line if you move it within eight screen pixels of the line.

When View > Snap is on (and depending on which document features are enabled on the View > Snap To submenu), as you move a selection border, layer, path, type, or shape near a guide, grid line, layer, or the edge of the canvas area, the pointer or item will snap (to the item) with a subtle tug. (Personally, we prefer to use smart guides...)

To use the Snap feature:

1. Choose View > Snap To > **Guides, Grid, Layers, Slices, Document Bounds,** or **All** (of the above). Note: For the Snap To > Guides, Grid, or Slices option to be available, that feature must have a check mark on the View > Show submenu.

2. Make sure View > **Snap** has a check mark (Ctrl-Shift-;/Cmd-Shift-;). This command enables whichever options are currently checked on the Snap To submenu.

A With the help of smart guides, the type layer is being aligned horizontally to the left edge of the boat layer and vertically to the midpoint of that layer.

B Smart guides are being used here, too, except this time the top of the type is being aligned to the midpoint of the boat layer.

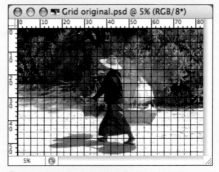

C The grid is displayed.

If you find the grid to be overbearing but still yearn for guides that will stay onscreen, try working with ruler guides. You can place ruler guides wherever you need them and remove them individually at any time—plus they have the same magnetic "Snap To" behavior as the grid.

To create ruler guides:

Show the rulers (Ctrl-R/Cmd-R), then drag from the horizontal or vertical **ruler** into the document window.**A–B** A guide will appear where you release the mouse.

As you create guides, you can do the following:

Snap a guide to a **selection** or to a **selected layer**.

Make sure View > Snap is checked, then Shift-drag slowly to snap a guide to a **ruler** increment.

➤ You can move any existing guide with the Move tool (the pointer will become a double arrow), provided the guides aren't locked.

➤ If the grid is showing and View > Snap To > Grid is on, you can snap a guide to a grid line.

➤ Obscure tip: Alt-drag/Option-drag as you create a guide to switch its orientation from vertical to horizontal, or vice versa.

When guides are locked, they can't be moved with the Move tool.

To lock or unlock all ruler guides:

Choose View > **Lock Guides** (Ctrl-Alt-;/Cmd-Option-;). Rechoose the command to unlock.

➤ Guides will keep their relative positions if you resize your image—provided they're not locked.

To create a ruler guide at a specific location:

1. Choose View > **New Guide**.

2. In the New Guide dialog, click **Orientation**: **Horizontal** or **Vertical**, enter a **Position** relative to the 0 (zero) point on that axis in any measurement unit used in Photoshop, then click OK.

To remove ruler guides:

Do either of the following:

To remove **one** guide, choose the **Move** tool (or hold down V), then drag the guide out of the document window (this works only if guides aren't locked). Don't press Delete, or you will delete the current layer!

To remove **all** guides, choose View > **Clear Guides**.

A A guide is dragged downward from the horizontal ruler.

B We created four ruler guides to surround the type layer. (Note: In the Guides, Grid & Slices panel of the Preferences dialog, we changed the guide color to red to contrast better with the colors in this image.)

To measure the distance and angle between two points:

1. Choose the **Ruler** tool ✐ (I or Shift-I).

2. Drag in the document window. The angle (A) and length (L) of the measure line will be listed on the Options bar and the Info panel. (Shift-drag to constrain the angle to a multiple of 45°.)

➤ Choose another tool when you're done using the Ruler, then hold down I for a temporary Ruler tool—the measure line will redisplay. Each document can contain only one measure line.

➤ To remove the measure line, choose the Ruler tool, then click Clear on the Options bar.

➤ With the Ruler tool, you can move a measure line to another area of the document, or drag an endpoint to change the angle of the line.

Aligning and distributing layers

Similar to the way you might align objects in a drawing program, you can align the visible parts of one layer to another layer—or align multiple layers to one another—via buttons on the Options bar.

To align layers to one another:

1. Choose the **Move** tool ⊹ (V), then check **Auto Select** and choose **Layer** on the Options bar.

2. Click one image or type layer, then Ctrl-click/Cmd-click one or more additional layers.**A**

3. Click one of the six **align** buttons on the Options bar (use tool tips to identify them).**B–C**

➤ Before using the align buttons, click a layer that one or more other layers are linked to; the linked layers will align to the one you click.

➤ To align layers to the edges of a selection, create the selection before step 1, above.

The distribute buttons equalize the spacing among multiple selected or linked layers. You must select three or more layers first.

To equalize the spacing among layers:

1. Choose the **Move** tool ⊹ (V), then check **Auto Select** and choose **Layer** on the Options bar.

2. Click a layer, then Ctrl-click/Cmd-click at least two other layers (not the Background).

3. Click one of the six **distribute** buttons on the Options bar.**D–E**

➤ Oops, you clicked the wrong button? Undo the last command before applying a different one.

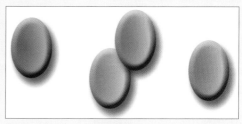

A We chose the Move tool and we selected four layers.

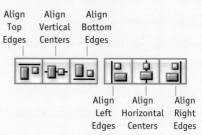

Align Top Edges   Align Vertical Centers   Align Bottom Edges

Align Left Edges   Align Horizontal Centers   Align Right Edges

B These are the align buttons on the Options bar.

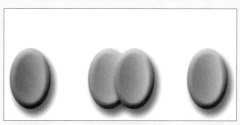

C We clicked Align Bottom Edges.

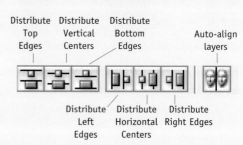

Distribute Top Edges   Distribute Vertical Centers   Distribute Bottom Edges   Auto-align layers

Distribute Left Edges   Distribute Horizontal Centers   Distribute Right Edges

D These are the distribute buttons on the Options bar.

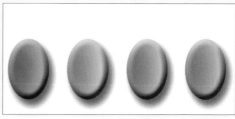

E We clicked Distribute Horizontal Centers.

Using the History panel, you can selectively undo or restore previous stages (called "states") of a work session. In this chapter, you'll learn how to restore, delete, and clear history states; preserve states by using snapshots; create a new document from a state or snapshot; and restore areas of an image to a prior state by using the History Brush or by filling a selection or layer with a history state.

Choosing History panel options

The History panel displays a list of the most recent states (edits) made to the currently open document. The bottommost state is the most recent. Click a prior state, and the document will be restored to that stage of the editing process. What happens to the panel when you do this depends on whether it's in linear or nonlinear mode,**A** so you need to learn how these two modes differ.

Choosing a mode for the History panel

To choose a mode for the panel, choose History Options from the panel menu, then in the History Options dialog, check or uncheck **Allow Non-Linear History**.

Continued on the following page

IN THIS CHAPTER

Choosing History panel options 165

Changing history states. 167

Deleting and clearing history states. .168

Using snapshots 169

Creating documents from states 171

Using the History Brush tool 172

Filling an area with a history state . .174

Source for the History Brush tool

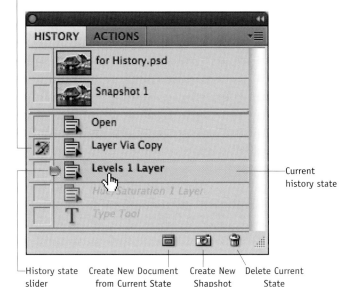

History state slider — Create New Document from Current State — Create New Snapshot — Delete Current State

Current history state

A The History panel shown here is in linear mode. Note that all the steps below the current state are dimmed.

We recommend keeping the History panel in **linear mode** (unchecking the Allow Non-Linear History option). In this mode, if you click an earlier state and resume image editing from that state or delete it, all subsequent (dimmed) states will be discarded. This gives you the option to revert back to an earlier state with a nice, clean break.

In **nonlinear mode**, if you click on or delete an earlier state, subsequent states won't be deleted or become dimmed. If you resume image editing when an earlier state is selected, your next edit will show up as the latest state on the panel, and all the states in between will be preserved. That is, the latest state will incorporate the earlier stage of the image plus your newest edit. If you change your mind, you can click any in-between state whenever you like and resume editing from there.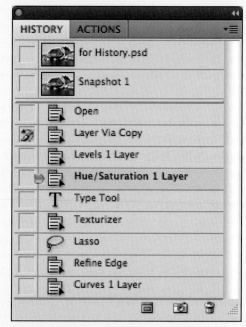 Nonlinear is the more flexible of the two modes, but it's also potentially more confusing and disorienting. (We offer a more complete explanation of nonlinear mode, including an example that demonstrates how to use it, in our *Visual QuickPro Guide* to Photoshop.)

Choosing other options for the History panel

The last option in the History Options dialog, **Make Layer Visibility Changes Undoable**, controls whether the hiding and showing of layers via the visibility icon on the Layers panel is listed as a state on the History panel. We prefer to keep this option off.

To specify the number of states that can be listed on the panel at a time, go to Preferences (Ctrl-K/Cmd-K) > Performance and enter a **History States** value (1–1000; default 20). If the maximum number of history states is exceeded during an editing session, earlier steps will be removed automatically to make room for the new ones. The maximum number of states may be limited by various factors, including the image size, the kind of edits that are made to the image, and currently available memory. Each open document has its own list of states. Note! Regardless of the preference setting, when you close a document, all the history states are deleted!

A In the History Options dialog, check whether or not to Allow Non-Linear History.

B Because this History panel is in nonlinear mode, all the states are available, even those that are listed below the current state.

Changing history states

To summarize, if the History panel is in linear mode (the Allow Non-Linear History option is off) and you click an earlier state, all the states below the one you click will become dimmed. If you then delete the state you clicked or continue editing the image with that earlier state still selected, all the dimmed states will be deleted. (If you change your mind, you can choose Undo immediately to restore the deleted states.) If the panel is in nonlinear mode and you click an earlier state, then perform another edit, the new edit will become the latest state, but the prior states won't be deleted.

To change history states:

1. Perform some edits on an image.

2. Do one of the following:

   Click a **state** on the History panel.  **A**

   On the left side of the panel, drag the **History State slider** upward or downward to the desired state.

   To **Step Forward** one state, press Ctrl-Shift-Z/Cmd-Shift-Z; or to **Step Backward** one state, press Ctrl-Alt-Z/Cmd-Option-Z.

➤ When you choose File > Revert, it becomes a state on the History panel, and like other states, all the states preceding it are preserved. You can restore the image to a state prior to the Revert one.

A This is after we clicked a prior state, with the History panel in linear mode.

Deleting and clearing history states

If you followed our advice and your History panel is in linear mode (the Allow Non-Linear History option is unchecked) and you delete a state, that state and all subsequent ones will be deleted.

To delete a history state:

Do one of the following:

Right-click/Control-click a state on the History panel and choose **Delete** from the context menu,**A** then click Yes when the alert dialog appears.**B**

To bypass the alert, drag the state to be deleted over the **Delete Current State** button 🗑 on the History panel.

To delete previous states sequentially, click a state, then Alt-click/Option-click the **Delete Current State** button as many times as needed. (Note: The Undo command will restore only the last state you deleted.)

To clear the History panel:

To clear all the states (but not the snapshots) from the History panel for all currently open documents in order to free up memory, choose Edit > Purge > **Histories**, then click OK. This command can't be undone!

To clear all states (not snapshots) from the History panel for just the current document, Right-click/Control-click any state and choose **Clear History**. This command can be undone.

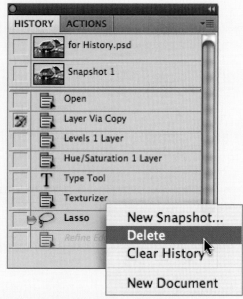

A Right-click/Control-click a state and choose Delete from the context menu, then click Yes in the alert dialog.

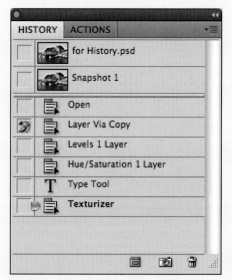

B Because our History panel was in linear mode (Allow Non-Linear History unchecked) when we deleted the "Lasso" state (see the previous figure), all the subsequent states were deleted in addition to that one.

Using snapshots

A snapshot is like a copy of a history state, with one major difference: Unlike a state, a snapshot remains on the panel even if the state from which it was created is deleted because the maximum number of history states was reached or the panel was cleared or purged. Like history states, however, all snapshots are deleted when you close your document.

In these instructions, you'll choose snapshot options, which affect all Photoshop files; on the next page, you'll learn how to create snapshots for a particular file.

To choose snapshot options:

1. Choose **History Options** from the History panel menu. The History Options dialog opens.**A**

2. Check or uncheck any of the following options:

   Automatically Create First Snapshot to have Photoshop create a snapshot every time you **open** a file (this option is checked by default).

   Automatically Create New Snapshot When Saving to have Photoshop create a snapshot every time you **save** a file. The time of day that the snapshot was created will be listed next to the snapshot thumbnail.

   Show New Snapshot Dialog by Default to have the **New Snapshot** dialog appear whenever you click the New Snapshot button, allowing you to choose options.

3. Click OK.

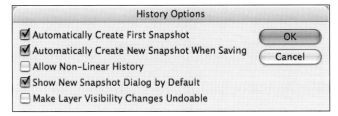

A There are three snapshot options in the History Options dialog.

If the Automatically Create New Snapshot When Saving option is off, you should get in the habit of creating snapshots periodically as you work and before running any actions on your document. If you use the New Snapshot dialog (the second method below), you'll be able to choose whether the snapshot is made from the full document, from merged layers, or from just the current layer.

To create a snapshot of a state:

Method 1 (without choosing options)

1. Edit your document so it contains the changes that you want to capture as a snapshot.

2. If the Show New Snapshot Dialog by Default option is off in the History Options dialog, click the **New Snapshot** button. If this option is on, Alt-click/Option-click the New Snapshot button. A new snapshot thumbnail will appear after the last snapshot in the upper section of the panel.

Method 2 (choosing options)

1. To create a snapshot of a layer, click that layer on the Layers panel.

2. Right-click/Control-click a history state and choose **New Snapshot**.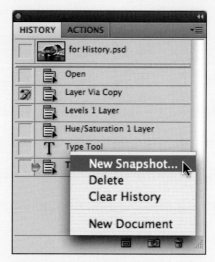 The New Snapshot dialog opens.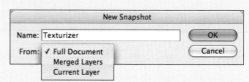

3. Type a **Name** for the snapshot.

4. Choose an option from the **From** menu:

   Full Document to create a snapshot from all the layers on the Layers palette. This is useful if you want to preserve all the edits at a particular stage of your document.

   Merged Layers to merge all the layers on the Layers panel at that state into the snapshot.

   Current Layer to make a snapshot from only the currently selected layer in its current editing state.

5. Click OK.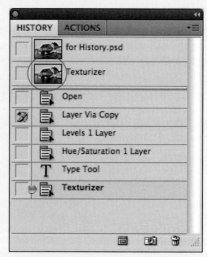

▶ If the Show New Snapshot Dialog by Default option is on in the History Options dialog, you can also open the New Snapshot dialog by clicking a state, then clicking the New Snapshot button at the bottom of the panel. Or if the dialog option is off, Alt-click/Option-click the New Snapshot button to open the dialog.

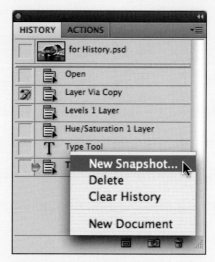

A Right-click/Control-click a state and choose New Snapshot from the context menu.

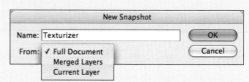

B In the New Snapshot dialog, enter a name and choose which part of the image you want the snapshot to be created from.

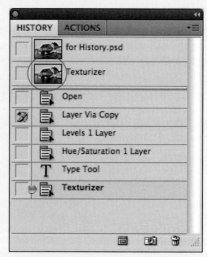

C A thumbnail for the new snapshot appears on the History panel.

To make a snapshot become the current state:

Do either of the following:

Click a snapshot thumbnail. If the History panel is in linear mode (as we recommend), the document will revert to the snapshot stage of editing, and all the states will be dimmed. If you now resume editing, all the dimmed states will be deleted.

Alt-click/Option-click a snapshot thumbnail to have earlier states remain available and to have that snapshot become the latest state. This is a useful option if you want to preserve earlier edits.

To delete a snapshot:

Do either of the following:

Click the snapshot, right-click/Control-click and choose **Delete** (or click the Delete Current State button), then click Yes.

To bypass the prompt, click the snapshot, then Alt-click/Option-click the **Delete Current State** button.🗑

Creating documents from states

By using the New Document command, you can spin off versions of your current document based on any state or snapshot.

To create a new document from a history state or snapshot:

Do either of the following:

Right-click/Control-click a snapshot or a state, then choose **New Document** from the context menu.**A**

Click a snapshot or a state, then click the **New Document from Current State** button.▣

A new document window will appear onscreen, bearing the title of the snapshot or state from which it was created, and "Duplicate State" will be the name of the starting state for the new document.**B** Be sure to save this new document.

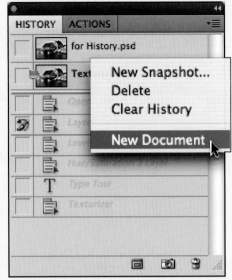

A Right-click/Control-click a snapshot or state and choose New Document.

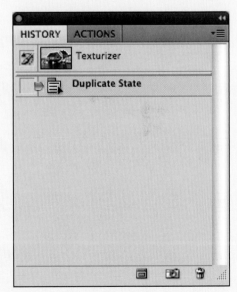

B This is the History panel for the new document.

Using the History Brush tool

When you draw strokes on a document with the History Brush tool, pixels below the pointer are restored from whichever state or snapshot you have designated as the history source.

Note: The History Brush tool can't be used if certain kinds of edits were made after the document was opened, such as cropping, changing the document color mode or canvas size, or adding or deleting layers. Furthermore, the tool can't restore deleted or modified layer effects, vector data (type or shapes), pixels from a deleted layer, or the effects of an adjustment layer. Moral: Keep your layers!

To use the History Brush tool:

1. Open an image, and make some edits. (For the image shown at right, we duplicated an image layer via Ctrl-J/Cmd-J, renamed the duplicate, and applied a filter to it.) **A–C**

2. Choose the **History Brush** tool 𝒵 (Y or Shift-Y).

3. On the Options bar:

   Click the Brush Preset picker arrowhead, then click a **brush** on the picker.

   Choose a blending **Mode**, **Opacity** percentage, and **Flow** percentage.

4. On the **History** panel, click in the leftmost column for the state or snapshot to be designated as the source for the History Brush tool; the history source icon 𝒵 moves to that slot.**D**

5. On the **Layers** panel, click the layer that you want to restore pixels to, and make sure Lock Transparent Pixels ▣ is off.

A This is the original image.

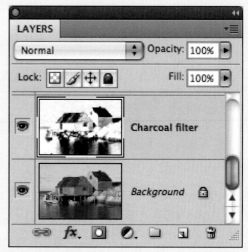

B We duplicated the image layer, then applied the Charcoal filter to the duplicate layer.

C The Charcoal filter is applied to a duplicate image layer.

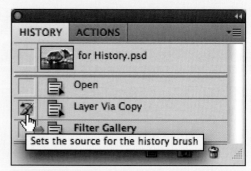

D To set the history source icon, we clicked in the leftmost column for a state prior to the filter edit but after the layer addition (in this case, it's the state called "Layer Via Copy").

6. Draw strokes on the image. Pixel data from the prior state of that layer will replace the current data where you apply strokes.**A–C**

➤ Say you apply some brush strokes to a layer, then decide a few editing steps later that you want to remove them. If you click the state above the one labeled "Brush Tool," the edits that you want to keep will be deleted when you resume editing. Instead, set the source for the History Brush tool as the state above "Brush Tool," click the layer on the Layers panel that you applied brush strokes to, then with the History Brush tool, paint out your strokes in the document window.

A On the duplicate layer that we applied the filter to, we applied strokes with the History Brush tool (we chose an Opacity of 55% and a big scratchy Spatter brush for the tool).

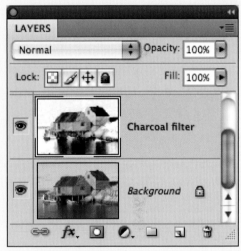

B In the Layers panel for the final image (shown below), you can see that the original color was restored to some areas of the duplicate layer.

SNAPSHOT AS HISTORY BRUSH SOURCE

To use a snapshot instead of a state as the source for the History Brush tool, try this exercise: Modify a layer (e.g., apply a filter or Image > Adjustments command or draw brush strokes), then create a snapshot of the current state. Make further modifications to the image, then create a second snapshot. Set the history source icon to the first snapshot, make sure the layer you want to restore pixels to is selected, then with the History Brush tool, draw strokes to restore areas from that snapshot. Set the history source icon to the second snapshot, then use the History Brush tool again to restore some later edits that you may have removed.

When using a snapshot as the source for the History Brush, you'll be able to choose which layer you restore pixels to if you chose the Full Document or Merged Layers option in the New Snapshot dialog when you created the snapshot. If you chose Current Layer in the New Snapshot dialog, you'll be able to paint only on the single layer that was preserved in the snapshot.

C Some of the original color is visible in this final image.

Filling an area with a history state

The Fill command, when used with the History option, fills a layer or selection with pixels from a designated history state or snapshot. Our note on page 172 also applies to this command.

To fill a selection or layer with a history state or snapshot:

1. Edit your document, and click an image layer.**A**

2. *Optional:* Create a selection. You can either leave the selection edges sharp or use Refine Edge to feather them.**B**

3. On the History panel, click in the leftmost column for the state or snapshot you want to use as the fill data. The history source icon will appear where you click.

4. Choose Edit > **Fill** (Shift-Backspace/Shift-Delete). The Fill dialog opens.**C**

5. Choose **Use: History**.

6. Choose a **Blending Mode** and an **Opacity** percentage.

7. Check **Preserve Transparency** to replace only existing pixels, or leave it unchecked to allow pixels to appear anywhere on the current layer. This option is available only if the layer contains transparent pixels.

8. Click OK.**D**

A This is the original image.

B We applied the Conté Crayon filter to a duplicate image layer, selected the bottom area of that layer, then feathered the selection by using the Refine Edge command.

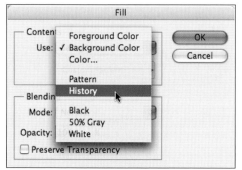

C In the Fill dialog, we chose Use: History. (You can also change the Blending Mode and Opacity, if desired.)

D The selection is filled with the unedited imagery at an Opacity of 75%.

You're happy with the composition of a photo, but it looks a bit dull or the contrast is too strong? Enter the digital darkroom. Photoshop offers so many commands for adjusting images, we couldn't fit them all into this chapter! First, we'll show you how to create adjustment layers—a super-flexible method for applying adjustment commands. After that you'll learn how to use the simple Threshold and Posterize commands, the Histogram panel, the Levels command, and the Brightness/Contrast command. And finally, you'll learn how to burn (darken) or dodge (lighten) areas via a removable neutral color layer.

Creating adjustment layers ★

A command applied via the Image > Adjustments submenu causes permanent changes directly to the layer it's applied to, whereas the effects of an adjustment layer become permanent only when you merge the layer downward into the underlying layer or flatten your document. We strongly recommend that you use adjustment layers whenever possible because they're flexible, meaning you can change the settings for them as often as you like; restack, hide, show, or delete them at any time; and even drag-copy them from one file to another. And they don't increase the file size, so you can create and keep as many as you need without hesitation. Note: The last six commands on the Image > Adjustments submenu can be applied only via a dialog, not via an adjustment layer.

A new feature in Photoshop is the **Adjustments** panel, which makes creating and using adjustment layers even easier than before. In addition to providing quick access to 15 of the Photoshop adjustment commands, the panel also provides new features, such as adjustment presets and preview and resetting options.

TONAL ADJUSTMENTS

11

IN THIS CHAPTER

Creating adjustment layers 175

Editing adjustment layer settings . . .177

Saving adjustment presets 178

Merging and deleting adjustment
    layers 179

Adjustment layer techniques 180

Editing adjustment layer masks 181

Applying a Threshold adjustment . . .182

Applying a Posterize adjustment 183

Using the Histogram panel 184

Creating a Levels adjustment layer . .186

Adjusting brightness and contrast . .189

Dodging and burning 190

ADJUSTMENT COMMANDS TO EXPLORE IN OTHER CHAPTERS			
Command	Page	Command	Page
Black & White	206–207	Match Color	280–281
Color Balance	211–212	Photo Filter	260
Curves	218–221	Replace Color	284–286
Hue/Saturation	213	Shadows/Highlights	257–259
Levels (for color)	214–217	Vibrance	208–210

When creating an adjustment layer, you can choose custom settings for any command or, for some commands, choose a settings preset instead. You can also customize the settings after applying a preset. By using the presets, you can quickly apply basic adjustments, such as to increase contrast using three progressively stronger settings via Levels, or increase saturation using progressively stronger settings via Hue/Saturation.

To create an adjustment layer: ★

1. Click the image layer you want the adjustment layer to appear above.

2. *Optional:* To restrict the effect of the adjustment to a specific area, create a selection.

3. Display the **Adjustments** panel.🔵 The **Add an Adjustment** buttons and scroll list display.**A**

   ► To redisplay the Add an Adjustment list when controls for an adjustment layer are displaying, click the Return to Adjustment List button 🔵 at the bottom of the panel.

4. Do either of the following:

   Click the **button** for the desired adjustment type. They are arranged as follows: tonal adjustments in the top row, color adjustments in the middle row, and miscellaneous adjustments in the bottom row.

   Click a triangle on the scroll list to expand a category of **presets**, then click a preset (not all adjustment types have presets).

5. Controls for the adjustment layer will display on the panel (no need to open a dialog!). A new adjustment layer will appear on the Layers panel, containing a thumbnail icon for that particular adjustment type and an editable mask **B** (and **A–B**, next page). If you clicked a preset, the controls will be set for you already.

6. Choose the desired settings (if you chose a preset, you can customize the settings or leave them as is).

   ► To create an adjustment layer the old-fashioned way, choose a command from the New Fill/ Adjustment Layer menu 🔵. at the bottom of the Layers panel.

   ► To expand the Adjustments panel, click the Switch Panel to Expand View button 🔵 at the bottom of the panel; click the button again to restore it to Standard view.

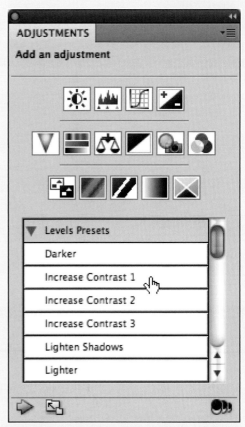

A On the Add an Adjustment list of the Adjustments panel, click a button to display controls for that adjustment type; or click a preset, if available, on the scroll list, to display the predefined settings for that preset.

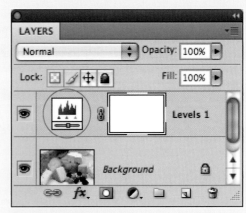

B Each kind of adjustment layer has a unique icon, which displays in the layer thumbnail and in its button on the Adjustments panel.

A This image lacks contrast.

B Via the Adjustments panel, we applied the Increase Contrast 1 preset in the Levels Presets category.

Editing adjustment layer settings

To change the settings for an adjustment layer: ★

1. On the Layers panel, double-click an adjustment layer **thumbnail** to select the layer and show the Adjustments panel (or click an adjustment layer and show the Adjustments panel).

2. The controls for that adjustment layer display on the Adjustments panel. Do either or both of the following:

   Edit the settings.**A–C**

   For the Levels, Curves, Exposure, Hue/Saturation, Black & White, or Channel Mixer adjustment type, choose a preset from the **Preset** menu at the top of the panel. (To create and save adjustment presets, see pages 178–179.)

By holding down the **View Previous State** button, you can temporarily display the image without the current adjustments (the settings won't change).

To view the image without the current adjustments: ★

1. On the Layers panel, double-click an adjustment layer **thumbnail** to select the layer and show the Adjustments panel, then edit the settings.

2. Press and hold the **View Previous State** button 💬 or press the \ key, then release the button or \ to toggle the latest edits off and on.

C We fine-tuned the contrast by editing the settings for the Levels adjustment layer. We dragged the midtones (gray) Input Levels sliders slightly to the right, to darken the midtones and add depth to the image.

To hide the effect of an adjustment layer: ★

Click the visibility icon 👁 on the Adjustments panel or Layers panel; click it again to redisplay.

By clicking the Reset button, you can undo the most recent changes made to an adjustment layer, if any (since the document was opened), or restore the default settings. The button icon changes depending on whether the settings for the adjustment layer were edited. Run through the following steps, just to see how the button works.

To reset an adjustment layer: ★

1. On the Layers panel, double-click an adjustment layer **thumbnail** to select the layer and show the Adjustments panel.

2. Edit the settings.

3. Click the **Reset to Previous State** button 🔄 to cancel the current changes (restore the last settings).

4. Click the **Reset to Adjustment Defaults** button 🔄 to restore the default settings.

➤ To undo the last individual slider, check box, or other adjustment edit, press Ctrl-Z/Cmd-Z.

➤ Although the creation of each adjustment layer appears as a state on the History panel, new presets chosen for, or settings changed in, an adjustment layer aren't listed as separate states (probably a good thing, to keep the panel from becoming overloaded with unnecessary listings).

Normally, an adjustment layer affects all the layers below it, but you can clip (restrict) its effect to just the layer directly below it.

To restrict the effect of an adjustment layer to the layer directly below it: ★

1. On the **Layers** panel, click an adjustment layer. **A**

2. On the **Adjustments** panel, click the **Clip to Layer** button. 🔗 (Click it again to "unclip.") **B**

Saving adjustment presets

Regardless of how you arrive at custom settings (whether by choosing a preset first or not), you can save your settings for future use.

To save custom adjustment settings as a preset: ★

1. Create and choose settings for an adjustment layer.

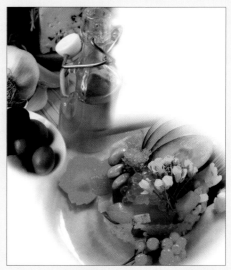

A A Levels adjustment layer is intensifying the contrast in this image.

B We clipped the effect of the adjustment layer to just the layer directly below it (the "olive oil" layer).

2. From the Adjustments panel menu, choose **Save** [adjustment type] **Preset**. In the Save dialog, enter a name, keep the default location, then click Save. Your user preset is now available for any document on the Add an Adjustment list on the Adjustments panel (see Figure **A** on page 176), and also on the preset menu at the top of the panel when the controls for that adjustment type are displaying.

➤ To delete a user preset, choose that preset, then choose Delete Current Preset from the panel menu.

Merging and deleting adjustment layers

When you merge down an adjustment layer, the adjustments are applied permanently to the image layer below it. If you change your mind, either choose Edit > Undo (right away!) or click the prior state on the History panel.

To merge an adjustment layer:

Do either of the following:

Click the adjustment layer you want to merge downward,**A** then press **Ctrl-E/Cmd-E**.**B**

Right-click/Control-click near the adjustment layer name and choose **Merge Down**.

Note: Adjustment layers don't contain pixels, so you can't merge them with one another. However, you can merge multiple adjustment layers into an image layer (or layers) by using either the Merge Visible or Flatten Image command (see pages 120–122).

It's as easy to delete adjustment layers as it is to create them.

To delete an adjustment layer: ★

Do either of the following:

Click an adjustment layer on the **Layers** panel, then press **Backspace/Delete**.

Click an adjustment layer on the **Layers** panel, then click the **Delete Layer** button on the same panel, 🗑 or on the **Adjustments** panel, click the **Delete Adjustment Layer** button. 🗑 Click Yes if an alert appears. *Optional:* Click Don't Show Again to prevent the alert from reappearing.

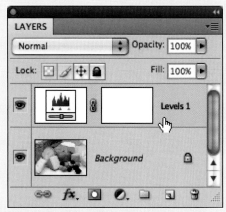

A Click the adjustment layer you want to merge downward.

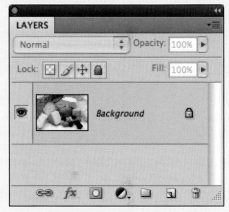

B The Merge Down command applied the Levels values from the adjustment layer to the underlying layer — in this case, to the Background.

Adjustment layer techniques

➤ Change the effect of an adjustment layer on underlying layers by choosing a different **blending mode** from the menu on the Layers panel (press Shift-+ or Shift-− to cycle through the blending modes). Try Saturation to heighten the saturation, Luminosity to adjust only the tonal values, or Darken or Lighten to darken or lighten, respectively.

➤ Lower the **opacity** of an adjustment layer to lessen its impact.

➤ Create multiple adjustment layers, then **hide** and **show A** them one by one to see how the image is affected.

➤ Create **multiple presets** for the same adjustment type, then choose the presets one by one to compare their respective effects. ★

➤ To copy adjustment layers between open documents, see page 222.

➤ To limit an adjustment to a specific area of an image, create a **selection** before creating the adjustment layer. The selection area will be represented by the white areas in the layer mask thumbnail.**B–E**

➤ To limit the effect of an existing adjustment layer, click the **layer mask** thumbnail, then apply brush strokes with the Brush tool or a gradient with the Gradient tool. For the Gradient tool, select the "Black, White" preset on the Gradient Preset picker (access the picker from the Options bar); see page 371.

USING MULTIPLE ADJUSTMENT LAYERS

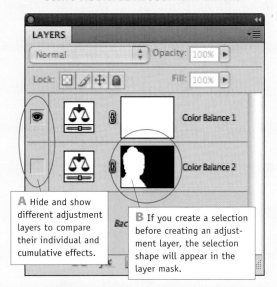

A Hide and show different adjustment layers to compare their individual and cumulative effects.

B If you create a selection before creating an adjustment layer, the selection shape will appear in the layer mask.

C The original image has a magenta cast.

D We used a Color Balance adjustment layer to neutralize the color cast.

E Then we selected the large Buddha on the left with the Magnetic Lasso tool and made it look warmer via a second Color Balance adjustment layer (note the layer mask thumbnail in Figure **A**).

Editing adjustment layer masks

By default, all new adjustment layers have a layer mask, which you can either ignore or use to control which area of the image the adjustment layer affects. In these instructions, you'll edit the adjustment layer mask either by creating and filling a selection or by applying brush strokes.

To partially mask an adjustment layer:

1. Click an adjustment layer.

2. Press D to choose the default colors, then press X to switch to black as the Foreground color (note the two color squares on the Tools panel).

3. To partially mask the adjustment layer effect, do either or both of the following:

   Create a **selection** with any selection tool (e.g., Rectangular Marquee, Lasso, or Magic Wand), choose Edit > Fill (Shift-Backspace/Shift-Delete), choose Use: Foreground Color, then click OK.

   Choose the **Brush** tool ✐ (B or Shift-B). On the Options bar, choose a brush tip, Mode: Normal, and Opacity 100% (or a lower opacity to create a partial mask), then paint on the image. **A–C**

4. *Optional:* To restore the adjustment layer effect by painting out the black mask, press X to switch the colors again (the Foreground color is now white), then with the Brush tool, draw brush strokes in the document window.

➤ To remove all the black areas from the mask, deselect, click the adjustment layer, choose Edit > Fill, choose Use: White, then click OK. To confine the adjustment layer effect to a small area, start with a fully black mask (click Invert on the Masks panel or apply Edit > Fill, Use: Black), then paint with white.

C Our brush strokes appeared in the thumbnail for the adjustment layer mask.

A We applied the Posterize command to this image via an adjustment layer first.

B Then we applied brush strokes to the layer mask to soften the harsh highlights in the background.

WORKING WITH LAYER MASKS

To turn off any of the features listed below, simply repeat the shortcut.

View the mask in the document window	Alt-click/Option-click the layer mask thumbnail
View the mask in the Quick Mask color (default color is red)	Alt-Shift-click/Option-Shift-click the layer mask thumbnail
Deactivate or activate the mask	Shift-click the layer mask thumbnail or click the Disable/Enable button 👁 on the Masks panel
Convert the unmasked area into a selection	Ctrl-click/Cmd-click the layer mask thumbnail or click the Load Selection from Mask button 🔲 on the Masks panel

Applying a Threshold adjustment

Next we'll show you how to apply a couple of easy two-step adjustments that produce marked changes: Threshold and Posterize.

A Threshold adjustment layer converts all the colors in the underlying layer to either black or white. The histogram on the panel graphs the distribution of pixels (to learn about the Histogram panel, see pages 184–185).

To create a Threshold adjustment layer:

1. Click a layer or the Background. **A**

2. On the Adjustments panel, click the **Threshold** button. ★ The Threshold controls display. **B**

3. Modify the **Threshold Level** (1–255) to increase or decrease the number of black pixels. Pixels that are lighter than the current Threshold Level will become white; pixels that are darker than that level will become black. **C–D**

4. Hold down the **View Previous State** button to view the original state of the image temporarily, then release. ★

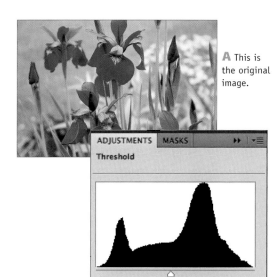

A This is the original image.

B We used the Threshold Level slider to set the cutoff point for the black and white values.

C The Threshold adjustment is applied.

CREATING A "WOODCUT"

Apply Filter > Other > High Pass to a duplicate image layer (try a Radius setting of around 4 or 5), then create a Threshold adjustment layer. Move the Threshold slider to the left for black lines on white or to the right for white lines on black.

D To restore some of the original image color, we lowered the adjustment layer opacity to 50%.

Applying a Posterize adjustment

The Posterize command reduces the number of color or value levels in an image to a specified number. When applied at a low number of Levels, the results look like a silkscreen.

To create a Posterize adjustment layer:

1. Click a layer or the Background. **A**

2. On the Adjustments panel, click the **Posterize** button. ▨ The Posterize controls display. ★

3. Choose the desired number of Levels (2–255). To make the layer look like a poster or silkscreen, choose a low value of, say, 4, 5, or 6. **B–D**

USING THE CUTOUT FILTER

For an effect that's similar to Posterize, apply Filter > Artistic > Cutout. The Filter Gallery opens (see pages 334–335). Adjust the settings as needed.

A This is the original image.

B The Posterize command was applied at 4 Levels.

C The Posterize command was applied at 5 Levels.

D The Posterize command was applied at 6 Levels.

Using the Histogram panel

The **Histogram** panel displays a graph of the current tonal (light and dark) values in an image, and it updates dynamically as you edit your document. It's always accessible, even when the Adjustments panel is being used or an adjustment dialog is open. By monitoring changes to the histogram as you apply adjustments, you'll be better equipped to gauge their impact.

After opening a scanned image or digital photo in Photoshop—but before you begin editing—study the histogram to evaluate the existing distribution of tonal values in the image. The horizontal axis on the graph represents the grayscale or color levels between 0 and 255; each vertical bar represents the number of pixels at that particular level; and the overall contour of the graph represents the current tonal range.

From the Histogram panel menu, choose a **view** for the panel: Compact View (just the histogram),**A** Expanded View (the histogram plus data and access to individual channels),**B** or All Channels View (all the features of Expanded View, plus a histogram for every channel). From the **Channel** menu, you can choose RGB,**C** a specific channel, Luminosity, or Colors, depending on what you want the panel to graph.

While a large file is being edited, Photoshop maintains the redraw speed of the Histogram panel by reading the data from the histogram cache—not the actual image data. As this occurs, a **Cached Data Warning** icon appears on the panel. Be sure to keep updating the panel, as in the instructions below (even while editing the settings for an adjustment layer), so it continues to reflect the present tonal values of the image.

To update the Histogram panel:

Do one of the following:

Double-click anywhere on the **histogram**.

Click the **Cached Data Warning** icon.

Click the **Uncached Refresh** button.

➤ To specify a Cache Levels value in the Preferences dialog, see page 393.

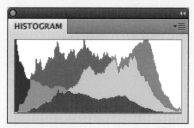

A This Histogram panel is in Compact View.

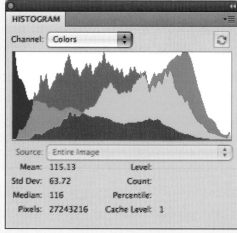

B This panel is in Expanded View. By default, the panel graphs the color pixels in an image (Colors is chosen on the Channel menu). ★

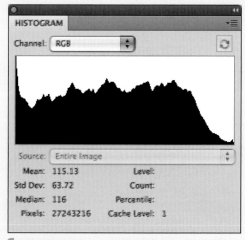

C With RGB chosen on the Channel menu, the current tonal values in the image are represented by black areas on the graph.

Interpreting the Histogram panel

A histogram is a dynamic graph of the tonal range (distribution of pixels) in an image. Pixels are represented by black areas, with shadows on the left, midtone pixels in the middle, and highlight pixels on the right.

   If an image is low key (relatively dark, such as a night scene), pixels will be clustered primarily on the left side of the histogram. If an image is average key (has balanced lights and darks), the distribution of pixels will be more uniform across the histogram. And if an image is high key (light, with little or no shadow areas, such as a polar bear on ice) pixels will be clustered primarily on the right.

   If an image has a wide tonal range (optimal), pixels will stretch from the left to the right edges of the whole graph, and will be distributed fairly equally in the shadow, midtone, and highlight zones. Also, the graph will be mostly solid and will have a relatively smooth (not spiky) contour. **A** If an image lacks detail in a particular tonal range, on the other hand, the graph will show gaps and/or spikes, like teeth on a comb. These are some graph profiles that you might see:

➤ In an average-key but **underexposed** image, pixels will be clustered primarily on the left side of the histogram, indicating that the image lacks detail in the highlights. **B**

➤ In an **overexposed** image, pixels will be clustered mostly on the right side of the histogram, indicating that it lacks detail in the shadows. **C**

➤ If pixels were **clipped** (details discarded) from the extreme shadow or highlight areas in an image, a line or cluster of pixels will rise sharply off the left or right edge of the histogram. **D**

➤ If an image has lost detail as a result of editing (say from applying filters or adjustments), there will be **gaps** or **spikes** in the histogram. **E** Gaps indicate a loss of specific tonal or color levels; spikes indicate that pixels from different levels have been averaged together and assigned the same value (the bar becomes taller at that level). A few gaps or spikes are an acceptable result of editing, whereas large gaps signify posterization and a loss of too many continuous tonal values (bad, for a photo). On the other hand, a lousy-looking histogram doesn't always signify failure —it can be thrown off by something as simple as adding a white border. If you like the way the image looks, simply ignore the histogram!

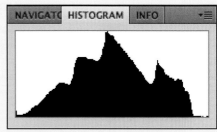

A This image has a good tonal range.

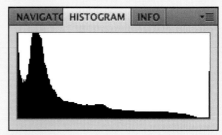

B This image is underexposed.

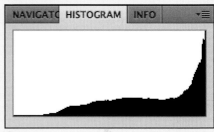

C This image is overexposed.

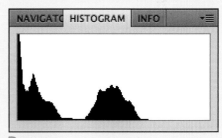

D This histogram has clipped shadow pixels.

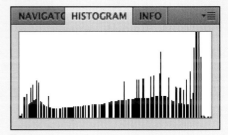

E This histogram has gaps and spikes.

Creating a Levels adjustment layer

Now that you know what a "good" histogram looks like, you're ready to create a Levels adjustment layer; Levels has a histogram of its own. We usually use Levels when we bring a photograph into Photoshop, then again during the course of editing. In these instructions, via the Input Levels and Output Levels sliders, you'll adjust highlight, midtone, and shadow values to intensify or diminish contrast.

To correct the light-to-dark balance of an image:

1. Click a layer,**A** then on the Adjustments panel, click the **Levels** button. 🔛 The Levels panel displays. ★

2. Do any of the following: **B**

    Use the sliders to adjust the contrast. For example, to intensify the contrast, move the white **Input Levels** highlights slider to the left to brighten the highlights and move the black **Input Levels** shadows slider to the right to darken the shadows. Any pixels located to the left of the black slider will be shifted to the darkest tonal value; any pixels located to the right of the white slider will be shifted to the lightest tonal value. This shifting of values is called "clipping."

    Another way to figure out where to position the highlights and shadows sliders is to activate Threshold mode, a temporary, high-contrast clipping display of the image. **Alt-drag/Option-drag** the highlights slider, and release the mouse when only a few areas of color or white appear (**A**, next page); these pixels will become the lightest tonal value. Also Alt-drag/Option-drag the shadows slider, releasing the mouse when only a few areas of color or black

A The original image looks dull (it lacks contrast).

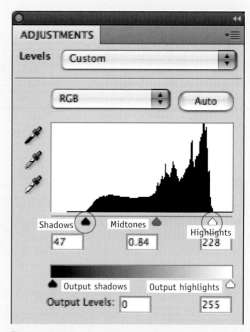

B The histogram in this Levels panel doesn't extend to the edges, signifying that our photo has a narrow tonal range. To correct this problem, we moved the shadows and highlights Input Levels sliders inward to align with the outer edges of the histogram (to expand the tonal range), and moved the midtones slider to the right to darken the midtones.

appear **B**; these pixels will become the darkest tonal value.

3. With the shadows and highlights sliders now in their proper place, move the gray **Input Levels** midtones slider to lighten or darken the midtones separately from the shadows or highlights. **C–D**

➤ To apply the current Levels settings to other open images (perhaps images that were taken under similar lighting conditions that require the same adjustments), choose Save Levels Preset from the Adjustments panel menu. Enter a name for the preset, then click Save. Click on another document window or tab. Click an image layer, expand the Levels Presets list on the Adjustments panel, then click your new preset (it will be at the bottom of the list). A Levels adjustment layer will be created, using your saved settings. ★

➤ The Shadow/Highlight command, another of our favorite commands, gives you more options and controls for adjusting lights and darks in an image than Levels. See pages 257–259.

A This is Threshold mode as we Alt-drag/Option-drag the white Input Levels (highlights) slider.

B This is Threshold mode as we Alt-drag/Option-drag the black Input Levels (shadows) slider.

C Our Levels adjustments enhanced the light/dark contrast, as reflected in the histogram at right.

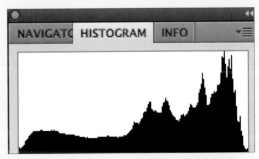

D The histogram after the Levels adjustments shows that the tonal range of the image was expanded (now the graph extends all the way to the ends). The shadows and highlights are stronger and the contrast is better.

Printing dark text on top of a photo can be tricky. The picture has to be light enough to allow the text to be readable, yet visible enough to be interpreted as an image. Screening back an image is yet another great use for a Levels adjustment layer.

To screen back a layer:

1. Open an image.

2. *Optional:* To limit the screened-back effect to a specific area of the image, create a selection.

3. Click an image layer or the Background, **A** then on the Adjustments panel, click the **Levels** button. The Levels controls display. ★

4. To reduce contrast in the image, move the **Input Levels** highlights (white) slider slightly to the left, and the **Output Levels** shadows (black) slider to the right.

5. To lighten the midtone values in the image, move the **Input Levels** midtones (gray) slider to the left. **B–C**

6. *Optional:* Hold down the View Previous State button to view the original state of the image temporarily, then release. ★

A The original document contains an editable type layer and an image layer.

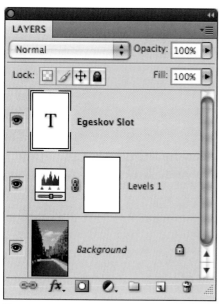

B We used a Levels adjustment layer to lighten the image.

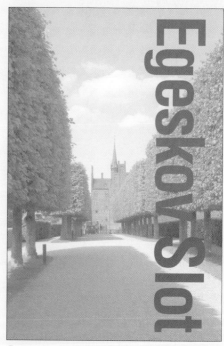

C With the image screened back, the type is more prominent and easier to read.

Adjusting brightness and contrast

For applying subtle brightness and/or contrast adjustments, try creating a Brightness/Contrast adjustment layer.

To adjust brightness and contrast:

1. Click a layer or the Background.

2. On the Adjustments panel, click the **Brightness/Contrast** button. ⚙ The Brightness/Contrast controls display. ★

3. Move the **Brightness** and/or **Contrast** sliders. **A–D**

➤ Keep the Use Legacy option for Brightness/Contrast unchecked, as it would permit tonal levels to be eliminated from the image. With this option off, Brightness/Contrast will preserve pixel data from the entire tonal range; after adjustment, you'll see evidence in the histogram of only a minor redistribution in tonal values.

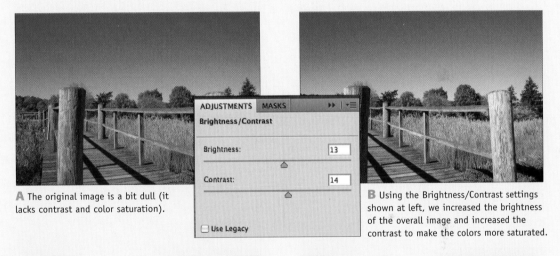

A The original image is a bit dull (it lacks contrast and color saturation).

B Using the Brightness/Contrast settings shown at left, we increased the brightness of the overall image and increased the contrast to make the colors more saturated.

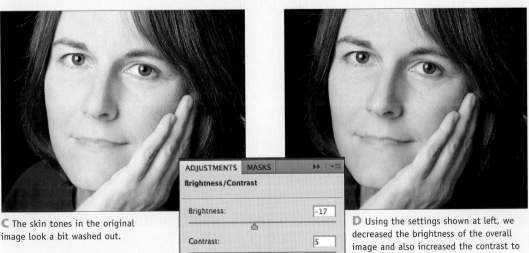

C The skin tones in the original image look a bit washed out.

D Using the settings shown at left, we decreased the brightness of the overall image and also increased the contrast to make the skin tones more saturated.

Dodging and burning

If you need to lighten and darken pixels by hand in small areas, the Dodge and Burn tools might seem like obvious contenders. However, these tools, even with their new enhancements, permanently alter layer pixels, which we try to avoid doing. A good alternative technique is to dodge and burn areas with the Brush tool on a removable, editable, neutral color layer, as in the following instructions.

To dodge and burn areas by using a neutral color layer:

1. If the document isn't already in RGB Color mode, choose Image > Mode > **RGB Color**.

2. Click an image layer or the Background,**A** then Alt-click/Option-click the **New Layer** button. The New Layer dialog opens.

3. Choose Mode: **Overlay** and check **Fill with Overlay-Neutral Color (50% gray)**; click OK.

4. Choose the **Brush** tool (B or Shift-B). From the Options bar, choose a large, Soft Round brush and an Opacity of 20%.

5. Press D to make the Foreground color black, then apply brush strokes to darken areas of the image. Press X to swap the Foreground and Background colors, then paint with white to lighten areas.**B–C**

6. *Optional:* To correct any stroke errors, hide the image layer. Alt-click/Option-click to sample the gray in an unpainted area, then paint with a full opacity brush over any strokes you want to remove. Redisplay the image layer.

➤ To lessen the overall dodge or burn effect, click the neutral gray layer on the Layers panel, then lower the layer opacity or choose Soft Light as the blending mode.

A The center of this image, where the focal point should be, lacks contrast. We'll adjust the reflected light on the cobblestones to draw more attention to the figure.

B This is what the neutral gray layer looks like, when displayed by itself.

We painted with black to darken the shadows on the sides of the buildings.

We painted with white to lighten the cobblestones around the figure.

C We painted on the neutral gray layer to dodge the road and burn the houses, then lowered the layer opacity to 78% to soften the overall effect.

In the first part of this chapter, you'll learn how to choose colors to use with various tools and commands. The last part of this chapter is a reference guide to the blending modes, which are available for tools, layers, and commands. In other chapters, you'll learn how colors are actually applied.

Choosing colors

The current **Foreground color** is applied when you draw strokes with the Brush or Pencil tool, create type, enlarge the canvas area, or use other tools and commands. The current **Background color** is applied by other procedures, such as when you apply a transform command to, or move a selection on, the Background.

These two colors are displayed in the Foreground and Background color squares on the Tools panel **A** and on the Color panel.**B** (Written with an uppercase "F" or "B," these terms refer to the two colors, not to foreground or background areas of a picture.) On the following pages, you'll choose Foreground and Background colors by using these methods:

➤ Enter values or click the large color square in the **Color Picker**.

➤ Pluck a color from an image with the **Eyedropper** tool.

➤ Choose a premixed color from a matching system via the **Color Libraries** dialog.

➤ Enter values or move the sliders on the **Color** panel.

➤ Click a swatch on the **Swatches** panel.

12

(COLORS & BLENDING MODES)

IN THIS CHAPTER

Choosing colors 191

Using the Color Picker. 192

Choosing colors from a color library. .193

Using the Color panel 194

Using the Swatches panel 195

Using the Eyedropper tool 197

Copying colors as hexadecimals 197

Choosing a blending mode. 198

The Default Foreground and Background Colors button (D) makes the Foreground color black and the Background color white.

The Switch Colors button (X) swaps the current Foreground and Background colors.

The currently selected square has a black border.

Foreground color square

Background color square

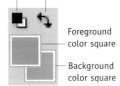

Foreground color square

Background color square

A The color controls on the Tools panel

B Use the Color panel to mix colors.

Color bar

Using the Color Picker

To choose a color using the Color Picker:

1. Do one of the following:

   Click the Foreground or Background color square on the **Tools** panel.

   Click the Foreground or Background color square on the **Color** panel, 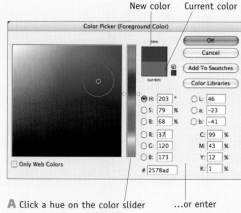 if it's already selected (has a black border).

   Double-click the Foreground or Background color square on the **Color** panel, if it's not already selected.

   Note: If the square you click contains a custom color from a matching system, the Color Libraries dialog will open instead of the picker. Click the **Picker** button to get to the Color Picker dialog.

2. *Optional:* In the Photoshop Color Picker, you can check Only Web Colors to make only Web-safe colors available.

3. Do one of the following:

   Click a color on the vertical color slider or drag the slider upward or downward to choose a **hue**, then click a variation of that hue in the large square on the left.**A**

   To mix a specific process color for print output, enter **C**, **M**, **Y**, and **K** percentages from a printed color matching system swatchbook (you can use the scrubby sliders).

   For onscreen output, enter **R**, **G**, and **B** values (0–255). A value of 0 in all three fields produces black; a value of 255 in all three fields produces white.

4. Click OK. The color will appear in the Foreground or Background color square on the Tools and Color panels. To store the color on the Swatches panel for future use, see page 195.

➤ To access the color picker for your system, in Preferences > General, choose Color Picker: Windows/Apple; or to use the Photoshop Color Picker (the default picker), choose Adobe. Only one color picker can be accessed at a time.

➤ You can also enter numbers in the **H**, **S**, and **B** or **L**, **a**, and **b** fields in the Color Picker.

New color   Current color

A Click a hue on the color slider or drag the slider, then click a color in the large square...

...or enter percentages in a group of fields.

WHAT DO THESE ICONS MEAN?

An out-of-gamut icon ⚠ in the Color Picker or Color panel signifies that the current color is outside the printable gamut, meaning it can't be printed with inks. If you're planning to print your Photoshop file, you can change any out-of-gamut color to an in-gamut color by clicking the exclamation point; Photoshop will substitute the closest printable color, as shown in the swatch next to or below the exclamation point. Keep in mind that when your image is converted to CMYK Color mode, all the image colors are brought into the printable gamut anyway. The out-of-gamut range is defined by the CMYK output profile, which is specified in Edit > Color Settings on the Working Spaces: CMYK menu.

A non-Web-safe icon 🔲 in the Color Picker signifies that the chosen color isn't Web-safe. You can click the swatch below the cube to have Photoshop substitute a similar Web-safe color, but note that with the wide proliferation of 16-bit monitors, it's unlikely that you'll need to restrict yourself to Web-safe colors for Web graphics.

Choosing colors from a color library

To help you pick colors from the many color libraries or systems that are accessible in Photoshop, such as PANTONE and FOCOLTONE, you can buy and refer to a printed fan book, or matching system guide, from a third-party supplier. For Web publishing or small-scale desktop printing, you don't need to do this, but it is imperative that you do so for commercial printing. Even the most carefully calibrated display can't show matching system colors with perfect accuracy, so if you pick colors willy-nilly based on whether they look appealing onscreen, you may in for a surprise when you see the printed result.

Before choosing colors in Photoshop for print output, the first step is to ask your commercial printer which brand of ink they're planning to use. Get the printed fan book for that system, and flip through it to decide which colors you're going to use. To choose those colors in Photoshop, use the Color Libraries dialog.

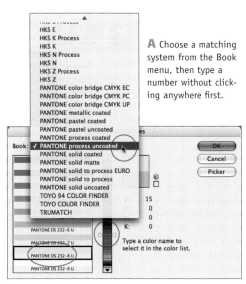

A Choose a matching system from the Book menu, then type a number without clicking anywhere first.

B Or click a color on the vertical color slider, then click a swatch on the scroll list.

To choose a color from a color library:

1. Do one of the following:

   Click the Foreground or Background color square on the **Tools** panel.

   Click the Foreground or Background color square on the **Color** panel, if it's already selected (has a black border).

   Double-click the Foreground or Background color square on the **Color** panel, if it's not already selected.

2. If the color square you clicked isn't a custom color, the Color Picker dialog will open. Click **Color Libraries** to get to the Color Libraries dialog.

3. From the **Book** menu, choose the matching system that your commercial printer has recommended.**A**

4. Do either of the following:

   Without clicking anywhere, type the number assigned to the desired color (refer to your swatch book); that swatch will become selected.

   Click a color on the vertical color slider, then click a swatch on the left side of the dialog.**B**

5. Click OK.

► To load a library of matching system colors onto the Swatches panel, see page 196.

CHOOSING A LIBRARY FOR PRINT OUTPUT

► ANPA colors are used in newspaper printing.

► DIC Color Guide and TOYO Color Finder colors are used in Japan.

► FOCOLTONE is a process color system that was developed to help prevent registration problems; it can be used in the United States.

► HKS process colors and HKS spot colors (without "Process" in the name) are used primarily in Europe.

► PANTONE process colors and PANTONE spot colors (without "Process" in the name) are widely used in the United States.

► TRUMATCH is a process color system that is organized differently than PANTONE. This system is used worldwide.

SPOT OR PROCESS?

By default, when color-separating an image for printing, Photoshop separates all colors — both process and spot — into the C, M, Y, and K process colors. If you want to output a spot color to a separate plate from Photoshop, you have to create a spot color channel for it.

Using the Color panel

For Web output, you can mix RGB or HSB colors directly on the Color panel by using the color bar, sliders, or fields.

To choose an RGB or HSB color using the Color panel:

1. Click the Foreground or Background color square on the Color panel, 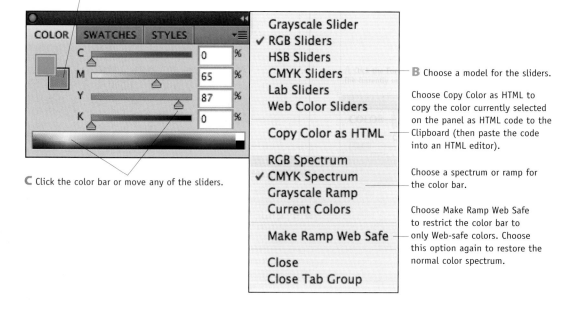 if the desired square isn't already selected.**A**

2. From the Color panel menu, choose a color **model** for the sliders (one of the first six choices).**B** For Web output, choose RGB Sliders, HSB Sliders (hue, saturation, and brightness), or Web Color Sliders (for Web-safe colors).

3. Do any of the following: **C**

   Move any of the **sliders**.

   Click on or drag in the **color bar**.

   Enter values in the **fields**.

➤ To choose a different spectrum style for the color bar, right-click/Control-click the color bar.

➤ Alt-click/Option-click the color bar to choose a color for whichever color square (Foreground or Background) isn't currently selected.

➤ If Dynamic Color Sliders is checked in Preferences (Ctrl-K/Cmd-K) > General, colors in the bars above the sliders will update interactively as you drag inside the color bar.

➤ In the RGB model, white (the presence of all colors) is produced when all the sliders are at the far right, black (the absence of all colors) is produced when all the sliders are at the far left, and gray is produced when all the sliders are aligned vertically with one another at any other location.

HUE, BRIGHTNESS, AND SATURATION

The hue (H) is the wavelength of light that a color is named for (such as "red" or "blue"); brightness (B) is the relative lightness of a color; and saturation (S) is the purity of a color (how much gray it contains).

A Click the Foreground or Background color square. The currently selected square has a black border.

C Click the color bar or move any of the sliders.

B Choose a model for the sliders.

Choose Copy Color as HTML to copy the color currently selected on the panel as HTML code to the Clipboard (then paste the code into an HTML editor).

Choose a spectrum or ramp for the color bar.

Choose Make Ramp Web Safe to restrict the color bar to only Web-safe colors. Choose this option again to restore the normal color spectrum.

Using the Swatches panel

Note: For convenience, detach the Swatches panel from the Color panel group before following these instructions.

To choose a color from the Swatches panel:

Do either of the following:

To choose a color for the currently selected color square (Foreground or Background), click a color swatch.

To choose a color for the square that isn't currently selected, Ctrl-click/Cmd-click a color swatch.

➤ To append other libraries of swatches to the panel or to replace the existing swatches, follow the instructions on the next page.

Colors you add to the Swatches panel stay there unless you delete them or reset the panel, and are available for all documents.

To add a color to the Swatches panel:

1. Mix or choose a **Foreground** color by using the Color panel or the Color Picker.

2. On the Swatches panel, ⊞ do either of the following:

Click the blank area below the swatches on the panel (paint bucket pointer), **A–B** or right-click/Control-click any existing swatch and choose **New Swatch**. Name the swatch, then click OK.

To create a new swatch without entering a custom name, click the **New Swatch of Foreground Color** button ◩ at the bottom of the Swatches panel.

Regardless of the method used, the new swatch will appear as the last swatch on the panel.

➤ To rename a swatch, double-click it, change the name, then click OK. To see the swatch name, use the tool tip, or choose Small List or Large List from the panel menu.

You can't undo the deletion of a swatch.

To delete a color from the Swatches panel:

Alt-click/Option-click the swatch to be deleted (scissors pointer); or right-click/Control-click a swatch and choose **Delete Swatch**, then click OK.**C**

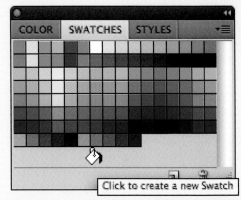

A To add a color to the Swatches panel, click the blank area below the swatches.

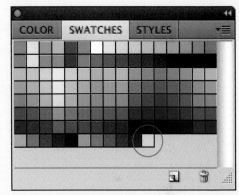

B The new swatch appears on the panel.

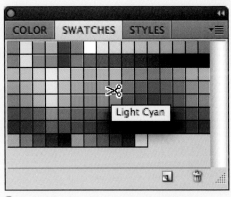

C Alt-click/Option-click a swatch to delete it.

If you save the current swatches as a library, you'll be able to load that library of swatches onto the panel at any time.

To save the current swatches as a library:

1. Make sure all the colors you want to save in the new library are on the Swatches panel, then choose **Save Swatches** from the panel menu.

2. In the **File Name/Save As** field, enter a name for the library (keep the .aco extension).

3. Choose a location in which to save the library (see the sidebar on this page).

4. Click Save.

➤ To edit an existing user-created library, follow step 1 above, click the existing library in the scroll window, click Save, then click Replace in the alert dialog.

You can load any user-created library or any of the preset swatch libraries that ship with Photoshop into the Swatches panel. You can either replace the existing swatches with the new ones or append the additional swatches while keeping the existing ones on the panel.

To replace or append a swatches library:

1. From the lower portion of the Swatches panel menu, choose the desired library name.

2. Do either of the following:

   Click **Append** to add the new library of swatches to the current panel.

   Click **OK** to replace the current swatches with the new ones. A prompt may appear, giving you the option to save the existing swatches on the panel as a library.**A**

➤ If you want to use your current swatches in another Creative Suite 4 application, save them via the Save Swatches for Exchange command on the Swatches panel menu.

➤ If you do interior design work, you may already know that some paint companies let you download swatches from their website (such as benjaminmoore.com, under Professional > Architects and Designers). Install the files in the default location, as listed in the sidebar at right, then relaunch Photoshop. Load the new swatch library from the Swatches panel menu.

You'll need to follow these instructions to load a swatches library only if the library isn't in the default location (as listed in the sidebar below); otherwise, follow the previous set of instructions.

To load a swatches library:

1. From the Swatches panel menu, choose **Load Swatches**.

2. Locate and click the desired library.

3. Click **Load**. The newly loaded swatches will appear below the existing swatches.

To restore the default swatches:

Choose **Reset Swatches** from the Swatches panel menu, then click OK. A prompt may appear, offering you the option to save the existing swatches as a library.

CHOOSING COLORS FOR WEB OUTPUT

When creating images for the Web, use the RGB color model on the Color panel or Color Picker. Bear in mind that RGB colors may not exactly match the color palette of your viewer's Web browser. For the most dependable results, load a Web or VisiBone palette onto the Swatches panel, and from the Color panel menu, choose Web Color Sliders and Make Ramp Web Safe.

WHERE TO STORE YOUR SWATCH LIBRARIES

To have your color swatch libraries appear automatically on the Swatches panel menu for all users of your system when you launch Photoshop, you must store them in the following location:

➤ In Windows, in Program Files\Adobe\Adobe Photoshop CS4\Presets\Color Swatches.

➤ In the Mac OS, in Applications/Adobe Photoshop CS4/Presets/Color Swatches.

A This prompt will appear in the Mac OS as you replace your current Swatches panel colors with a new library if the current swatches haven't yet been saved. In Windows, the buttons are Yes, No, and Cancel.

Using the Eyedropper tool

Being able to pluck a color from an image is useful for color matching when, say, retouching a photo or creating type. For this, use the Eyedropper tool.

To choose a color from an image using the Eyedropper:

1. Choose the **Eyedropper** tool (or hold down I for a temporary Eyedropper tool).

2. On the Options bar, choose a **Sample Size** (see the sidebar on this page) and **Sample: Current Layer** (then click a layer) or **All Layers**. ★

3. When you do either of the following, the sampled color will appear in the currently selected color square on the Tools and Color panels:

   Click a color in any open document window.**A**

   Drag in any document window. The currently selected color square will change dynamically as you drag. Release the mouse when the pointer is over the desired color.

➤ Alt-click/Option-click or drag in the document window with the Eyedropper tool to choose a Background color when the Foreground color square is selected, or vice versa.

Copying colors as hexadecimals

For Web output, you can copy colors as hexadecimal values from a file in Photoshop and paste them into an HTML file.

To copy a color as a hexadecimal value:

Method 1

1. Choose the **Eyedropper** tool (I or Shift-I) and choose Options bar settings.

2. Right-click/Control-click a color in the document window, then choose **Copy Color as HTML**. The color you selected will be copied to the Clipboard as a hexadecimal value.

3. To paste the color into an HTML file, display the HTML file in your HTML-editing application, then choose Edit > Paste (Ctrl-V/Cmd-V).

Method 2

1. Choose a **Foreground** color via the Color panel, Color Picker, or Swatches panel.

2. From the Color panel menu, choose **Copy Color as HTML**. The Foreground color will be copied to the Clipboard as a hexadecimal value.

3. To paste the color into an HTML file, open the destination application, display the HTML file, then choose Edit > Paste (Ctrl-V/Cmd-V).

A A color is sampled from an image with the Eyedropper tool.

CHOOSING A SAMPLE SIZE

➤ To change the size of the area the Eyedropper tool samples from, on the Options bar, choose Sample Size: Point Sample (the exact pixel you'll click on) or one of the Average options (e.g., an average within a 5-by-5-pixel square).

➤ You can also right-click/Control-click in the document window with the Eyedropper tool and choose a sample size from the context menu.

➤ 3 by 3 Average and 5 by 5 Average are useful for sampling continuous tones, such as skin tones in a portrait photo or the background area in a landscape. The 11 by 11 Average through 101 by 101 Average options work best for very high-resolution images.

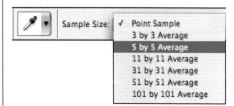

Choose a Sample Size for the Eyedropper tool from the Options bar (or from the context menu).

Choosing a blending mode

The **blending mode A** that you choose for a tool or layer affects how that tool or layer interacts with underlying pixels. You can choose from a list of blending modes in many locations in Photoshop, such as the Options bar (for most painting and editing tools), the Layers panel, and the Layer Style dialog.

In the text that accompanies the figures in this section, the colors of underlying pixels are called the **base colors**; the color in the upper layer or that you apply with a tool (such as the Brush), and that you choose a mode for, is called the **blend color**. In the images, we used the same three color squares, as shown in the first figure below (Normal mode). To avoid confusion, we kept the blend layer opacity at 100% (except for Dissolve mode).

➤ For most blending modes, Photoshop compares the colors of the two layers (or the layer and the paint color being applied by a tool) on a channel-by-channel basis. For example, the lightness of a pixel in the Red channel of the blend layer would be compared to the lightness of a corresponding pixel in the Red channel of the base layer.

➤ When choosing an Opacity percentage for a tool via the Options bar, keep in mind that the impact of the tool is also affected by the opacity of the layer that you apply strokes to. For example, strokes applied with the Brush tool at 50% opacity on a layer opacity of 50% will appear lighter than the same strokes on a layer that has an opacity of 100%.

Normal Dissolve Behind Clear	Basic
Darken ✓ Multiply Color Burn Linear Burn Darker Color	Darken
Lighten Screen Color Dodge Linear Dodge (Add) Lighter Color	Lighten
Overlay Soft Light Hard Light Vivid Light Linear Light Pin Light Hard Mix	Contrast
Difference Exclusion	Comparative
Hue Saturation Color Luminosity	Component

A The blending modes are organized in groups based on their function.

CYCLING THROUGH THE MODES

To cycle through the blending modes for the current painting or editing tool, or for the currently selected layer if a nonediting tool is selected (such as the Move tool or a selection tool), press Shift - + (plus) or Shift - – (minus).

Basic blending modes **replace** the base colors

Normal
All the base colors are modified. (When an image is in Bitmap or Indexed Color mode, this mode is called Threshold.)

Dissolve (50% Opacity)
Creates a chalky, dry-brush texture using the blend color. The higher the pressure or opacity of the tool or the higher the opacity of the layer, the more solid the color.

Darken blending modes **darken** the base colors

Darken
The blend color tints the base color.

Multiply
A dark blend color produces darker base colors; a light blend color merely tints the base colors. Good for creating semitransparent shadows.

Color Burn
Increases contrast in the base colors by making the shadow areas darker and the highlights lighter.

Linear Burn
Uses the blend color to darken the base colors by decreasing the brightness.

Darker Color
The blend color replaces base colors lighter than itself without affecting darker base colors. The blend color is fully opaque. Could be used to "paint out" light colors on a figure or object without having to use a selection.

The light blue strokes were applied to a blank layer above the image layer. Darker Color blending mode is chosen for the layer that contains the brush strokes.

See also the figures on the following page

Lighten blending modes **lighten** the base colors

Lighten
Modifies only base colors that are darker than the blend color, not base colors that are lighter than the blend color.

Screen
A light blend color produces lighter, bleached base colors; a dark blend color lightens the base colors less.

Color Dodge
A light blend color lightens the base colors by decreasing the layer's contrast; a dark blend color tints the base colors slightly.

Linear Dodge (Add)
A light blend color lightens the base colors by increasing the layer's brightness; a dark blend color tints the base colors slightly.

Lighter Color
The blend color replaces base colors darker than itself without affecting lighter base colors. The blend color will be fully opaque. Could be used to "paint out" dark colors around a light figure or object without having to use a selection.

The light blue strokes were applied to a blank layer above the image layer. Lighter Color blending mode is chosen for the layer that contains the brush strokes.

Contrast blending modes increase or decrease overall **contrast**

Overlay
Multiplies (darkens) dark base colors and screens (lightens) light base colors while preserving luminosity (light and dark) values. Black and white pixels aren't changed, so details are preserved.

Soft Light
Softens the base color by applying a light tint. Preserves luminosity values in the base colors.

Hard Light
Screens (lightens) the base colors if the blend color is light; multiplies (darkens) the base colors if the blend color is dark. Increases contrast in the blend color. Good for composite effects or for painting glowing highlights.

Vivid Light
Burns (darkens) the base colors by increasing contrast if the blend color is dark; dodges (lightens) the base colors by decreasing contrast if the blend color is light.

Linear Light
Burns (darkens) the base colors by decreasing their brightness if the blend color is dark; dodges (lightens) the base colors by increasing their brightness if the blend color is light.

Pin Light
A light blend color replaces the base colors; a dark blend color merely tints the base colors.

See also the figures on the following page

Contrast blending modes (continued)

Hard Mix
Posterizes (reduces) the base colors to approximately 5–8 flat colors. A dark blend color produces more black in the base colors; a light blend color produces more white in the base colors.

Comparative blending modes **invert** the base colors

Difference
Inverts the base and blend colors. The lighter the blend color, the more saturated the inverted color.

Exclusion
Grays out the base colors where the blend color is dark; inverts the base colors where the blend color is light. Lowers contrast.

HSL blending modes apply a specific **color component**

Hue
Applies the hue of the blend color without changing saturation and luminosity values in the base colors. Whites and blacks in the base colors are unchanged.

Saturation
Applies the saturation of the blend color without changing hue and luminosity values in the base colors.

Color
Applies the saturation and hue of the blend color without changing light and dark (luminosity) values in the base colors. Details are preserved, making this a good mode to use for tinting.

Luminosity
Replaces luminosity values in the base colors with luminosity values from the blend color without changing hue and saturation values in the base colors.

From professional-level correction to exotic color shifts, Photoshop has adjustment controls to suit your needs. First try to figure what needs correcting, then decide what kind of adjustment layer will help you reach your goal. For figurative photography, that goal will probably be color fidelity, whereas for a montage, you might aim for a unified color "temperature" that strikes the right mood. Some controls (such as Color Balance and Levels), are easier to get the hang of than others (Curves, Hue/Saturation), but when you forego simplicity, you gain more options and power.

To reiterate a point we made in Chapter 11, we recommend applying adjustments using adjustment layers and the Adjustments panel instead of applying them directly to a layer via the Image > Adjustments dialogs. You can easily edit the settings for an adjustment layer, and the adjustments won't become permanent until you merge it downward into the underlying layer. (To learn how to create and use adjustment layers, see our detailed instructions on pages 175–181.)

Important notes: Make sure your monitor is calibrated before performing any color adjustments (see pages 7–9). Also, unless you're working with a CMYK scan, keep your files—and perform all your color adjustments—in RGB Color mode (digital photos are already in this mode). And finally, should you need to make adjustments for a specific CMYK output device, be sure to work on a copy of your file—not the original.

13

IN THIS CHAPTER

Creating fill layers 204

Converting layers to grayscale 206

Creating a Vibrance adjustment
    layer 208

Creating a Color Balance
    adjustment layer 211

Creating a Hue/Saturation
    adjustment layer 213

Applying an Auto Color Correction. . . .214

Creating a Levels adjustment layer . .216

Creating a Curves adjustment layer . .218

SETTING THE STAGE FOR COLOR ADJUSTMENTS

Before performing color corrections, we suggest you choose Standard Screen Mode from the Screen Mode menu 🔲 on the Application bar. Mac OS users, also display the Application frame. The large gray area around the image will provide a good neutral backdrop for judging your color adjustments.

Creating fill layers

Like an adjustment layer, a fill layer affects the layers below it, except in this case it applies a solid color, gradient, or pattern. Like adjustment layers, fill layers can be edited or removed easily, and their content can be changed at any time. We'll explore two common uses for fill layers: applying a pattern or texture (below) and applying a color tint (next page).

To add a texture using a pattern fill layer:

1. On the Layers panel, click the layer that you want the fill layer to appear above. **A**

2. From the **New Fill/Adjustment Layer** menu ⬤. on the Layers panel, choose **Pattern**. The Pattern Fill dialog opens.

3. Click the **Pattern** Preset picker thumbnail to open the Pattern Preset picker. **B**

4. From the picker menu (click the arrowhead), choose a pattern library. When the alert prompt appears, click Append to add the library to the current picker.

5. Click a pattern thumbnail in the picker. You can move the pattern fill by dragging in the document window.

6. Click OK to close the Pattern Fill dialog.

7. With the fill layer still selected, change the layer blending mode and/or opacity. **C**

➤ Click the mask thumbnail on the fill layer, then apply brush strokes with black to block the effect of the fill layer, or with white to restore it. To lessen the overall effect of the mask, lower the Density value on the Masks panel.

➤ To create a custom pattern, on an image layer, draw brush strokes or apply filters to create an abstract design. Select an area of the layer with the Rectangular Marquee tool (Feather value of 0), choose Edit > Define Pattern, enter a Name, click OK, then deselect all (Ctrl-D/Cmd-D). Your new pattern is now available on the Pattern Preset picker.

➤ To limit the effect of an adjustment layer to just the layer directly below it, Alt-click/Option-click the line between the two (this creates a clipping mask).

A This is the original image.

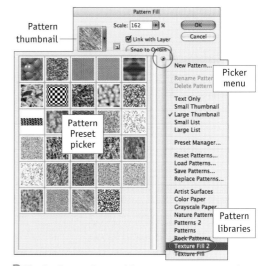

B Via the Pattern Preset picker menu, you can append a pattern library to the current picker. (Here, we're choosing the Texture Fill 2 library.)

C A pattern fill layer (Weave 5, Scale 162) above the image layer is creating the paper texture. The fill layer opacity is 50%.

If you apply a color to a layer (or to a selection on a layer) via a Solid Color fill layer, you'll have the option to edit or remove it at any time. When first applied, a Solid Color fill layer is completely opaque. If you wish, you can lighten it by using the layer opacity control or change the layer blending mode to make it interact differently with the underlying layers. This is a simple but effective way to correct a color cast or to apply a color tint to a whole image—or more typically, to part of an image.

To apply a tint using a solid color fill layer:

1. *Optional:* To restrict the tint to part of the image, create a selection. (For Figure **A**, we chose the Quick Selection tool, choose a brush Diameter of 10 px via the Brush Preset picker on the Options bar, then dragged across the sky. Next, we clicked the sky area below each arm, then Alt/Option dragged to deselect any selected snow areas.)

2. From the **New Fill/Adjustment Layer** menu ⬤, on the Layers panel, choose **Solid Color**. The Color Picker dialog opens.**B**

3. Choose a color for the tint, but don't sweat over it; you can change the color later if you wish. Click OK.

4. With the fill layer selected, choose a blending mode on the Layers panel.**C** You can also lower the layer opacity to lighten the color fill.

➤ To change the tint for a color fill layer, double-click the adjustment layer thumbnail; this reopens the Color Picker.

➤ You can limit a Solid Color, Gradient, or Pattern fill layer by editing its layer mask. You cannot do this for the Color Overlay, Gradient Overlay, or Pattern Overlay layer effect.

➤ You can also apply a tint via a Photo Filter adjustment layer (see page 260).

A We selected the sky before creating a Solid Color fill layer.

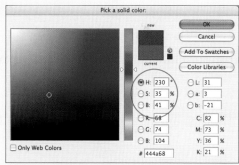

B In the Color Picker, we chose a color with percentages of H: 230, S: 35, B: 41.

C To enliven the sky, we applied a blue tint to the selection via a Solid Color fill layer. (We also changed the adjustment layer blending mode to Vivid Light, which restored some definition to the clouds.)

Converting layers to grayscale

Next, we'll show you three ways to strip color from a layer without changing the document color mode. Our favorite way is to use a Black & White adjustment layer because it enables us to control how the R, G, B and C, M, Y color channel values contribute individually to the resulting gray levels.

To convert an RGB image to grayscale using Black & White controls: ★

1. Click a layer or the Background. **A**

2. On the Adjustments panel, ◑ click the **Black & White** button. ◢ The Black & White controls appear on the panel.

3. If you're working on an RGB image, try adjusting the Reds, Greens, and Blues sliders first. If you like, you can click Auto to have the program choose settings for you, or select from the Preset menu, then adjust the settings. **B** The **Reds**, **Greens**, and **Blues** sliders control how each color is converted to a particular gray level (**A–B**, next page). Drag a slider to the left to produce a darker gray equivalent for that color or to the right to produce a lighter gray.

   ➤ If you want to preserve the original tonal range of the image, keep the combined sum of the Reds, Greens, and Blues values close to 100%; or if you don't mind altering the overall tone, ignore this sum (**C–D**, next page).

> **SAVING YOUR ADJUSTMENT SETTINGS**
>
> To save your custom settings for future use, see pages 178–179.

4. Fine-tune the conversion by adjusting the **Yellows**, **Cyans**, and **Magentas** sliders. You can use the Yellows slider to lighten or darken a portrait or to correct a landscape image that contains a lot of green.

5. Do any of the following optional steps:

   Click the On-Image Adjustment tool, 🖑 then drag horizontally over an area in the image to lighten or darken that shade. The corresponding slider on the panel for the most dominant color in that area will shift. ★

   To apply a tint to the whole image, check Tint, click the color swatch, then choose a color from the Color Picker.

   To restore some of the original color uniformly to the whole layer, lower the opacity of the adjustment layer. Or to restore color in some areas, click the adjustment layer mask thumbnail, make the Foreground color black, then with the Brush tool, draw strokes on the image (lower the tool opacity for a subtle effect).

A In this color image, the central figure commands our attention because of her position and outstretched hands, the light on her face and hands, and the stripes on her sweater.

B The Auto setting in the Black & White adjustment layer produced an adequate grayscale conversion, but we'll adjust the gray values next to draw more attention to the central figure, which was the focal point in the color image.

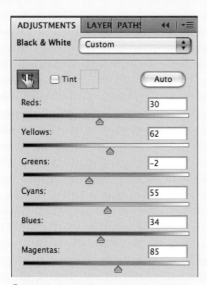

B As a result of the slider settings shown at left, the three figures are darker and more uniformly gray except for the face and cupped hands of the central figure, which are lighter. Now the focus is where we intend it to be, but the central figure could use more "punch."

A We reduced Reds and Yellows to darken the man's jacket, reduced Cyans and Blues to darken the women's clothing, and reduced Greens to darken the stripes on the sweater.

D As an experiment, we tried the slider settings shown at left to enhance the contrast in the striped sweater—and it worked. Now the central figure commands the most attention, as in the color version.

C We reduced Reds, Yellows, and Blues to darken the outer two figures and increased Greens to lighten the stripes on the sweater.

ORCHESTRATING A SCENE

In our environment, as in art and photography, colors define spatial and shape relationships and draw our eye to specific parts of a scene. When converting an image to grayscale, you can orchestrate visual movement with lights and darks instead of color. Choose gray levels based on how you want to reinterpret the composition and which areas you want to draw the viewer's attention to. For example, say there was a bright red shape in the center of the original composition. Using the Black & White controls, you could lighten or darken that shape to distingish it from the surrounding grays.

Creating a Vibrance adjustment layer

Using a Vibrance adjustment layer, you can either strip the color completely from a layer or desaturate a layer partially and then adjust the Vibrance to control the color intensity.

To desaturate a layer using a Vibrance adjustment layer: ★

1. Click a layer or the Background. **A**

2. On the **Adjustments** panel, ⬤ click the **Vibrance** button. Ⅴ

3. Do either of the following:

   For a simple, full desaturation, reduce the **Saturation** to its lowest value (to −100).

   To adjust the color vibrance as you desaturate a layer, lower the **Saturation** to between −60 and −80, then to control the color intensity in the almost grayscale layer, raise or lower the **Vibrance** value. **B–D** The Vibrance option boosts the intensity of the less saturated colors the most.

A This is the original image.

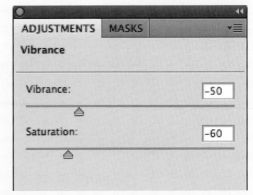

B For a Vibrance adjustment layer, we lowered the Saturation to −60 to desaturate the color partially and set the Vibrance option to −50.

C This is the image after applying the Vibrance adjustment layer settings shown in the preceding figure.

D This image has the same Saturation value of −60 but a higher Vibrance value of +100.

To desaturate a color layer and restore the color selectively: ★

1. Click a layer or the Background.

2. On the **Adjustments** panel, ⬤ click the **Vibrance** button. V

3. Reduce the **Saturation** all the way to –100. **A**

4. Choose the **Brush** tool, and from the Options bar, choose an Opacity of 50% or less. Press D for the default colors, then press X to swap them.

5. Keep the adjustment layer selected, then apply strokes where you want to restore the original colors. **B–D** You can change the brush opacity between strokes. To restore grayscale areas, press X and paint with white.

A To strip the color from this image, we lowered the Saturation to –100 by using a Vibrance adjustment layer.

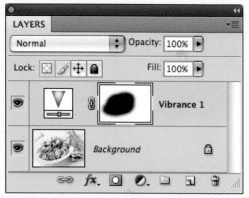

B We applied brush strokes to the adjustment layer mask to restore color in the center of the image, where we want to draw the viewer's attention.

C Now the color is visible only in the center of the image.

D For a variation, we selected the bottom two-thirds of this image, clicked the layer mask thumbnail for the Vibrance adjustment layer, filled the mask with black, then adjusted the Feather value on the Masks panel (see page 304).

The Vibrance controls can also be used to adjust the color intensity while keeping the layer almost fully saturated. Play around with the two simple controls.

To adjust the vibrance of a color layer: ★

1. Click a layer or the Background. A

2. On the **Adjustments** panel, ⬤ click the **Vibrance** button. Ⅴ

3. Do either of the following:

   Increase the **Vibrance** value, then reduce the **Saturation** value slightly. B

   Reduce the **Vibrance** value, then increase the **Saturation** value slightly. C

A The color in this portrait is oversaturated.

B For the Vibrance adjustment layer, we set the Saturation value to –25 and the Vibrance value to +40. Now the color and the contrast are less intense.

C For a subtle variation, we set the Saturation value to +25 and the Vibrance value to –40. The color is also less intense here, but the contrast is slightly stronger.

Creating a Color Balance adjustment layer

You can use a Color Balance adjustment layer to apply a warm or cool cast to an image or to neutralize an unwanted cast. Each slider affects a pair of cool and warm colors. For example, you could move a slider toward green to reduce magenta, or add yellow to reduce blue. See how the overall image is affected as you add or reduce individual colors.

Note: Although the Color Balance controls enable you to restrict your adjustment to the shadows, midtones, or highlights tonal range, Curves and Hue/Saturation let you adjust the values in even more restricted tonal ranges.

To make an image cooler or warmer using the Color Balance controls: ★

1. Click a layer or the Background.**A**

2. On the Adjustments panel,✐ click the **Color Balance** button.⚖

3. For the **Tone**, click the range to be adjusted: **Shadows**, **Midtones**, or **Highlights**.

   Optional: Keep Preserve Luminosity checked to preserve the tonal values of the layer as you make corrections; or when adjusting highlights, such as in skin tones, uncheck this option to apply soft color adjustments. (For the image shown on this page and the next, our adjustments were more successful with this option off.)

4. Each slider pairs a cool color with a warm one. Move a slider toward any color you want to add more of or away from any color you want to diminish **B–C** (also **A–D**, next page).

   ► To make the image warmer or cooler, move multiple sliders toward similar colors. For example, to add a cool cast, you could move the first slider toward Cyan and the third slider toward Blue. Or to make an image warmer, move the first slider toward Red and the third slider toward Yellow.

5. Click any other Tone button, then adjust the color sliders for that range. You can click the visibility icon 👁 to compare the adjusted image with the original.

   See also the figures on the following page

A The original image has a harsh magenta cast.

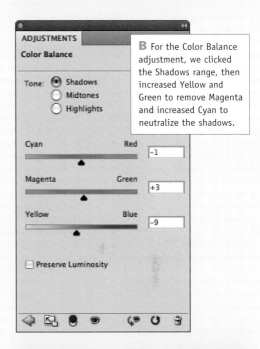

B For the Color Balance adjustment, we clicked the Shadows range, then increased Yellow and Green to remove Magenta and increased Cyan to neutralize the shadows.

C The Shadows adjustment produced a subtle improvement (note that the dark shadows on the columns are slightly grayer than before), but there's more work to do.

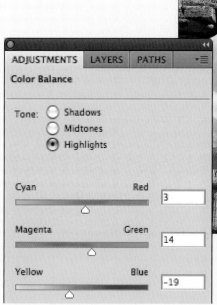

B The adjustment to the Midtones using the settings shown at left added blue to the sky and distant landscape and made the stone lighter and more neutral. However, the highlights still contain too much Magenta.

A With the Midtones range chosen, we added Yellow and Green (to remove Magenta).

D An adjustment to the Highlights using the settings shown at left neutralized the last traces of the magenta cast. Note that now the clouds are whiter and the stone is a warm, natural-looking cream color.

C With the Highlights range chosen, we added Yellow and Green (to remove Magenta). We also added Red to warm the yellow-green of the stone. Now the magenta cast is gone and the highlights look lighter.

Creating a Hue/Saturation adjustment layer

For making precise hue and saturation corrections without having to make a selection, try using a Hue/Saturation adjustment layer (instead of Levels or Curves). With the Hue/Saturation controls, you can target specific colors, then shift just those colors to a different hue or adjust their saturation or lightness. This is a good way to swap out colors in a product or fashion shot.

To create a Hue/Saturation adjustment layer: ★

1. Click a layer.**A**

2. On the **Adjustments** panel, ⬤ click the **Hue/Saturation** button. ▤

3. Do any of the following:

   To change all the document colors, keep **Master** as the choice on the second menu, then move the **Hue** slider to shift all the colors to different hues; or move the **Saturation** slider to adjust the saturation for all the colors; or move the **Lightness** slider to lighten or darken all the colors. After adjusting the Lightness, you may need to increase the

A We will change the blue napkin in this image to yellow to coordinate better with the lemons.

Saturation to revive any colors that became too light or dark.

To change the **hue** for a specific color, **B** click the **On-Image Adjustment** tool 🖑 on the panel, then Ctrl-drag/Cmd-drag horizontally over a color in the image. **C** The menu will list the color range you dragged over and the adjustment slider will shift to that color on the color bar.

To change the **saturation** for a specific color, drag horizontally with the On-Image Adjustment tool over a color in the image.

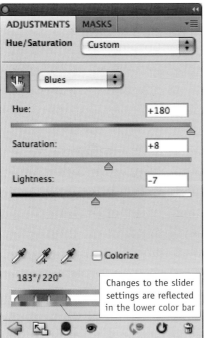

B We created a Hue/Saturation adjustment layer and clicked the On-Image Adjustment tool. Holding down Ctrl/Cmd, we dragged over the blue of the napkin until the hue shifted into the yellow range. Finally, we increased the Saturation and lowered the Lightness for the adjusted colors.

C Now the napkin is yellow.

Applying an Auto Color Correction

Via the Auto Color Correction Options, you can adjust the color, tonal range, and contrast in an image by using preset algorithms (formulas)—or, better yet, by using target values that you specify for the midtones.

To apply an Auto Color Correction: ★

1. Open an image.A

2. On the **Adjustments** panel, click the **Levels** button, then Alt-click/Option-click the **Auto** button.

3. The Auto Color Correction Options dialog opens.**B** Move it out of the way, if necessary, so you'll be able to monitor the Levels histogram as you choose options.

4. Click the **Find Dark & Light Colors** algorithm (the algorithms are described in the sidebar on the next page).

5. Check **Snap Neutral Midtones**. Photoshop will adjust any colors that are close to neutral to match the Midtones target color swatch in the dialog.

6. To adjust the color temperature of the image, you can assign a subtle color tint to the midtones. Click the **Midtones** swatch. The Select Target Midtone Color dialog opens.**C**

   Click the **H** button in the **HSB** group, then drag the circle in the large square slightly to the right (keep the **S** value around 10–30). Next, on the vertical Hue bar, click a red-yellow hue to make the overall temperature of your image warmer, or a green-blue hue to cool it down. To change the midtone brightness, drag the circle slightly upward or downward (keep the **B** value around 45–55).

   Note: Midtones is the only swatch you need to change; the other two swatches will adjust automatically when the document is prepared for printing.

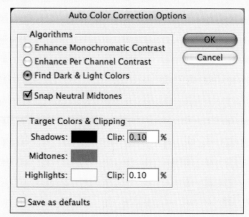

A The original image looks "too cool," due to a blue-green cast in the midtones.

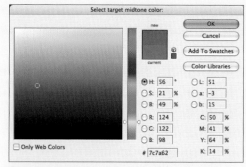

B In the Auto Color Correction Options dialog, we'll use the Target Colors & Clipping options to specify target values.

C This dialog opens when you click the Midtones swatch. We're choosing a warmer yellow-green that we think will work for the moss, sand, and evergreens in our beach photo.

7. Click OK to exit the Select Target Midtone Color dialog, then again to exit the Auto Color Correction Options dialog. **A**

When the alert dialog appears, offering you the option to save the new target colors as defaults, click No (we prefer to choose settings on a case-by-case basis than establish global default settings).

➤ For the most control when redefining the mid-tone color, we recommend editing the Midtones swatch via the Auto Color Correction Options dialog, as in the instructions on the previous page. A less reliable method would be to adjust the midtones using the gray point (middle) eyedropper in the Levels or Curves dialog—less reliable because the results vary depending on where you click. If you can locate (and click) a neutral gray area, fine and dandy, but it's not as easy to do as it sounds. **B–C**

A As a result of a midtones adjustment by way of the Auto Color Correction Options dialog, the image now looks warmer and more natural.

B Clicking in the original image with the gray eyedropper from the Levels dialog in the location shown above set the midtone color to a cool gray, which wasn't the change we were aiming for.

THE AUTO COLOR CORRECTION ALGORITHMS

➤ Enhance Monochromatic Contrast moves the black and white Input Levels sliders inward, which lightens the highlights and darkens the shadows. Because the sliders are moved the same amount for each channel, color relationships among the channels are preserved. (The Image > Auto Contrast command also uses this algorithm.)

➤ Enhance Per Channel Contrast moves the Input Levels sliders inward by a different amount for each channel, and produces more noticeable color shifts and changes in contrast than the other algorithms. (The Image > Auto Tone command also uses this algorithm.)

➤ Find Dark & Light Colors positions the black and white Input Levels sliders in each channel based on the average darkest and lightest pixels in the image, resulting in heightened contrast. We like this algorithm the best. (The Image > Auto Color command also uses this algorithm.)

(These algorithms are also accessible when you Alt-click/Option-click the Auto button for a Curves adjustment layer.)

C Clicking in the original image in the location shown above with the gray eyedropper from Levels also failed to correct the cool cast in the midtones.

When we need to make comprehensive color corrections, we use the Levels or Curves controls, because they enable us to apply corrections to individual color channels. Which one should you use? It depends on what needs correcting. Study the image to figure out what the exact problem is first. Is it under- or overexposed? If so, we suggest using Levels because it lets you correct broad ranges of color, such as in the midtones. Or perhaps the image has an unnatural color cast. For this, Curves would be a better choice because it lets you correct not only a broad color range, such as the color of a sky, but also a specific color cast in a particular tonal range, such as in the upper midtones.

Creating a Levels adjustment layer

The instructions below are general, whereas the captions below the figures refer to a specific image.

To adjust colors in an RGB image using the Levels controls: ★

1. Study the image and try to figure out which of the RGB color components need correction.**A** You'll adjust those colors in step 4.

2. On the **Adjustments** panel,⬤ click the **Levels** button.📊

3. Correct any exposure problems in the full RGB channel first **B–C** (see also pages 186–187).

4. To start removing a color cast, do as follows:

   Choose **Red** from the **Channel** menu.

   To reduce red in the midtones (and thereby increase green and blue), move the gray Input Levels slider to the right; or to increase red, move the slider to the left.

   To add red to the highlights, move the white Input Levels slider to the left. To reduce red in the shadows, move the black Input Levels slider to the right.

5. Choose the **Green** channel, then the **Blue** channel, and in each case increase or decrease the amount of that color by moving the sliders as in the previous step (**A–D**, next page).

   ► Don't overadjust any single channel or you'll throw off the color balance of the whole image. Also, we don't recommend moving the Output Levels sliders to adjust an individual color channel, as this could actually produce a color cast.

A The original image is underexposed and has a greenish cast.

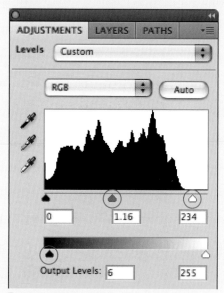

B On the Adjustments panel, we moved the gray Input Levels slider to the left to lighten the midtones, moved the white Input Levels slider inward to brighten the highlights, and moved the black Output Levels slider inward to lighten the shadows.

C Adjustments to the RGB channel (shown in the previous figure) made the image lighter. So far, so good.

6. To finalize the correction, switch back and forth between the color channels and readjust them, if necessary.

7. *Optional:* To remove the adjustment in some areas, with the adjustment layer mask selected, paint on the image with the Brush tool, Foreground color black.

► As contrast increases, so does color saturation. To reduce oversaturation caused by a Levels or Curves adjustment layer, choose Luminosity as the blending mode for the adjustment layer.

► To save your adjustment settings as a preset, see pages 178–179.

USING LEVELS ON A CMYK IMAGE

When adjusting individual color channels via Levels in a CMYK document, to decrease or increase the amount of a color, move the sliders in the opposite direction from our instructions in step 4 on the previous page. For instance, for the Cyan channel, you would move the gray Input slider to the left to decrease cyan or to the right to increase it.

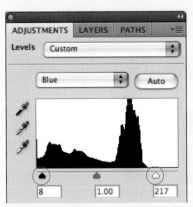

A Red channel: We added red to the midtones (moved the gray Input Levels slider to the left) and removed red from the shadows (moved the black slider to the right).

B Adjustments to the Red channel removed a green cast from the bricks and stones, but that area now looks too rosy and the sky and water still look dull. For the Green channel (not shown), we moved the gray slider to 1.04 to make the bricks less pink.

C Blue channel: We moved the black Input Levels slider to the right to remove blue from the shadows and moved the white Input Levels slider to the left to add blue to the highlights (the sky, path, and water).

D Although adjustments to the Blue and Green channels successfully removed the green cast, the castle, path, and other stone work still look too pink. In the next section, we'll color-correct the same (original) image using Curves.

Creating a Curves adjustment layer

The controls for Curves are even more powerful than those for Levels because they enable you to adjust a narrow tonal range, such as the highlights, quarter tones, midtones, three-quarter tones, or shadows. And, as with Levels, you can apply precise corrections to the composite channel (all the channels combined) or to individual color channels.

To adjust the color in an RGB image using the Curves controls: ★

Part 1: Apply tonal adjustments

1. Open an image that needs color adjustment. **A** (We'll apply Curves to the same unadjusted image that we used for our Levels adjustment so you can compare the results.)

2. On the **Adjustments** panel, ◑ click the **Curves** button.⊞ (We also chose Curves Display Options from the Adjustments panel menu, and checked all four Show options; see the sidebar on this page.)

3. First, adjust the shadows and highlights by doing any of the following:

   The **Input** sliders affect the lightest and darkest tonal values in the image. To increase the contrast, drag the black shadow Input slider and the white highlight Input slider inward to align with the ends of the histogram.**B** This will darken the shadows and brighten the highlights (the steeper the curve, the greater the contrast).

   To set the lightest and darkest values and thereby increase the contrast in **Threshold** mode (a high-contrast display of clipping), Alt-drag/Option-drag the black slider until a few areas of black appear; Alt-drag/Option-drag the white slider until a smidgeon of white appears. (You can do this for Levels, too!)

4. Do any of the following:

   A point is created when you move any part of the curve. As you do this, note the **Input** value, which is the current brightness value of the pixel you're adjusting, and the **Output** value, which is the value of that pixel after adjustment. If the Output value is higher than the Input value, you've lightened that pixel; an Output lower than Input shows you have darkened it.

   To **lighten** the **midtones**, drag the middle of the curve upward, or to **darken** the midtones, drag the middle of the curve downward.

A This image is underexposed and has a greenish cast.

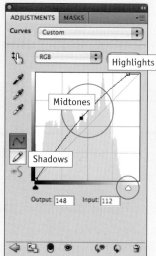

B In the Curves dialog, we moved the white slider inward toward the right end of the histogram to brighten the highlights and moved the middle of the curve upward to lighten the midtones.

USING THE DISPLAY OPTIONS IN CURVES

The four Show options in the Curves Display Options dialog are as follows:

Channel Overlays	Color channel curves and the composite curve
Histogram	Static histogram for the image
Baseline	Straight diagonal line representing no adjustments, for comparison
Intersection Line	Axis guides that appear as you move a point on the curve

Click the large grid button ⊞ to display quarter-tone grid lines, or click the small grid button ⊞ to display a finer grid.

To apply an adjustment by dragging in the image, click the **On-Image Adjustment** tool 🖑 and move the pointer over the image—a small circle appears on the curve. Drag upward to lighten or downward to darken those tonal values. A corresponding point appears on the curve.**A–C**

To nudge a selected point, press an arrow key. To remove a point, click it, then press Backspace/Delete; or Ctrl-click/Cmd-click it.

Keep the Curves controls showing. To correct the color, follow the instructions on the next page.

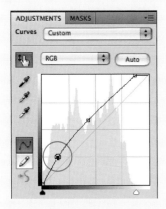

A We clicked the On-Image Adjustment tool, then dragged upward slightly on the trees to lighten the shadows. A curve point appeared.

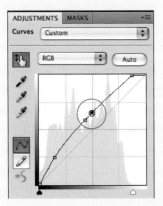

B Next, we dragged upward slightly with the tool on the brick to lighten the midtones in that area. Another curve point appeared.

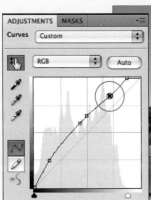

C Finally, we dragged downward on the clouds with the tool to recover details in the sky and path. Our adjustments improved the light/dark balance, but the image still has a greenish cast and looks undersaturated.

Part 2: Correct the color

1. With the Curves adjustment layer still selected, from the second menu, choose **Red** to adjust that channel separately.

2. Drag the midpoint of the curve upward to add more **red** to the **midtones** or downward to reduce red (this adjustment will also affect reds in the shadows and highlights slightly). This midtone adjustment is usually all that's required.

    You can also add or reduce red in the shadows by dragging the lower part of the curve or add or reduce red in the highlights by dragging the upper part of the curve.**A–B**

    ➤ Don't add too many points to the curve; try to keep it as smooth as possible.

3. Choose the **Green** channel, then the **Blue** channel, increasing or decreasing the amount of each color in the image by moving the curves, as in the previous step. You can switch back and forth between the color channels to readjust them as needed (**A–E**, next page).

4. *Optional:* To reduce the impact of the Curves adjustment layer, lower the layer opacity; or click the adjustment layer mask, then paint on the image with the Brush tool and the Foreground color set to black.

➤ With the On-Image Adjustment tool selected ![icon] and an individual color channel chosen from the menu, Ctrl-Shift-click/Cmd-Shift-click on the image to place a corresponding point on all the color channel curves (alas, no point will appear on the RGB curve).

➤ To save your adjustment settings as a preset, see pages 178–179.

USING CURVES ON A CMYK IMAGE

The Curves options work the opposite way for a CMYK Color image than for an RGB image:

➤ Readouts from the Curves graph are listed as percentages of ink. Black = 100%; white = 0%.

➤ Shadow values are in the upper right part of the curve, and highlights are in the lower left. Drag the curve downward to lighten a tonal value or upward to darken it. Similarly, for each individual color channel, you can drag the curve upward to add more of a color or downward to reduce it.

➤ The color pairs (cyan/red, magenta/green, and yellow/blue) work in tandem. For example, lowering cyan adds red, lowering magenta adds green, and lowering yellow adds blue.

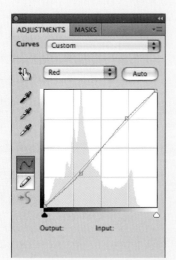

A We dragged the bottom part of the curve downward slightly to reduce red in the shadows and moved the upper part of the curve upward to add red to the highlights.

B Our adjustments to the Red channel in Curves were successful. We were able to add red only where needed: to the light areas on the building facade, sky, and path.

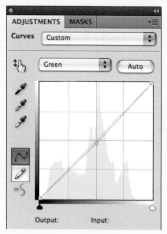

A We dragged the Green channel curve downward slightly to reduce green throughout the image.

B Reducing green by adjusting the Green channel added more red and blue to the image, which was our goal.

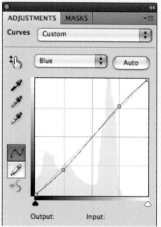

C We dragged the lower part of the Blue curve downward to reduce blue in the shadows and raised the upper part to increase blue in the sky.

D This is the cumulative result of all our Curves adjustments.

WHICH ONE DID A BETTER JOB?

➤ Curves **D** brought out more shadow details in the trees on the right side, whereas Levels **E** left those areas fairly flat.

➤ Using Curves, we were able to control the color of the brick more precisely (it's neither too red nor too green), whereas Levels left the brick too pink.

➤ Using Curves, we were able to adjust specific highlights and achieve a better balance between the reds and blues in the sky and the path, while keeping the stone railing neutral. Levels left those areas too red.

E For comparison, this is the result of our Levels adjustments.

APPLYING ADJUSTMENT SETTINGS TO MULTIPLE IMAGES ★

Gather a series of photos that were shot under the same lighting conditions and require the same color correction, and open them into a tabbed window. Adjust one of them via a Levels, Curves, Exposure, Hue/Saturation, Black & White, Channel Mixer, or Selective Color adjustment layer, then save your settings as a preset via the panel menu.**A** Click another document tab,

create the same type of adjustment layer, then choose your saved preset from the Preset menu.**B** Or to copy adjustment settings for controls that can't be saved as a preset, on the Arrange menu on the Application bar, click an appropriate "Up" button to tile the documents. Drag and drop the adjustment layer from the Layers panel of the corrected document into each of the other documents.

A We corrected a photo via a Levels adjustment layer, then saved our settings as a preset.

B We clicked the tab for another photo in the same series, created a Levels adjustment layer, then chose our saved settings preset from the Preset menu on the Adjustments panel.

You'll need to choose brush settings when using the Brush tool, and also for many other tasks, such as when editing a Quick Mask or layer mask "by hand" or when using the History Brush or Healing Brush tool. In this chapter, you'll master the Brush tool, use the Brush Preset picker and Brushes panel to customize your brush settings, smudge colors with the Smudge tool, and erase parts of a layer with the Eraser and Magic Eraser tools.

Using the Brush tool

Before getting into the complexities of custom brush presets, take a few minutes to get acquainted with the Brush tool. In these instructions, you'll choose an existing brush preset (brush tip) for the Brush tool and choose Options bar settings to control the tool's behavior. In the next section, you'll learn how to customize brush presets via the Brushes panel.

To use the Brush tool:

1. Click an image layer or create a new layer.
   Optional: Create a selection if you want to confine your brush strokes to a specific area.

2. Choose the **Brush** tool ✐ (B or Shift-B).

3. Choose a **Foreground** color.

4. On the Options bar, do the following:

   Click the **Brush Preset** picker arrowhead or thumbnail, then click a preset.**A**

   Choose a blending **Mode** (see pages 198–202).

   Choose an **Opacity** percentage. At 100%, the stroke will completely cover underlying pixels.

   Choose a **Flow** percentage to control how fully and smoothly the brush applies paint.

Continued on the following page

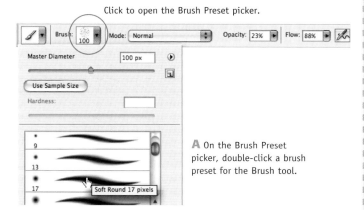

Click to open the Brush Preset picker.

A On the Brush Preset picker, double-click a brush preset for the Brush tool.

IN THIS CHAPTER

Using the Brush tool. 223

Choosing temporary brush settings . .224

Using the Brushes panel 225

Customizing brushes. 226

Smudging colors 230

Using the Eraser tool 231

Using the Magic Eraser tool 232

Click the **Airbrush** button 🖌 to have paint spread and build up when you hold down the mouse, as in traditional airbrushing.

5. Draw strokes in the document window. If the Airbrush option is on and you press and hold in one spot, the paint drop will gradually widen (up to the maximum diameter of the brush) and become more dense and opaque.**A–B** Feel free to change Options bar settings between strokes.

➤ On the Layers panel, click the Lock Transparent Pixels button ⊠ for the current layer to allow the tool to recolor only nontransparent pixels.

➤ To draw a straight stroke, hold down Shift while dragging; or click in a starting location, then Shift-click to end the stroke.

➤ To sample colors with a temporary Eyedropper while using a painting tool, Alt-click/Option-click anywhere in the document window.

Choosing temporary brush settings

Each brush preset has its own built-in Master Diameter and Hardness settings, but you can make temporary changes to either setting via a context menu or the Options bar.

To choose temporary settings for a brush preset:

1. Choose any tool that uses brush presets, such as the Brush, Pencil, Dodge, Burn, or Eraser tool.

2. Do either of the following:

   Right-click/Control-click in the document window, then change the **Master Diameter** and, if available, the **Hardness** setting.**C** These settings can also be changed on the Brush Preset picker (see **A**, previous page).

   To change the brush diameter interactively, Alt-right-click-drag/Control-Option-drag to the left or right. If OpenGL is turned on in Preferences > Performance, a color will display within the brush cursor as you scale it. ★

3. Press Enter/Return or just start dragging in the document window. Your settings will remain in effect only until you choose a different preset.

A This brush stroke was created with the Airbrush option off.

B This brush stroke was created with the Airbrush option on.

C You can change the Master Diameter and Hardness for a preset quickly via the context menu.

SHORTCUTS FOR CHANGING TOOL SETTINGS

When using the Brush, Burn, Clone Stamp, Dodge, Healing Brush, Paint Bucket, Pencil, or Smudge tool, you can use some or all of these shortcuts:

Cycle through the blending modes for the tool	Shift- + (plus) or Shift- - (minus)
Decrease or increase the master diameter for a brush preset	[or]
Change the opacity, exposure, or strength percentage* (Shift-press a number to change the Flow level**)	0–9 (e.g., 2 = 20%) or quickly type a percentage (e.g. "38"); 0 = 100%

*If the Airbrush option is on, press a number to change the Flow percentage or Shift-press a number to change the Opacity percentage.

**When Shift-pressing in Windows, use the numbers on the main keyboard, not on the keypad.

Using the Brushes panel

The Brushes panel offers a huge assortment of options for customizing brush presets. The presets, in turn, are available for the Brush, Pencil, History Brush, Art History Brush, Clone Stamp, Pattern Stamp, Eraser, Blur, Sharpen, Smudge, Dodge, Burn, and Sponge tools.

The first step is to familiarize yourself with the Brushes panel. This is "Brushes Panel 101"; in the next set of instructions, you'll explore panel settings.

To use the Brushes panel:

1. Choose one of the tools listed in the first paragraph on this page.

2. To show the Brushes panel, click the panel tab or icon 🖌; or choose Window > Brushes (F5); or click the Toggle Panel button 🖹 on the Options bar.

3. If you don't see a list of option sets on the left side of the panel, A choose **Expanded View** from the panel menu. To resize the panel, drag any corner or edge. ★

4. Check the **box** for any of the first six option sets to **activate** the features for that set. If a set name is dimmed, it means it's not available for the current tool. The option sets are discussed in depth in the next set of instructions.

5. To display the **options** for an option set, click the set **name**, such as Scattering or Texture. The bottom five options can be checked on and off, but you can't choose settings for them.

6. To choose a different **display** type for the panel, click **Brush Presets** in the upper left corner of the panel, then from the panel menu, choose Text Only, Small Thumbnail, Large Thumbnail, Small List, Large List, or Stroke Thumbnail. The "Small" choices make the list more compact, whereas the "Large" choices enable you to see the brush tips more easily.

► To learn how to load additional brush preset libraries onto the picker, see page 403.

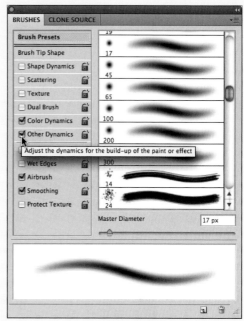

A Use the Brushes panel to choose and customize brush presets.

Customizing brushes

The options that you can use to customize a brush preset are organized into sets on the Brushes panel, except for a handful of options that you can simply switch on or off. Some features apply specifically to input devices for a stylus. Your choices for customizing brush presets are infinite, but we'll make the job manageable for you by listing the features we use most often separately from the ones we rarely touch (writing a book is more fun when you can reveal your biases). You can pick and choose among the various options to create your dream brush.

Note: Custom settings you choose for a preset are lost as soon as you choose another preset. In step 9, we'll show you how to save your custom brush as a new preset. Note also that brush presets are used with many other tools besides the Brush tool. Keep this in mind when you read the word "pigment" in our instructions.

To customize a brush preset (main course):

1. Choose a tool that uses brush presets, and show the Brushes panel. 🖌

2. Click **Brush Presets A** in the upper left corner of the Brushes panel, then click a preset on the right side of the panel (scroll down the list, if necessary).

3. To change basic shape and/or size settings for the chosen preset, click **Brush Tip Shape** at the top of the list, **B** then keep an eye on the brush preview at the bottom of the panel as you make any of these changes:

   To change the **Diameter** (brush size), move the slider or enter a value (1–2500 pixels).

   To change the **Angle** (brush slant), use the scrubby slider, or drag the arrowhead around the circle, or enter a new Angle.

   To change the **Roundness** (brush shape), **C** use the scrubby slider (0–100%) or drag either of the two tiny dark circles on the ellipse inward or outward.

   To change the **Hardness** (feather or sharpen the edge of the brush), **D** move the slider or enter a value (0–100%). This option isn't available for all brush tips.

   To control the distance between marks within the stroke, check **Spacing**, then move the slider (1–1000%). **E–F**

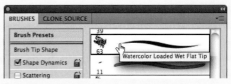

A Click Brush Presets on the left side of the Brushes panel, then click a preset on the right.

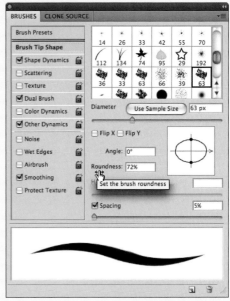

B The preview at the bottom of the Brushes panel updates dynamically as you change settings.

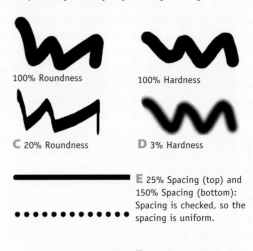

100% Roundness

100% Hardness

C 20% Roundness

D 3% Hardness

E 25% Spacing (top) and 150% Spacing (bottom): Spacing is checked, so the spacing is uniform.

F A slow stroke (top) and a fast stroke (bottom): Spacing is unchecked, so the spacing is uneven.

4. To control how much variation is allowable in the brush tip shape, click **Shape Dynamics** (click the words—the box will become checked automatically), then do any of the following:

Change the **Size Jitter,** 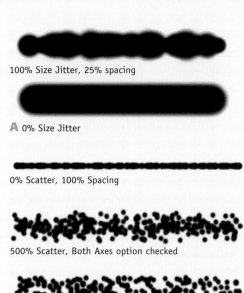 **Angle Jitter**, and **Roundness Jitter** values to establish variation parameters for those attributes. "Jitter" is the amount of random variation allowable for that option. These variations are more noticeable when the Spacing value (in the Brush Tip Shape option set) is greater than 10%.

From the **Control** menus, choose a feature for your stylus to control that option's variation directly. Note that variations will occur even if you choose Off.

Change the **Minimum Diameter** value for the brush size variations.

5. To control the placement of pigment in the stroke, click **Scattering**, then do any of the following:

Check **Both Axes** **B** to scatter pigment along and perpendicular to the path you draw, or uncheck Both Axes to scatter pigment perpendicular to, but not along, the path. Also choose a Control option, if desired.

Change the **Scatter** value (1–1000%) to control how far pigment can veer off the path you draw. The lower the Scatter value, the more solid the stroke.

Change the **Count** value (1–16) to control the overall density (amount of pigment) in the stroke.

Change the **Count Jitter** value **C** (0–100%) to control how much the Count (density) can vary.

6. To control how randomly the overall stroke opacity can vary as you use the tool, click **Other Dynamics**, then do any of the following:

Change the **Opacity Jitter** (0–100%) **D–F** for the amount the opacity can vary. Choose a Control option to control fading.

Change the **Flow Jitter** (0–100%) to control how smoothly the pigment is applied. A high Flow Jitter will make the stroke blotchy, but that may be the look you're after. Choose a Control option.

Continued on the following page

100% Size Jitter, 25% spacing

A 0% Size Jitter

0% Scatter, 100% Spacing

500% Scatter, Both Axes option checked

B 500% Scatter, Both Axes option unchecked

0% Count Jitter, 100% Spacing

C 100% Count Jitter: The Count varies randomly from 1% to 100% of the Count value.

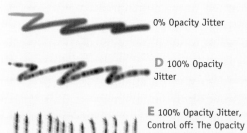

0% Opacity Jitter

D 100% Opacity Jitter

E 100% Opacity Jitter, Control off: The Opacity varies randomly from 1% to 100%.

F 0% Opacity Jitter, Control set to Pen Pressure: The Opacity is controlled by the amount of pressure exerted on the tablet by the stylus.

7. And last but not least (you're almost done!), check any or all of these options:

Noise to add random grain to your brush strokes to make them more rough-looking.

Wet Edges to simulate the buildup of pigment that occurs at the edges of brush strokes in traditional watercoloring. **A–D**

Airbrush to allow a stroke to build up for as long as the mouse button is held down in the same spot. Clicking the Airbrush ✍ button on the Options bar does the same thing.

Smoothing to draw smoother curves.

Protect Texture to apply the same texture pattern and scale to other brushes that currently use the Texture option, or to which you add a texture option, for a uniform surface texture across the entire canvas.

8. *Optional:* Click an open lock icon 🔓 next to the name of any option set to prevent the current settings for that set from being edited, even if you change presets (note the closed lock icon). Locked settings are applied, but not saved, to any other preset you choose. Click a closed lock icon to make those settings editable again. (To unlock all locked settings, choose Reset All Locked Settings from the panel menu.)

9. Changes made to a preset remain in effect only until you choose a different preset. To save your custom preset for future use (which we recommend), click the **New Brush** button 🔳 at the bottom of the panel or choose **New Brush Preset** from the panel menu. Change the name in the Brush Name dialog, if desired, then click OK. To learn about saving and managing brush preset libraries, see pages 400–403.

A This image was created with the Brush tool using various presets and settings.

B The Wet Edges option produced the pooling effect in this image.

C This stroke was drawn with Wet Edges unchecked.

D This stroke was drawn with Wet Edges checked.

To customize a brush preset (side dishes):

1. Choose a tool that uses brush presets, and show the Brushes panel.

2. To use the texture from a pattern in your brush strokes, click **Texture** on the left side of the panel, then monitor the preview as you do any of the following:

   Click the **Pattern Preset** arrowhead, then click a pattern in the picker.

   Check **Invert** to swap the light and dark areas in the pattern.

   Change the **Scale** of the texture (1–1000%).

   Check **Texture Each Tip** to allow the Depth (see below) to vary within each stroke, or uncheck to keep the Depth value constant.

   Choose a blending **Mode** to control how the texture mixes with the brush stroke.

   Choose a **Depth** value (0–100%) **B** to control how deeply paint sinks into the texture. At a high Depth value, paint is applied only to the high points in the texture, which makes the texture more prominent.

   If you checked Texture Each Tip, you can choose a **Minimum Depth** to keep the texture from looking too flat. Some brushes reveal texture more than others. Also choose a **Depth Jitter** value to control how much the Depth can vary, and choose an option from the Control menu to specify if and how the stroke can fade.

3. To make the brush preset more interesting, you can add another tip to it. Click **Dual Brush,C** click a tip; choose a Mode to control how the two tips interact with each other, then choose Diameter, Spacing, Scatter, and Count values.

4. To control how much the color can vary as you use the brush, click **Color Dynamics**, then do any of the following:

   Choose a **Foreground/Background Jitter** value **D** for the amount of allowable variation between the Foreground and Background colors. Choose an option from the Control menu to specify if and how colors can fade.

   Choose **Hue Jitter**, **Saturation Jitter**, and **Brightness Jitter** values to establish variation parameters for those attributes.

   Choose a **Purity** value to control the degree of color saturation in the stroke.

GETTING BACK TO A SAVED PRESET

To restore the saved settings to a brush preset, click Brush Presets on the Brushes panel, then click the preset again.

A These strokes were drawn using a texture preset, with Pen Pressure chosen as the Opacity Jitter Control.

50% Texture Depth

B 100% Texture Depth

Primary brush tip

Secondary brush tip

C Tips combined using the Dual Brush option, Linear Burn mode

0% Foreground/Background Jitter

D 100% Foreground/Background Jitter

Smudging colors

To smudge colors:

1. Click an image layer.

2. Choose the **Smudge** tool 🖐 (it's on the Blur tool pop-out menu).

3. On the Options bar, do the following:

   Click a brush preset on the **Brush Preset** picker.

   Choose a blending **Mode**. **Normal** smudges all shades or colors; **Darken** pushes only dark colors into lighter ones; **Lighten** pushes only light colors into darker ones; **Hue**, **Saturation**, and **Color** smudge only that color attribute without changing the tonal (light and dark) values; and **Luminosity** smudges tonal values without changing the hues.

   Choose a **Strength** percentage to control how forcefully the stroke smudges pixels.

   Check **Sample All Layers** to smudge colors found on all the currently visible layers and send the results to the active layer (uncheck Finger Painting if you use this option); or uncheck Sample All Layers to smudge colors from only the currently selected layer.

   To start the smudge with the current Foreground color, check **Finger Painting**; or leave this option unchecked to have the smudge start with the color under the pointer where the stroke begins. (For your first use of the Smudge tool, we recommend keeping this option off.)

4. Press [or] or Alt-right-click-drag/Control-Option-drag sideways if you want to adjust the diameter of the brush tip, then drag across any area of the image.**A–D** Pause between strokes, if necessary, to allow the screen to redraw.

➤ To toggle the Finger Painting option on or off for the Smudge tool, hold down Alt/Option.

A This is the original image.

B With Normal mode chosen for the Smudge tool, all colors were smudgeable.

C With Lighten mode chosen, only light colors smudged.

D With Color mode chosen, hues smudged but luminosity values did not.

Using the Eraser tool

The Eraser tool is handy for removing stray blobs, perhaps to tidy up after deleting most of the background area behind an object or for erasing part of a layer in an isolated area.

Note: The Eraser tool results are permanent, so you may want to work on a duplicate layer. As an alternative to using this tool, you can block out part of a layer with an editable and removable layer mask (see pages 302–303).

To use the Eraser tool:

1. Choose the **Eraser** tool ⬬ (E or Shift-E).

2. On the Options bar, do the following:

   Choose a brush preset from the **Brush Preset** picker.

   Choose **Mode: Brush**, **Pencil**, or **Block**. For the Block option (a square-shaped eraser), no Options bar settings are available.

   Choose an **Opacity** percentage.

   If you chose Brush mode, you can choose a **Flow** percentage to control the uniformity of the erasure.

   Click the **Airbrush** button off.

3. Click a layer or the Background (or create a duplicate layer).

4. Decide whether to click the **Lock Transparent Pixels** button ▣ on or off:

   If Lock Transparent Pixels is on for the currently selected layer (or you clicked the Background), the area you erase is going to fill with the current Background color; choose that color now.**A**

   If Lock Transparent Pixels is off for the current layer, the erased area will fill with transparency.

5. To change the brush **diameter** interactively, press [or] or Alt-right-click-drag/Control-Option-drag sideways. If you want to adjust the diameter of the brush tip, then click on or drag across the area(s) of the image that you want to erase.**B–C**

A We used the Eyedropper tool to sample the white background color first, then pressed X to swap the Foreground and Background colors.

B Next, we're using the Eraser tool (80% Opacity) to erase four of the "dots" of sauce. Because we clicked Lock Transparent Pixels on for the layer, the erased area is being replaced by the current Background color (the color we sampled with the Eyedropper).

C All the dots are erased in the final image.

Using the Magic Eraser tool

With the Magic Eraser, you erase only by clicking with the mouse, not by dragging. The tool erases only pixels that are similar in color to the pixel you click on, within a user-defined tolerance range. Unlike the Background Eraser, you can lower the Magic Eraser tool opacity to render areas of a layer semitransparent.

To use the Magic Eraser tool:

1. Click an image layer; or click the Background, duplicate it, and keep the duplicate selected.**A** If you edit a layer with transparency unlocked, the erased pixels will be replaced with transparency; if you edit a layer with transparency locked, choose a Background color to replace the erased pixels.

2. Choose the **Magic Eraser** tool 🧽 (E or Shift-E).

3. On the Options bar, do the following:

    Choose a **Tolerance** value (you could start with a value of around 30). The higher the Tolerance, the wider the range of colors the tool can erase. To erase only colors that are very similar to the color you click on, choose a lower Tolerance of around 5–8; or to erase just one color, make the Tolerance 0.

    Check **Anti-alias** to slightly soften the edges of the erasure.

    Check **Contiguous** to erase only pixels that are adjacent to one another, or uncheck this option to erase similarly colored pixels throughout the currently selected layer.

    Check **Sample All Layers** to erase colors found on all the currently visible layers, or uncheck this option to erase colors found only on the current layer. We find it easier to control what we're erasing when this option is unchecked.

    Choose an **Opacity** percentage of 100% to replace colored pixels with transparent ones, or choose a lower opacity to replace them with semitransparent pixels.

4. In the document window, click the area that you want to erase.**B–C** To make it easier to position the pointer, press Caps Lock to turn the pointer into crosshairs.

➤ If the erasure is too large or small, either undo or click a prior state on the History panel, change the Tolerance value on the Options bar, then click again with the Magic Eraser tool.

A The sky in this image is mostly uniform in color and is lighter than the areas adjacent to it, so the Magic Eraser tool should be able to remove it with just a couple of clicks. Our first step was to duplicate the Background, then hide it.

B The first click of the Magic Eraser tool removed most of the sky (tool settings of Tolerance 38, Contiguous on, and Opacity 100%), and a click on the remaining section of sky finished the job.

C After removing the sky, we created a new layer, filled it with a solid color, and restacked it below the duplicate image layer.

The beauty of the Adobe Camera Raw plug-in is that it lets you apply corrections to your photos before opening them into Photoshop. In this chapter, in addition to learning how to open digital photos via the Camera Raw plug-in (it's called "Camera Raw," for short), you'll also use the many tabs in Camera Raw to correct photos for exposure, color, and lighting deficiencies and other defects.

Why use Camera Raw?

Whereas amateur-level digital cameras store images in the JPEG or TIFF format, advanced amateur and pro models offer the option to save images as raw files, which offers substantial advantages. For the JPEG or TIFF format, the camera also performs internal processing operations, such as sharpening, setting the white balance, and making color adjustments. With raw files, you get only the raw information that the lens captured onto its digital sensor, leaving you with full control over subsequent image processing and correction. Each camera manufacturer creates its own variation of a raw file. (See our comparison of JPEG vs. raw on page 235.)

The following are some of the key features of the Camera Raw plug-in:

➤ Camera Raw processes raw files from most of the current camera manufacturers, as well as digital TIFF and JPEG photos.

➤ Camera Raw offers powerful features for adjusting the exposure, color, tonal range, noise, and other attributes of your photos, and you can monitor your corrections via a large preview.

➤ For raw files, Camera Raw edits (stored as instructions) are saved in a "sidecar" file or the Camera Raw database. For TIFF and JPEG files, the instructions are saved in the photo itself. In either case, when you open a file from Camera Raw into Photoshop, the instructions are applied to a copy of the file; the original digital files are preserved (like traditional film negatives).

➤ Camera Raw lets you convert photos to a few standard formats, such as PSD or TIFF. You can also save your files in any standard format after opening them in Photoshop.

Note: Don't confuse raw files from a camera with Photoshop Raw, which is available as a Format in the File > Save/Save As dialog.

Continued on the following page

CAMERA RAW

15

IN THIS CHAPTER

Why use Camera Raw?. 233

Choosing preferences for opening
    photos 236

Opening photos into Camera Raw . . .237

The Camera Raw tools 239

Cropping and straightening photos . .240

Retouching photos. 241

Changing the Workflow options 241

Using the Basic tab 242

Using the Tone Curve tab. 246

Using the HSL/Grayscale tab 248

Using the Detail tab 250

Saving and applying Camera
    Raw settings 251

Using the Adjustment Brush 252

Synchronizing Camera Raw settings. .254

Opening and saving Camera
    Raw files 255

Opening and placing photos as
    Smart Objects 256

More reasons to use Camera Raw

The Camera Raw plug-in offers some powerful and unique features that you won't find in Photoshop. In case you're not fully convinced, we'll outline some compelling reasons for using the Camera Raw plug-in instead of opening your digital photos directly into Photoshop.

Raw preview: The only way to preview an actual raw photo (not the JPEG version of a file) is via a raw converter, such as Camera Raw.

Less destructive: Exposure, white balance, and color adjustments that you apply in Camera Raw cause less destruction to an image than adjustment commands in Photoshop. Remember, the goal is to preserve as much original data as possible.

16 bits per channel: To preserve the full tonal range of a raw photo, you can use Camera Raw to produce a 16-bits-per-channel file. Starting with all the original data at the outset helps offset the data loss that image edits cause in Photoshop. The end result is a better-quality image.

Tonal redistribution: A bonus feature of Camera Raw is that it fixes a "problem" inherent in all digital photos: the fact that the digital sensor in a camera records data in a linear fashion. The sensor captures the existing range of tonal values in a scene without altering the resulting data. More data is used to capture lights values than dark values.**A** The human eye, however, is more sensitive to lower levels of light than to brighter levels. That is, we're more likely to notice a lack of detail in the shadows and less likely to notice extra details in the highlights. By shifting data into the midtone and shadow ranges, Camera Raw produces an image that more closely approximates human vision. The graph of this restribution is curved rather than straight.**B** When there is insufficient data in the shadow areas, tonal adjustments

---

CAPTURING TONAL VALUES: A CAMERA VERSUS THE HUMAN EYE

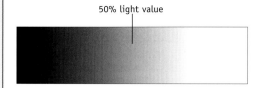

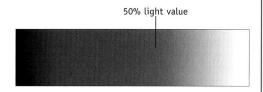

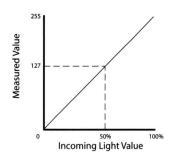

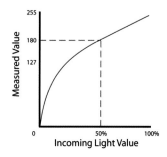

A The digital sensor in a camera captures tonal values in a linear fashion, from light to dark. The incoming data isn't altered, so this graph of the linear capture shows a straight line. A light value of 50% is located in the center of the tonal range.

B Camera Raw performs tonal redistribution to shift data to the lower levels. Incoming data is altered, so the graph is now curved. The 50% light value was shifted to the right of center (of the tonal range), so there is now more detail in the lower levels, the range the human eye is more sensitive to.

in Photoshop cause posterization and a loss of detail. With its extra midtone and shadow data, an image converted by Camera Raw is better able to withstand Photoshop edits.

Noise reduction and **sharpening**: The noise reduction and sharpening features in Camera Raw are simpler, less destructive, and more effective than similar commands in Photoshop.

You're halfway there: Camera Raw features that you'll use to adjust the tonal and color balance in your photos are similar to adjustment controls (such as Levels, Curves, and Hue/Saturation) that you learned about in earlier chapters, so you'll be able to build on your present skills.

The skinny: To correct and enhance digital photos in preparation for work in Photoshop, Camera Raw is an ideal launch pad.

Raw, JPEG, or TIFF?

In addition to raw files, photos that a camera saves in the JPEG or TIFF format can also be opened and edited in Camera Raw. Although more Camera Raw features are available for raw photos than for JPEG and TIFF photos, if your camera doesn't shoot raw photos or you acquire JPEG or TIFF photos from other sources, you can still use most of the Camera Raw features to process them.

Unfortunately, Camera Raw can't correct deficiencies in JPEG and TIFF photos as fully as it can in raw photos, for several reasons. First, the camera records the tonal range of JPEG and TIFF photos in only 8 bits per channel. Second, color and tonal processing is applied to JPEGs and TIFFs by the camera ("in camera"). Camera Raw reinterprets this processed data, with less successful results than when it has access to the raw, unprocessed data. And finally, the editing instructions are saved in the files themselves (processing is applied to the original pixels), not in the sidecar or database file, as is the case with raw files.

Nonetheless, you can use the many outstanding correction and adjustment features in Camera Raw to improve your JPEG and TIFF photos.

Note: In this chapter, we focus only on processing raw and JPEG files in Camera Raw—not TIFFs, and we mention the JPEG format in our steps only when a feature behaves differently for JPEGs.

JPEG...

JPEG pluses

JPEG files are smaller in storage size than raw files, so your digital camera can store more of them. JPEG files have shorter transfer speeds, so they can be created and stored more quickly by a camera than raw files. This allows for faster shot sequencing, which is a necessity for sports, nature, and other quick-motion photography.

Most software programs can read JPEG files.

JPEG drawbacks

JPEG compression methods lower the image quality and can produce defects, such as artifacts, banding, and loss of detail.

When a camera processes and saves photos in the JPEG format, it performs in-camera image-processing operations that alter the original pixel data. The camera also reduces the original tonal range to 8 bits per channel for the JPEG format. Although you can apply adjustments to your photos in Camera Raw, you can't retrieve all of the original pixel data.

...VERSUS RAW

Raw pluses

The raw compression methods are lossless.

Raw preserves the original, unprocessed pixel information that was captured by your camera.

Raw files can be opened as 16-bits-per-channel files into Photoshop.

Raw files contain the full range of tonal levels that were captured by the camera.

Because the white point setting isn't applied to raw pixels when a photo is shot (it's just stored in the metadata of the file), you can adjust this setting in Camera Raw.

In Camera Raw, higher-quality adjustments can be made to raw files than to JPEG files.

Camera Raw does a better job of redistributing tonal values in raw files, which makes them better candidates for Photoshop edits.

Raw drawbacks

Digital cameras create and store raw files more slowly than JPEG files.

Raw files have larger storage sizes than JPEG files.

The bottom line

Although JPEG offers the advantage of speed, which is useful for action photography, for most purposes, raw is the clear winner.

Choosing preferences for opening photos ★

Setting a preference to have your JPEG or TIFF photos open directly into Camera Raw instead of Photoshop is simpler in Photoshop CS4 than it was in CS3.

To ensure that your raw photos open directly into Camera Raw:

In Photoshop, choose Edit (Adobe Photoshop CS4, in the Mac OS) > Preferences, then click File Handling on the left side. Check Prefer **Adobe Camera Raw for Supported Raw Files**, then click OK. With this option on, raw files will open into the Camera Raw dialog (as opposed to other software that converts raw files) when double-clicked.

To ensure that your JPEG or TIFF photos open directly into Camera Raw:

In Bridge, choose Edit (Adobe Bridge CS4, in the Mac OS) > Camera Raw Preferences. At the bottom of the dialog, from the JPEG menu, choose **Automatically Open JPEGs with Settings**, and from the TIFF menu, choose **Automatically Open TIFFs with Settings**.

Now when you click a JPEG or TIFF photo thumbnail in Bridge, and then click the Open in Camera Raw button 🔄 or press Ctrl-R/ Cmd-R, the file will open into Camera Raw.

► If you have chosen the pertinent Automatically Open… options but for some reason you want to open a JPEG or TIFF photo directly into Photoshop instead of into Camera Raw (and if the file hasn't yet been edited in Camera Raw), click the thumbnail, then press Ctrl-O/Cmd-O.

► If the Open in Camera Raw button is available when you click a thumbnail, you know that image can be opened into Camera Raw.

To choose a host for Camera Raw:

In Bridge, choose Edit (Adobe Bridge CS4, in the Mac OS) > Preferences (Ctrl-K/Cmd-K), then click General on the left side. Check **Double-Click Edits Camera Raw Settings in Bridge** if you want the Camera Raw dialog to be hosted by Bridge when you double-click the thumbnail for a raw, JPEG, or TIFF thumbnail photo in Bridge. If this preference is unchecked and you double-click the thumbnail for a raw, JPEG, or TIFF photo, it will open into Camera Raw, hosted by Photoshop.

Note: If Bridge is the host for Camera Raw, the default button for exiting the dialog is labeled Done, whereas if Photoshop is the host for Camera Raw, the default button is Open Image.*

WHAT WE DO

If you shoot only raw or JPEG photos (as we do) — not TIFF photos — you can follow the two suggestions below to have your raw and JPEG photos always open into Camera Raw and your TIFF files always open directly into Photoshop.

► In Camera Raw Preferences, under JPEG and TIFF Handling, choose JPEG: Automatically Open JPEGs with Settings and choose TIFF: Disable TIFF Support.

► In Bridge Preferences, check Double-Click Edits Camera Raw Settings in Bridge.

WHAT'S THAT FUNNY SYMBOL?

If a file has been opened and edited previously in Camera Raw, it will have this badge 🔄 in the upper right corner of the thumbnail in Bridge, and the current Camera Raw settings will be reflected in the thumbnail and preview. Also, if the currently selected file has been edited in Camera Raw, the Metadata panel will have a Camera Raw category.

► Each digital camera model attaches a different extension to its raw file names, such as .nef for Nikon, .crw or .cr2 for Canon, and .dcr for Kodak.

---

*If you see an Open Object button instead of an Open Image button, see the first tip on page 256.

Opening photos into Camera Raw

Note: If you shoot JPEG photos, follow the second set of instructions on the previous page before proceeding.

To open a raw or JPEG digital photo into Camera Raw:

1. Launch Bridge, display the thumbnail for the raw or JPEG photo you want to open, then do one of the following:

   Double-click the thumbnail.

   Click the thumbnail, then press Ctrl-R/Cmd-R.

   Click the thumbnail, then click the **Open in Camera Raw** button 🔄. ★

2. The Camera Raw dialog opens.**A** An alert symbol displays in the upper right corner of the preview window while the image data is reading in, and disappears when it's done.

   Information about your photo (taken from the metadata the camera embedded into it) is listed in several locations: the camera model, in the title bar at the top of the dialog; the file name, below the preview; and the camera

settings used to take the photo (aperture, shutter speed, ISO sensitivity, and focal length), below the histogram. The underlined link below the preview gets you to the Workflow Options dialog (see page 241).

The image adjustment options are distributed among eight tabs—Basic, Tone Curve, Detail, HSL/Grayscale, Split Toning, Lens Corrections, Camera Calibration, and Presets—which you'll use to correct your photo (**A–B**, next page). We'll explore most of them in this chapter.

When you're done making adjustments, you can either click Open Image to open the photo into Photoshop or click Done to close Camera Raw without opening the photo. In either case, the Camera Raw settings stick with the photo and the original data is preserved.

A The Camera Raw dialog

Camera model

Toggle Full-Screen Mode/previous dialog size (F)

Toolbox

Histogram

Camera settings

Tabs for accessing settings

Camera Raw Settings menu

Preview

Zoom controls

See also the figures on the following page

Link to the Workflow Options dialog to set the color space, bit depth, dimensions, and resolution

Tone Curve   HSL/Grayscale   Lens Corrections   Presets

Basic   Detail   Split Toning   Camera Calibration

A Click a tab icon to access specialized options.

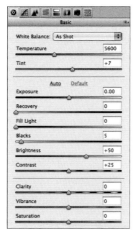

Use the Basic tab to adjust the white balance and exposure (see pages 242–245).

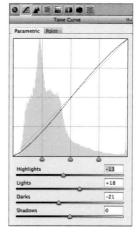

Use the Tone Curve tab to fine-tune the exposure (see pages 246–247).

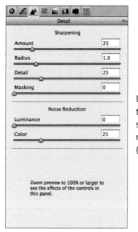

Use the Detail tab to apply sharpening and noise reduction (see page 250).

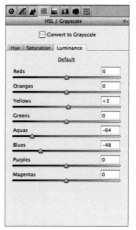

Use the HSL/Grayscale tab to adjust colors individually (see pages 248–249).

B Four of the eight tabs in Camera Raw are illustrated here. We tend to do most of our correction work in the Basic, Tone Curve, and HSL/Grayscale tabs.

KEEPING CAMERA RAW UP TO DATE

Of the many proprietary raw "formats," some are unique to particular manufacturers (such as Nikon or Canon) and some are unique to particular camera models. To ensure that the latest interpreters for the raw formats that Camera Raw supports are installed in your system, visit www.adobe.com periodically and download any Camera Raw updates that are available for your camera.

The Camera Raw tools

In the upper left corner of the dialog, A click the **Zoom** tool 🔍, then click the image preview to zoom in or Alt-click/Option-click it to zoom out.

Use the **Hand** tool 🖐 to move a magnified preview image in its window. Hold down Spacebar for a temporary Hand tool.

For the **White Balance** tool 🖋, see page 242.

Choose the **Color Sampler** tool 🖋, then click in the image preview to place up to nine samplers. Readouts of the RGB components for the pixels below each sampler display below the tools, and update as you make color and tonal adjustments to the photo. To reposition a sampler, drag it with the Color Sampler tool. To remove all samplers, click Clear Samplers.

To use the **Crop** ⛶, **Straighten** ⟋, and **Spot Removal** ⟋ tools, see the following two pages.

The **Red Eye Removal** tool 🔴 works like the Red Eye tool in Photoshop (see page 296).

For the **Adjustment Brush** tool 🖌, see pages 252–253. ★

For the **Graduated Filter** tool ▭, see Photoshop Help. ★

Click the **Open Preferences Dialog** button ☰ (Ctrl-K/Cmd-K) to open the Camera Raw Preferences dialog.

Use the **Rotate 90° Counterclockwise** button ↺ or **Rotate 90° Clockwise** button ↻ to rotate the image; the results preview in the dialog.

Check **Preview** (P) to preview changes made in all the tabs; or uncheck it to see changes made in all tabs except the current one so you can evaluate your most recent changes.

Click the **Toggle Full Screen Mode** button ⬚ (F) to enlarge the dialog to fill your screen; click it again to restore the previous dialog size.

Note: If tool settings are displaying in the Camera Raw dialog (say you were using the Adjustment Brush tool) and you want to redisplay the tabs, click one of the first six tools.

➤ The tools in Camera Raw are "memory-loaded," meaning you can press a tool shortcut key to select a tool, then press the same key again to reselect the last tool. ★

MORE WAYS TO ZOOM

➤ Press Ctrl –/Cmd – (hyphen) to zoom out or Ctrl-+/Cmd-+ to zoom in.

➤ Use the Zoom Level menu or zoom buttons (– or +), located below the image preview.

➤ Double-click the Zoom tool to change the zoom level to 100%.

➤ Double-click the Hand tool to change the zoom level to Fit in View.

BUTTON TOGGLES

When you hold down Alt/Option in the Camera Raw dialog, the functions of these buttons change:

➤ Save Image… becomes Save Image, which bypasses the Save Options dialog.

➤ Open Image becomes Open Copy (see page 255).

➤ Cancel becomes Reset, which restores all of the original dialog settings.

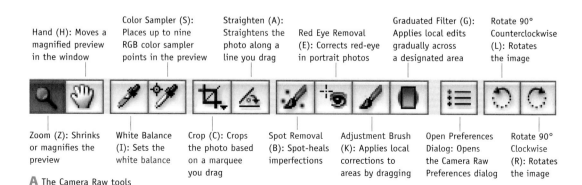

| Hand (H): Moves a magnified preview in the window | Color Sampler (S): Places up to nine RGB color sampler points in the preview | Straighten (A): Straightens the photo along a line you drag | Red Eye Removal (E): Corrects red-eye in portrait photos | Graduated Filter (G): Applies local edits gradually across a designated area | Rotate 90° Counterclockwise (L): Rotates the image |

| Zoom (Z): Shrinks or magnifies the preview | White Balance (I): Sets the white balance | Crop (C): Crops the photo based on a marquee you drag | Spot Removal (B): Spot-heals imperfections | Adjustment Brush (K): Applies local corrections to areas by dragging | Open Preferences Dialog: Opens the Camera Raw Preferences dialog | Rotate 90° Clockwise (R): Rotates the image |

A The Camera Raw tools

Cropping and straightening photos

With the Crop tool, you can control which portion of a photo opens in Photoshop. You can readjust the crop marquee at any time, and it will remain available even after you click Save, Done, or Open. All the raw pixels are preserved.

To crop a photo:

1. Open a photo into Camera Raw (see page 237). Choose the **Crop** tool ⊔ (C).

2. Drag a marquee on the preview image.**A** To move the marquee, drag inside it; to resize it, drag a handle. Only the area within the marquee will import into Photoshop.

You can also straighten a photo before opening it into Photoshop.

To straighten a crooked photo:

1. Choose the **Straighten** tool ⊿ (A).

2. Drag across the preview along an edge in the photo that you want to align to the horizontal or vertical axis.**B** A crop marquee will display, aligned to the angle you drew. When you open the image in Photoshop, that edge will be aligned with the document window.**C**

➤ To redisplay a crop or straighten marquee after using another tool, choose the tool again. To remove it, press Esc.

A Drag a marquee with the Crop tool in the preview window.

B With the Straighten tool, drag across the preview along an edge that you want to align to the horizontal axis.

C The straightened image is opened into Photoshop.

Retouching photos

To repair blemishes or imperfections:

1. Choose the **Spot Removal** tool ✏. (B).

2. Drag across the blemish; a red and white target circle displays.**A** Drag inward or outward to scale the target circle to cover the blemish (the Radius slider will move accordingly). Release the mouse, and a green and white source circle appears, linked to the target circle.

3. Drag the **source** circle over an area to copy those pixels to the target circle.**B**

4. From the **Type** menu, choose **Heal** to blend source pixels into the luminosity of the target pixels or **Clone** to copy the source pixels exactly.

5. *Optional:* Lower the Opacity value to lessen the retouching effect. ★ You can also drag the edge of either circle to resize them in unison, add more circle pairs to correct other blemishes, or reposition the circles at any time. To hide them, choose a different tool.

➤ The retouch circles will remain available even after you click Save, Done, or Open. To redisplay them, choose the Retouch tool; to remove a selected pair, press Backspace/Delete; to remove them all, click Clear All.

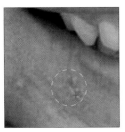 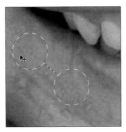

A With the Spot Removal tool, drag to scale the target circle over a blemish...

B ...then drag to position the linked source circle. Source pixels will copy to the target circle.

Changing the Workflow options

Via the Workflow Options dialog, you can change the color space, dimensions, bit depth, and resolution of a photo before opening it into Photoshop—all without changing the original digital file.

To change the color space, dimensions, bit depth, and resolution of a photo:

1. Open a photo into Camera Raw, then at the bottom of the Camera Raw dialog, click the underlined link that lists the color space, bit depth, etc. The **Workflow Options** dialog opens.

2. From the **Space** menu, choose the color profile to be used for converting the raw file to RGB: Adobe RGB (1998), ColorMatch RGB, ProPhoto RGB, or sRGB IEC61966-2.1 (or "sRGB," for short). In Chapter 1, you assigned Adobe RGB as the default color space for color management, so we suggest choosing it here, too.

3. From the **Depth** menu, choose a color depth of 8 Bits/Channel or 16 Bits/Channel (see page 21). If you have a large hard drive and a fast system with a lot of RAM, go ahead and choose 16 Bits/Channel. With the extra pixels, more of the original tonal levels in your photo will be preserved as you edit it in Photoshop.

4. If you need to resize the image, from the **Size** menu, choose a preset size (in megapixels) that matches the proportions of your raw image. (The default image size has no – or + after it.) Resampling will occur if you choose a larger size than the original. If a crop marquee is present, the crop size will be the default size. (Experts disagree on whether it's better to resample an image in Camera Raw or in Photoshop. Until they reach a consensus, you get to decide.)

5. Enter a **Resolution**. This value affects only the print output size of the photo. (For example, a resolution of 240 to 300 would be appropriate for a 2000 x 3000-pixel image to be output on an inkjet printer or a commercial press.)

6. Click OK. The new document info will be listed below the preview.

➤ To learn about the Open in Photoshop as Smart Objects option, see page 256.

Using the Basic tab

As you use the Basic tab to perform white balance, exposure, and other tonal adjustments, keep your eye on the histogram so you can monitor changes in the distribution of tonal values in your photo.**A** The histogram graphs the red, green, and blue pixels, superimposed upon one another at each tonal level. Shadow pixels are on the left, highlights are on the right, and the white areas indicate where the three colors overlap.

For the first round of adjustments, we recommend using the Basic sliders in the order in which they're listed. Unlike the color adjustment controls in Photoshop, these sliders cause minimal destruction to image pixels.

To apply white balance adjustments:

1. Click the **Basic** tab 🌑 (**A**, next page), and choose Fit in View as the zoom level for the preview.

2. You should adjust the white balance (color temperature) first, because this setting affects the overall photo. Do either of the following:

   From the **White Balance** menu, choose a preset setting that best describes the lighting conditions in which the photo was taken (this is for raw files only). Choose As Shot at any time to restore the initial camera settings (**B**, next page).

   To correct the color temperature more specifically, lower the **Temperature** value to add blue and make the image cooler (**C**, next page), or raise it to add yellow and make the image warmer (**D**, next page). To fine-tune the temperature correction, move the **Tint** slider slightly to the left (–) to add green or to the right (+) to add magenta. (Note that the White Balance menu listing is now "Custom.")

➤ You could adjust the white balance quickly based on a sampled area by choosing the White Balance tool ✎ (I) and then clicking a grayish white area that contains some detail. However, deciding which area to click can be tricky, so we recommend using the Temperature and Tint sliders instead.

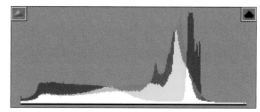

A The Camera Raw histogram charts the number of pixels at each tonal level in a photo for its red, green, and blue components. As in all the histograms in Photoshop, shadow pixels are on the left and highlight pixels are on the right.

THE CAMERA RAW SETTINGS DEMYSTIFIED

When you open a file into Camera Raw, by default, it's adjusted according to the built-in profile for your camera model. To assign a different collection of settings to your file or to restore the original settings, choose one of these settings from the Camera Raw Settings menu:

➤ Image Settings to restore the settings that were attached to the file from either the initial photo shoot or a prior Camera Raw session. When you open a photo initially, these settings will match the Camera Raw Defaults settings.

➤ Camera Raw Defaults to remove any custom settings and reapply the built-in default settings for the current camera model.

➤ Previous Conversion to apply the settings from the last image you adjusted in Camera Raw.

➤ Custom Settings to reapply the last settings chosen during the current Camera Raw session.

➤ The next item on the menu may be the name of an applied user-saved preset.

RESTORING DEFAULT SETTINGS

➤ Double-click a slider to restore the default value to just that slider.

➤ Click Default in the Basic or HSL/Grayscale tab to reset the sliders in only that tab to their default values (no adjustments).

➤ Choose Camera Raw Defaults from the Camera Raw Settings menu (see above) to reset all the sliders in all the tabs to their default settings.

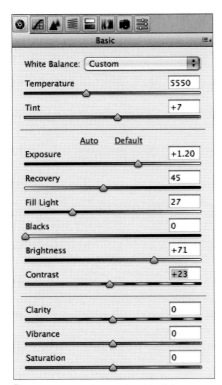

A Use the Basic tab to apply white balance, exposure, and other adjustments.

WHITE BALANCE IN PHOTOGRAPHY

The color temperature of the environment or lighting in which a photo is shot determines the relative amounts of red, green, and blue that the camera records. A digital camera uses a technique called white balance to balance red, green, and blue to create an accurate white, and adjusts other colors in the photo relative to that value.

B With As Shot chosen on the White Balance menu, the color temperature is well balanced.

C A lower Temperature value makes the image cooler. The metal is noticeably blue and the grass looks bluer.

D A higher Temperature value makes the image warmer (note the metal and the grass again).

To make tonal adjustments:

1. When the Camera Raw dialog first opens, the tonal sliders in the **Basic** tab—Exposure, Recovery, Fill Light, Blacks, Brightness, and Contrast—are set to their default values (the word "Default" is dimmed). You can click **Auto** to see which slider settings Camera Raw deems appropriate for your photo, but for even better results, we recommend making custom adjustments. Click **Default** to reset the above-mentioned sliders to their default settings, then follow the remaining steps.

2. The **histogram** reflects the current Camera Raw settings and redraws as you change those settings. Study the graph to see if any high-light or shadow pixels are being pushed to the edge (clipped). Clipping occurs if the tonal range of a scene is wider than the range the camera can capture. Your goal will be to bring the pixels into the range of your chosen RGB color space, and thereby minimize clipping. (In our setup, the Adobe RGB color space is chosen for our camera and for Camera Raw.)

3. To minimize the clipping of highlight and shadow pixels, do the following:

   In the top left corner of the histogram, click the **Shadow Clipping Warning** button (U) to display a representation of any shadow clipping in the preview, and in the top right corner, click the **Highlight Clipping Warning** button (O) to display any highlight clipping **A** (and **A**, next page). If you refer to the clipping warnings (blue for shadows, red for highlights), your corrections will be better informed.

   Use the Exposure and Recovery sliders as a duo to improve the highlight details. For an overexposed photo, move the **Exposure** slider to the left and the **Recovery** slider well to the right until only a trace remains of the red highlight warning color (you can use the sliders or scrubby sliders) (**B**, next page).

   Use the Blacks and Fill Light sliders as a pair to improve the shadow details. For an under-exposed photo, move the **Fill Light** slider slightly to the right and the **Blacks** slider to the left until only a trace remains of the blue shadow warning color (**C**, next page).

To minimize clipping a different way, Alt-drag/Option-drag the **Exposure** and/or **Recovery** slider and release the mouse when small amounts of white (representing all three color channels) display in the black preview. Alt-drag/Option-drag the **Blacks** slider and release the mouse when small amounts of black display in the white preview. Color areas, if any, represent clipping in those channels.

4. Adjust the **Brightness** to enhance details in the midtones, and adjust the **Contrast** to increase or decrease contrast (**D**, next page).

Finally, you'll use the Clarity slider in the Basic tab to adjust edge contrast and the Vibrance slider to adjust color saturation. Note: Although both the Vibrance and Saturation sliders adjust color saturation, the latter can cause oversaturation and highlight clipping, whereas the former does not (move the Saturation slider to the right, and your photo starts looking unnatural). In fact, we've found that even a high Vibrance setting doesn't cause skin tones to become oversaturated.

To adjust edge contrast and color saturation:

1. To add depth by adjusting the edge contrast in the midtones, increase the **Clarity** value. Or reduce this value to soften a photo, such as portrait or landscape.

2. Adjust the **Vibrance** value to increase or reduce the color saturation (**E**, next page).

➤ To adjust the saturation of specific colors, see pages 248–249.

Shadow Clipping
Warning button

Highlight Clipping
Warning button

A Click either or both of the Clipping Warning buttons above the histogram (a white frame around a button means that warning is on). This is the histogram for the original photo, shown in **A** on the next page. Most of the pixels are clustered at the left edge of the graph, which signifies that the image is underexposed.

CORRECTING AN UNDEREXPOSED PHOTO

A The original photo is underexposed, as is evidenced by the blue and red clipping warning colors in **A** on the previous page.

B We increased the Exposure value to lighten and recover detail in the highlights and midtones. We also increased the Recovery value to recover some detail in the metal highlights, but left some clipping because the specular highlights on these bright, metallic surfaces are supposed to be pure white, without details.

C We used the Fill Light and Blacks sliders to recover detail in the shadows (on the lower front area of the car and in the grass).* The blue and red clipping warnings are now minimal.

D We increased the Brightness value to recover more detail in the midtones, and also increased the Contrast value, which intensified the shadows.

E Finally, we raised the Clarity value to increase the edge contrast and raised the Vibrance value to boost the color saturation. Now this classic MG really shines!

*The settings on this page were applied to a raw photo. If you downloaded and are working on the JPEG version, choose a Fill Light value of 20, a Blacks value of 0, and a Brightness value of +28.

Using the Tone Curve tab

After making adjustments in the Basic tab, the next step is to use the Tone Curve tab to fine-tune specific sections of the tonal range (highlights, midtones, or shadows). You can adjust the curve in either of two ways: by manually placing points, employing the same techniques that you'd use for a Curves adjustment layer in Photoshop (pages 218–221), or by using the Parametric sliders. We'll show you the latter method because we think it produces higher-quality corrections. A slider is provided for each part of the tonal range (no need to guess which part of the curve to bend), and you can't misshape a curve, so the image is protected from posterization.The Parametric curve and sliders were first introduced in Adobe Photoshop Lightroom and are an adjustment method of the future.

To make tonal adjustments using the Parametric sliders:

1. Click the **Tone Curve** tab,  then click the nested **Parametric** tab.**A–B** Behind the curve you'll see a static shape of the current histogram. As in all the tabs, you can drag the sliders or use the scrubby sliders.

2. Increase the **Highlights, Lights, Darks,** or **Shadows** value to lighten that tonal range (and thus raise the corresponding portion of the curve above the diagonal line),**C** or reduce it to darken that tonal range (and thus lower that portion of the curve below the diagonal line)(**A–B**, next page).

    ► When using these sliders, we recommend adjusting one, two, or maybe three sections of the tonal range—but not all four. Remember, your goal is just to fine-tune the exposure.

3. After adjusting the sliders, you can move the **region control** (located below the graph) to expand or contract the range of each slider adjustment. The left region control affects the Shadows slider, the right region control affects the Highlights slider (**C–F**, next page), and the middle region control affects the Lights and Darks sliders. The more a control moves the curve away from the diagonal line, the more adjacent tonal ranges are affected; the more a control moves the curve closer to the diagonal line, the fewer adjacent tonal ranges are affected.

A The highlights in this photo lack detail and the midtones lack contrast.

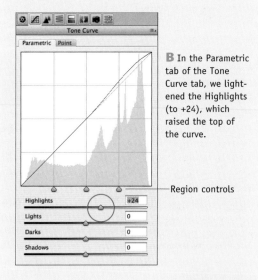

B In the Parametric tab of the Tone Curve tab, we lightened the Highlights (to +24), which raised the top of the curve.

Region controls

C Now the highlights are lighter, especially in the cloud areas. We'll darken the midtones next.

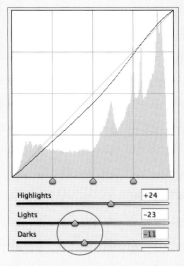

A We reduced the Lights and Darks values, which in turn lowered the midsection of the curve.

B The Lights adjustment lightened the upper midtones, and the Darks adjustment darkened the lower midtones. Overall, the image contrast is improved.

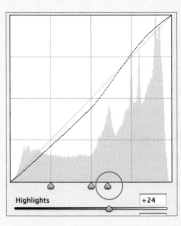

C We moved the right region control to the left, which raised the top and middle sections of the curve.

D The control adjustment expanded the effect of the lightened highlights to the midtones, which isn't our aim.

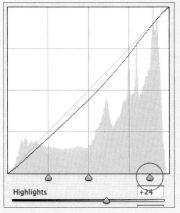

E We moved the right region control to the right, which lowered the top and middle sections of the curve.

F The control adjustment narrowed the lightening effect of the Highlights slider to just the highlights; the result was that details were recovered in the clouds. Now the exposure is just right.

Using the HSL/Grayscale tab

In the HSL/Grayscale tab, you can adjust the hue, saturation, or luminance of colors individually. This is a powerful tab!

To adjust individual colors:

1. Click the **HSL/Grayscale** tab ☰ and choose Fit in View as the zoom level for the preview. You can use the sliders or scrubby sliders. **A**

2. Click the nested **Hue** tab. Move any slider to shift that color toward its adjacent hues, as shown in the bar. For example, you could shift the Greens toward yellow to make a photo warmer, or toward aqua to make it cooler.

3. Click the **Saturation** tab (**A–B**, next page). Move a slider to the left to desaturate a color (make it grayer) or to the right to make it more saturated (more pure). Try to avoid oversaturation, which makes a photo look unnatural.

➤ To make a sky more vivid, increase the saturation of Blues and Aquas; or for a warm sunset effect, increase the saturation of the Yellows or Greens; or to make the lighting look gray and hazy, lessen the saturation of Yellows or Greens.

4. Click the **Luminance** tab (**C–D**, next page). Move a slider to the left to make that color darker (add black) or to the right to make it lighter (add white). Avoid overlightening colors, to prevent highlight clipping.

A In the original photo, the sky lacks contrast and the greens and yellows in the field are overpowering.

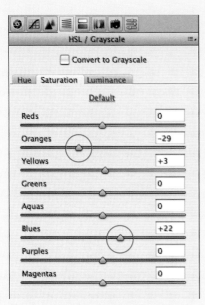

B The Saturation adjustments lowered the intensity of oranges in the field and made the blues in the sky look richer.

A In the Saturation tab of the HSL/Grayscale tab, we lowered the saturation of Oranges and increased the saturation of Blues.

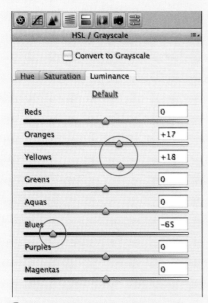

D By using the Luminance sliders, we were able to change the quality of light in the field from orange-yellow to neutral, and also darkened the blues in the sky. In summary, we desaturated the colors in the field and increased the saturation and contrast in the sky. Now the colors in the photo look richer and better balanced.

C In the Luminance tab, we lightened the Oranges and Yellows and darkened the Blues. The result of the Blues adjustment is similar to the effect of using a polarizing filter at the time of the shoot.

Using the Detail tab

Via sliders in the Detail tab, you can preview and adjust the sharpness of your photo, and also reduce color noise.**A**

To sharpen edges and reduce color noise:

1. Click the **Detail** tab  **B** and choose a zoom level of 100% for the preview.

2. If the words "(Preview Only)" display in the Detail tab, click the **Open Preferences** button ≣ on the toolbox. In the Camera Raw Preferences dialog, choose **Apply Sharpening To: All Images**, then click OK.

3. In the **Sharpening** area, use the **Amount** slider to adjust the edge definition. For subject matter that needs a lot of sharpening, such as hard objects or architecture, set the Amount to 100; if less sharpening is needed, try a value of 50–60. For a portrait, keep the Amount between 50 and 70.

   ➤ To judge a sharpening value in a grayscale preview (without the distraction of color), set the zoom level to 100%, then Alt-drag/ Option-drag the slider.

4. All digital cameras produce some undesirable noise, such as visible artifacts and stray pixels. Budget cameras tend to produce the most noise, but noise can also result from using high ISO (light sensitivity) settings in high-end cameras in poorly lit scenes. Noise can become accentuated by image editing, so if possible, it should be removed before the photo is opened into Photoshop. To reduce noise in the dark areas, move the **Luminance** (smoothing) slider (try a value between 10 and 15).

   ➤ The higher the Luminance value, the more the photo will need to be sharpened.

5. Finally, move the **Color** (noise reduction) slider to the right to eliminate color artifacts and random speckling from all the tonal levels of the photo.**C** These defects tend to be most noticeable on solid-color surfaces, especially in the shadow areas. The default value is 25, but you can raise it to 40–60, depending on the type of photo you're working with (figure, landscape, interior, etc.).

   ➤ In our *Visual QuickPro Guide* to Photoshop, we show an example of how to use the Sharpening sliders.

A In this photo, the sky and background contain too much color noise and, overall, the edges look too soft.

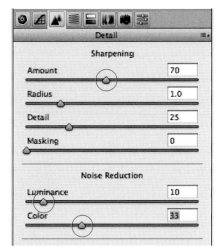

B In the Detail tab, we set the Amount value for Sharpening to 70, and in the Noise Reduction area, we raised the Luminance and Color values.

C The settings shown in the preceding figure made the sky and background smoother and sharpened the edges.

Saving and applying Camera Raw settings

After carefully choosing custom settings for a photo in Camera Raw, you'll be happy to know that you can save those settings for future use as a settings preset. The preset can then be applied to other files (say, from the same photo session) that need the same or similar corrections. You can apply it to a single image via Camera Raw, to multiple selected thumbnails via Bridge, or to multiple files via batch processing.

To save Camera Raw settings as a preset:

1. With your corrected image open in Camera Raw, choose **Save Settings** from the Settings menu. The Save Settings dialog opens.**A**

2. Check which categories of settings you want saved to the settings file; or to narrow the number of checked boxes, choose a category (tab name) from the **Subset** menu (and check any additional boxes that you want to include).

3. Click Save. In the Save Settings dialog, enter a name (preferably one that describes the type of settings being saved), keep the .xmp extension and the location as the Settings folder, then click Save.

4. The saved settings preset can now be chosen in the Presets tab for any photo (see the next set of instructions).

You can apply a user-defined preset (saved collection of settings) to any photo in Camera Raw.

To choose a Camera Raw preset:

In Camera Raw, do either of the following:

Click the **Presets** tab, ⊞ then click a preset name.

From the **Apply Preset** submenu on the Settings menu, choose a preset.

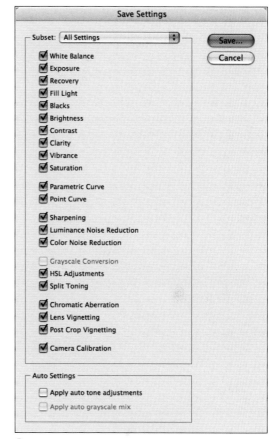

A In the Save Settings dialog, specify which of your custom Camera Raw settings are to be saved in a preset.

Using the Adjustment Brush ★

Unlike settings chosen in the Camera Raw tabs which apply to the overall photo, the Adjustment Brush lets you apply "local" adjustments to specific areas by applying brush strokes. For example, you could adjust the exposure or color saturation of a few key details in a composition that you want to emphasize. You choose values for the tool first, then apply strokes to the preview. If most of the sliders look familiar to you, it's because they're like the ones in the Basic tab. With the Show Mask option on, a tint displays over the adjusted areas.

To apply Adjustment Brush edits:

1. After making adjustments in the Basic and Tone Curve tabs,**A** click the **Adjustment Brush** ✎ (K). The sliders for the tool display. You will paint over specific areas to mask them first, then adjust the sliders for the masked areas.

2. To "zero out" all the other sliders except one to make the tool operational, click the + button for one of the sliders.

3. Adjust the brush size by pressing [or]. Choose a Feather value of 60–95 to allow the edits to fade into surrounding areas. Keep the Flow at

A The original photo is lit evenly. We want to apply local exposure edits to lighten and darken some areas in the center.

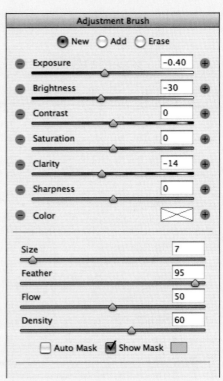

B On the Adjustment Brush panel, we chose the settings shown above so the areas that we'll drag across will be darkened.

C With Show Mask checked, we are able to see where we brushed on the darkening adjustment.

50 (for the smoothness of the stroke) and set the Density to 60 (for the adjustment strength) (**B**, previous page).

4. Check **Show Mask**, then draw strokes over areas of the photo you want to mask (**C**, previous page). Release the mouse, then paint over any other noncontiguous areas that you want to add to the mask.

5. Uncheck Show Mask, then move the various sliders to apply adjustments to the masked areas.

6. To apply a local adjustment to another area of the photo, click New, then follow steps 2–5 again. **A–C**

➤ To edit an adjustment, click an existing pin (a black dot appears in the pin), then add to the mask and/or change the slider settings.

To remove Adjustment Brush edits:

1. With the Adjustment Brush tool selected, check **Show Mask** to display the current mask.

2. To remove adjustments locally, click an existing pin, click **Erase**, then brush where you want to erase the mask.

To remove an entire mask and its adjustments, click a pin, then click **Backspace/Delete**.

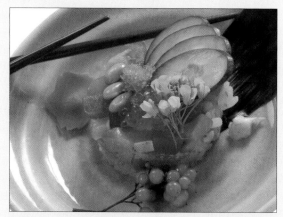

A Our adjustments slightly darkened the shadowy area around the food in the center.

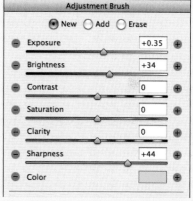

B We clicked New again, and applied a lightening adjustment to the food and yellow flowers in the center (using the settings shown above). We also clicked the color swatch to apply a yellow tint to the areas we had lightened.

C We used local darkening and lightening adjustments to accent the food and flowers in the center.

USING THE AUTO MASK OPTION

To mask a specific color area, zoom in on it, check Auto Mask, scale the brush to cover only that area, and start your Adjustment Brush stroke over that color. The mask will cover only the areas that match that color. We used this method to limit an exposure adjustment to the yellow on the flowers.

Synchronizing Camera Raw settings

When you open multiple photos into Camera Raw, the files are represented by thumbnails in a film-strip panel on the left side of the dialog. In theory, you could, say, open several files from the same photo shoot into Camera Raw, choose settings, then click Synchronize to apply those settings to all the photos. In practice, it's unlikely that all the adjustments for one photo will work perfectly on the rest. The Synchronize option is useful, however, for applying settings incrementally. For example, you could apply some Basic adjustments to all your photos first (perhaps to correct the white bal-ance and exposure), then select smaller batches of thumbnails for more targeted adjustments. Click Synchronize after each adjustment to apply the changes to all the currently selected thumbnails.

To synchronize the Camera Raw settings of multiple photos:

1. In Bridge, select two or more thumbnails for photos that were shot under the same light-ing conditions and that need the same type of correction (they should be all raw files or all JPEG files). Double-click one of the selected thumbnails.

2. In Camera Raw, the filmstrip panel displays.**A** Click one of the thumbnails.

3. Make the necessary adjustments to the selected image, including cropping if you want to crop all the images exactly the same way.

4. Click **Select All** at the top of the filmstrip panel or Ctrl-click/Cmd-click multiple thumbnails, then click **Synchronize**. The Synchronize dialog opens. (This dialog is very similar in appearance and layout to the Save Settings dialog, which is shown on page 251.)

5. Either check the setting(s) you want to apply or choose a category from the Synchronize menu (and check any additional boxes).

6. Click OK to apply the current settings in the categories you checked to all the selected thumbnails.

A If you open two or more digital photos simul-taneously, whether via Bridge or via File > Open in Photoshop, image thumbnails will display in the film-strip panel on the left side of the Camera Raw dialog. Click the thumbnail for the photo you want to either apply corrections to or open.

Opening and saving Camera Raw files

Still with us? Great! Finally, you get to open your Camera Raw file into Photoshop. (After reading this page, be sure to also see our instructions for opening a Camera Raw file as a Smart Object layer on the next page.)

To open a Camera Raw file, saving settings:

When you're done choosing settings in the Camera Raw dialog, click **Open Image** to convert and open the corrected file in Photoshop. The current settings will be saved as instructions for converting the raw or JPEG photo; the original raw or JPEG file is unchanged.

Note: The settings for a raw photo will be saved either as part of the internal Camera Raw database in your system or as a hidden sidecar .xmp file in the same folder as the raw file. This internal file is different from any user-created settings file that you may have created via the Save Settings command on the settings menu.

➤ To close Camera Raw without opening your file, click Done; your current settings will still be saved as instructions for modifying the file.

WHAT IS DNG?

Have you wondered what the best file format is for saving digital photos — for the present and the future — so they can be accessed and printed over, say, a 20-year period or longer? Currently, there is no one standard raw format, as each camera maker uses a unique proprietary method for creating raw files. And should a manufacturer discontinue its proprietary method, raw photos from their cameras might then be rendered unreadable by commonly used image-editing applications.

DNG, an open-standard file format that was developed by Adobe, may some day become a popular long-term solution. It preserves all the raw, unprocessed pixel information that the camera records. Adobe has made the coding for DNG publicly available ("open standard") to interested companies in the hope that it will be adopted for a wide range of hardware devices and software applications. Sometime in the future, hopefully, DNG files will be universally readable.

You can also open a copy of a Camera Raw file without recording the settings into the metadata of the raw file or into the actual JPEG file.

To open a copy of a Camera Raw file:

In the Camera Raw dialog, hold down Alt/ Option and click **Open Copy**. The file will be converted using the current settings and will open into Photoshop, but those settings won't be recorded over any existing instructions in the raw or JPEG file.

You can rename your photo files and convert them to the DNG (digital negative), JPEG, TIFF, or Photoshop format without opening them into Photoshop.

To save a file via Camera Raw:

1. In the lower left corner of the Camera Raw dialog, click **Save Image**. The Save Options dialog opens.

2. Do all of the following:

   For the Destination, choose **Save in Same Location** or **Save in New Location**. For the latter, choose a location in the Select Destination Folder dialog, then click Select.

   In the **File Naming** area, enter a file name; also choose a naming or numbering convention from the adjacent menu, if desired.

   Choose a **Format** (we recommend the Photoshop format), then choose format-related options. For example, if you cropped the photo in Camera Raw, for the Photoshop format, check whether you want to Preserve Cropped Pixels.

   Click **Save**.

➤ Via the Save Image button, you can save more than one version of a photo, each with a different set of adjustments (such as two different exposure adjustments). In this case, in the Save Options dialog, be sure to change the file name.

Opening and placing photos as Smart Objects

If you open or place a Camera Raw file into Photoshop as a Smart Object, you'll be able to readjust it at any time via Camera Raw. To learn more about Smart Objects, see pages 314–316.

To convert a Camera Raw file into a Smart Object:

Method 1 (open as a new document)

When you're done applying your Camera Raw edits, hold down Shift and click **Open Object.** A new file opens in Photoshop, and the image appears on a Smart Object layer.

➤ If you prefer to have Camera Raw open all files as Smart Objects by default, click the underlined link at the bottom of the Bridge window to open the Workflow Options dialog, then check Open in Photoshop as Smart Objects. The Open Image button becomes an Open Object button.

Method 2 (place into an existing document)

1. Open a Photoshop document.

2. In Bridge, click the thumbnail for a raw or JPEG photo that has been edited in Camera Raw (look for the badge ⏣ in the upper right corner).

3. Choose File > Place > **In Photoshop.** The Camera Raw dialog opens.

4. Make any further adjustments to the photo, if desired, then click **OK.** It will appear on its own layer in the currently active Photoshop document, within a transform box.**A–B**

5. Apply any scale or shape transformations, then to accept the placed image and convert it to a **Smart Object** layer, press Enter/Return or double-click inside the transform box.

To edit a Smart Object photo:

1. Double-click a Smart Object layer thumbnail to reopen an embedded copy of the photo into Camera Raw.

2. Make any desired adjustments, then click OK to apply your edits to the Smart Object layer. The original file won't be affected by your edits.

➤ You can scale a Smart Object layer at any time. Photoshop will use the pixel data from the original file to scale the image, so its quality won't be diminished (that is, provided you don't enlarge it beyond its original size).

A We opened a Photoshop document, then from Bridge, chose File > Place > In Photoshop. When the photo opened in the Camera Raw dialog, we clicked OK; the photo appeared in the Photoshop file. Here, we are Shift-dragging a corner handle of the transform box to scale it.

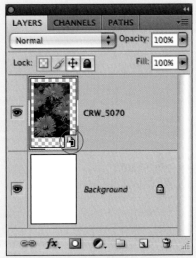

B The photo appears on a Smart Object layer. Note the icon.

When you first open a photograph in Photoshop, take a few minutes to study it. Does it have any overall deficiencies or problems? Is it over- or underexposed? Does it have a color cast (ghostly blue, sickly green)? There are a number of commands that you can use to rectify these kinds of problems. If you captured the photo as a raw file or in the JPEG or TIFF format, you were able to apply exposure corrections via the Camera Raw plug-in. If you didn't use Camera Raw, you can apply exposure corrections in Photoshop.

In this chapter, you'll perform shadow and highlight corrections; adjust the color temperature to compensate for improper lighting; correct over- or underexposure by rebalancing light and dark values; and add drama or illumate a dark area by applying lighting effects.

Using the Shadows/Highlights command

Shadows/Highlights is one of our favorite tonal adjustment commands because it provides very targeted controls. It adjusts the luminance of each individual pixel in an image depending on the darkness or lightness of neighboring pixels, and lets you apply corrections to a specific tonal range without overadjusting other areas of the image. The command does a good job of recovering details in the shadows and highlights, making it invaluable for correcting overexposed and underexposed areas, such as subjects that may be in shadow due to strong side or back lighting.

Shadows/Highlights preserves more pixels in each tonal range than Levels and Curves (you can confirm this by viewing the Histogram panel).**A** And because Shadows/Highlights lets you pinpoint the tonal ranges to be corrected, you won't have to use multiple adjustment layers and layer masks to limit the area of adjustment, as you do when using Levels and Curves.

Continued on the following page

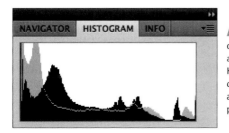

A No gaps or spikes appear on the Histogram panel as you apply Shadows/Highlights because the command preserves an adequate number of pixels in each tonal range.

16

IN THIS CHAPTER

Using the Shadows/Highlights
  command. 257

Applying a Photo Filter adjustment. .260

Correcting exposure via the Layers
  panel. .261

Applying the Lighting Effects filter . .262

To apply the Shadows/Highlights command:

1. Click a layer or the Background, A and display the **Histogram** panel 📊 so you'll be able to monitor your tonal adjustments. Shadows/Highlights can't be applied via an adjustment layer, but it can be applied to a Smart Object layer.

2. Choose Image > Adjustments > **Shadows/Highlights**. The Shadows/Highlights dialog opens and the image is adjusted automatically using preliminary settings. Check **Show More Options** to display the full set of options.

3. For the **Shadows:**

   Adjust the **Amount** value to lighten the shadows.**B** We usually find the default Amount of 50% produces too strong a correction, so we lower it; leave the slider at 50% if a strong shadow correction works for your image.

Change the **Tonal Width** value to expand or reduce the range of midtones that the adjustment affects. To limit the adjustment to only very dark shadows, keep the Tonal Width value low (**A–B**, next page).

Raise or lower the **Radius** value to expand or reduce how many neighboring pixels will be compared to a specific pixel in a shadow area in order to produce the adjustment. Don't raise the Radius value too much, though; allowing too many pixels to be compared could reduce the contrast and counteract the benefits of the adjustment.

4. For the **Highlights:**

   Increase the **Amount** value to darken the highlight areas (0% produces no darkening).

A Because this original photo was exposed for the sky, the trees in the foreground are underexposed and lack detail.

B In the Shadows/Highlights dialog, our initial Shadows settings of Amount 40 and Radius 52 successfully lightened the shadows but at the same time made the midtones too light and reduced the contrast too much.

By lowering the brightness of the highlights, you'll recover detail in those areas and also enable the midtones to stand out more.

Adjust the **Tonal Width** and **Radius** sliders to control the range of midtones that are affected by the Highlights adjustment.**C–D**

5. Uncheck, then recheck **Preview** to compare the original and adjusted images.

6. If raising the Shadows: Amount caused the image to become oversaturated, lower the **Adjustments**: **Color Correction** value to reduce the saturation. (Or raise this value to increase the saturation.)

7. Raise the **Midtone Contrast** to increase contrast in the midtones, or lower this value to decrease contrast in the midtones.

8. *Optional:* To save your Shadows/Highlights settings as a preset to use with other images, click Save, enter a descriptive name (keep the .shh extension), choose a location, then click Save again. To load a saved settings preset, click Load.

9. Click OK.

➤ To restore the default settings in the dialog, hold down Alt/Option and click Reset.

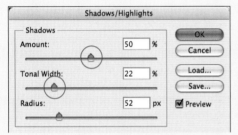

A Next, we lowered the Shadows: Tonal Width value to prevent the command from adjusting the midtones, and raised the Shadows: Amount value to lighten just the shadows.

B To preserve the original midtone values, we lowered the Shadows: Tonal Width value before adjusting the Shadows: Amount.

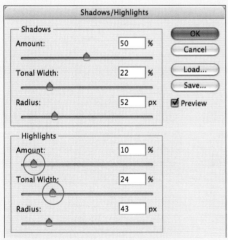

C We also increased the Highlights: Amount slightly to reduce the brightness of the sky. Finally, we removed the midtones from the adjustment once more by reducing the Highlights: Tonal Width value.

D By using the Shadows/Highlights command, we were able to lighten the shadows in the trees, darken the sky, and improve the contrast between the midtones, shadows, and highlights.

Applying a Photo Filter adjustment

To change the color temperature of a scene (make it look warmer or cooler), photographers use colored lens filters at the time of the shoot. In Photoshop, you can simulate the effect of a camera filter by using the Photo Filter command. You can choose from 20 preset filter tints or choose a custom color via the Color Picker, and best of all, you can apply the command via the Adjustments panel. When using this feature, go for subtle or extreme, but not in between.

To apply a Photo Filter adjustment:

1. Click a layer or the Background.**A**

2. On the **Adjustments** panel, click the **Photo Filter** button. ★ The Photo Filter controls display.**B**

3. Do either of the following:

   Click **Filter**, then from the menu, choose a preset warming or cooling filter or filter color. The filter color will appear in the swatch.

   Click the **Color** swatch, choose a color for the filter from the Color Picker, then click OK.

   ➤ Pick a related color for a subtle change or a complementary color (opposite on the color wheel) for a more obvious change.

4. Using the slider or scrubby slider, choose a **Density** (opacity percentage) for the tint. Try a modest value between 10% and 25%, or higher for a dramatic change. You can also lower the adjustment layer opacity after clicking OK.

5. Check **Preserve Luminosity** to preserve the overall brightness and contrast of the image. With this option unchecked, the contrast will be softer in the highlights, but the resulting colorization effect may be too pronounced. For portraits, you may prefer the results with this option unchecked.

6. To compare the original and adjusted images, click the **Layer Visibility** button 👁 on the Adjustments panel, then click it again.**C**

A The original image has a magenta cast.

B For our Photo Filter adjustment, we chose Cyan from the Filter menu and left the Density at 25%.

C The Photo Filter command toned down the magenta while preserving the warmth of the afternoon sun.

Correcting exposure via the Layers panel

Here's a quick and easy way to correct an over- or underexposed photo: Choose a lightening or darkening blending mode for an adjustment layer, then duplicate the adjustment layer multiple times. It's not the most precise method in the world, but if it works, it works (and if it makes your art director happy, maybe you can go home early).

To correct over- or underexposure via the Layers panel:

1. Open an over- or underexposed photo,**A** and click the Background or a layer.

2. On the **Adjustments** panel, click the **Levels** button.⚏ ★ The Levels controls display; don't change any of the settings.

3. On the Layers panel, click the adjustment layer, then choose a **blending mode** that has a lightening or darkening effect. For example, to darken an overexposed image, try **Multiply** mode, or to lighten an underexposed image, try **Screen** mode.

4. If the image is still too light or dark, **duplicate** the adjustment layer by pressing Ctrl-J/Cmd-J.**B** Repeat the shortcut until you reach a point where the image is slightly overcorrected and you need to step it back a bit.

5. Lower the **opacity** of the topmost adjustment layer until the exposure is just right.**C**

6. *Optional:* To restore some color saturation, choose Color Dodge as the blending mode for the bottom adjustment layer.**D**

A The original image is underexposed.

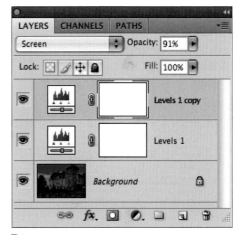

B We created an adjustment layer, chose Screen blending mode for the new layer, then duplicated it.

C The two Levels adjustment layers produced this result.

D Our last step was to choose Color Dodge as the blending mode for the lower of the two adjustment layers.

Applying the Lighting Effects filter

By using the Lighting Effects filter, you can place up to 16 light sources in your image, and you can assign a different color, intensity, and angle to each source. To produce its effect, the filter darkens the whole layer, then casts a light. It's not the easiest interface to use, but it does offer a lot of options.

To cast a light on an image:

1. Click a layer in an RGB document.**A** We suggest using an image that's relatively dark.

   Note: To enable the filter settings to be readjusted later, we recommend that you right-click/Control-click the layer and choose Convert to Smart Object. (We usually find that the settings need to be tweaked.)

2. Choose Filter > Render > **Lighting Effects**. The Lighting Effects dialog opens (**A**, next page).

3. From the **Style** menu, choose Default or one of the lighting presets.

4. In the **Light Type** area:

   Check **On** to access the Light Type options.

   From the **Light Type** menu, choose Directional, Omni, or Spotlight.

   Move the **Intensity** slider to adjust the brightness of the light.

   For the Spotlight Light Type, you can move the **Focus** slider to adjust the width of the beam that fills the ellipse.

   To change the **color** of the light, click the color swatch, then choose a color from the picker.

5. In the preview window, do any of the following:

   To **move** the entire light, drag the center point.

   To **rotate** the ellipse without reshaping it, and thereby change the direction of the light, Ctrl-drag/Cmd-drag one of the outer points.

   To make the light more **diffuse**, drag the angle endpoint away from the center.

   To **widen** or **narrow** the light, drag either of the side points.

6. Use the **Properties** sliders to adjust the surrounding light conditions on the layer:

   Gloss controls the amount of surface reflectance on the lit surfaces.

Steps continued on page 264

A The original image looks dull and lacks contrast.

A low light Intensity looks more realistic in an outdoor scene.

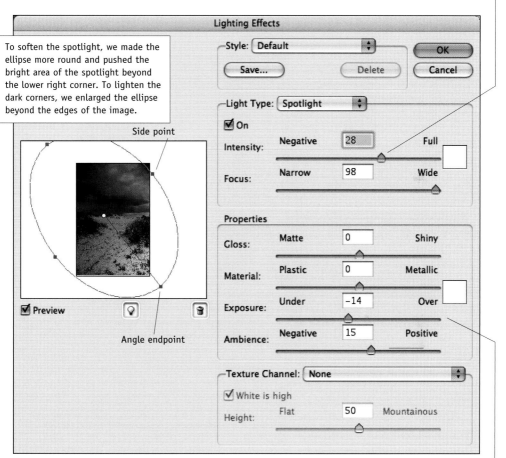

To soften the spotlight, we made the ellipse more round and pushed the bright area of the spotlight beyond the lower right corner. To lighten the dark corners, we enlarged the ellipse beyond the edges of the image.

Side point

Lighting Effects

Style: Default

Save...   Delete   OK   Cancel

Light Type: Spotlight

☑ On

Intensity: Negative [28] Full

Focus: Narrow [98] Wide

Properties

Gloss: Matte [0] Shiny

Material: Plastic [0] Metallic

Exposure: Under [–14] Over

Ambience: Negative [15] Positive

Texture Channel: None

☑ White is high

Height: Flat [50] Mountainous

☑ Preview

Angle endpoint

A In the Lighting Effects dialog, choose a preset, then adjust the lighting ellipse and/or the Light Type and Properties settings.

We chose a slightly negative Exposure value and a low Ambience value to lower the overall light in the scene (note the clouds in the preview) and to enhance the spotlight effect.

Material (Plastic or Metallic) changes the way the light reflects off the surfaces.

Exposure lightens or darkens the whole light, within the ellipse.

Ambience controls the overall amount of light on the layer and establishes the maximum lightness for the Exposure option.

To choose a different color for the ambient light around the spotlight, click the **Properties** color swatch and choose a color from the Color Picker.

7. Do any of these optional steps:

   To add the current configuration of settings to the Style menu for use with other images, click Save, enter a name, then click OK.

   To add more light sources, drag the light bulb icon 🔦 into the preview window.

   To delete a light source, drag its center point over the trash icon. 🗑 One light source must remain.

   To duplicate a light source, Alt-drag/Option-drag its center point.

8. Click OK.**A–B**

➤ The last-used settings of the Lighting Effects filter will remain in the dialog until you change them or exit/quit Photoshop. To restore the default settings, choose Default from the Style menu; or if you customized the Default style, choose a different preset, then choose Default again. To remove the current Style preset, click Delete, then click Delete again in the alert dialog.

A To add a bright foreground light, we applied the Lighting Effects filter using the settings shown on the previous page.

B Here, we applied the Lighting Effects filter to a copy of the original landscape using Style: Soft Omni, for an even more dramatic effect.

Photographers use focusing techniques to orchestrate a scene, such as blurriness to convey motion or a shallow depth of field to contrast an in-focus subject with its background. In Photoshop, you can apply similar special effects (e.g., blur areas that were previously in focus) or correct for photographic errors (e.g., sharpen an image that lacks focus). In this chapter, you'll apply the Lens Blur filter and use vignettes to create a focal point in your photo; apply the Motion Blur filter to simulate motion; apply the Lens Correction filter to correct for lens distortion; and apply the Smart Sharpen and Unsharp Mask filters to sharpen.

Using the Lens Blur filter

When you use a camera, you know that some parts of a scene end up being more in focus than others. If your camera lets you adjust exposure and shutter settings, as opposed to the "point-and-shoot" type of camera, you can control how much of the image will be in focus (the depth of field) via the f-stop setting. Objects that fall outside the depth of field—either in front of it or behind it—will be blurred. The appearance of the blurred area will vary depending on the individual camera lens and camera model. For example, blurred white highlights, which photographers call specular highlights, can vary in shape and brightness.

The Lens Blur filter in Photoshop attempts to replicate this type of blurring. What formerly required the use of multiple channels, gradients, and editing steps can now be accomplished via this single command. All of this number crunching comes at a price, however: it can be slow when applied to a large image.

To apply the Lens Blur filter:

1. Click an image layer (or duplicate the Background via Ctrl-J/Cmd-J), then click the **Add Layer Mask** button ▣ on the Layers panel.

2. Keep the layer mask thumbnail selected, choose the **Gradient** tool ▣ (G or Shift-G), click the Gradient Picker arrowhead on the Options bar, click the "Black, White" preset, then drag across the entire document window to apply a gradient. The Lens Blur filter will use this gradient "invisibly." Keep this in mind when you choose a Blur Focal Distance setting in step 5. (Don't concern yourself with where the white and black areas of

Continued on the following page

REFOCUS

17

IN THIS CHAPTER

Using the Lens Blur filter 265

Using the Motion Blur filter 268

Changing the focus with a vignette. . .270

Using the Lens Correction filter 272

Using the sharpening filters 274

the gradient land; you'll be able to swap them in the Lens Blur dialog.)

3. Shift-click the layer mask thumbnail to disable the layer mask (you don't want to mask out the imagery). Click the layer thumbnail, then choose Filter > Blur > **Lens Blur**. The Lens Blur dialog opens (resize it, if you like). **A**

4. At any time while making adjustments, you can uncheck, then recheck **Preview** to compare the original and blurred images.

   Click a **Preview** speed. For a large file (larger than 100 MB), click **Faster;** for a smaller file, click **More Accurate.**

   You can also change the **zoom level** for the preview via the zoom buttons or menu in the lower left corner of the preview window. We like to use the Fit in View setting.

5. The grayscale values in a depth map will control where the blur is applied, mimicking the depth of field in a camera. In the **Depth Map** area:

   From the **Source** menu, choose **Layer Mask** as the source for the depth map. The change in grayscale values in the source will control which areas remain in focus. (A setting of None blurs the whole image uniformly.)

   To set the **Blur Focal Distance**, either specify which grayscale value (from 0, black, to 255, white) in your depth map will remain in full focus via the scrubby slider, or in the preview, click the area that you want to keep in focus. In either case, what you're doing is choosing a grayscale value from the hidden gradient in the layer mask (**A**, next page). Shades lighter or darker than this value will become progressively more blurry. You'll see the change more readily after moving the Radius slider in the next step.

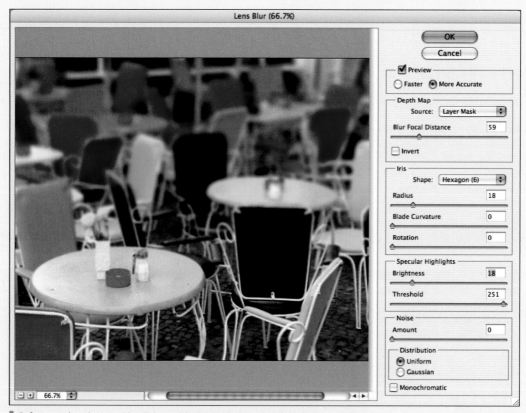

A Before opening the Lens Blur dialog, with the Gradient tool and the layer mask thumbnail selected, we dragged upward from the bottom of our image.

Optional: Check Invert to swap the white and black areas in the depth map, and thereby swap the areas in focus with the areas that are not.

6. In the **Iris** area, use the **Radius** value to control the intensity of the blur. This produces the most pronounced effect of any option in the dialog. (The other Iris sliders are used for creating intricate "photographic" highlights).

7. Blurring averages the values of neighboring pixels and tends to gray out white specular highlights. In the **Specular Highlights** area, you can use the **Brightness** slider to brighten highlight areas that have become blurred and use the **Threshold** slider (move it slightly) to control which tonal range the Brightness setting affects. At 255, only pure white pixels will be affected; at low settings, most of the pixels in the blurry areas will be brightened.

8. Blurring can also affect the film grain in an image, producing a nonuniform texture. If you want to reintroduce noise to the blurred areas, do any of the following:

   Move the **Noise: Amount** slider slightly.

   Click **Distribution: Uniform** or **Gaussian**.

   Check **Monochromatic** to limit the noise to just grayscale pixels instead of color pixels.

9. Click OK. **B–C**

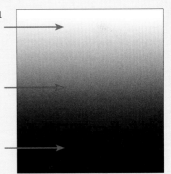

Light grayscale values will produce total blurring in this part of our photo.

Intermediate grayscale values will produce partial blurring in this part of our photo.

Because we chose a dark grayscale value (59) as our Blur Focal Distance, no blurring will occur in this part of the photo.

Image

Layer mask

A When you click the preview in the Lens Blur dialog or move the Blur Focal Distance slider, you're choosing a grayscale value in the layer mask, which establishes the Blur Focal Distance value. Pixels at that grayscale value will stay in focus; the remaining pixels will become progressively more blurry.

B The original image

C We used a layer mask in conjunction with the Lens Blur filter to blur the background of this photo. Our settings are shown in the figure on the previous page, and our layer mask is shown in figure **A**, above.

Using the Motion Blur filter

One way to capture the blur of motion in photography is by panning the camera as a subject moves. In Photoshop, you can create an illusion of motion by using the Motion Blur filter. In the following instructions, you'll blur the whole image first by applying the filter as a Smart Filter, then remove the effect from part of the image by painting on the filter mask to bring a key area back into focus.

To apply the Motion Blur filter to part of an image:

1. Click an image layer and duplicate it by pressing Ctrl-J/Cmd-J (**A**, next page).

2. With the duplicate layer selected, choose Filter > **Convert for Smart Filters**, then click OK if an alert dialog appears; or choose Convert to Smart Object from the Layers panel menu.

3. Choose Filter > Blur > **Motion Blur**. The Motion Blur dialog opens (**B**, next page).

4. Choose an **Angle** value (use the scrubby slider or move the dial), choose a **Distance** for the degree of blurring, then click OK (**C**, next page). For a high-resolution image (300 ppi), a Distance of 80–100 will substantially blur the image while preserving some recognizable details in the background.

5. On the Layers panel, click the Smart Filter mask thumbnail.

6. Choose the **Brush** tool ✎ (B or Shift-B).

7. On the Options bar, choose a medium-sized Soft Round tip and an Opacity of 80%. Press X, if necessary, to make the Foreground color black.

8. Paint over the area(s) of the image that you want to keep in focus (**D–E**, next page). By painting with black, you will hide the blur effect on the object and create a visual separation between the object and the background. Paint over an area more than once to hide more of the motion blur.

   If you hide too much of the motion blur, press X to make the Foreground color white and draw strokes to restore the effect of the filter.

9. *Optional:* Double-click the Motion Blur listing on the Layers panel (**F**, next page). In the Motion Blur dialog, change the Angle or Distance settings, then click OK. The beauty of Smart Filters is that you can readjust the settings!

B We used these settings in the Motion Blur dialog, including setting the Angle dial to match the angle and direction of the motorcycle.

A This is the original photo.

C Apply the Motion Blur filter to the whole image first.

D Click the Smart Filter mask thumbnail, then paint with black where you want to hide the Motion Blur effect.

E The final results convey fast motion. We were careful not to remove the Motion Blur from the tires, since they would be moving too fast to stay in focus.

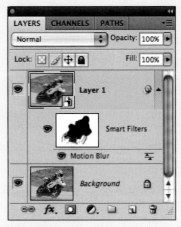

F The Layers panel shows the Smart Object layer (Layer 1), Smart Filter, and filter mask.

Changing the focus with a vignette

In these instructions, you'll create an area of focus by using a Smart Filter and a Smart Filter mask. An advantage of this method is that you can modify the filter settings and edit the mask to change which part of the image is in focus.

To create an area of focus (vignette) by using a mask:

1. Open an image in which you want to emphasize the center.**A**

2. On the Layers panel, click an image layer or the Background, then press Ctrl-J/Cmd-J to duplicate it.

3. Select the area of the image that you want to **emphasize** (keep in focus). For example, you could use the Elliptical Marquee tool (M or Shift-M) then Alt-drag/Option-drag to create an oval (as we did), or use the Lasso tool to create an irregular selection.

4. On the Options bar, click **Refine Edge**. Check Preview, click Default, soften the selection edge via the Feather slider, then click OK.

5. Press Ctrl-Shift-I/Cmd-Shift-I (Select > Inverse) to switch the selected and unselected areas.**B**

6. Choose Filter > **Convert for Smart Filters**, then click OK if an alert dialog appears.

7. Choose Filter > Blur > **Gaussian Blur**. The Gaussian Blur dialog opens. Click the zoom out (–) button so you can see the whole image in the preview window, increase the **Radius** to blur the image, then click OK.**C–D**

➤ To change the Radius amount, double-click the Gaussian Blur (Smart Filter) listing on the Layers panel. The dialog reopens.

A The original image is fully in focus.

B We created an oval selection, used Refine Edge to feather it (a Feather value of 40 px for this 300 ppi photo), and chose Select > Inverse. Now everything outside the oval marquee is selected.

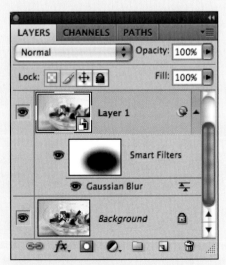

C For our focus vignette, we used a Radius value of 5.7 pixels in the Gaussian Blur dialog.

D The Layers panel shows our Smart Object layer (Layer 1), filter mask, and Smart Filter.

Another way to create a vignette is by manipulating light and dark values. In this case, you'll use (and move) the layer mask on a Levels adjustment layer to control the location of the vignette on the image.

To create a darkening vignette via Levels:

1. Open an image in which you want to emphasize an area in or near the center.

2. Follow steps 2–4 on the previous page, and keep the duplicate layer selected.

3. On the Adjustments panel, ⊘ click the **Levels** button. ⊡ ★ Ignore the Levels settings for the moment.

4. With the adjustment layer thumbnail selected, press Ctrl-I/Cmd-I to **invert** the mask.

5. On the Adjustments panel, move the white **Output Levels** slider for Levels to the left to darken all but the masked part of the image.**A–B**

6. *Optional:* To change the location of the darkening vignette, on the Layers panel, click the Levels adjustment layer, click the Link Layer Mask icon 🔗 to unlink the mask from the adjustment layer, click the layer mask thumbnail, then with the Move tool ⊹ (V), drag the mask shape to the desired location in the document window (it's like moving a spotlight).**C–D** Click again on the Layers panel to restore the link icon.

A We darkened Layer 1 via a Levels adjustment layer (we moved the white Output Levels slider to 180).

B For a more dramatic lighting effect, we changed the blending mode of the Levels adjustment layer to Difference and lowered the layer Opacity to 80%.

C We unlinked the layer mask from the adjustment layer thumbnail (the link icon disappeared), then, with the Move tool, moved the layer mask to the left.

D Because we moved the layer mask to the lower left, the light area (the area blocked by the mask) is now on the left side.

Using the Lens Correction filter

The Lens Correction filter lets you correct many types of lens distortion, such as when the top of a tall building or column appears to be tilting away from the camera (called "keystoning"), color fringes along high-contrast edges (chromatic aberrations), under- or overexposure along the edges of a photo (vignetting), and horizontal or vertical perspective.

To correct lens distortion:

1. Open an RGB image.**A** On the Layers panel, click an image layer or the Background, then press Ctrl-J/Cmd-J to duplicate it.

2. With the duplicate layer selected, choose Filter > **Convert for Smart Filters**, then click OK if an alert dialog appears.

3. Choose Filter > Distort > **Lens Correction**. The Lens Correction dialog opens.**B** You can use the sliders or scrubby sliders for these steps.

4. In the **Settings** area, do any of the following:

   Lower the **Remove Distortion** value to spread the image out (to fix pincushion distortion),**C** or raise this value to pinch the image inward (to fix barrel distortion).

   Use the **Chromatic Aberration** sliders to correct any color fringes along high-contrast edges.

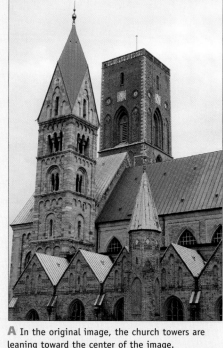

A In the original image, the church towers are leaning toward the center of the image.

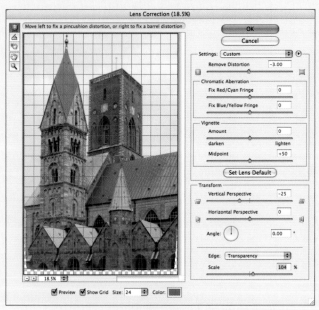

B The Lens Correction dialog lets you correct various types of optical distortion. The final settings we used are shown here.

C We moved the Remove Distortion slider to the left to keep the horizontal elements level (such as the red brick in the foreground).

➤ If the grid is distracting, uncheck Show Grid below the preview window.

Use the **Vignette** sliders to help correct for under- or overexposure on the outer edges of the image.

5. In the **Transform** area, do any of the following:

Lower the **Vertical Perspective** value to widen the top of the image, **A** or raise it to widen the bottom. You may have to readjust the Remove Distortion value to level the horizontal shapes.

Lower the **Horizontal Perspective** value to widen the left edge of the image, or raise it to widen the right edge of the image.

To rotate the image, change the **Angle** via the scrubby slider (it provides better control than the dial).

6. If empty canvas areas appear at the edges of the image, from the **Edge** menu, choose whether those areas will fill with an Edge Extension (extension of the image), Transparency, or the current Background Color.

Other options are to enlarge the image by raising the **Scale** value or to crop the image after exiting the dialog.

7. You can use any of the options below the preview window:

Click the **zoom in** or **zoom out** button or choose a preset zoom level from the menu.

Uncheck, then check **Preview** to compare the original and edited images.

Choose a grid size via the **Size** slider or click the **Color** swatch to change the grid color.

8. *Optional:* To save the current settings as a preset, from the settings menu choose Save Settings, enter a name (keep the .lcs extension), then click Save. Saved settings can be chosen from the Settings menu for any image.

9. Click OK.**B**

➤ To learn about any tool or option in the Lens Correction dialog, rest the pointer on it and read the description at the top of the dialog.

➤ To edit the Lens Correction results, double-click its Smart Filter listing on the Layers panel.

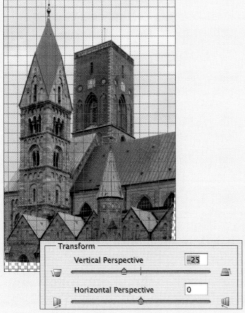

A We moved the Vertical Perspective slider to the left to widen the tops of the towers; now they're aligned better vertically.

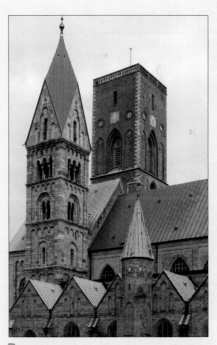

B In the corrected (and slightly cropped) photo, the horizontals and verticals are properly aligned.

Using the sharpening filters

Deciding which sharpening filter to use

Most digital photos need sharpening, and the need becomes greater if you change a document's dimensions or resolution with the Resample Image option checked, convert your document to CMYK Color mode, or apply a transformation command. You can correct unwanted blurring by using the **Smart Sharpen** filter **A** or the **Unsharp Mask** filter (the latter, despite its name, has a focusing effect).

These filters can add noise to an image and therefore should be applied at the end of the image-editing, adjustment, and color correction cycle—unless your image source is a scan, in which case we recommend applying some minimal sharpening before editing and once again afterward.

High-resolution printing also causes some minor blurring due to dot gain. You can anticipate and compensate for this by sharpening the image as you prepare it for output. Experience will teach you how much sharpening is needed.

(Note: We don't recommend using the Sharpen tool, because it creates unwanted artifacts. Instead, if you want to confine the sharpening effect, select an area before applying the filter.)

Although the Unsharp Mask filter has been an industry standard for years and is a powerful sharpening tool, Smart Sharpen may very well replace it in your workflow because it offers many advantages:

▶ **More control:** The Tonal Width sliders extend the sharpening through a broader tonal range. Also, Smart Sharpen gives you the ability to sharpen, then fade the sharpening, in the shadow and highlight areas separately, whereas Unsharp Mask doesn't provide that control.

▶ **More power:** The More Accurate option in Smart Sharpen performs multiple sharpening passes on the image automatically.

▶ **Fewer halos:** Smart Sharpen has the ability to detect edges, so fewer color halos are produced.

▶ **Flexibility:** Smart Sharpen offers a choice of three algorithms (to correct Gaussian Blur, Lens Blur, or Motion Blur), whereas Unsharp Mask corrects just Gaussian blur.

▶ **Better workflow:** Smart Sharpen lets you save and reuse your settings, for an improved workflow and better consistency.

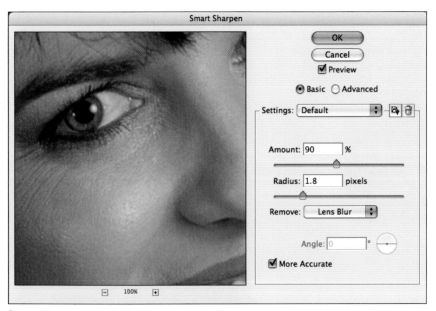

A Because the Smart Sharpen filter gives you a lot of control over how tonal areas in an image are sharpened, it's a good choice for sharpening portraits.

If your photo is slightly blurry to begin with, you can use the Smart Sharpen filter to sharpen it. Or if your photo became less sharp as a result of image edits or resampling, this filter can do an effective job of resharpening it.

To apply the Smart Sharpen filter:

1. Open a photo that needs sharpening.**A** On the Layers panel, click an image layer or the Background, then press Ctrl-J/Cmd-J to duplicate it. Choose Filter > **Convert for Smart Filters**, then click OK if an alert dialog appears.

2. Choose Filter > Sharpen > **Smart Sharpen**. The Smart Sharpen dialog opens (**A**, previous page). Keep the zoom level for the preview at 100%.

3. Check **More Accurate** to produce high-quality sharpening by allowing multiple passes of the filter. This takes longer but is worth the wait.

4. From the **Remove** menu, choose an algorithm for the correction: **Gaussian Blur** is a good, all-purpose choice; **Lens Blur** sharpens details with fewer resulting halos (we prefer this option); and **Motion Blur** is useful for correcting blurring due to movement of the camera or subject, but you need to know the angle of movement.

5. Try a **Radius** value between 1 and 2.5 pixels, and an **Amount** of 60–150% (you can use the scrubby slider for all the sliders in this dialog). The image should now look slightly oversharpened;**B** next, you'll fade the effect.

6. To control the amount of sharpening in the shadow and highlight areas, click **Advanced**, then click the **Shadow** tab.**C** Drag in the preview to display an area of the image that contains both shadows and midtones, then make the following adjustments:

   Choose a **Radius** value (between 5 and 10) to control how many neighboring pixels will be compared to a specific pixel. The higher the Radius, the larger the area to be compared.

   Change the **Tonal Width** value to control the range of midtones to be affected by the Fade Amount. The higher the width, the wider the range of midtones affected and the more evenly the sharpening fades into the shadows.

   Move the **Fade Amount** slider until you see the desired reduction of oversharpening in the shadows. If the Tonal Width value is too low, the effectiveness of this slider will be limited.

Continued on the following page

A The original 300 ppi resolution image is blurry.

B The settings we used in the Basic panel of the Smart Sharpen dialog (shown on the previous page) properly sharpened the key details, such as the eyes, teeth, and lips, but in the process also oversharpened the skin.

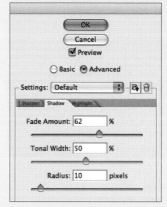

C In the Shadow tab of the Smart Sharpen dialog (Advanced), we used a high Fade Amount to soften the sharpening in the shadows (e.g., around the eyes) and a moderate Tonal Width amount to make the fade affect the shadows fully but the midtones only slightly.

7. Click the **Highlight** tab.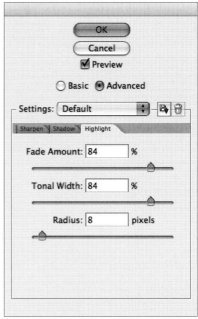 Drag the image in the preview to display an area that contains both highlights and midtones. Adjust the **Radius**, **Tonal Width**, and **Fade Amount** values, as in the previous step.

8. Hopefully, sharpness has been restored to the key details or features (such as the eyes and mouth in a portrait) but not to the broader or less important areas (cheeks, forehead). If the overall image now looks too sharp, click the **Sharpen** tab and lower the **Amount** value slightly. After making adjustments in one tab, you may need to readjust the settings in the other two.

9. Click OK.**B–C**

➤ To save the current settings as a preset, click the Save a Copy button, 🖫 enter a name, then click OK. Saved settings can be chosen from the Settings menu for any image.

➤ To compare the unsharpened and sharpened versions of the image, press on the dialog preview, then release.

➤ To restore all values in the dialog to their default settings, hold down Alt/Option and click Reset.

➤ To modify the Smart Sharpen results, double-click the Smart Sharpen listing on the Smart Object layer; the dialog reopens. Your new settings will be applied to the original blurry image, not to the sharpened one.

A In the Highlight tab of the Smart Sharpen dialog, we used a high Fade Amount again to soften the sharpening on the broad, flat highlight areas of skin (to make them look smoother) and a high Tonal Width amount to allow the fade to affect the highlights and lighter midtones.

B Finally, we used the sliders in the Shadow and Highlight tabs to soften the sharpening on the cheeks, nose, and forehead and around the eyes.

C Here is the original image, for comparison.

To sharpen an image, the Unsharp Mask filter increases the contrast between adjacent pixels. You can specify how much the contrast increases (the Amount), the number of surrounding pixels that the filter affects (the Radius), and the degree of contrast adjacent pixels must have to be affected by the filter (the Threshold).

To apply the Unsharp Mask filter:

1. Choose a zoom level of 100% for your image, then duplicate an image layer (Ctrl-J/Cmd-J).**A**

2. Right-click/Control-click the duplicate layer and choose **Convert to Smart Object**.

3. With the Smart Object layer selected, choose Filter > Sharpen > **Unsharp Mask**. The Unsharp Mask dialog opens.**B**

4. Choose an **Amount** value for the percentage increase in contrast between pixels. Use a low setting (try 80–100) for figures or natural objects or a higher setting (150–170) for sharp-edged objects. For a high-resolution image (say, 2000 x 3000 pixels or higher), try an Amount of 130–170.

   Uncheck, then recheck Preview to compare the original and sharpened images.

5. The **Radius** controls how many pixels surrounding high-contrast edges will be modified. Choosing an appropriate Radius can be tricky, as you need to consider the total number of pixels and the subject matter of the image.**C** The more pixels the image contains, the higher the Radius value needed to achieve the desired result. For a low-contrast image that contains large, simple objects and smooth transitions, try a high Radius of 2 (you'll rarely need to use a higher value); for an intricate, high-contrast image with sharp transitions, use a lower Radius (around 1).

   Note: The Amount and Radius settings are interdependent, meaning if you raise the Radius, you'll need to lower the Amount, and vice versa.

6. Choose a **Threshold** value (0–255) for the minimum amount of contrast an area must have to be affected by the filter (**A**, next page). Start with a Threshold of 0 (to sharpen the entire image), then raise it slowly. At a Threshold of 5–10, high-contrast areas will be sharpened and areas of lesser contrast will be sharpened less. When raising the Threshold, you can also increase the Amount and Radius to sharpen

Continued on the following page

A The original 300 ppi image is slightly blurry.

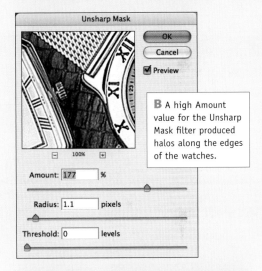

B A high Amount value for the Unsharp Mask filter produced halos along the edges of the watches.

C And a high Radius value (3.3) produced halos around the watch hands and numerals.

edges (thankfully, the filter won't oversharpen the low-contrast areas).

7. Click OK.**B** You can double-click the Unsharp Mask listing on the Layers panel at any time to reopen the dialog and adjust the settings.

➤ With the Unsharp Mask dialog open, if you click in the document window, that area will display in the dialog preview.

➤ If the sharpening produced color halos along the edges of objects, double-click the Blending Options icon ⬙ for the Unsharp Mask listing, choose Mode: Luminosity, then click OK. This will limit the sharpening to luminosity values and remove it from hue and saturation values.

SUGGESTED SETTINGS FOR UNSHARP MASK

Try using these values for a 3000 x 2000-pixel image:

Landscapes and other soft-edged subjects	Amount 100–150, Radius 1–1.5, Threshold 6–10
Portraits	Amount 100–120, Radius 1–2, Threshold 4–6, or to the point where skin areas start looking smoother
Buildings, objects for which contrast is a priority	Amount 150–200 or more, Radius 1.5–3, Threshold 0–3

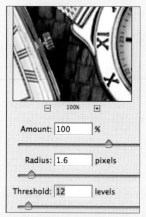

A At a high Threshold value (12) for the Unsharp Mask filter, only high-contrast edges were sharpened but the watchbands and background are still blurry.

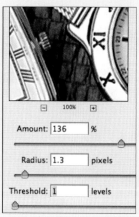

➤ To learn more about sharpening images, see our *Visual QuickPro Guide* to Photoshop.

B We used the values shown at left (a lower Threshold value) to produce this final, properly sharpened image.

Photoshop has a tool to fix every
kind of small imperfection, from
blemishes and crow's feet to creases
or stains in precious vintage photos.
We're seeing more middle-aged fashion models nowadays, but the pursuit of perfection persists. To a design
director, even a seemingly perfect portrait may need
some repair—perhaps the model has a birthmark
or a slightly imperfect smile—horrors! Or perhaps
you have an old, damaged family photo that you
want to salvage. In this chapter, you'll perform color
changes—such as changing product colors or whitening teeth—by using the Match Color command, the
Replace Color command, and the Color Replacement
tool; clone areas with the Clone Stamp tool; smooth
textures, such as skin, by using the Surface Blur filter;
smooth or remove wrinkles with the Healing Brush
and Spot Healing Brush tools; repair tears, dust marks,
or creases with the Patch tool; **A–B** and remove
red-eye with—yup! You guessed it—the Red Eye tool.

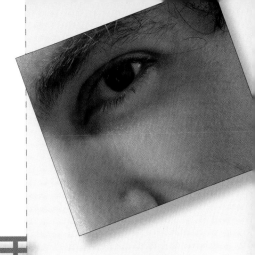

RETOUCH

18

IN THIS CHAPTER

Using the Match Color command. . . .280

Cloning 282

Using the Replace Color command. . .284

Using the Surface Blur filter. 287

Using the Color Replacement tool. . .288

Using the Healing Brush tool 290

Using the Spot Healing Brush tool . .293

Using the Patch tool. 294

Using the Red Eye tool 296

A The original photo
has some creases.

B The Patch tool magically repaired them.

Using the Match Color command

You can use the Match Color command to match the overall color and tonal values in one document with those of another document. This is useful, say, for correcting a series of product shots that were shot under slightly different lighting conditions or with different camera settings and have different color values. Match Color works best on images of the same subject matter (e.g., food, figures) or of similar content, such as a series of landscapes.

To match colors between documents by using the Match Color command:

1. Open a one-layer RGB document to be used as the source for the desired color and tonal values, and a second one-layer RGB document to be the recipient (target) of the color match.**A–B**

2. *Optional:* Display the Histogram panel  to observe a graph of the tonal changes.

3. With the target document active, on the Layers panel, click the Background, press Ctrl-J/Cmd-J to duplicate it, and keep the duplicate selected.

4. Choose Image > Adjustments > **Match Color**. The Match Color dialog opens. Check Preview.

5. From the **Source** menu, choose the name of the source document that you opened in step 1.**C**

A The two original images include a scene with bright midday sunlight...

B ...and a misty scene with overcast light.

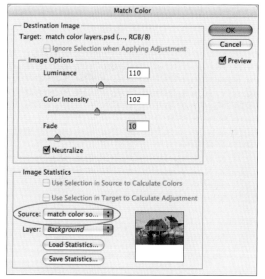

C In the Match Color dialog, we chose an image from the Source menu.

D By using the Match Color command, we made the "overcast" image adopt the warmer tones of the "midday sun" image.

The target document will instantly adopt the color tones of the chosen source document.

6. In the **Image Options** area, do any of the following:

   Move the **Luminance** slider to adjust the overall brightness of the image.

   Move the **Color Intensity** slider to adjust the color saturation.

   Move the **Fade** slider to restore some of the original color to the image, blending the old and the new.

   Check **Neutralize** to remove any color casts from the target document. If this causes too great a color shift, try lessening the effect via the Fade slider.

7. Readjust any of the sliders as needed, then click OK (**D**, previous page).

➤ To limit the choice of colors you match from (to help prevent peculiar color shifts from occurring), create a selection in the source document before choosing Match Color. In the Match Color dialog, check Use Selection in Source to Calculate Colors.

Another use for the Match Color dialog is to quickly remove a color cast from an image. It doesn't always work, but when it does, it works beautifully.

To remove a color cast by using the Match Color command:

1. Open an RGB image.**A** Choose Image > Adjustments > **Match Color**. The Match Color dialog opens.**B** Check Preview.

2. Don't select a Source document, but do check **Neutralize**.

3. Do any of the following (you can use the scrubby sliders):

   Adjust the **Luminance** and **Color Intensity** as needed.

   If the color correction is too severe, adjust the **Fade** value to restore some of the original image color.

4. Click OK.**C**

A The original image has a cool, bluish cast.

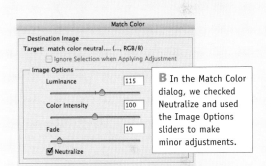

B In the Match Color dialog, we checked Neutralize and used the Image Options sliders to make minor adjustments.

C This corrected the cool color cast.

Cloning

You can use the Clone Stamp tool to clone imagery on the same layer or from one layer to another within the same document, or from one document to another.

To clone imagery:

1. Open an RGB document.**A**

2. Choose the **Clone Stamp** tool ⬒ (S or Shift-S).

3. On the Options bar,**C** do the following:

    Click the **Brush** Preset picker arrowhead, then click a Soft Round brush in an appropriate size for the area you want to clone.

    Choose a blending **Mode**.

    Choose an **Opacity** percentage.

    Choose a **Flow** percentage to control the rate of application.

    Check **Aligned** to maintain the same distance between the source point and the area that you drag across, even if you release the mouse, switch modes, or switch brushes between strokes (to clone a large area seamlessly); or uncheck Aligned to sample from the original source point each time you release the mouse (to produce repetitive clones of a smaller area).

    From the **Sample** menu, choose **All Layers** to sample pixels from all the currently visible layers that you Alt-click/Option-click over (see the sidebar on the next page).

    Optional: Click the Ignore Adjustment Layers When Cloning button ◼ if the document contains adjustment layers and you want the Clone Stamp tool to ignore their effects when sampling.

4. Create a new layer in the target document, and keep it selected.

5. Alt-click/Option-click the area you want to clone from to establish a source point.**B**

6. Drag the Clone Stamp tool back and forth where you want the clone to appear.

    Two pointers will appear onscreen: a cross pointer over the source point and a brush

A We want to remove the metal pipes from the side of the building (wall) and add more leaves to fill in the front of the trellis.

B We Alt-clicked/Option-clicked with the Clone Stamp tool to sample a blank area of the wall.

C We chose these Options bar settings for the Clone Stamp tool.

pointer where you drag the mouse.**A** Imagery from the source point will display within the brush cursor.**B** Note: If the whole layer displays in the overlay as you clone, display the Clone Source panel,▤ then check Clipped. ★

7. *Optional:* If you want to establish a new source point to clone from, Alt-click/Option-click a different area in the source document.**C–D** You can also change Options bar settings for the Clone Stamp tool between strokes.

➤ To create a "double-exposure" effect, with underlying pixels partially showing through the cloned pixels, choose a low Opacity percentage for the Clone Stamp tool.

➤ Read about the Clone Source panel (pages 156–157), which lets you keep track of source points in multiple documents when using the Clone Stamp tool.

SAMPLING LAYERS

With the Sample: All Layers option checked/chosen on the Options bar for the current editing tool, the tool will sample pixels from all the visible layers and send the results to the current layer. If the current layer is a new, blank layer, you'll be able to show and hide your edits — or erase any unwanted edits — at any time.

B We're continuing to sample the wall and clone away the pipe. Multiple sampling prevents a noticeable (tacky!) repetition of the texture.

A We're dragging with the Clone Stamp tool to replace the pipe with pixels from the blank wall.

D Compare this final image with Figure **A** on the previous page.

C We're sampling the vine leaves because we want to add more leaves to the trellis.

Using the Replace Color command

By using the Replace Color command, you can adjust the hue, saturation, or lightness of colors in specific areas that you click (in either the document window or the dialog) without using any selection tools. This powerful command works best for adjusting soft-edged areas, such as in a landscape, that don't require a sharp-edged selection.

To use the Replace Color command:

1. *Optional:* For an RGB document that you're going to send to a commercial printer, choose View > Proof Setup > Working CMYK to see a soft proof of the image in CMYK color.

   Once you've made a choice from the Proof Setup submenu, you can toggle the proof on and off while the Replace Color dialog is open by pressing Ctrl-Y/Cmd-Y. Regardless of whether the proof is on or off, the Color and Result swatches in the Replace Color dialog always display in RGB.

2. Click a layer or the Background.**A**

3. *Optional:* Create a selection to confine the color replacement to.

4. Choose Image > Adjustments > **Replace Color**. The Replace Color dialog opens.

5. Initially, the preview window will be all or mostly black. In the document window, click on or drag across the color that you want to replace.**B** That color will appear in the **Color** swatch at the top of the dialog.**C**

   Click **Selection** to preview the current selection in the preview window, or click **Image** to display the entire document. You can press, then release Control to toggle the two display modes.

6. Do either of the following:

   To add more color areas to the selection, with the first **eyedropper,** Shift-click or drag in the preview window or document window.

   Move the **Fuzziness** slider to the right to add similar colors to the selection or to the left to narrow the range of selected colors.

   Check **Localized Color Clusters** to limit the selection to similar, contiguous colors. ★ (We've gotten similar but better results by lowering the Fuzziness value.)

   (To create a new selection, click with the eyedropper without holding down Shift.)

A We want to replace the red on the three watering cans in the middle of this image with a soft tan.

B When we click the small red can...

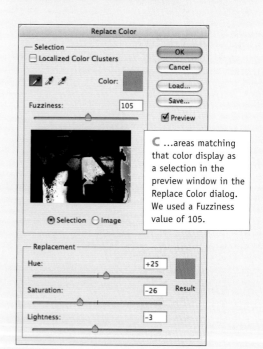

C ...areas matching that color display as a selection in the preview window in the Replace Color dialog. We used a Fuzziness value of 105.

7. If you've added colors to the selection that you now want to subtract, with the first eyedropper, ☒ Alt-click/Option-click or drag in the preview window or document window.**A–C** Or choose the ☒ eyedropper, then click or drag without holding down Alt/Option.

8. To replace the selected colors, do either of the following:

In the **Replacement** area, choose replacement **Hue**, **Saturation**, and **Lightness** values. The Result swatch will update as you do so. A Saturation value greater than +25 may produce a nonprintable color.

Click the **Result** swatch, choose a color from the Color Picker, then click OK. The sliders will shift to reflect the attributes of the new color.

Note: The Replacement sliders will stay put, even if you click a different area of the image or add to or subtract from the selection.

9. Click OK.**D**

➤ The Replacement sliders won't change the amount of Black (K) in a color for a CMYK document. That component is set separately by the Black Generation feature in Photoshop.

➤ To restore the original settings to the dialog, hold down Alt/Option and click Reset.

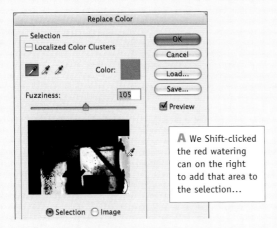

A We Shift-clicked the red watering can on the right to add that area to the selection...

B ...but this applied the replacement color (gold) to the orange can in the background too, which wasn't our intention.

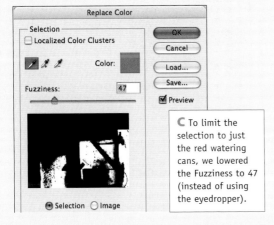

C To limit the selection to just the red watering cans, we lowered the Fuzziness to 47 (instead of using the eyedropper).

D As shown in this final image, only the colors on the three formerly red cans in the foreground were replaced.

Another use of the Replace Color command is for whitening teeth or the whites of the eyes. By selecting those problem areas in an image before using the Replace Color command, you can quickly correct any discoloration.

To whiten teeth or eyes:

1. Open a portrait photo that you want to correct, and duplicate the Background. Choose the **Lasso** tool, zoom in on the teeth or eye area, then drag to create a tight selection of the teeth **A** or of the white areas on one of the eyes. (If you prefer, you can create a selection by painting a Quick Mask instead of using the Lasso tool; see page 143.)

2. On the Options bar, click **Refine Edge**. In the Refine Edge dialog, click **Default**, choose a **Feather** value of 6–12 px, then click OK.

3. Choose Image > Adjustments > **Replace Color**.

4. Using the **eyedropper** from the Replace Color dialog, **B** click the preview or click the selection in the document window.

5. To add related shades of white to the selection, move the **Fuzziness** slider or Shift-click on, or drag across, any unselected areas.

6. *Optional:* Check Localized Color Clusters to limit the selection to contiguous colors. ★

7. Lower the **Saturation** to desaturate the selected area and remove the off-white tinge (you can use the scrubby slider), and raise the **Lightness** slightly to brighten the selected area.

8. Click OK. Deselect the selection. **C**

9. If you're whitening eyes, repeat the steps above to select and whiten the off-white areas in the other eye.

A We used the Lasso tool to select the teeth.

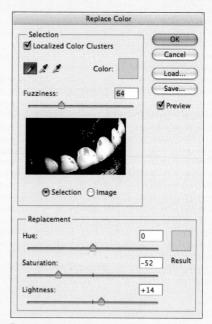

B Then we used the eyedropper in the Replace Color dialog to refine the selection.

C The teeth were whitened using the settings shown in the preceding figure — no whitening strips required!

Using the Surface Blur filter

With the Surface Blur filter, it's easy to smooth out skin pores or mottled surfaces on objects.

To smooth skin or other surfaces:

1. Press Ctrl-J/Cmd-J to duplicate the Background in an image that needs surface smoothing. **A**

2. Choose Filter > Blur > **Surface Blur**. The Surface Blur dialog opens. Check Preview.

3. Choose a low **Threshold** value (try 3–6) to blur only low-contrast areas, such as the cheeks and forehead in a portrait, while preserving the contrast in key details, such as facial features.

4. To soften skin (cheeks, forehead again), choose a **Radius** of around 6–12. Increase the Radius just enough to produce the desired degree of smoothing. If the Radius is too low, the poster-izing effect of the filter may make the skin look blotchy.

5. Readjust the **Threshold** to either increase or decrease the amount of blurring in low-contrast areas. Too much smoothing could make a face look artificial—but then again, this whole task is a lesson in artifice!

6. Click OK. **B**

7. *Optional:* To restore details from the original image, either lower the opacity of the dupli-cate layer slightly or follow the next set of instructions.

➤ We don't recommend applying the Surface Blur filter as a Smart Filter (to a Smart Object). If fur-ther retouching were needed, you would have to double-click the Smart Object layer, but you wouldn't see the smoothing effect onscreen.

To selectively restore details that were blurred by the Surface Blur filter, apply strokes to a layer mask.

To restore details selectively after using the Surface Blur filter:

1. With the duplicate layer selected, click the **Add Layer Mask** button on the Layers panel.

2. Choose the **Brush** tool (B or Shift-B).

3. On the Options bar, choose a small, Soft Round tip and an Opacity of 80–90%.

4. With black as the Foreground color, draw strokes on any areas you want to restore sharpness to, such as lips, eyes, eyebrows, or hair. **C** To restore the blur effect to areas that you mask uninten-tionally, paint with white.

A The pores on this woman's skin look too prominent.

B With a Radius setting of 7 pixels and a Threshold set-ting of 5 levels chosen for our 300 ppi file, the Surface Blur filter successfully smoothed the skin texture while keeping the facial details crisp. Compare the cheeks and under-eye areas in this image with the previous figure.

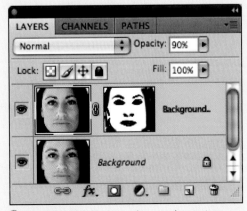

C We painted with black on a layer mask to restore facial details from the underlying layer.

Using the Color Replacement tool

Like the Replace Color command, the Color Replacement tool lets you change color, hue, saturation, and luminosity values—but here, instead of using a dialog, you apply changes manually with a brush. You can also specify mode, sampling, limits, and tolerance parameters for the tool. And unlike the Brush tool, which applies flat colors, the Color Replacement tool preserves the original texture, when possible, as it changes colors. This tool, like the Replace Color and Match Color commands, might be of interest to advertising and catalog designers in particular.

To use the Color Replacement tool:

1. Open an RGB image.

2. Choose the **Color Replacement** tool 🖊 (B or Shift-B).

3. To choose a **replacement** color, do either of the following:

   Choose a Foreground color from the Color or Swatches panel.

   Alt-click/Option-click in the image with the Color Replacement tool to sample a color (temporary Eyedropper).

4. If the color you chose isn't already on the Swatches panel, ⊞ save it to the panel now by clicking the **New Swatch of Foreground Color** button 🔲, then clicking OK.

5. From the Options bar (**A**, next page) choose parameters for the tool:

   Click the **Brush Preset** picker arrowhead and choose a suitable Diameter, a high Hardness value, and a low Spacing value (you can also press [or] to change the brush diameter).

   To control which color characteristics the tool applies, choose a blending **Mode: Hue, Saturation, Color,** or **Luminosity**. We like the results we've gotten with Color mode.

   Click a **Sampling** button: **Continuous** 🖊 to apply the current Foreground color to all pixels the brush passes over (we prefer this option because it lets us replace both light and dark colors); or **Once** 🖊 to sample the first pixel the brush crosshairs click on and then apply the Foreground color only to pixels that match that initial sampled color (since this option confines the sampling to just one color, if you need to replace, say, different shades of a particular color, you would have to sample each one separately); or **Background Swatch** 🖊 to replace only colors that match or are similar to the current Background color (choose a Background color for this option).

   From the **Limits** menu, choose **Discontiguous** to recolor only pixels under the pointer; or **Contiguous** to recolor pixels under the pointer plus adjacent pixels; or **Find Edges** (our favorite option) to recolor pixels under the pointer while keeping the color replacement within discrete shapes. For all three choices, the tool replaces only pixels that fall within the current Sampling parameters.

   To control the range within which a color can differ from the sampled color yet still be recolored, choose a **Tolerance** value (1–100%). A high Tolerance value permits a wide range of colors to be recolored; a low value limits recoloring to only pixels that closely match the sampled color.

   Optional: Check Anti-alias to smooth the transitions between the original and replacement colors.

6. Click a layer, then drag across the areas you want to recolor (**B–E**, next page). Only pixels that fall within the chosen Mode, Sampling, Limits, and Tolerance parameters will be recolored.

➤ For the most targeted control when using the Color Replacement tool, change the Options bar settings between strokes.

A Choose settings for the Color Replacement tool from the Options bar.

B We want to change the lighter green stripes on the woman's sweater to aqua blue.

C With the Color Replacement tool and the tool settings shown in the screen capture of the Options bar above, we're painting light blue (our current Foreground color) over the light green on the woman's sweater.

D Next, we zoom in to paint smaller areas. At a Tolerance of 40%, we're able to replace both the highlights and shadows within the green stripes. To replace the green along the edges of the stripes but not in the darker stripes, we'll lower the Tolerance to 15%, then paint again with light blue, while making sure to keep the center of the brush cursor (the +) within the green areas.

E With Limits: Contiguous as the setting, we were more likely to (and did) accidentally recolor the dark stripes. To repair our mistaskes, we Alt-click/Option-click to sample the original color in the darker stripe (as shown here), then paint with that color. Last of all, we'll click to select the light blue swatch that we saved to the Swatches panel, then continue to apply more light blue to replace the green.

The three tools discussed next sample a texture, apply it to the target area, then blend the texture into the existing color and brightness values, for a seamless repair. (The Clone Stamp tool merely copies a source color without blending it into the target area.) With these tools, it's easy to fix imperfections such as facial blemishes and paper creases.

With the **Healing Brush** tool, you Alt-click/Option-click an unblemished (sample) area, then apply strokes to repair the blemish.**A** The blemish pixels are replaced with the sampled pixels.

With the **Patch** tool, you select the blemish area first, then drag the selection marquee over an unblemished area for sampling. Here again, the blemish pixels are replaced with the sampled pixels.

And with the **Spot Healing Brush** tool, you simply stroke over blemishes without sampling. Pixels are magically replaced based on data from neighboring pixels.

Using the Healing Brush tool

To use the Healing Brush tool:

1. Choose the **Healing Brush** tool ![brush icon] (J or Shift-J).

2. Create a new, blank layer.**B**

3. *Optional:* To prevent the Healing Brush from picking up colors from surrounding areas and to confine the repair to a specific area, create a selection with the Lasso tool.

4. On the Options bar,**C** do all of the following:

   Click the **Brush Preset** picker arrowhead, make the brush **Diameter** slightly wider than the area you want to retouch, and choose a high **Hardness** value. (Also, in Preferences > Cursors, click Full Size Brush Tip and check Show Crosshair in Brush Tip.)

   Choose **Mode:** Normal to preserve the grain, texture, and noise of the area surrounding the target; or choose a different mode if you don't need to preserve those attributes, such as Lighten for subtle retouching or for wrinkles or creases that are very close together, to prevent them from cloning onto one another.

   Click **Source:** Sampled.

A We appreciate this woman's natural beauty, but advertisers might not like her crow's feet (maybe they will appreciate her nice, bright teeth?).

B We'll draw strokes on a new, blank layer, with Sample: All Layers chosen for the Healing Brush tool.

C We chose these Options bar settings for the Healing Brush tool.

Uncheck Aligned to create repetitive strokes anywhere in the image, always sampling from the same source point; or check **Aligned** to maintain the same distance between the source point (which will change) and the target area that you drag across.

Since you'll be working on a new, blank layer, from the **Sample** menu, choose **All Layers** to sample pixels from all the layers below the pointer.

5. Alt-click/Option-click an area to use as the source texture.**A** The sampled area will display within the brush cursor. ★

6. With the new, blank layer still selected, drag across the area you want to repair.**B** When you release the mouse, the source texture will be applied to the target area and will be blended with its surrounding pixels. It will render in two stages, so be patient.**C**

7. To establish a new source point for further repairs, Alt-click/Option-click a different area, then apply more strokes (you can press [or] to change the diameter of the brush tip).

8. *Optional:* For more realistic results, lower the opacity of the new layer slightly to blend it with the original image layer.

➤ To correct mistakes made with the Healing Brush tool, hide the image layers below the new layer that you applied strokes to (so you'll be able to see your strokes more easily), then with the Eraser tool, erase any unwanted strokes. This is easier than stepping back through brush stroke states on the History panel.

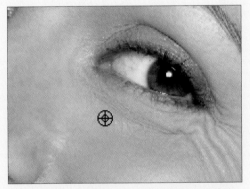

A With the Healing Brush tool, Alt-click/Option-click the area you want to use as replacement pixels...

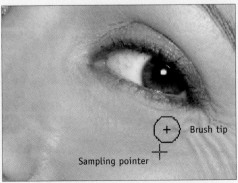

Brush tip

Sampling pointer

B ...then drag across the area you want to repair. A brush tip and a sampling pointer appear onscreen.

C We softened the lines around the right eye; we could do the same for the left.

REMOVING FACIAL HOT SPOTS

A The Healing Brush tool is also useful for removing shiny hot spots from a portrait, which are caused by harsh, uneven lighting. Choose Mode: Darken on the Options bar for the tool, then Alt-click/Option-click to sample a medium-toned area of skin.

B Drag once or twice over a hot spot, letting your stroke follow the contours of the face.

C With Darken chosen as its Mode, the tool repaired only the light areas of skin. Now the nose looks less shiny.

D With the Spot Healing Brush tool and a small brush tip, drag once along a fold of skin, in the direction of the wrinkle.

Using the Spot Healing Brush tool

The Spot Healing Brush tool is an effective blemish and wrinkle remover, and it's cheaper than Botox. Skin folds tend to be close together and have highlights and shadows, which can make it difficult to pick a sample area. An advantage of this tool is that you can correct imperfections without sampling.

To use the Spot Healing Brush tool:

1. Do either of the following:

   Press Ctrl-J/Cmd-J to duplicate the Background, and leave the duplicate layer selected.

   Create a new, blank layer to contain your correction strokes, and keep it selected.

2. Choose the **Spot Healing Brush** tool ✏️ (J or Shift-J), and set the zoom level to 100%.

3. In Preferences > Cursors for Painting Cursors, click Full Size Brush Tip and check Show Crosshair in Brush Tip.

4. On the Options bar, do the following:

   Choose a **Mode**. For preserving skin tones, we've gotten good results with Normal and Lighten modes. In Replace mode, the tool may pick up unwanted facial details in the stroke, such as hair or eyelashes.

   To help preserve tonal values in skin tones when correcting large or long facial lines, click **Type: Proximity Match;** or to even out the tonal values when retouching a small area, click **Type: Create Texture**.

   To allow the brush to sample pixels from all layers below the pointer, check **Sample All Layers** (check this option if you created a new, blank layer in step 1); or if you're working on an image layer, uncheck Sample All Layers to allow the brush to sample pixels from only the current layer.

5. Make the brush slightly wider than the area to be repaired (such as a wrinkle) by pressing [or], then drag once across it (**D**, previous page and **A** this page). Repeat to repair other areas. **B** We've found that a small brush produces the most subtle changes.

6. To make the results look more natural, lower the opacity of the duplicate or new layer slightly to blend it with the original image layer.

➤ If you applied your Spot Healing strokes to a new layer, you can erase any unwanted strokes from that layer.

A The wrinkles we dragged over are removed.

B We dragged again with the Spot Healing Brush tool to remove more lines from the corner of the eye.

Using the Patch tool

The Patch tool is a good choice for retouching bags or wrinkles below eyes and for repairing tears, stains, and dust marks in vintage photos. With this tool, you select an area before applying the repair.

To use the Patch tool:

1. Choose the **Patch** tool ⟳ (J or Shift-J).

2. On the Options bar, click **Patch**: **Source**.

3. Press Ctrl-J/Cmd-J to duplicate the Background, and keep the duplicate layer selected.

4. Drag a marquee around the area to be repaired.**A**

5. *Optional:* Shift-drag to add to the selection or Alt-drag/Option-drag to subtract from it.

6. Drag from inside the selection to the area you want to sample from.**B** When you release the mouse, imagery from the sampled area will appear within the original selection. Deselect (Ctrl-D/Cmd-D).**C**

7. *Optional:* When retouching a portrait, if you notice a color change in the patched skin, try changing the blending mode of the duplicate layer to Lighten.

➤ If you're not satisfied with the Patch tool results but you want to reuse the Patch selection, click the "Patch Tool" state on the History panel, then drag to sample a different area.

➤ Before using the Patch tool, you can create a selection with any tool (or create a selection by using a Quick Mask), then with the Patch tool, drag the selection to the desired sample area.

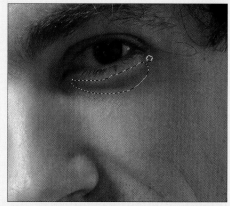

A With the Patch tool, select the area to be retouched.

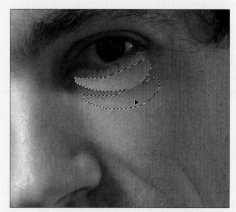

B Drag from the selected area to the area you want to sample pixels from. To better preserve the skin texture, we're sampling an area near the eye.

C The patch sample is applied to the selection.

REPARING A DAMAGED PHOTO WITH THE PATCH TOOL

A The original photo has some areas of damage.

B With the Patch tool, an area is selected for repair.

C Next, the selection is dragged across an undamaged area, for sampling.

D The sampled pixels replaced the damaged area. (We'll use the tool again to repair the other damaged areas.)

REMOVING DUST MARKS AND SCRATCHES

You can also use Filter > Noise > Dust & Scratches to quickly remove dust marks or small flecks of white from an old photo. Move the Radius slider slightly until most of the white dust marks disappear, then move the Threshold slider until some image detail is restored, but not to the point that the dust marks reappear.

Using the Red Eye tool

Red-eye in portrait photography results from light emitted by a camera-mounted or built-in electronic flash reflecting off the retina when a subject is looking straight at the camera. You're less likely to run into this problem if your camera has a built-in red-eye control or if you use a flash bracket and an off-camera flash, and if the subject looks away from the camera. For photos taken without such controls, you can remove the red-eye with a click of the Red Eye tool in Photoshop.

To remove red-eye from a portrait:

1. Open a portrait photo, and zoom on the eye area to 200%– 300% view.

2. Choose the **Red Eye** tool 🐷 (J or Shift-J).

3. On the Options bar, do the following:

    Choose a **Pupil Size** for the recolored pupil; try 60–80%. You don't want the tool to enlarge the pupil.

    Choose a **Darken Amount** to control how dark the resulting pupil will be; try 30–40%. Light eyes need a lower setting than dark eyes. If the Darken Amount setting is too high, the tool will make the pupils too dark.

4. Click once on the red area on each pupil. The tool will remove all traces of red. **A–B**

➤ If the tool enlarged the pupil too much, undo the initial click, lower the Pupil Size value, then click again. Similarly, to try a different Darken Amount value, undo the initial click first.

➤ You don't need to drag across the eye with the Red Eye tool; the tool is smart enough to find the pupil area automatically when you click.

➤ The Camera Raw dialog has a nifty Red Eye Removal tool that's similar to the one in Photoshop.

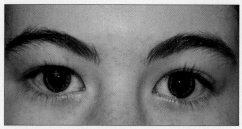

A With the Red Eye tool, click once on each eye.

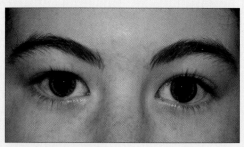

B The red-eye is gone.

REMOVING THE LAST TRACES OF RED

If the Red Eye tool fails to remove traces of red from the iris of the eyes (the area around the pupils), do the following: Zoom in on an eye (200%–300%), then choose the Color Replacement tool. 🖌 On the Options bar, choose a very small brush tip, Mode: Color, Sampling: Once, ⊕ Limits: Contiguous, and Tolerance: 30%. Alt-click/Option-click to sample an iris color to replace the red, then draw strokes to paint out the remaining red traces.

CONTINUING YOUR STUDIES

To explore the topic of retouching in more depth, see our *Visual QuickPro Guide* to Photoshop.

By this point, hopefully, you've got the hang of using the Layers panel and basic layer features and are ready to explore the panel further. In this chapter, we'll show you how to blend pixels between layers; create and use layer masks; create and use clipping masks; link layers; transform and warp layers; create and edit Smart Object layers; and fill areas with a solid color.

Changing layer opacity and fill values

The Opacity setting on the Layers panel controls the opacity of a layer, including any layer effects, whereas the Fill setting controls the opacity of a layer, excluding any layer effects (for layer effects, see the next chapter). Both settings are available for image, type, adjustment, Smart Object, and shape layers. Each layer has its own Opacity and Fill percentages.

To change the opacity or fill of a layer:

1. Click a layer (not the Background).

2. From the Layers panel, choose an **Opacity** or **Fill** percentage (you can use the scrubby slider).**A–B** The lower the opacity or fill, the more pixels from the layer below will be visible through the currently selected layer.

A The original image contains four layers, including an editable type layer.

B We lowered the Opacity of the three image layers; and we lowered just the Fill percentage of the type layer to keep the drop shadow (a layer effect) at full opacity.

MORE LAYERS

19

IN THIS CHAPTER

Changing layer opacity and
  fill values 297

Blending layers 298

Creating layer masks. 302

Editing layer masks 303

Working with layer masks 306

Using clipping masks 308

Linking layers 309

Transforming layers 310

Warping layers. 313

Using Smart Object layers 314

Filling areas with a solid color 316

Blending layers

The blending mode you choose for a layer controls how that layer blends with the layer directly below it. You can change the blending mode for any kind of layer, be it image, type, adjustment, shape, or Smart Object. Some modes, such as Soft Light, tend to produce subtle effects, whereas others, such as Difference, produce dramatic color shifts. The default mode is Normal. The individual blending modes are described and illustrated on pages 198–202.

To choose a blending mode for a layer:

1. Click a layer (not the Background). **A**

2. Choose a **blending mode** from the menu in the upper left corner of the Layers panel. **B–D**

➤ If you don't have a painting or editing tool selected, you can press Shift- + (plus) or Shift - – (minus) to cycle through the blending modes for the current layer. If a painting or editing tool is selected, the same shortcut will change the mode for the tool instead.

➤ To change the blending mode for a Smart Filter on a Smart Object layer, see page 337.

A We duplicated the Background in the original image.

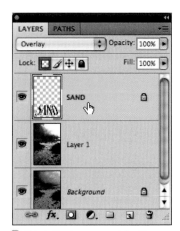

B To the duplicate layer, we applied the Desaturate command to make it grayscale, then chose Screen as the blending mode.

C We lowered the Opacity of the duplicate layer to 70%. The type layer has its own blending mode of Overlay.

D This is the Layers panel for the previous figure.

In these instructions, you'll edit a duplicate layer and then blend the original and duplicate layers by using the opacity and blending mode controls on the Layers panel. You can use this method to soften the effect of a filter or other image-editing command or to try out various blending modes. If you don't like the results, simply discard the duplicate layer (or Smart Filter) and start over.

To blend a modified layer with the original layer:

1. Click a layer, **A** then press Ctrl-J/Cmd-J to duplicate it. (Or if you know how to use Smart Filters, duplicate an image layer, then right-click/Control-click the duplicate and choose Convert to Smart Object.)

2. Modify the duplicate layer by applying one or more image-editing commands (such as filters) or by using an image-editing tool.

3. On the Layers panel, adjust the **Opacity** of the duplicate layer to achieve the desired degree of transparency **B–D** and/or choose a different **blending mode**.

A This is the original image.

B We applied the Dry Brush and Grain filters to a duplicate layer (which we had converted to a Smart Object), then lowered the layer opacity.

C This is the original image.

D We applied the Charcoal filter to a duplicate of the Background, then lowered the layer opacity.

The Blending Options in the Layer Style dialog offer, in addition to the blending mode, opacity, and fill controls we've already discussed, a number of advanced settings for controlling how a layer and layer effects blend with underlying layers.

To choose blending options for a layer:

1. Double-click next to a layer name on the Layers panel, or right-click/Control-click a layer and choose **Blending Options**. The Layer Style dialog opens, with Blending Options selected in the upper left.**A**

2. Check Preview.

3. *Optional:* In the General Blending area, change the Blend Mode or Opacity (the same options as on the Layers panel).

4. To control the opacity of the layer, excluding any layer effects, in the Advanced Blending area, adjust the **Fill Opacity** (this has the same function as the Fill option on the Layers panel).

5. Using the **Blend If** sliders, you can control which pixels in the current layer stay visible and which pixels from the underlying layer show through the current layer (**A–D**, next page):

Move the black **This Layer** slider to the right to remove shadow areas from the current layer.

Move the white **This Layer** slider to the left to remove highlight areas from the current layer.

Move the black **Underlying Layer** slider to the right to restore shadow areas from the underlying layer.

Move the white **Underlying Layer** slider to the left to restore highlight areas from the underlying layer.

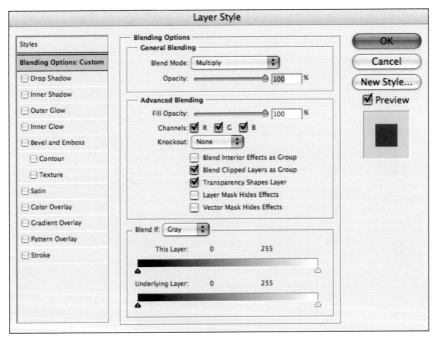

A The Blending Options in the Layer Style dialog offer an assortment of layer blending techniques.

To adjust the midtone colors independently of the lightest and darkest colors, Alt-drag/Option-drag a slider; it will divide in two.**E**

6. Click OK.

➤ For the sake of simplicity, you can work with all the channels at once by leaving the Blend If menu set to Gray, or if you want to experiment with blending each color channel separately, choose a channel from the Blend If menu before moving the sliders.

A This is the original image.

B We chose black as the Foreground color and a light tan as the Background color, duplicated the Background, then applied the Sketch > Charcoal filter to the duplicate layer (the filter used the colors we chose).

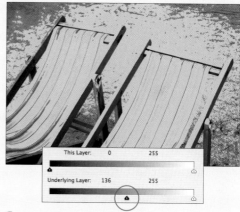

C To allow some of the dark tones in the photo to peek through the filter layer, we moved the black Underlying Layer slider in the Blending Options panel of the Layer Style dialog.

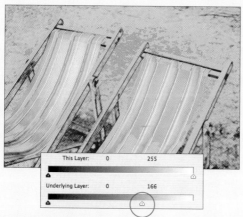

D A second option was to restore some of the light tones from the photo by moving the white Underlying Layer slider.

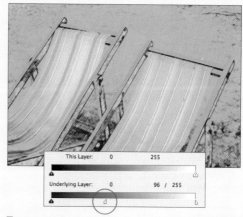

E And a third option was to restore only the midtone colors (not the lightest colors) by dividing and moving the white Underlying Layer slider.

Creating layer masks

A layer mask is an editable and removable 8-bit grayscale channel that serves the function of hiding all or some of the pixels on a layer. White areas in a layer mask permit pixels to be seen, black areas hide pixels, and gray areas mask pixels partially. With the layer mask thumbnail selected, you can edit or deactivate the mask, or move or copy it to other layers. When you're done working with the mask, you can either apply it to make the effect permanent or discard it to undo its effect completely. The new Masks panel provides access to most of the masking options in one convenient location.

A The original image contains two layers. Before creating a mask, we selected the archway, then clicked the tile layer.

To create a layer mask: ★

1. *Optional:* Create a selection, to become the mask shape.

2. On the **Layers** panel, click an image or type layer or a layer group.**A**

3. Display the **Masks** panel.▣

4. To create a white mask in which all the layer pixels are visible or to reveal layer pixels only within the selection area, click the **Add Pixel Mask button** ▣ at the top of the Masks panel

(or click the Add Layer Mask button ▣ at the bottom of the Layers panel).**B–D**

5. *Optional:* To swap the black and white areas in the mask, click Invert on the Masks panel.

➤ Another way to create a black mask in which all the layer pixels are hidden or in which just the pixels inside a selection are hidden is to Alt-click/Option-click either the Add Pixel Mask button on the Masks panel or the Add Layer Mask button on the Layers panel.

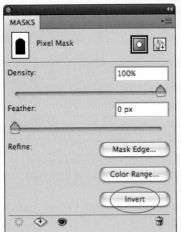

B We used the Masks panel to add a layer mask to the tile layer and clicked Invert on the panel to swap the black and white areas in the mask.

C Finally, to blend the mosaic layer with the stone wall, on the Layers panel, we chose Pin Light blending mode and lowered the layer opacity.

D The tile imagery is hidden by the arch-shaped layer mask.

Editing layer masks

In the instructions on this page, you'll edit a layer mask by applying strokes with the Brush tool. In the instructions on the following two pages, you'll edit a mask by using controls on the Masks panel.

To reshape a layer mask:

1. Choose the **Brush** tool ✐ (B or Shift-B).

2. On the Options bar, click a brush on the **Brush Preset** picker, choose **Mode: Normal**, and choose an **Opacity** of 100% to hide layer pixels fully or a lower opacity to hide them partially.

3. Do either of the following:

   To display the mask as a **colored overlay** on top of the image, Alt-Shift-click/Option-Shift-click the layer mask thumbnail on the Layers panel.**A–B** (Repeat the shortcut at any time to restore the normal display.)

   To display the mask as **black** and **white** without the image showing underneath, Alt-click/Option-click the layer mask thumbnail on the Layers panel. (Repeat the shortcut to restore the normal display.)

4. Do any of the following:

   Paint with **white** as the Foreground color to **reduce** the mask and reveal pixels on the layer.**C**

   Paint with **black** as the Foreground color to **enlarge** the mask and hide pixels on the layer.**D**

   ▶ You can change the diameter, hardness, or opacity for the Brush tool between strokes. To draw straight strokes, click, then Shift-click.

5. When you're finished modifying the layer mask, click the layer thumbnail.

If it's hard to see the overlay because it's too similar to the image color, you can change the overlay color and/or opacity.

To choose layer mask display options:

1. Double-click a layer mask thumbnail on the Layers panel (or click a mask thumbnail, then choose Mask Options from the Masks panel menu ★). The Layer Mask Display Options dialog opens.**E**

2. Change the **Opacity** percentage; or click the **Color** square, choose a different overlay color from the Color Picker, then click OK. Click OK again. To see the change, follow the first option in step 3 in the preceding set of instructions.

A We're painting out (removing) areas of the mask, with the mask displayed as a red overlay on top of the image.

B The mask is reshaped.

C We're reducing the mask (adding white) with only the mask displaying in the document window.

D Here we're enlarging the mask by painting with black as the Foreground color.

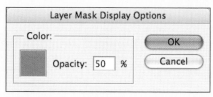

E By using the Layer Mask Display Options dialog, you can change the Color and/or Opacity of the mask overlay.

The Density control on the Masks panel affects the opacity of the overall mask, whereas the Feather control affects the opacity of the edge of the mask. Both controls are nondestructive, meaning they don't alter the original mask and can be readjusted at any time.

To adjust the Density and/or Feather value for a layer mask: ★

1. Click a layer that has a layer mask, and display the **Masks** panel. ▣ **A**

2. Click the **Select Pixel Mask** button, ▣ then do either or both of the following:

   Reduce the **Density** value to lighten the black area of the mask and partially reveal layer pixels. **B–C** The lower the Density, the more transparent the mask and thus the more fully hidden layer pixels are revealed.

   Increase the **Feather** value to reduce the contrast of (soften) the edge of the mask, for a more gradual transition between the masked and unmasked areas (**A**, next page).

To swap the black and white areas in a layer mask: ★

Do either of the following:

Click a layer that has a layer mask, display the **Masks** panel, then click the **Invert** button.

Click a layer mask thumbnail on the **Layers** panel, then press Ctrl-I/Cmd-I.

To refine the edges of a layer mask: ★

1. Click a layer that has a layer mask, and display the **Masks** panel. Zoom to around 100%.

2. Click **Mask Edge**; the Refine Mask dialog opens (you don't need to create a selection first).

3. Use the Refine Mask controls to adjust the softness or sharpness of the edge of the mask, as you would for a selection in the Refine Edge dialog (see pages 132–134). We've found these sliders to be helpful for cleaning up the edge of a mask: a low Radius value (1–2), a low Contrast value (5–10), and a slightly negative Contract/Expand value to shrink the mask inward (to hide more background pixels).

➤ We recommend keeping the Feather slider in the Refine Edge dialog at 0 and using the Feather slider on the Masks panel instead, since only the latter is nondestructive.

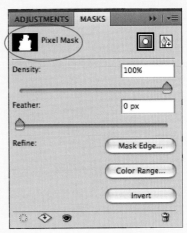

A The Masks panel is indicating that a Pixel Mask is selected.

B A mask is revealing just the two flowers on an image layer above a white Background.

C Now a lower Density value on the Masks panel is permitting the mask to partially reveal layer pixels.

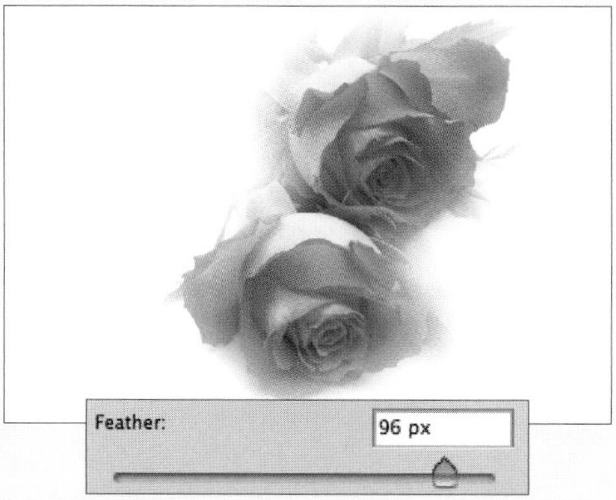

A Raising the Feather value on the Masks panel softens the transition between the masked and unmasked areas.

FOCUSING ATTENTION TO PART OF AN IMAGE BY USING THE MASKS PANEL ★

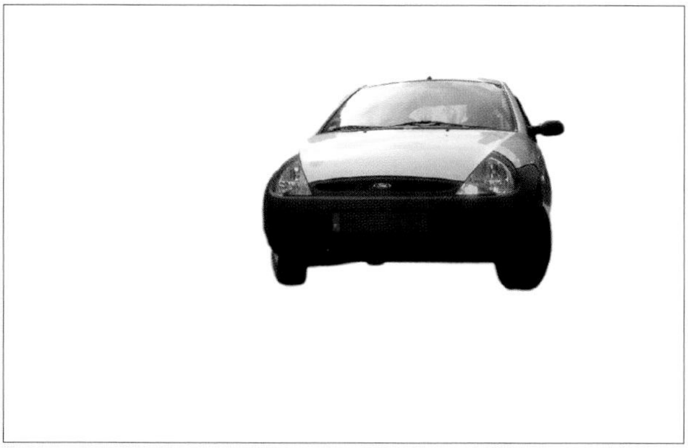

B The original hard-edged mask is revealing just the car on an image layer above a white Background.

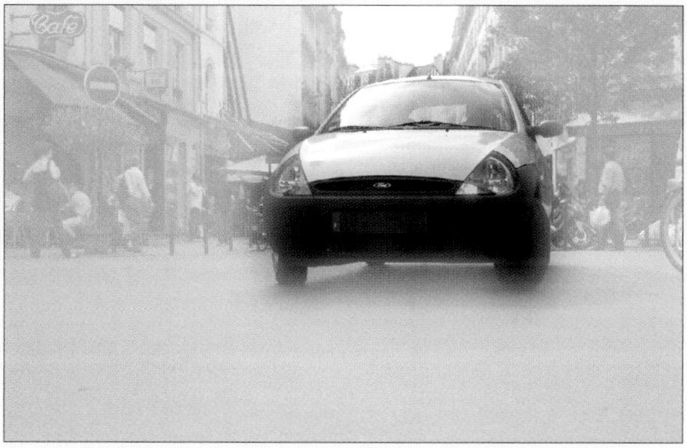

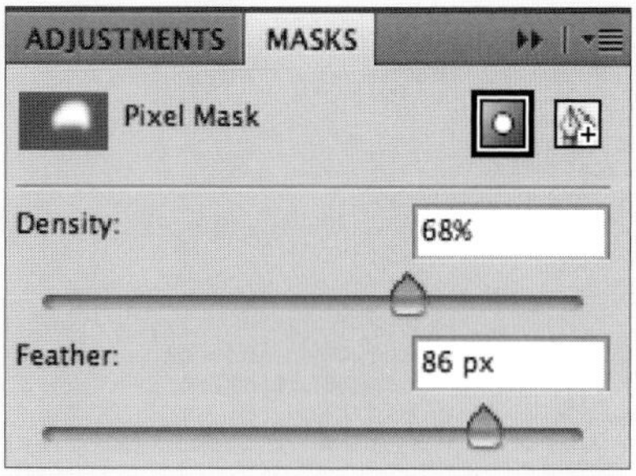

C We reduced the Density value and increased the Feather value for the layer mask to make the transition between the masked and unmasked areas more gradual. The car is still the star of the show, but the soft imagery around it complements it well.

Working with layer masks

By default, a layer and its layer mask are linked and, when moved, travel as a unit. If you want to move either component separately, you have to unlink them first.

To move the layer content or mask independently:

1. On the Layers panel, click the **Link** icon 🔗 between the layer and layer mask thumbnails.*A–B The icon will disappear.

2. Click either the layer thumbnail or the layer mask thumbnail, depending on which one you want to move.

3. Choose the **Move** tool, ⊹ then drag in the document window (or hold down the V key, drag, then release V ★).**C**

4. Click again between the layer and layer mask thumbnails to reinstate the link.

To move or duplicate a layer mask to another layer:

Do either of the following:

To **move** a mask, drag its thumbnail onto another layer (not onto the Background).

To **duplicate** a mask, Alt-drag/Option-drag its thumbnail onto another layer.

When you load a mask as a selection, it appears in the document window with the usual "marching ants" marquee.

To load a mask as a selection: ★

1. On the **Layers** panel, click a layer that contains a layer mask.

2. On the Masks panel, click the **Load Selection from Mask** button. ▦

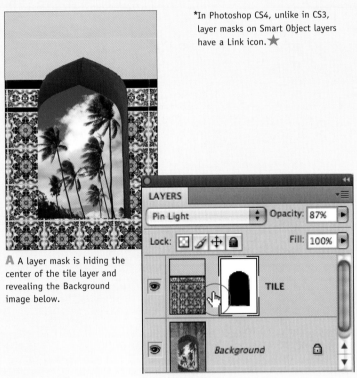

*In Photoshop CS4, unlike in CS3, layer masks on Smart Object layers have a Link icon. ★

A A layer mask is hiding the center of the tile layer and revealing the Background image below.

B We clicked the Link icon to disengage the layer image from the mask, and also clicked the layer mask thumbnail.

C With the Move tool, we dragged the mask in the document window to reveal a different part of the Background. (If you want to move the layer imagery instead, click the layer mask thumbnail before dragging.)

To deactivate a layer mask temporarily:

Do either of the following:

At the bottom of the **Masks** panel, click the **Disable/Enable Mask** button. ☻ **A** ★

On the **Layers** panel, Shift-click the layer mask thumbnail **B** (the thumbnail won't become selected).

A red X will appear over the thumbnail on both the Layers and Masks panels, and the entire layer will become visible.

➤ To reactivate a mask, repeat either method above.

One disadvantage of using layer masks is that they occupy storage space (albeit a small amount), so when you're done using them, consider applying the ones whose effects you like to make them permanent and deleting those you don't need.

Note: Before applying or deleting any masks, use the File > Save As command to copy the file, and keep the original file with layer masks in reserve for future editing.

To apply or delete a layer mask:

Do either of the following:

On the Layers panel, click a layer mask thumbnail, then on the **Masks** panel, click the **Delete Mask** button 🗑 to delete the mask or the **Apply Mask** button ⊗ to apply it. ★

On the **Layers** panel, right-click/Control-click a layer mask thumbnail and choose **Delete Layer Mask** or **Apply Layer Mask**.

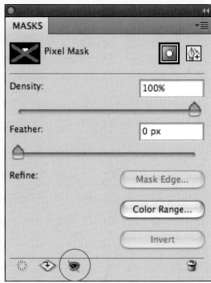

A To deactivate or activate a layer mask by using the Masks panel, click the Disable/Enable Mask button. A red X will appear over the thumbnail and button.

B To deactivate or activate a layer mask via the Layers panel, Shift-click the layer mask thumbnail. A red X will appear over the thumbnail.

MASK TOPICS IN OTHER CHAPTERS

➤ Create an adjustment layer mask (page 181).

➤ Use type shapes in a layer mask (pages 365 and 367).

Using clipping masks

When layers are formed into a clipping mask, the bottommost layer, called the "base" layer, clips (limits the display of pixels on) the layers above it. The base layer also controls the mode and opacity of the clipped layers. As the base layer, you can use a type, image, Smart Object, or shape layer.

To create a clipping mask:

1. Do either of the following:

   Alt-click/Option-click the line between two layers (the pointer will turn into two overlapping circles),**A–B** or right-click/Control-click the layer to be clipped and choose **Create Clipping Mask**.

   Note: The layers used in a clipping mask must be listed consecutively. When clipping layers in a group, all the layers must reside within the group.

   The base layer name will be underlined; the thumbnail for each clipped layer will have a downward-pointing arrow ⬇ and will be indented.

2. *Optional:* Repeat the previous step to add more consecutive layers to the mask.**C–D**

▶ You can also create a clipping mask by Shift-clicking the layers to be clipped, then pressing Ctrl-Alt-G/Cmd-Option-G. The same shortcut also releases selected layers from a clipping mask.

When you release a layer from a clipping mask, any masked layers above the one you're releasing are released, too.

To release a layer from a clipping mask:

Do one of the following:

Alt-click/Option-click the line below the layer you want to release.

Right-click/Control-click a layer to be released (not the base layer) and choose **Release Clipping Mask**.

To release an entire clipping mask:

1. Click the base layer in the group.

2. **Alt-click/Option-click** the line between the base layer and the next layer above it.

A The original image contains five layers. (An editable type layer is obscured by the image layers.)

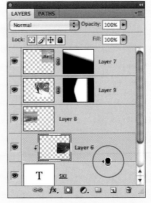

B When we Alt-click/Option-click the line between two layers to create a clipping mask, the clipped layer becomes indented and the base layer name becomes underlined.

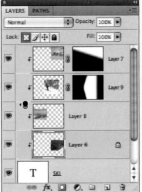

C Next, we Alt-click/Option-click each layer above Layer 6. All four image layers are now being clipped by the base ("SKI") layer.

D The type layer is clipping the four image layers.

Linking layers

Linked layers will move as a unit in the document window and drag-and-drop as a unit to other files. If you align, distribute, or transform (e.g., scale or rotate) a linked layer, your edits will also be applied to all the layers it's linked to.

To link layers:

1. On the Layers panel, select two or more layers (Ctrl-click/Cmd-click to select nonconsecutive layers).**A–B**

2. Click the **Link Layers** button 🔗 at the bottom of the Layers panel. If you subsequently click any one of the linked layers, a link icon will appear to the right of that layer and all the other layers it's linked to.**C**

➤ To unlink a layer, click the layer, then click the Link Layers button. The link icon disappears.

➤ To align or distribute layers, see page 164.

To move linked layers: ★

1. Click a linked layer.

2. Hold down the **V** key for a temporary Move tool, drag in the document window, then release V.**D**

➤ Don't link layers to the Background, because you won't be able to move them.

A This image contains multiple layers and a clipping mask.

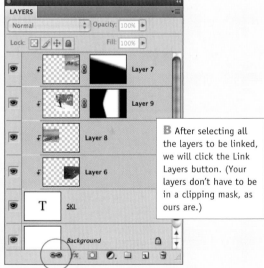

B After selecting all the layers to be linked, we will click the Link Layers button. (Your layers don't have to be in a clipping mask, as ours are.)

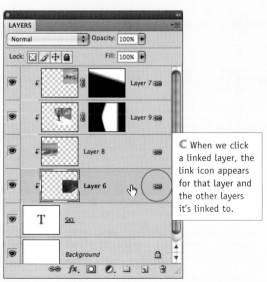

C When we click a linked layer, the link icon appears for that layer and the other layers it's linked to.

D We moved the linked image layers to the left.

Transforming layers

In Photoshop, you can apply scale, rotate, skew, distort, and perspective transformations to a layer, layer group, selection, or linked layers. We'll explore the individual transformation commands first so you can see how they work, then show you how to apply multiple transformations via the Free Transform command and the Move tool—the quicker and more intuitive methods that we prefer. Finally, we'll show you how to apply transformations by entering values on the Options bar.

To transform a layer or group via an individual command:

1. On the Layers panel, click a layer or group, or Shift-select multiple layers (linked layers will transform as a unit). You can scale, rotate, or skew editable type layers. To transform the Background, you must create a selection first.

2. *Optional:* For an image layer (not a group), create a selection to limit what gets transformed.

3. Choose Edit > Transform > **Scale**, **Rotate**, **Skew**, **Distort**, or **Perspective**. A transform box will surround either the opaque part of the layer or the whole selection.

4. *Optional:* To transform the layer or selection from a point other than the center, drag the reference point. You can move it outside the transform box.

5. To **Scale** the layer horizontally and vertically, drag a corner handle; **A** to scale only the horizontal or vertical dimension, drag a side handle; to scale it proportionally, Shift-drag a corner handle; or to scale it from the reference point, Alt-drag/Option-drag a handle (add Shift to scale it proportionally from the reference point).

   For **Rotate**, position the pointer either just inside or outside the transform box, near a handle on the box (the pointer becomes a curved, double-headed arrow), then drag in a circular direction. **B** Shift-drag to constrain the rotation to a multiple of 15°.

   For **Skew**, drag a side handle on the transform box to skew on the horizontal or vertical axis, or Alt-drag/Option-drag to skew symmetrically from the reference point (**A–B**, next page).

   For **Distort**, drag a corner or side handle. Alt-drag/Option-drag to distort symmetrically from the reference point.

A A Scale transformation

B A Rotate transformation

C A Perspective transformation

For **Perspective**, drag a corner handle along the horizontal or vertical axis to create one-point perspective along that axis C (and C, previous page). The adjacent corner will move symmetrically.

➤ If you're going to perform multiple transformations, choose them from the Edit menu and apply them before accepting the transformation. This will help preserve the image quality.

6. To accept the transformation, do one of the following:

Double-click inside the transform box.

Click the Commit Transform button ✔ on the Options bar.

Press Enter/Return.

(To cancel the transformation, click the Cancel Transform button ⊘ or press Esc.)

➤ To undo the last handle modification, choose Edit > Undo.

➤ To move the entire layer (or selection) while the transform box is still showing onscreen, drag inside the transform box.

➤ To rotate a layer along an angle that you define, choose the Ruler tool (I or Shift-I), drag in the document window to define an angle, then with the tool still selected, choose Edit > Transform > Rotate.

➤ For the Warp command, see page 313.

A This editable type contains layer effects.

B We applied a skew transformation to the editable type.

C To apply a perspective transformation, as shown here, you have to rasterize the type first (Layer > Rasterize > Type).

TRANSFORM TIPS

➤ The current Image Interpolation method setting in Preferences (Ctrl-K/Cmd-K) > General applies to transformations, among other things. The Bicubic methods, although slower, degrade the image the least.

➤ To repeat the last transformation, choose Edit > Transform > Again (Ctrl-Shift-T/Cmd-Shift-T).

➤ As you transform a layer or a selection, your edits will be indicated in the readouts on either the Options bar or the Info panel.

WHAT'S LEFT AFTER A TRANSFORMATION?

➤ If you transform an image layer or a selection on an image layer, any empty space created by the transformation will be replaced with transparency.

➤ Before you can transform the Background, you must create a selection. Any empty space created by a transformation of the Background will be filled with the current Background color.

Now that you're acquainted with the individual Transform commands, you're ready to try using the Free Transform command, or the Move tool with its transform controls. Using these methods, you can apply multiple transformations without having to choose individual commands from a menu. And image data is resampled once—when you accept the edits—which helps preserve the image quality.

A The original image

To transform a layer or layer group using the Free Transform command or Move tool:

1. Click a layer, multiple layers, or a group.**A** Any layers that are linked to the selected layer will also be transformed. To transform the Background, you must create a selection first.

2. To display the transform controls, do either of the following:

   Choose Edit > **Free Transform** (Ctrl-T/Cmd-T).

   Choose the **Move** tool, then check **Show Transform Controls** on the Options bar. For editable type or a Smart Object, click a handle.

B We selected the car, then copied it to a new layer. Here, we're scaling the new layer.

3. Do one or more of the following:

   To **scale** or **rotate**, follow the instructions in step 5 on page 310.**B**

   To **skew**, Ctrl-drag/Cmd-drag a side handle. (Include Shift to constrain the movement.)

   To **distort,*** Ctrl-drag/Cmd-drag a corner handle.

   To apply **perspective,*** Ctrl-Alt-Shift-drag/Cmd-Option-Shift-drag a corner handle.**C**

   You can also use the **Options** bar to apply many transform edits.**D** For example, to change the reference point for the transformation, click a square on the Reference Point Location icon.

C We're applying perspective to make the front of the car wider than the back.

4. To accept the transformation, double-click inside the bounding box or click the ✔ on the Options bar (Enter/Return). To cancel the transformation, click the ⊘ (Esc). You must either accept or cancel to resume normal editing.

*In Photoshop CS4, unlike in CS3, you can apply Distort and Perspective transformations to a Smart Object layer. ★

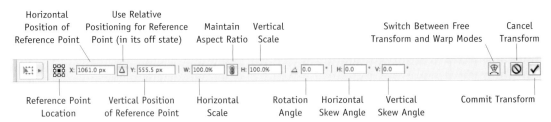

Horizontal Position of Reference Point — Use Relative Positioning for Reference Point (in its off state) — Maintain Aspect Ratio — Vertical Scale — Switch Between Free Transform and Warp Modes — Cancel Transform

Reference Point Location — Vertical Position of Reference Point — Horizontal Scale — Rotation Angle — Horizontal Skew Angle — Vertical Skew Angle — Commit Transform

D When you choose a Transform command, features become available on the Options bar for applying transform edits. It's not the fastest method on the planet, but it's definitely the most precise.

Warping layers

The Warp command lets you distort an entire layer by manipulating an editable grid. You can choose preset warp shapes, an orientation, and other controls for the warp via the Options bar.

To warp a layer:

1. Click a layer on the Layers panel.**A**

2. Choose Edit > Transform > **Warp**. A grid with handles will display over the image layer.

3. Do either of the following:

   To distort the layer manually, choose **Warp: Custom** on the Options bar, then drag any of the squares, diamond-shaped points, grid lines, or direction line handles on the grid.

   To warp the layer via the Options bar, choose a preset style from the **Warp** menu;**B–C** then, if desired, click the **Warp Orientation** button to toggle between horizontal and vertical distortion; or reshape the grid by using the scrubby sliders for **Bend**, **H** (horizontal distortion), or **V** (vertical distortion).

4. To accept the warp, press Enter/Return or click ✔ on the Options bar (to cancel it, press Esc or click the ⊘).**D**

➤ To undo a warp on a standard layer, use the History panel; for a Smart Object layer, see the sidebar at right.

RESAMPLE ONCE!

When performing multiple transformations (or a transform plus a warp), applying them consecutively and accepting them in one pass helps preserve the image quality, because resampling occurs once rather than for each command. When transforming multiple layers, do so simultaneously, for the same reason. While warp or transform controls are showing in your document, you can click the Switch Between Free Transform and Warp Modes button 🏛 on the Options bar to toggle between the two modes.

WARPING A SMART OBJECT

To edit the warp settings for a selected Smart Object layer, choose the Warp command again, then use the warp controls on the Options bar. To undo the warp, choose None from the Warp menu.

A This image contains a type layer and an image layer.

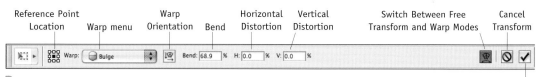

| Reference Point Location | Warp menu | Warp Orientation | Bend | Horizontal Distortion | Vertical Distortion | Switch Between Free Transform and Warp Modes | Cancel Transform |

B When the Edit > Transform > Warp command is chosen, these commands appear on the Options bar.   Commit Transform

C The type layer is being warped using the Bulge style.

D We applied Overlay mode to the type layer to blend the type better with the lime rind.

Using Smart Object layers

A Smart Object layer is created manually when you convert one or more layers in a Photoshop image into a Smart Object, or automatically when you place an Adobe Illustrator, Acrobat, or Camera Raw file, or another Photoshop file, into a Photoshop document. If you double-click the thumbnail for a Smart Object made from Photoshop layers, a separate document window or tab opens in Photoshop, containing the embedded layers; if you double-click the thumbnail for a Smart Object made from imported contents, the embedded file opens in the creator application. In either case, when you edit, save, and close the window for the embedded file, the Smart Object in the Photoshop document updates automatically to reflect your edits.

To create a Smart Object:

Do one of the following:

Select one or more layers (e.g., image, type, shape, or Fill layer) on the Layers panel, then right-click/Control-click the panel and choose **Convert to Smart Object** (or choose the command from the panel menu).**A–B**

Via the File > **Place** command in Photoshop or Bridge, import a raw photo, another Photoshop file, or a file from another application into the current document. Scale and position the bounding box as needed, then press Enter/Return. The file is now embedded in the document as a new Smart Object layer.

Open a photo into **Camera Raw**, apply adjustments, if desired, then hold down Shift and click **Open Object** (see page 256).

Use File > **Open as Smart Object** to open a file as a Smart Object layer in a new document.

▶ When you apply filters to a Smart Object layer, they become Smart Filters (see pages 336–337).

To edit a Smart Object:

1. On the Layers panel, double-click the **Smart Object layer** thumbnail, then click OK when the alert dialog appears.**C**

2. If the Smart Object layer contains Photoshop layers, a separate document will open in Photoshop, containing those layers; if the Smart Object layer contains imported content (imagery or graphics), that content will appear in a document window in the creator application. Edit the document.

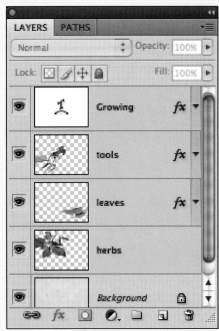

A Select one or more layers to be converted into a Smart Object.

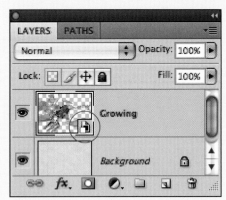

B The layers were converted into one Smart Object (note the icon in the layer thumbnail). You can apply filters, layer effects, and transformations to a Smart Object layer. The individual layers will remain accessible in the embedded file.

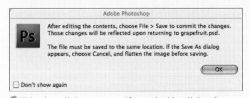

C This alert dialog appears if you double-click a Smart Object layer thumbnail. Click OK.

3. Save the file without changing the file name or location, and close it. You'll get back to the Photoshop document automatically, and your edits will display on the Smart Object layer. Only the embedded copy of the object is affected by edits, not the original file used to create it.

The Replace Contents command lets you swap existing Smart Object content with a replacement file. If you edit the original file that a Smart Object was created from, you can use this command afterward to update the content of the Smart Object.

To replace the contents of a Smart Object with another file:

1. Right-click/Control-click a Smart Object layer (not the thumbnail) and choose **Replace Contents**. The Place dialog opens.

2. Locate the replacement file (one you've edited or an altogether new file), then click **Place**. The Smart Object updates with the new image.**A–C**

▶ Changes made to Layers panel settings (e.g., opacity, blending mode, mask, or effects) on a Smart Object layer affect only the layer appearance—not the embedded Smart Object file. If you edit or replace the contents of a Smart Object, your layer settings are preserved.

Photoshop layers that are converted into a Smart Object become part of an embedded file. If you want to put any of those layers back into your Photoshop file, you may.

To reclaim Photoshop layers from a Smart Object:

1. On the Layers panel, double-click the thumbnail for a **Smart Object** layer, then click OK if an alert dialog appears.

2. The embedded file will open in a separate document tab or floating window. For tabbed windows,★ click a 2-Up button on the Arrange Documents menu,▣ drag the layers into the original document, then click the Consolidate All button ▣ on the Arrange Documents menu. For a floating window, click in it, then drag the layers you want to reclaim from the Layers panel into the original document window.

3. Close the window for the embedded file.

▶ Smart Filters, transformations, and layer effects from the original Smart Object layer won't be present in the reclaimed layers.

A We applied layer effects to this Smart Object layer.

B We edited the original file the Smart Object originated from (we added the three solid-color squares).

C The Replace Contents command replaced the contents of the Smart Object with the edited file. Note that the layer effects were preserved.

CONTEMPLATING A MERGE?

When you're contemplating whether to merge or flatten layers, consider grouping them into a Smart Object layer instead. You'll achieve the same reduction of layers, plus you'll gain the ability to edit the original layers individually by double-clicking the Smart Object layer thumbnail.

When you rasterize a Smart Object layer (convert it to a standard image layer), the contents of the embedded file become inaccessible, so we recommend copying the file by using File > Save As first.

To rasterize a Smart Object layer:

Right-click/Control-click the Smart Object layer and choose **Rasterize Layer**.

Filling areas with a solid color

You can fill a whole layer, or a selection on a layer, with a solid color.

To fill a selection or a layer with a solid color:

1. Click a layer, or create a new layer.

   Optional: Create a selection. If you clicked an image layer, you can use the Select > Color Range command to select a particular color or the highlight, midtone, or shadow areas.

2. To choose a fill color, do either of the following:

   Choose a Foreground color via the **Color** or **Swatches** panel.

   Choose the **Eyedropper** tool, then click a color in the image (or hold down the **I** key to use a temporary Eyedropper).

3. Choose Edit > **Fill**. The Fill dialog opens. **A**

4. Choose **Use: Foreground Color**. (You could also choose Color, then choose a color from the Color Picker.)

5. Check **Preserve Transparency** to recolor only opaque pixels in the selection or layer, or uncheck this option to fill the entire selection or layer.

6. *Optional:* Choose a blending Mode or change the Opacity percentage for the color fill.

7. Click OK.

➤ For a more flexible way to apply a solid color, gradient, or pattern, use the New Fill/Adjustment Layer menu on the Layers panel (see pages 204–205).

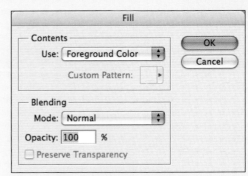

A You can use the Fill dialog to fill a selection or layer with a solid color or pattern.

SHORTCUTS TO FILL A SELECTION OR LAYER

Windows

Fill with the Foreground color, 100% Opacity	Alt-Backspace
Fill with the Background color, 100% Opacity	Ctrl-Backspace
Fill only nontransparent pixels with the Foreground color	Alt-Shift-Backspace
Fill only nontransparent pixels with the Background color	Ctrl-Shift-Backspace

Mac OS

Fill with the Foreground color, 100% Opacity	Option-Delete
Fill with the Background color, 100% Opacity	Cmd-Delete
Fill only nontransparent pixels with the Foreground color	Option-Shift-Delete
Fill only nontransparent pixels with the Background color	Cmd-Shift-Delete

As a Photoshop user, you're in the business of creating illusions, and layer effects let you do so in short, easy steps. The effects that you can apply alone or in combination include Drop Shadow, Inner Shadow, Outer Glow, Inner Glow, Bevel and Emboss, Satin, Color Overlay, Gradient Overlay, Pattern Overlay, and Stroke.A Once applied, layer effects can be edited, hidden, or removed at any time. And best of all, when you modify layer pixels, the effects update accordingly (they should be called "Smart Effects"!).

In this chapter, we offer generic instructions for applying, copying, moving, and removing layer effects, separate instructions for each effect, and finally, instructions for saving and applying effects combined with other Layers panel settings as styles by using the Styles panel.

Applying layer effects (general info)

Layer effects can be applied to any layer (even to editable type), but not to the Background. They affect all the visible pixels on a layer and update instantly if you add, modify, or delete pixels from the layer they're applied to. Each individual effect can be turned on or off at any time via its own visibility icon.

Layer effects are applied and edited via the Layer Style dialog and are listed on the Layers panel below the layer they belong to. Before exploring the individual effects, take a look at these generic instructions:

To apply layer effects (generic instructions):

1. Do any of the following:

   Double-click to the right of a layer name. (Or for an image layer—not a type, Smart Object, or shape layer—you can double-click the layer thumbnail instead.)

   Click a layer, then choose an effect from the **Add Layer Style** menu *fx* at the bottom of the Layers panel.

Continued on the following page

A The Drop Shadow, Bevel and Emboss, and Gradient Overlay effects are applied to this editable type.

LAYER STYLES

20

IN THIS CHAPTER

Applying layer effects
(general info) 317

Applying a shadow effect 320

Applying a glow effect 322

Applying a bevel or emboss effect. . . .324

Applying a satin effect 326

Applying the overlay effects. 327

Applying a stroke effect 329

Copying, moving, removing layer
effects. 330

Applying layer styles. 331

Creating layer styles 332

The Layer Style dialog opens.**A**

2. Click an effect name on the left side, then choose settings. Check Preview to preview the effect in the image.

3. *Optional:* Click other effect names to apply additional effects to the same layer.

4. Click OK.

5. Edit the **layer** and watch the "smart" effect update!

On the Layers panel, any layer that contains effects will have this icon: *fx* Click the arrowhead next to the icon to expand or collapse the list of effects on that layer (**A**, next page).

To change the **settings** for an effect or to add more effects, double-click the layer or double-click the effect name nested below the layer name.

To **hide** or **show** one layer effect, expand the effects list for the layer in question, then click the visibility icon 👁 for the effect.

To **hide all** the effects on a layer, click the visibility icon for the "Effects" listing.

▶ If you move layer pixels, any effects on that layer will tag right along with them.

▶ To restore the settings that were in place (in all the panels) when you opened the Layer Style dialog, Alt-click/Option-click Reset (Cancel becomes Reset).

▶ Once you become familiar with the individual effects, read the helpful tips in the "Becoming a Layer Effects Pro" sidebar on page 323.

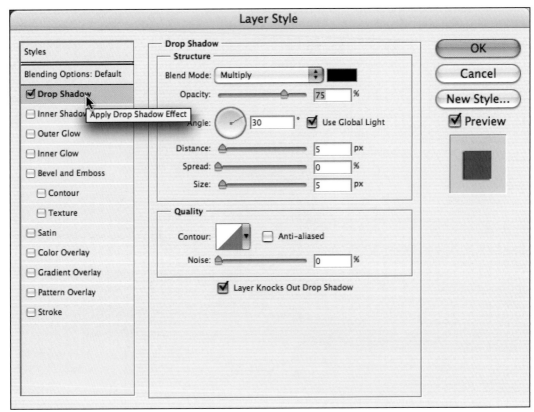

A In the Layer Style dialog, click the name for the layer effect (the box will become checked automatically) that you want to display and choose settings for.

What kind of imagery should you use?

► We recommend applying the layer effects that work inward or outward from edges—Drop Shadow, Inner Shadow, Outer Glow, Inner Glow, Bevel and Emboss, and Stroke—to a type layer, shape layer, or any layer imagery that's surrounded by transparent pixels. You can select an area of a layer, then use Layer via Copy (Ctrl-J/Cmd-J) to isolate a subject from its background before applying layer effects.

► You can apply the Satin, Color Overlay, Gradient Overlay, and Pattern Overlay effects either to fully opaque layers or to layers that contain transparency.

Note: Don't bother creating a selection before applying a layer effect; your selection will be ignored.

LAYER OPACITY AND FILL SETTINGS

A quick reminder from the previous chapter: the Opacity setting on the Layers panel controls the opacity of layer imagery, including any layer effects, whereas the Fill setting controls only the opacity of layer imagery—not layer effects.

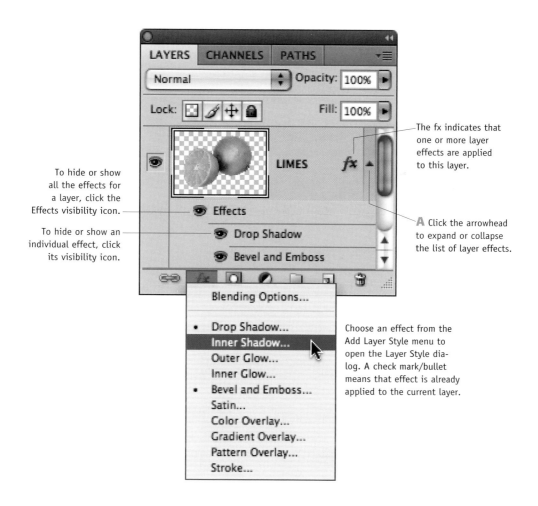

To hide or show all the effects for a layer, click the Effects visibility icon.

To hide or show an individual effect, click its visibility icon.

The fx indicates that one or more layer effects are applied to this layer.

A Click the arrowhead to expand or collapse the list of layer effects.

Choose an effect from the Add Layer Style menu to open the Layer Style dialog. A check mark/bullet means that effect is already applied to the current layer.

Applying a shadow effect

You can create drop shadows and inner shadows with just a few clicks of the mouse.

To apply the Drop Shadow or Inner Shadow effect:

1. On the Layers panel, double-click next to a layer name.**A** The Layer Style dialog opens.

2. Click **Drop Shadow** or **Inner Shadow**.

3. Change any of the following settings:

   Choose a **Blend Mode** from the menu. We usually keep the default setting of Multiply.

   To choose a different shadow **color**, click the color swatch, then choose a color from the Color Picker or click a color in the document window with the eyedropper (the new color will preview immediately). Click OK. If you change the shadow color, you may also want to change the Blend Mode to Normal.

   Choose an **Opacity** percentage for the transparency level of the shadow.

   Choose an **Angle** for the angle of the shadow relative to the original layer shapes. Note: If you readjust the Angle for an individual effect while Use Global Light is checked, the angle for any other effects that utilize the Global Light option will update accordingly. This option unifies the lighting across multiple layer effects.

   Choose a **Distance** for the distance (in pixels) of a drop shadow from the original layer shapes **B** or for the width of an inner shadow.**C–D**

   ➤ You can also change the position of the shadow by dragging in the document window while the dialog is open, but be aware that this will also reposition any other effects that utilize the Global Light option.

   Choose a **Spread** (for a Drop Shadow) or **Choke** (for an Inner Shadow) percentage to control the point at which the shadow starts to fade.

   Choose an overall **Size** for the shadow (in pixels).

   Optional: In the Quality area, click the Contour arrowhead and choose a preset from the picker for the edge profile of the shadow. We usually stick with the default Contour.

   Check **Anti-aliased** to soften the jagged edges between the shadow and the layer imagery.

A The original image consists of some garden tools on one layer and a background pattern on another layer (we created the pattern via Filter > Render > Clouds).

B The Drop Shadow effect is applied.

C The original image consists of editable type on one layer and a blue-gray background pattern on another.

D The Inner Shadow effect is applied.

Adjust the **Noise** level. Noise (speckling) can help prevent banding on print output, but keep this option at a low value.

For the Drop Shadow effect, if the layer Fill opacity was lowered, check **Layer Knocks Out Drop Shadow** to prevent the shadow from showing through transparent areas on the layer.

4. Click OK. If you're not satisfied with the shape of the resulting shadow, follow the next set of instructions.

➤ When we apply the Drop Shadow effect, we usually raise the Distance, Spread, and Size values and lower the Opacity slightly from the default setting.

Depending on the time of day and the angle of the sun or other light source, cast shadows may be short or elongated. You can reshape a drop shadow via the Distort command.

To transform a Drop Shadow effect:

1. Apply the Drop Shadow effect as per the previous instructions, and keep that layer selected.

2. To transfer the shadow effect to its own layer, right-click/Control-click the Effects listing on the Layers panel, choose **Create Layer(s)** from the context menu, then click OK in the alert dialog.

3. Click the new Drop Shadow layer.**B**

4. Choose Edit > Transform > **Distort**, drag the handles of the transform box to achieve the desired slanted shape, then press Enter/Return.**C** (If you don't see all the handles, press Ctrl-0 (zero)/Cmd-0 to enlarge the document window.) For a symmetrical perspective distortion, hold down Ctrl-Alt-Shift/Cmd-Option-Shift as you drag a corner handle.

➤ Turn on the Lock Transparent Pixels option (Layers panel) to limit any painting or fill changes to just the shadow shape.

➤ Select the shadow layer and the original image layer, then click the Link Layers button 🔗 at the bottom of the Layers panel; now they will move and transform as a unit.

A The original layer has a Drop Shadow effect.

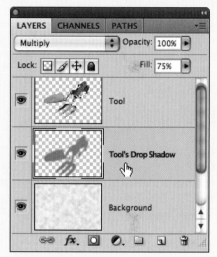

B We clicked the new Drop Shadow layer.

C Then we elongated the shadow to make it more prominent.

Applying a glow effect

The Outer Glow and Inner Glow effects add a soft, airbrushed accent to the edges of layer imagery or type.

To apply the Outer or Inner Glow effect:

1. Display the **Swatches** panel.▦
2. On the Layers panel, double-click a layer to open the Layer Style dialog.A
3. Click **Outer Glow** or **Inner Glow**.
4. Choose **Structure** settings: **B–C**

   Choose a **Blend Mode**.

   Choose an **Opacity** level for the glow.

   Adjust the **Noise** level. Noise (speckling) helps to prevent banding on print output.

   To change the glow color, click the color square in the **Structure** area, choose a color from the Color Picker (or, while the picker is open, choose from the Swatches panel or click a color in the document window). Click OK. The new color will preview in the image.

   ➤ Choose a color that contrasts with the background color. It might be hard to see a light Outer Glow color against a light background.

5. Choose **Elements** settings:

   From the **Technique** menu, choose **Softer** for soft edges or **Precise** for slightly crisper edges.

   For an Inner Glow, click **Source: Center** to create a glow that spreads outward from the center of the layer pixels (this looks nice on type), or click **Edge** to create a glow that spreads inward from the inside edges of the layer imagery.

   Choose a **Spread** (Outer Glow) or **Choke** (Inner Glow) percentage to control the point at which the glow starts to fade.

   Choose an overall **Size** for the glow.

6. Choose **Quality** settings:

   Optional: Click the Contour arrowhead and choose a preset from the picker to modify the edge of the glow.

   Choose a **Range** to control how smoothly (high value) or abruptly (low value) the glow transitions from the contour of the shape.

7. Click OK (**A**, next page).

A The original image contains a silhouetted image of a watch above a solid-color Background.

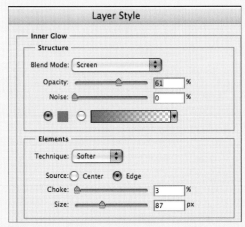

B We chose these Structure and Elements settings for the Inner Glow effect in the Layer Style dialog.

C And we chose these Structure and Elements settings for the Outer Glow effect.

A These inner and outer glow effects were produced by applying the Layer Style settings shown in the two preceding figures.

BECOMING A LAYER EFFECTS PRO

▶ When deciding which effect or effects to use, think about the surface texture you're trying to create. Stone? Metal? Paper? Embossed text that looks as if it's embedded into porous paper, or satin text that looks as if it's cast in metal? Choose an effect that will help you achieve the desired illusion.

▶ Except for Drop Shadow and Overlay, layer effects usually look better, or more convincing as an illusion, when applied in combination (see the figures below).

▶ If you achieve a layer effect or combination of effects and Layers panel settings that you like, save that collection of settings as a style on the Styles panel (see pages 331–332). This is a great timesaver.

▶ While the Layer Style dialog is open, you can click Blending Options on the upper left side, then change any of the settings, such as the layer blending mode or Fill opacity (you'll also find these settings on the Layers panel).

This is plain editable type (in the Bodoni Highlight font) on top of a pattern layer.

The Drop Shadow effect is applied.

We also added the Bevel and Emboss effect — two effects look better than one.

Three layer effects — Drop Shadow, Bevel and Emboss, and Gradient Overlay — look even better.

Applying a bevel or emboss effect

The Bevel and Emboss effect creates an illusion of volume by adding a highlight and some shading. The results can range from a chiseled bevel that looks factory-made to a pillowy emboss that looks as if it's been stamped onto porous paper. For variety, experiment with the Contour options.

To apply the Bevel or Emboss effect:

1. Display the **Swatches** panel.⬛

2. On the Layers panel, double-click a layer **A** to open the Layer Style dialog.

3. Click **Bevel and Emboss**.

4. Choose **Structure** settings: **B**

   Choose a **Style: Outer Bevel,C Inner Bevel,D Emboss, Pillow Emboss**, or **Stroke Emboss** (**A–C**, next page).

   From the **Technique** menu, choose **Smooth, Chisel Hard**, or **Chisel Soft**.

   Choose a **Depth** to control how far the high-light and shading are offset from the layer shapes.

   Click the **Up** or **Down** button to swap the positions of the highlight and shading.

   Choose a **Size** for the depth of the bevel or emboss effect.

   Raise the **Soften** value to blur the effect.

5. Choose **Shading** settings:

   Choose an **Angle** and an **Altitude** to change the location of the light source. These settings in turn will affect the highlight and shading. Check **Use Global Light** to use the same Angle and Altitude settings for all effects that utilize the Global Light option; or uncheck it to use a unique setting for this individual effect. Note: If you change the Angle or Altitude for an individual effect while Use Global Light is checked, any other effects utilizing the Global Light option will update accordingly.

   Click the **Gloss Contour** arrowhead, then choose a profile from the Contour Preset picker.

   Choose a **Highlight Mode** and **Opacity** and a **Shadow Mode** and **Opacity** for the highlight and shading.

   To change the highlight or shading **color**, click either color swatch, then choose a color from the Color Picker (or, while the picker is open,

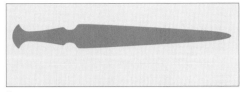

A The original image contains two layers.

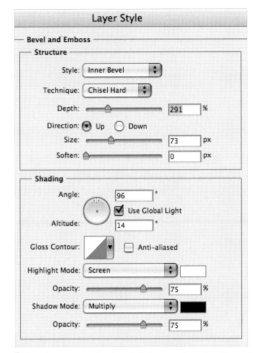

B We chose these Bevel and Emboss options for Figure D.

C The Outer Bevel effect is applied (plus a Drop Shadow).

D The Inner Bevel effect was created by using the settings shown in figure **B** (a Drop Shadow was also added).

choose from the Swatches panel or click a color in the document window). The color will preview in the image. Click OK.

6. To add a **Contour** to the edges of the bevel or emboss, click Contour on the left side of the dialog, below Bevel and Emboss. Click the Contour arrowhead, then click a preset contour in the picker. This option can dramatically change the appearance of the effect.

   Check **Anti-aliased** to soften the hard edges between adjoining areas.

   For the Outer Bevel and Inner Bevel Style options, adjust the **Range** (position of the bevel on the chosen contour) to minimize or maximize the prominence of the bevel.

7. To add a texture to a bevel or emboss, click **Texture** on the left side of the dialog, click the Texture arrowhead, choose a pattern from the picker, then do any of the following: **D**

   Adjust the **Scale** of the pattern.

   Change the **Depth** to adjust the contrast between the shadows and highlights in the pattern.

   Check **Invert** to swap the highlight and shading. This has the same effect as changing the Depth percentage from negative to positive, and vice versa.

   Check **Link with Layer** to ensure that the texture and the layer move as a unit.

   Drag in the document window to reposition the texture within the effect. Click **Snap to Origin** to realign the pattern with the upper left corner of the image.

   If you've changed settings for the current pattern, you can click the **New Preset** button ⬒ to add it as a new preset.

8. Click OK.

A This is the original editable type.

B Emboss (Chisel Soft) is applied.

C Pillow Emboss (Technique: Smooth), plus a Drop Shadow are applied.

D Pillow Emboss, with a Texture, plus a Drop Shadow are applied.

Applying a satin effect

Use the Satin layer effect to apply light and dark shades to the surfaces of objects or type to make them look reflective or metallic.

Notes: The default Blend Mode for the Satin layer effect, Multiply, deepens some tonal values and heightens contrast, so we recommend applying it to an image that has a good range of tonal values. To make the Satin effect show up well on type, apply a medium to light color to the type first and also apply a strong Inner Glow or Bevel and Emboss effect.

To apply the Satin effect :

1. Double-click a layer **A** on the Layers panel to open the Layer Style dialog.

2. Click **Satin**.

3. Do any of the following.**B**

   Change the **Blend Mode**.

   To change the overlay **color**, click the color swatch, then choose a color from the Color Picker or click a color in the document.

   Adjust the **Opacity** of the effect.

   Change the **Angle** of the effect. This angle is independent of the Global Light settings.

   Set the **Distance** and the **Size** of the effect. You can also drag in the document window to adjust the distance.

   Click the **Contour** arrowhead, then choose from the Contour Preset picker to change the edge profile of the effect.

   Check **Anti-aliased** to soften the hard boundary between the effect and the underlying shapes.

   Check **Invert** to swap the shadows and highlights in the effect.

4. Click OK.**C**

A The Bevel and Emboss effect is applied to this editable type.

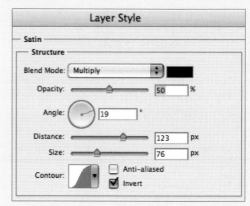

B We chose these options for the Satin layer effect.

C The addition of the Satin effect makes the surface of the letters look even more reflective.

Applying the overlay effects

The three overlay effects, Color Overlay, Gradient Overlay, and Pattern Overlay, can be applied to image, shape, and type layers.

To apply the Color Overlay effect:

1. Double-click a layer **A** on the Layers panel to open the Layer Style dialog.

2. Click **Color Overlay**.

3. Do any of the following:

   Choose a **Blend Mode**.

   Click the **color** swatch, then choose a different color for the overlay via the Color Picker.

   Adjust the **Opacity** of the overlay.

4. Click OK.**B**

➤ Compare the editable Color Overlay effect with the Fill command, which we give instructions for on page 316.

To apply the Gradient Overlay effect:

1. Double-click a layer on the Layers panel to open the Layer Style dialog.

2. Click **Gradient Overlay**.**C**

3. Do any of the following:

   Choose a **Blend Mode**.

   Adjust the **Opacity** of the overlay.

   Click the **Gradient** arrowhead, then choose a preset gradient from the Gradient Preset picker.

   Choose a **Style: Linear**, **Radial**, **Angle**, **Reflected**, or **Diamond**.

   Check **Reverse** to change the direction of the gradient.

   Check **Align with Layer** to confine the gradient to visible pixels in the layer, or uncheck it to have the gradient fill the whole canvas.

   Set the **Angle** of the gradient.

   Choose a **Scale** percentage to control the placement of the midpoint of the gradient.

   Drag in the document window to **reposition** the gradient.

4. Click OK.**D** Read more about creating and editing gradients in Chapter 23.

➤ If you apply two overlay effects, such as Gradient Overlay and Pattern Overlay, lower the opacity of the one that's listed first in the dialog; otherwise the second one won't be visible.

A The Bevel and Emboss effect is applied to this type.

B The Color Overlay effect is also applied.

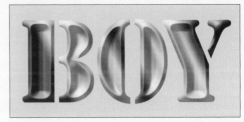

C We chose these options for the Gradient Overlay layer effect.

D The Gradient Overlay effect is applied to the original image (shown in figure **A**).

Patterns applied via the Pattern Overlay effect can range from ones with an obvious repeat, such as polka dots or stripes, to ones with an overall texture, resembling surfaces like gritty sandpaper, woven fabric, or variegated stone.

To apply the Pattern Overlay effect:

1. Double-click a layer on the Layers panel to open the Layer Style dialog. **A**

2. Click **Pattern Overlay**.

3. Do any of the following: **B**

   Choose a **Blend Mode**.

   Adjust the **Opacity** of the overlay.

   Click the **Pattern** arrowhead, then choose a pattern preset in the picker. To load patterns from another library, choose a library name from the lower part of the picker menu.

   Click **Snap to Origin** to align the pattern with the upper left corner of the document. You can also drag in the document window to reposition the pattern.

   Choose a **Scale** percentage for the size of the pattern.

   Check **Link with Layer** to link the pattern to the layer so they'll move as a unit if you move the layer.

   If you changed settings for the current pattern, you can click the **New Preset** button ⬛ to add it as a new preset.

4. Click OK. **C**

A The original type contains the Bevel and Emboss and Satin layer effects.

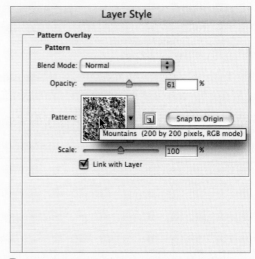

B For the Pattern Overlay layer effect, we chose the Mountains pattern, which is in the Texture Fill library.

C With the Pattern Overlay layer effect added to the mix, now the type looks like polished granite.

Applying a stroke effect

If you're partial to neon, you can achieve that illusion by using the Stroke effect.

To apply a Stroke effect:

1. Double-click a layer on the Layers panel to open the Layer Style dialog.

2. Click **Stroke**.

3. Do any of the following: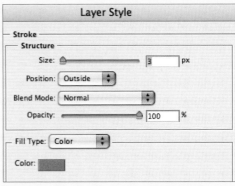A

   Choose a **Size** (width) for the stroke.

   From the **Position** menu, choose whether you want the stroke to be on the **Outside**, **Inside**, or **Center** of the layer shapes.

   Choose a **Blend Mode**.

   Choose an **Opacity** percentage.

   Choose **Fill Type: Color, Gradient,** or **Pattern,** and choose settings for the options that become available. See the information about Color Overlay or Gradient Overlay on page 327, or about Pattern Overlay on the previous page.

4. Click OK.**B–C**

A Options are chosen for the Stroke layer effect.

B The Bevel and Emboss, Gradient Overlay, and Stroke effects are applied to this type. If you want to achieve the same result, use the Styles panel to apply the Neutral Bevel layer style, which is in the Text Effects 2 style library; to load styles, see page 403.

C The Bevel and Emboss, Gradient Overlay, and Stroke effects are applied here too, but with different presets, colors, and settings. This is the Liquid Rainbow layer style, which is in the Text Effects style library.

PICKING FROM THE PICKER

Choices in the Contour preset picker change the profile of various effects. The gray areas in the thumbnail represent opaque pixels, and the white areas represent transparency. To close the picker, double-click a contour; or click the Contour arrowhead; or click anywhere outside the picker in the Layer Style dialog.

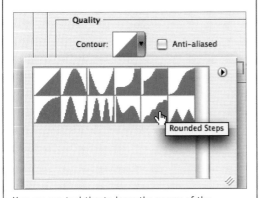

You can use tool tips to learn the names of the contours in the Contour Preset picker.

Copying, moving, and removing layer effects

If you like how an effect looks on one layer, you can copy it to another one. The more, the merrier.

To copy individual effects between layers:

Alt-drag/Option-drag any individual effect name from one layer to another.

You can move individual effects (take them out of) one layer and move them to another layer without deleting any effects on the target layer.

To move an effect from one layer to another without replacing existing effects:

Drag any individual effect **name** from one layer to another.

And finally, you can also move all the effects from one layer to another, replacing any existing effects on the target layer and removing them from the source layer.

To move all the effects from one layer to another, replacing existing effects:

Drag the **Effects** listing from one layer to another.

Clicking (removing) the visibility icon for a layer effect or unchecking the box for an effect in the Layer Style dialog doesn't remove the effect—it merely hides it from view. If you want to permanently delete effects from a layer, follow these instructions.

To remove layer effects:

Do either of the following:

Drag an individual effect **name** over the **Delete Layer** button 🗑 at the bottom of the Layers panel.

To remove all the effects from a layer, drag the **Effects** listing over the Delete Layer button.

➤ If you turn off an effect via the check box in the Layer Style dialog and then turn it back on again the same way, the last-used options for that effect will redisplay. (The same holds true if you reapply an effect that you dragged individually to the Delete Layer button.)

Applying layer styles

You can conveniently store a collection of layer settings—including layer effects and/or blending options, such as layer opacity, blending mode, fill opacity—collectively as a style on the Styles panel. Once stored, styles can be applied to any layer with a click of the mouse. To get acquainted with the Styles panel, start by applying one of the predefined styles to a type layer or to a layer that contains some transparency. You can edit the effects from any predefined style, or create and save your own styles, as in the steps on the next page.

To apply a style to a layer:

1. Show the **Styles** panel. Via the panel menu, you can change the display mode for the panel to Text Only or to a Thumbnail or List mode.

2. Do one of the following:

   Click a layer (not the Background) on the **Layers** panel, then click a style on the **Styles** panel.**A-G**

   Drag a style name or thumbnail from the **Styles** panel over any selected or unselected layer on the **Layers** panel.

   Double-click a layer to open the Layer Style dialog, click **Styles** at the top, click a style thumbnail, then click OK (**A**, next page).

➤ Normally, when you apply a style, it replaces any existing effects on the current layer. To combine the effects from a style with existing effects on a layer, Shift-click or Shift-drag the style. With Shift down or not, if two effects have the same name, effects in the new style will replace existing ones.

A Click a layer, then click a style thumbnail (or name) on the Styles panel.

B Web Styles library > Blue Paper Clip

C Text Effects library > Sprayed Stencil

D Text Effects library > Shaded Red Bevel

E Text Effects library > Overspray

F Textures library > Abstract Fire

G Image Effects library > Water Reflection

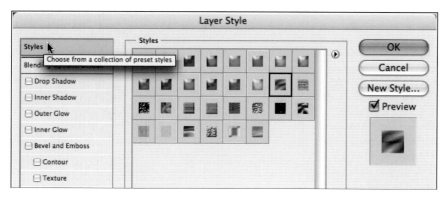

A Styles can also be applied to a layer via your old friend the Layer Style dialog. Click Styles at the top left side of the dialog, then click a style thumbnail.

Creating layer styles

As you create a layer style, you can control whether the style will include the layer effects and/or Blending Options settings (such as layer opacity, blending mode, and fill opacity) that are currently applied to the selected layer.

To save a style to the Styles panel:

1. Do either of the following:

   On the **Layers** panel, click a layer,**B** then on the **Styles** panel,**A** click either the blank area **C** or the **New Style** button.**≡**

   On the **Layers** panel, double-click a layer to open the Layer Style dialog, then click the **New Style** button.

2. Enter a **Name** for the new style, check whether you want to **Include Layer Effects** and/or **Include Layer Blending Options** in the style, then click OK. If the Layer Style dialog is open, click OK again. Your new style will appear as the last listing or thumbnail on the Styles panel.

▶ To load more style libraries onto the Styles panel, choose from the panel menu. To create a style library, see page 401. The styles that are included with Photoshop are in Adobe Photoshop CS4/Presets/Styles.

▶ To remove a style from a layer (including restoring the default opacity of 100% and the layer blending mode of Normal), right-click/Control-click a layer and choose Clear Layer Style.

▶ To copy the current settings from one layer to another, right-click/Control-click the layer that contains the desired settings and choose Copy Layer Style, click another layer, then right-click/Control-click and choose Paste Layer Style.

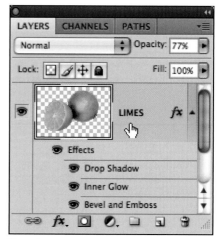

B On the Layers panel, click a layer that contains the effects and/or other settings that you want to save as a style...

C ...then on the Styles panel, click either the blank area or the New Style button.

You've probably already used a filter or two in an earlier chapter. In this chapter, they're star players. Depending on which filters you apply and which settings you choose for them, the results can range from barely noticeable to a total morph.**A** You can make an image look hand painted, silkscreened, or sketched; apply distortion or noise; create patterns or textures; make an image look like a mosaic or like it's being viewed through mottled glass—the creative possibilities are infinite. Once you start using the Filter Gallery, you'll see—time will fly by.

Using this chapter, you can learn techniques for applying filters, learn how to create and use Smart Filters, peruse an illustrated compendium of filters, and combine filters to make a photo look hand drawn or painted (quick exercises just to get you started).

Applying filters

You can apply filters to a whole layer or just to a selection on a layer. Most of the filters are applied either through the Filter Gallery or through an individual dialog; a small handful of filters, such as Clouds and Blur, are applied in one step simply by choosing the filter name from the menu. If you apply a filter to a Smart Object layer, it becomes an editable, removable Smart Filter (see pages 336–337).

If you try to select a filter and find that it's not available, the cause is most likely the current document color mode and/or bit depth. All the filters are available for RGB and Grayscale files; most filters are available for Lab Color files; fewer are available for CMYK Color and 16-bits-per-channel files; still fewer are available for 32-bits-per-channel files; and none are available for Bitmap and Indexed Color files.

IN THIS CHAPTER

Applying filters 333

Creating and using Smart Filters 336

Filter pro techniques 338

Most of the filters illustrated 341

Photos into drawings or paintings. . .349

A One tiger, three ways: The original image, the Charcoal filter applied, and the Diffuse Glow filter applied

The Filter Gallery dialog (**A**, next page) houses most of the Photoshop filters under one roof. Here you can preview dozens of filters and filter settings, show and hide each filter effect that you've previewed, and change the sequence in which they're applied.

To use the Filter Gallery:

1. Click an image layer or a Smart Object layer. See also "Choosing Colors First" in the sidebar on this page.

2. Choose Filter > **Filter Gallery**.

3. To change the zoom level for the preview, click the **Zoom Out** button ⊟ or **Zoom In** button ⊞ in the lower left corner of the dialog or choose a zoom level from the menu. You can drag a magnified preview in the window or move it via the scroll bar(s) or arrows.

4. Do either of the following:

   In the middle pane of the dialog, click an arrowhead to expand any of the six filter categories, then click a filter thumbnail.

   Choose a filter name from the menu below the Cancel button.

5. Choose settings for the filter on the right side. The filter you've chosen will be listed in the lower right area of the dialog.

6. Do any of the following optional steps:

   To apply an additional filter effect, click the **New Effect Layer** button, ⬛ click another filter thumbnail in any category, then choose settings.

   To **replace** one filter effect with another, click that filter effect name on the scroll list (don't click the New Effect Layer button), then choose a replacement filter and settings.

   To **hide** a filter effect, click the visibility icon 👁 next to the effect name (click in the same spot again to redisplay the effect).

   To change the **stacking order** of a filter effect to produce a different result in the image, drag the effect name upward or downward on the list.

   To **remove** a filter effect from the list, select it, then click the Delete Effect Layer button. 🗑

7. When you're satisfied with the filter(s) and settings that you've chosen, click OK.

➤ Alt-click/Option-click the visibility icon to hide or show all the previews except the one you click on.

➤ If you choose an individual filter from the Filter menu that also happens to be in the Filter Gallery, the Filter Gallery opens automatically.

➤ If you get tired of using Photoshop filters, you can purchase filter plug-ins from third-party suppliers.

CHOOSING COLORS FIRST

Some filters use the Foreground and/or Background colors:

➤ Artistic > Neon Glow (Foreground color)

➤ Distort > Diffuse Glow (Background color)

➤ Pixelate > Pointillize (Background color)

➤ Render > Clouds, Difference Clouds, Fibers (Foreground and Background colors)

➤ Sketch > Bas Relief, Chalk & Charcoal, Charcoal, Conté Crayon, Graphic Pen, Halftone Pattern, Note Paper, Photocopy, Plaster, Stamp, Torn Edges (Foreground and Background colors)

➤ Stylize > Tiles (Foreground and/or Background colors)

REAPPLYING FILTERS

➤ To reapply the last-used filter using the same settings, choose Filter > [last filter name] (Ctrl-F/Cmd-F).

➤ To reopen either the last-used filter dialog or the Filter Gallery with the settings for the last-used filter displayed, press Ctrl-Alt-F/Cmd-Option-F.

Click this button to hide the thumbnail pane and expand the
preview window; click it again to redisplay the thumbnail pane.

To preview a filter effect, click a thumbnail
or choose a filter name from the menu.

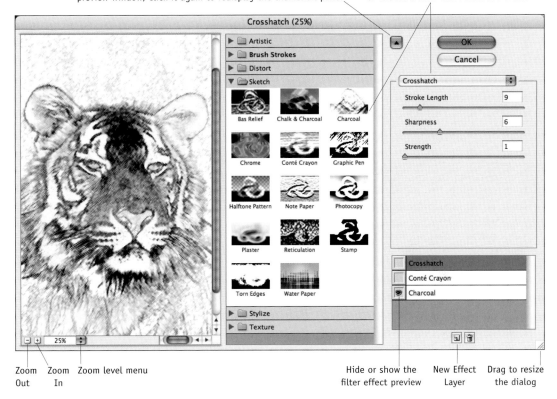

Zoom　Zoom　Zoom level menu
Out　In

Hide or show the　New Effect　Drag to resize
filter effect preview　Layer　the dialog

A The Filter Gallery dialog has three sections: a preview on the left; filter categories with thumbnails in the middle; and on the right, filter settings and a list of the filter effects you've previewed thus far.

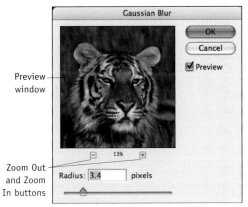

Preview
window

Zoom Out
and Zoom
In buttons

B Some filters are applied via a separate dialog. Of those, some have a preview window and some don't.

Using the preview in individual filter dialogs

➤ For individual filter dialogs that have a preview window, **B** you can click the + button to zoom in or click the – button to zoom out (we usually do the latter). When the preview is magnified, you can drag it inside the preview window. You can also click and hold in the preview, then release, to compare the image with and without the filter. Some filter dialogs also have a Preview check box that you can click on or off.

➤ In some filter dialogs, if you click with the square pointer in the document window, that area of the image appears in the preview window.

➤ When you change filter settings in a dialog that has a preview window, a line may blink on and off below the preview percentage while the preview is rendering.

Creating and using Smart Filters

When you apply a filter to a Smart Object, it becomes a Smart Filter. As with layer effects, you can edit, hide, or remove Smart Filters at any time, apply multiple filter effects to the same Smart Object layer, hide individual filter effects while keeping others visible, and move or copy filter effects from one Smart Object layer to another. In addition, you can edit the filter mask (which is created automatically), change the stacking order of the filter effects, and edit the Smart Object.

The file formats that support Photoshop layers —including PSD, PDF, and TIFF—also support Smart Filters. You can also apply some third-party filters as Smart Filters.

To create a Smart Filter:

1. Click a Smart Object layer (see pages 314–316). *Optional:* Create a selection to restrict the filter effect. (The selection shape will appear in the Filter Effects mask after you apply a filter).

2. Apply a filter. A Smart Filters listing and mask thumbnail will appear, and the filter effects list will expand to reveal the new filter name.**A**

▶ If you transform a Smart Object layer, as an alert dialog will tell you, any Smart Filters on that layer will be hidden temporarily until the transformation is completed.

The greatest advantage to using Smart Filters is that you can edit the filter settings at any time.

To edit the settings for a Smart Filter:

1. Do either of the following:

   Double-click next to the filter name on the Layers panel.

   Right-click/Control-click the filter name and choose **Edit Smart Filter** from the context menu.

2. If any Smart Filters are listed above the one you're editing, an alert will appear,**B** indicating that those filter effects will be hidden until you exit the Filter Gallery or the individual filter dialog. Check Don't Show Again to prevent the warning from appearing again, and click OK.

3. Make the desired changes in the filter dialog, then click OK.

▶ To reapply a filter that is normally applied in one step without a dialog appearing (such as Clouds), double-click the filter name.

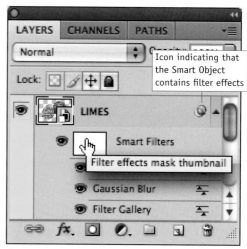

A When you apply a filter to a Smart Object layer, the layer gains a "Smart Filters" listing, filter mask, and nested list of filters. If you apply one or more filter effects by choosing Filter > Filter Gallery, the filter listing will be a generic "Filter Gallery"; if you apply an individual filter by choosing the filter name from the Filter menu, that name will be listed.

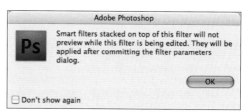

B This alert dialog will appear if you try to edit a Smart Filter and there are other filters listed above it on the same Smart Object layer. Click OK.

DISAPPEARING FILTER EFFECTS

When changing the document color mode or bit depth, if the document contains filters that aren't supported by the new color mode or depth, an alert dialog will appear. If you click Don't Rasterize and then click Don't Flatten, this symbol ⚠ will display next to the filter names, indicating that the filter effect is currently inaccessible. If you then convert the file to a mode or depth that does support the filter, the icon will disappear and the filter effect will become visible again. Note: The Liquify and Vanishing Point filters can't be applied as Smart Filters, regardless of the document color mode or bit depth.

Each filter effect can have its own blending mode and opacity, separate from the blending options for the Smart Object layer. Granted, all of this can be a lot to keep track of.

To edit the blending options for a Smart Filter:

1. Double-click the **Blending Options** icon ⬆ next to the filter name on the Layers panel, and click OK if an alert dialog appears. The Blending Options dialog opens.**A**

2. Choose a blending **Mode** and **Opacity** (use the latter to fade the filter effect), then click OK. You can change these settings at any time.

To hide/show Smart Filter effects:

Do either of the following:

Click the **visibility** icon 👁 for the **Smart Filters** listing to hide all the Smart Filters on that layer.

Click the **visibility** icon 👁 for any individual **Smart Filter**. This may take longer to process than clicking the visibility icon for all the filters.

To copy filter effects from one Smart Object layer to another:

Expand the list of filter effects for a Smart Object layer, then **Alt-drag/Option-drag** a filter effect or the Smart Filters listing into another Smart Object layer.

➤ You can also restack any filter effect within the same Smart Object layer or move (drag) a Smart Filter or a whole stack of Smart Filters from one Smart Object layer to another (pause while Photoshop processes the change).

When you delete a Smart Filter and there are other filters on that layer, it may take a moment for Photoshop to update the display.

To delete a Smart Filter:

Do either of the following:

Right-click/Control-click a Smart Filter and choose **Delete Smart Filter**.

Drag the filter to the **Delete Layer** button.🗑

To create a filter mask:

When you apply the first filter to a Smart Object layer, a filter mask appears automatically next to the Smart Filters listing. If you create a selection first, that selection shape appears in the mask. To create a filter mask if there is none (say you deleted it), create a selection, if desired, then right-click/Control-click the Smart Filters listing and choose **Add Filter Mask**, or click the **Add Filter Mask** button ⊕ on the Masks panel.★

WORKING WITH FILTER MASKS

You can do the same things to a filter mask (for Smart Filters) as you can to a layer mask, including:

➤ To delete a filter mask, drag it to the Delete Layer button; or on the Masks panel, click the Select Filter Mask 🔘 button, then click the Delete Mask button. ★

➤ Click the filter mask thumbnail, then paint with black to hide the filter effect, where needed, with white to reveal any areas you've hidden, or with black and a lower tool opacity to hide areas partially.

➤ Alt-click/Option-click the filter mask to display just the mask in the document window; repeat to redisplay the full Smart Object layer.

➤ Shift-click the filter mask thumbnail to disable the mask temporarily (a red X will appear over the mask thumbnail); repeat to reenable it.

➤ To load a filter mask as a selection, Ctrl-click/Cmd-click the filter mask thumbnail.

A Each filter effect can have its own Blending Options (blending mode and opacity). If you think this can get confusing, you're right! And unfortunately, no indicator appears on the Layers panel to show when the blend settings have been altered.

Filter pro techniques

➤ Before applying a filter, create a **selection** on a layer. The filter effect will be limited to pixels within the selection. If you create a selection before applying a Smart Filter, the selection shape will appear in the filter mask. For a soft transition between the filtered and nonfiltered areas, on the Masks panel, click the Select Filter Mask button, 🅠 then adjust the Feather or Density value.

➤ For greater flexibility, duplicate an image layer and apply filters to the duplicate—or even better, apply them as **Smart Filters** to a Smart Object layer.**A–B** You can edit, remove, mask, or change the opacity or blending mode of each Smart Filter effect individually at any time (see the first task on the preceding page).**C**

(Although the Edit > Fade command also lets you change the opacity or blending mode for the last edit, such as a filter, it requires more steps, must be applied right after applying the filter, and doesn't apply to Smart Object layers, so we don't recommend it.)

➤ To make your filter results look less uniform and "machine made," apply **more than one**; that way, no single effect will stand out.

➤ To intensify the results of a filter, before applying it, pump up the brightness and contrast of the image via a **Levels** adjustment layer. Move the black Input Levels slider slightly to the right and the white Input Levels slider slightly to the left.

➤ If you apply a filter to a Smart Object layer, you can click the **filter mask**, then with the Brush tool, paint with black to mask the filter effect (lower the tool opacity for a partial mask) or

---

FILTERS IN OTHER CHAPTERS

To see if a specific filter is discussed in another chapter, look in the index for the filter name.

A This is the original image.

B We duplicated the image layer, converted it to a Smart Object layer, then applied the Charcoal filter as a Smart Filter.

C We lowered the opacity of the Smart Object layer.

A We clicked the filter mask, then used the Brush tool at 50% Opacity with black as the Foreground color to partially restore the tiger's face to its original state.

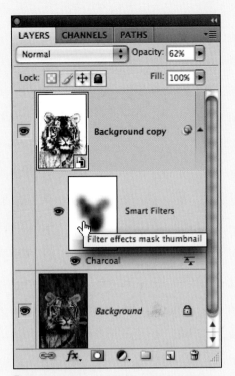

B This is the Layers panel for the preceding figure. The Smart Object layer has an Opacity of 62%. (Alternatively, we could have lowered the opacity of the Smart Filter effect via the Blending Options dialog.)

with white to reveal the filter effect. A–B If you apply a filter to a duplicate image layer, you can add a layer mask and paint on it the same way. See also the sidebar on page 337.

➤ If you get carried away and apply too many Smart Filters, you can simply drag them individually to the **Delete Layer** button. To remove a non-Smart Filter, revert to an earlier document state or snapshot via the **History** panel.

➤ If a filter has been applied to an image layer, you can selectively reduce its effect by using the **History Brush** tool. On the History panel, click in the leftmost column for a prefilter state to be designated as the source for the History Brush tool; the history source icon moves to that slot. Choose an opacity for the History Brush tool from the Options bar, then draw brush strokes on the image.

Continued on the following page

➤ To fade a filter effect gradually across the whole image, apply the **Black, White** gradient (linear or radial) to the filter mask on a Smart Object layer. The filter will apply fully to the image where the mask is white and fade to nil where the mask is black. **A–C**

A Continuing with the image from the preceding page, we erased our brush strokes from the layer mask with the Eraser tool.

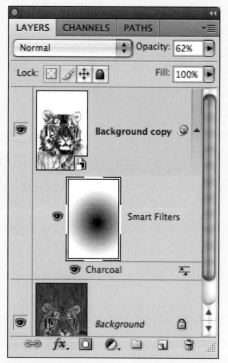

B To edit the filter mask in a different way, we applied the "Black, White" gradient (radial type).

C The gradient in the filter mask is diminishing the impact of the filter in the center of the image, where we want the focal point to be.

Most of the filters illustrated
Artistic filters

Original image

Colored Pencil

Cutout

Dry Brush

Film Grain

Fresco

Neon Glow (choose a Foreground color first, and choose a glow color in the Filter Gallery)

Paint Daubs

Palette Knife

Artistic filters (continued)

Original image

Plastic Wrap

Poster Edges

Rough Pastels

Smudge Stick

Sponge

Underpainting

Watercolor

Brush Strokes filters

Original image

Accented Edges

Angled Strokes

Crosshatch

Dark Strokes

Ink Outlines

Spatter

Sprayed Strokes

Sumi-e

Pixelate filters

Color Halftone

Crystallize

Facet

Fragment

Mezzotint

Mosaic

Two Render filters

Pointillize (choose a Background
color first)

Clouds (choose Foreground and
Background colors first)

Lens Flare

Sketch filters

Bas Relief*

Chalk & Charcoal*

Charcoal*

Chrome

Conté Crayon*

Graphic Pen*

Halftone Pattern*

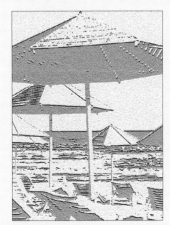

Note Paper*

Photocopy*

*Choose Foreground and Background colors first.

Sketch filters (continued)

Original image

Plaster*

Reticulation

Stamp*

Torn Edges*

Water Paper

A few of the Distort filters

Diffuse Glow (choose a Background color first)

Displace

Glass

*Choose Foreground and Background colors first.

Stylize filters

Diffuse

Emboss

Extrude

Find Edges

Glowing Edges

Solarize

Tiles (choose a Foreground and/or
Background color first)

Trace Contour

Wind

Texture filters

Original image

Craquelure

Grain (Soft)

Grain (Speckle)

Grain (Vertical)

Mosaic Tiles

Patchwork

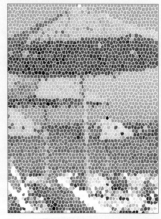

Stained Glass

Texturizer

Photos into drawings or paintings

In the instructions on this page and the next, you'll turn an image into a drawing or watercolor—in one case by reducing an image to lines and then painting on the filter mask, and in the other case by applying a series of filters. We hope this exercise inspires you to develop your own formulas.

To turn a photograph into a tinted drawing:

1. Duplicate an image layer, then right-click/Control-click the duplicate and choose Convert to Smart Object. Keep the new Smart Object layer selected.**A**

2. Choose Filter > Stylize > **Find Edges**.**B**

3. Click the filter mask thumbnail on the Layers panel.

4. Choose the **Brush** tool; ✎ choose a large, Soft Round brush tip, Normal mode, and an Opacity below 50% on the Options bar; make the Foreground color black; then draw strokes on the image to reveal parts of the underlying layer.**C–D**

5. *Optional:* Lower the opacity of the Smart Object layer.

A We converted an image layer into a Smart Object layer.

B We applied the Find Edges filter to the Smart Object layer.

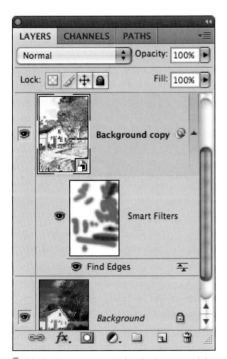

C This is the Layers panel for the image at right.

D We applied brush strokes to the filter mask to reveal some of the underlying image.

There are so many ways to combine filters. In these instructions, you'll turn an image into a watercolor by applying the Median and Minimum filters. A medium- to light-toned image would work best for this exercise.

To create a watercolor:

1. Duplicate an image layer, then right-click/ Control-click the duplicate and choose Convert to Smart Object. Keep the new layer selected.

2. Choose Filter > Noise > **Median**. In the Median dialog, move the Radius slider to between 2 and 8, then click OK.

3. Choose Filter > Other > **Minimum**. In the Minimum dialog, move the Radius slider to between 2 and 5, then click OK.

4. *Optional:* Choose Filter > Sharpen > Smart Sharpen, click Basic, try an Amount of 80–100% and a Radius of 4–8 px, then click OK. **B** Compare your results with those of the Watercolor filter, shown in Figure **C**.

A This is the original photo.

B This watercolor was created by following the instructions above.

C Compare the results at left with those of Photoshop's Artistic > Watercolor filter here.

We've never heard the phrase "A word is worth a thousand pictures," but in Photoshop, where you can do such artful things with type, the line between pictures and words is blurred (sometimes literally!). In this chapter, you'll learn how to create and select editable type and apply a host of character and paragraph attributes. You'll also learn some fancy tricks, such as how to transform, warp, fade, and screen back type, and how to fill it with imagery.

When you use the **Horizontal Type** tool or **Vertical Type** tool, a new layer appears and fully **editable** type appears instantly in the document window. You can easily change the attributes of editable type (such as the font, style, size, color, kerning, tracking, leading, alignment, and baseline shift), plus you can transform it, warp it, apply layer effects to it, change its blending mode, and change its opacity or fill percentage.

To apply some kinds of edits to type, such as filters or brush strokes, or to fill type with a gradient or a pattern by using the Fill command, you have to **rasterize** the type layer first. And you can't have your cake and eat it, too: once type is rasterized, you can't edit its character attributes, such as the font, or edit its paragraph attributes, such as the alignment.

To apply typographic attributes, you'll use the **Character** panel,**A A** the **Paragraph** panel,**¶** and the **Options** bar (see the next page).

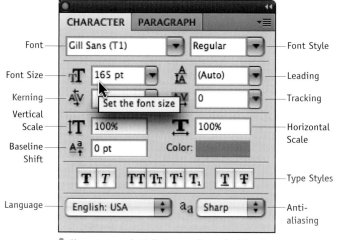

Font
Font Size
Kerning
Vertical Scale
Baseline Shift
Language

CHARACTER | PARAGRAPH

Gill Sans (T1) — Regular — Font Style

T 165 pt — Leading
A̲V̲ 0 — Set the font size — Tracking
I̲T 100% — T 100% — Horizontal Scale
A̲ᵃ 0 pt — Color:

T T TT Tʈ T¹ T₁ T T̶ — Type Styles

English: USA — aₐ Sharp — Anti-aliasing

A Character panel attributes can be applied to all the type on a layer, or to some characters or words.

22

IN THIS CHAPTER

Creating editable type 352

Selecting type 354

Converting type 355

Importing type from Adobe
   Illustrator as a Smart Object 355

Changing the font 356

Scaling type 356

Kerning and tracking type 357

Adjusting leading. 358

Changing the type style 359

Shifting type from the baseline 359

Changing the orientation of type . . .360

Applying paragraph settings 361

Transforming type via its
   bounding box 362

Warping type. 363

Rasterizing type. 364

Filling type with imagery. 364

Making type fade 366

Screening back type 367

Putting type in a spot color
   channel 368

Creating editable type

Because editable type automatically appears on its own layer, it can be edited, moved, transformed, warped, restacked, or otherwise modified without affecting any other layers. You can be very casual about where you position editable type initially and about which typographic attributes you choose for it, because it's so easy to move and edit.

To create an editable type layer:

1. Choose the **Horizontal Type** tool or **Vertical Type** tool (T or Shift-T).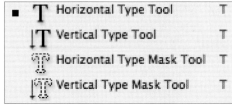

2. Read the sidebar at right, then do either of the following:

   To create **point** type, click to establish an insertion point.

   To create **paragraph** type, drag a marquee to define a bounding box for it to fit into.

3. On the Options bar, do the following:

   Choose a **font family**.**B** A sample of each font displays on the menu.

   Choose a **font style**.

   Choose or enter a **font size** (you can use the scrubby slider).

   Choose an **anti-aliasing** method: Sharp (sharpest), Crisp (somewhat sharp), Strong (heavier), or Smooth (smoothest). Photoshop will smooth the edges of the type by introducing partially transparent pixels along the edges of the characters. With anti-aliasing off (None), the edges of the type will be jagged.**C–D**

POINT TYPE OR PARAGRAPH TYPE?

► To create point type, click in the document window with the Horizontal Type tool or Vertical Type tool, then type some characters. The type will keep going, even disappearing off the edge of the canvas area, until you press Enter/Return. Use this method to create a few lines of text, and when you want to control hyphenation and line breaks manually.

► To create paragraph type, which is more suitable for larger text blocks, draw a marquee in the document window with the Horizontal or Vertical Type tool to define a bounding box for the type, then start typing. To learn about the Paragraph panel and commands, see page 361.

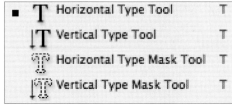

A To create editable type, choose the Horizontal Type tool or the Vertical Type tool. (Ignore the Type Mask tools, which create type-shaped selections.)

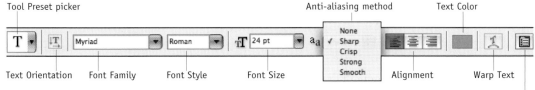

Tool Preset picker · Anti-aliasing method · Text Color

Text Orientation · Font Family · Font Style · Font Size · Alignment · Warp Text

B The Options bar offers many controls for the Horizontal Type tool.

Open or close the Character and Paragraph panel group

C With Anti-aliasing off, type edges look jagged.

D With Anti-aliasing on, type edges look smoother.

Click an **alignment** button to align point type relative to your original insertion point or to align paragraph type to the left edge, right edge, or center of the bounding box (see page 361).

Click the **Text Color** swatch, then choose a color from the Color Picker, the Swatches panel, or the Color panel, or click a color in the document window.

4. Type the desired text in the document window. If you're creating point type, press Enter/Return to create line breaks, where necessary. For paragraph type, let the type wrap naturally to the edges of the bounding box.

5. To accept the new text, press Enter on the keypad or click the ✔ button on the far right end of the Options bar. (To cancel the type, press Esc or click the ⊘ button.) Each time you use the Horizontal or Vertical Type tool, Photoshop creates a new layer automatically.**B**

Later in this chapter, we'll show you how to use the Character and Paragraph panels to change type attributes.

➤ For an explanation of the missing fonts alert icon, see page 60.

➤ You can right-click/Control-click an editable type layer name and choose a different anti-aliasing method from the context menu.

➤ You can turn font menu previewing on or off and change the preview size for the Font menu in Preferences > Type: Font Preview Size.

➤ Photoshop uses the vector outlines for a typeface when resizing editable type, when saving to the PDF and EPS formats, and when outputting to a PostScript printer. Editable type outputs at the printer resolution, not at the file resolution.

➤ If you create type in a Bitmap, Indexed Color, or Multichannel mode image, it will appear on the Background, not on a layer, and can't be edited.

A The Alignment buttons control the position of paragraph type relative to its bounding box (or the position of point type relative to the insertion point). After typing each word shown above, we pressed Enter/Return to make each word into a separate paragraph, then aligned the first, second, and third words to the Center, Right, and Left, respectively.

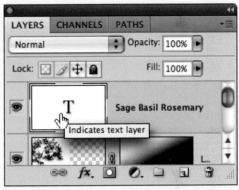

B Editable type layers always have a **T** in the thumbnail and are named automatically by the first word or first few words of the type they contain.

MANAGING YOUR TYPE LAYERS

If you place individual passages, words, or characters on separate layers, you'll be able to move them around or apply effects to them individually. If your type layers start to overpopulate, on the other hand, you can periodically delete any layers that you don't need and gather the ones you want to keep into layer groups.

Selecting type

Before you can change the character or paragraph attributes of type or make copy changes, you have to select the characters you want to edit. You can edit either all the type on a layer or just a few characters or words.

To select type for editing or style changes:

1. Do any of the following:

   To highlight type characters for editing, click a type layer, choose the **Horizontal Type** tool T or **Vertical Type** tool ‖T (T or Shift-T), click in the type to create an insertion point, then drag across **characters** or **words** to select them.**A** See also the methods listed in the sidebar at right.

   To select all the type on the layer, with any tool selected, double-click the **T** icon on the **Layers** panel. If the type was created with the Horizontal Type tool, the tool will also become selected.

   To change the attributes of all the type on the layer, such as the scale, tracking, leading, style, or paragraph settings such as alignment or justification, just click the **layer**. (This doesn't cause a type tool to become selected.)

2. After performing text edits or styling changes, to take the type tool out of edit mode and commit to your changes, do one of the following:

   Click the ✔ on the Options bar.

   Press Enter on the keypad.

   Click any other tool.

   Click a different layer.

   (To cancel your editing changes before committing to them, click the ⊘ on the Options bar or press Esc.)

➤ If you want to make the bounding box for a block of text visible, choose the Move tool (V), click the type layer on the Layers panel, and check Show Transform Controls on the Options bar. You can also use the Move tool to move the type block in the document window.

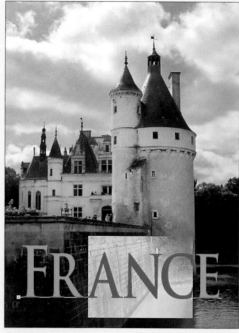

A Drag across the characters you want to select.

SELECTING TYPE CHARACTERS

Choose the Horizontal Type or Vertical Type tool, then do any of the following:

Select consecutive characters or words	Drag across them. Or click at the beginning of a series of words, then Shift-click at the end.
Select a word	Double-click a word
Select multiple words	Double-click a word, then drag
Select a line	Triple-click a line
Select a paragraph	Quadruple-click a line
Select all the characters in the type object	Double-click the **T** thumbnail on the Layers panel; or click in the text, then press Ctrl-A/Cmd-A

Converting type

To convert paragraph type to point type:

On the Layers panel, right-click/Control-click a type layer name and choose **Convert to Point Text**. A return will be added to the end of every line of type except the last one. If the type object contains hidden (overflow) text, an alert dialog will warn you that the hidden text will be deleted if you proceed.

➤ We don't know of a command in Photoshop that reveals hidden characters (paragraph returns and the like). We wish there was one.

To convert point type to paragraph type:

On the Layers panel, right-click/Control-click a type layer name and choose **Convert to Paragraph Text**. To reshape the resulting bounding box, follow the instructions on page 362. Be sure to delete any unwanted hyphens that Photoshop may have inserted.

Importing type from Adobe Illustrator as a Smart Object

If you create type in Adobe Illustrator and then import it into Photoshop by using either method outlined below, it will arrive as a Smart Object layer in Photoshop. You can edit or restyle the type at any time in Illustrator, and the file will update in Photoshop to reflect your changes.

Note: If the type you want to import has stroke attributes or layer effects that you want to keep editable, follow Method 1 below. If you follow Method 2, the type layer containing those attributes or effects will be rasterized.

To create "smart" type from Adobe Illustrator:

Method 1 (AI format)

1. In Adobe Illustrator, make sure the type is on its own layer, then save the file in the **Illustrator Document** (.ai) format.

2. Open a file in Photoshop, then do either of the following:

   In Photoshop or Bridge, use File > **Place** to import the type file (see page 27).

   Copy (Ctrl-C/Cmd-C) the type object in Illustrator, click in your Photoshop document,

then **Paste** (Ctrl-V/Cmd-V). In the Paste dialog, click **Paste As: Smart Object**, then click OK.

A new Smart Object layer will appear on the Layers panel. If you double-click the Smart Object layer thumbnail and click OK in the alert prompt (if it appears), the embedded file will open in Illustrator. You can edit the type or any of its attributes or layer effects. When you save and close the file, your changes will be reflected in the Photoshop document.

Method 2 (PSD format)

1. To create a Smart Object layer that can be edited as a separate Photoshop file, create type in Illustrator, then choose File > **Export**. The Export dialog opens.

2. Choose **Format: Photoshop (.psd)**, then click Export. The Photoshop Export Options dialog opens.

3. Choose Color Mode: RGB; check Resolution: Medium (150 ppi); click Write Layers; check Preserve Text Editability, Maximum Editability, and Anti-alias; then click OK.

4. Do either of the following:

   Open a Photoshop file, then in Photoshop or Bridge use File > **Place** to place the type file.

   Use File > **Open as Smart Object** to open the type file as a new Photoshop file, with the type on a Smart Object layer.

5. If you double-click the new Smart Object layer thumbnail and click OK in the alert dialog (if it appears), the embedded Photoshop file will appear onscreen, with the editable type in a layer group. You can edit the file at any time (e.g., add layer effects to the type layer). When you save and close it, the Photoshop document will update to reflect your edits.

Note: If the Illustrator type contained layer effects, those elements will become separate rasterized image layers in the embedded Smart Object file and won't be editable via the Layer Style dialog. The type will also be rasterized if it contained a stroke.

➤ To learn more about Smart Object layers, see pages 314–316.

Changing the font

1. Do either of the following:

   On the Layers panel, double-click a **T** icon, then select a sequence of characters or words.

   To change the font for all the characters on a layer, click the **layer**, but don't select anything.

2. On the Options bar or the Character panel, choose from the **Font Family** menu, then from the **Font Style** menu (to show the Character panel, see the sidebar on the following page).

Scaling type

To assign the same font size (point size) to all currently selected characters, use either the Options bar or the Character panel.

To scale type by choosing a value:

1. Select the type to be scaled (see step 1 in the preceding set of instructions).

2. Choose the **Horizontal Type** or **Vertical Type** tool; then, on the Options bar, use the **Font Size** icon **T** as a scrubby slider (Alt-drag/Option-drag for finer increments), **A** or enter a value, or choose from the menu. **B** You can also change the font size via the Character panel. **C**

If the type characters you select are in more than one point size and you want to preserve their relative differences as you change their scale, you can do so with the Move tool.

To scale type using the Move tool:

1. On the Layers panel, click a type layer.

2. Choose the **Move** tool (V) and check **Show Transform Controls** on the Options bar to make the transform controls appear for the type layer.

3. Click any handle on the transform box first, then do any of the following:

   To scale just the **height or width**, drag a side handle.

   To scale both the **height and** the **width**, drag a corner handle.

   To preserve the **proportions** of the characters as you scale them, Shift-drag a corner handle. **D**

4. To commit to the scale change, click the ✔ button on the Options bar or double-click the text block. (To cancel the scale change before committing to it, click the ⊘ button on the Options bar or press Esc.)

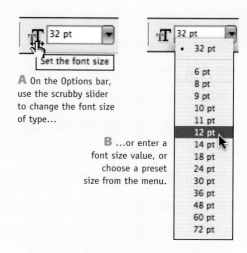

A On the Options bar, use the scrubby slider to change the font size of type...

B ...or enter a font size value, or choose a preset size from the menu.

C You can also change the font size via the Font Size scrubby slider, field, or menu on the Character panel.

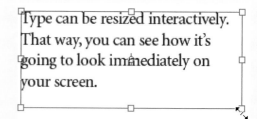

Type can be resized interactively. That way, you can see how it's going to look immediately on your screen.

D To preserve the proportions of type as you resize it interactively, Shift-drag a corner handle with the Move tool.

Kerning and tracking type

Kerning affects the spacing between a pair of text characters.

To apply kerning:

Method 1

1. On the Layers panel, double-click a **T** icon.

2. Click to create an insertion point between any two characters.

3. Show the **Character** panel (see the sidebar at right), then do either of the following:

   From the **Kerning** menu, choose **Metrics** to apply the kerning value built into the current font or **Optical** to let Photoshop control the kerning.

   Use the **Kerning** icon as a scrubby slider; **A** or enter or choose a positive or negative value.**B**

Method 2

   Choose a type tool, insert the cursor between two characters, then press **Alt/Option** plus the left or right **arrow** key. Add Ctrl/Cmd to the shortcut to kern in a larger increment.

Tracking is like kerning, except that it affects multiple characters instead of a pair of characters.

To apply tracking:

1. On the Layers panel, do either of the following:

   To apply tracking to a whole layer, click the **layer**.

   To apply tracking to part of a layer, double-click a **T** icon, then select some characters or words.

2. Do either of the following:

   On the Character panel, use the **Tracking** icon as a scrubby slider or enter or choose a positive or negative tracking value.**C**

   If type is selected, you can press **Alt/Option** and the left or right **arrow** key. Add Ctrl/Cmd to the shortcut to apply tracking in a larger increment.

   ► To reset the tracking value of selected characters to 0, press Ctrl-Shift-Q/Cmd-Control-Shift-Q.

DISPLAYING THE CHARACTER PANEL

► If the Character panel is open but collapsed to an icon, click the **A** icon.

► Choose the Horizontal Type tool or Vertical Type tool, then click the button on the Options bar.

► Choose Window > Character.

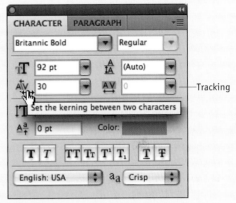

Tracking

A The Kerning and Tracking controls on the Character panel don't have equivalents on the Options bar. To change either value quickly, use the scrubby slider (or shortcut).

B Use a negative kerning value to close the gap between two characters (we chose –100).

TRACKING IT OUT

Tracking can aid or hinder readability, depending on how high a tracking value you use. Try not to overdo it!

C On occasion, we might spread out a few words, as in the header in this illustration, but never a whole paragraph (a typesetting no-no!).

Adjusting leading

For paragraph type, you can choose a Leading value to control how much space separates each line of text from the line above it. Although each character can have its own leading value (the highest value in a line controls the line), it's simplest just to apply one value to either a whole line or a whole block of text.

To adjust leading in horizontal type:

1. Do either of the following:

   On the Layers panel, double-click the **T** icon for a type layer. *Optional:* Select a line or lines of text that you want to limit the leading change to.

   Click a type **layer**.

   Note: Leading doesn't affect the spacing above the first line in a paragraph.

2. Show the **Character** panel,**A** then use the **Leading** icon 🅐 as a scrubby slider **A–C** (Alt-drag/Option-drag for finer increments), or enter a value in the field (.01 to 5000 pt.), or choose a preset value from the menu. The leading will change from Auto to a numerical value. If you're not sure what value to use, start with a number that's a couple of points larger than the current font size, then readjust it if needed.

► The Auto setting for leading is calculated as a percentage of the font size. Choose Justification from the Paragraph panel menu, and note the Auto Leading percentage; the default value is 120%. At the default value, for example, the leading for 30-point type would be 36 points. To restore the Auto setting to selected type, press Ctrl-Alt-Shift-A/Cmd-Option-Shift-A.

► To adjust the vertical spacing between characters in vertical type, highlight the characters you want to adjust, then change the Tracking (not the leading) value on the Character panel.

CREATING PRESETS FOR YOUR TYPE TOOL

After styling your type, choose the Horizontal or Vertical Type tool, click the type layer, then click the Tool Preset picker thumbnail or arrowhead T⸱ on the far left side of the Options bar. Click the New Tool Preset button,▣ then click OK. You can choose your new preset from the Tool Preset picker or the Tool Presets panel any time you create type. It's sort of like having a style sheet, because all your carefully chosen attributes are saved in the preset—but in this case you have to pick the preset before creating the type. Try creating different presets for your print and Web work.

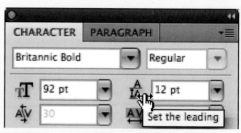

A This is the Leading area on the Character panel.

B This type has a leading value of 90 pt.

C A leading value of 70 pt. brings the bottom line of type closer to the top line.

Changing the type style

To change the type style:

1. To modify a whole type layer, click the **layer**; or to style some of the type on the layer, double-click a **T** icon, then select the type to be styled.

2. Click any **style** button on the **Character** panel. To identify the buttons, use the tool tips onscreen or refer to Figure **A** at right.

➤ The Fractional Widths option on the Character panel menu allows Photoshop to use fractions of pixels to control the spacing of type in order to optimize its appearance (this applies to the entire layer). Keep this option checked unless you're setting small type for Web output.

➤ The Reset Character option on the Character panel menu resets the panel and any selected type to the factory-default Character panel settings.

➤ To choose "real" italic, bold, and other type styles, see page 356.

Shifting type from the baseline

Use the baseline shift feature to raise or lower type characters from the baseline or from a path by one point at a time.

To shift characters from the normal baseline:

1. On the Layers panel, double-click a **T** icon, then select the characters or words you want to shift.

2. On the Character panel, use the **Baseline Shift** icon ᴬᵃ as a scrubby slider (Alt-drag/Option-drag for finer increments), or enter a baseline shift value.**B** A positive value raises characters upward from the normal baseline or path; a negative value moves them downward.**C–D**

➤ To shift whole lines of paragraph type, use leading—not baseline shift. To shift a whole layer, drag it with the Move tool.

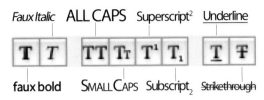

Faux Italic ALL CAPS Superscript² Underline

faux bold Small Caps Subscript₂ Strikethrough

A Click a style button on the Character panel.

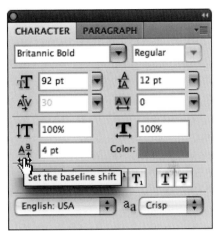

B Use the Baseline Shift feature to shift characters or words a few points upward or downward.

C This type has a Baseline Shift value of 0.

D This type has a Baseline Shift value of −7.

DIFFERENT VALUES

You can enter values in any of these nondefault units on the Character and Paragraph panels: in for inches, pt for points, mm for millimeters, cm for centimeters, px for pixels, or pica for picas. The value will be converted automatically to the current default unit, which is specified in Preferences > Units & Rulers > Units: Type.

Changing the orientation of type

You can change the orientation of type from horizontal to vertical, or vice versa.

To change the orientation of type:

Do either of the following:

On the Layers panel, right-click/Control-click a type layer name and choose **Horizontal** or **Vertical** (the opposite of the current orientation).

On the Layers panel, double-click a type layer thumbnail,**A** then, on the Options bar, click the **Change Text Orientation** button.**🖹 B**

Note: After changing the type orientation, you may need to reposition the type or adjust its tracking value.

➤ To rotate vertical type a different way, double-click the type layer thumbnail (and highlight the characters you want to rotate if you don't want to rotate them all), then choose Standard Roman Vertical Alignment from the Character panel menu to uncheck it.**C** This command isn't available for horizontal type.

MAKING TYPE WIDER OR NARROWER

If you need to typeset narrow or wide characters, we strongly recommend using a condensed or extended typeface, which has balanced proportions built into its design. That said, if you want to fiddle with the scale features in Photoshop, click the type layer first (or double-click the layer thumbnail, then select some characters), then use the scrubby slider for Vertical Scale 𝕀𝕋 or Horizontal Scale 𝕋 (0–1000%).

stretch   Horizontal Scale 50%

stretch   Horizontal Scale 100% (normal)

stretch   Horizontal Scale 200%

stretch   Vertical Scale 300%

Type can be scaled horizontally, vertically, or uniformly (both — and we think best!).

A This is the original vertical type.

B This is the same type after we clicked the Change Text Orientation button on the Options bar.

C And this is the original vertical type after we unchecked Standard Roman Vertical Alignment on the Character panel menu.

Applying paragraph settings

For paragraph type, Photoshop offers a range of formatting options. Although you forgo the manual control you have with point text, you gain powerful typesetting tools. Using the Paragraph panel, you can choose basic settings for justification, alignment, indents, and paragraph spacing.

Note: If your layout will be incorporating a large block of text, you may find it easier to create the imagery in Photoshop and add the type in a layout or Web page creation program.

To set paragraph alignment and justification for horizontal type:

1. Do either of the following:

   On the Layers panel, double-click a **T** icon, then click in a paragraph or select a series of paragraphs.

   To modify all the type in a layer, click the **layer**, but don't select anything.

2. If the **Paragraph** panel is open but collapsed to an icon, click the ¶ icon. If the panel isn't open, click the 🖹 button on the Options bar, then click the Paragraph tab.

3. Click an **alignment** and/or **justification** button at the top of the panel: **A**

   The buttons in the first group—**Left-Align Text**, **Center Text**, and **Right-Align Text**—align type to an edge or the center of the type bounding box. **B** (Note: These options can also be used on point type.)

   The buttons in the second group—**Justify Last Left**, **Justify Last Centered**, and **Justify Last Right**—justify the type, forcing all but the last line to span the full width of the bounding box.

   The last button, **Justify All**, forces all lines, including the last line, to span the full width of the bounding box.

4. Check **Hyphenate** at the bottom of the panel to enable automatic hyphenation. We suggest checking this option for justified text to help minimize any potential gaps that may occur between words.

➤ To change the alignment and/or justification for vertical type, the procedure is the same as described above, except the buttons are labeled Top Align Text, Center Text, and Bottom Align Text.

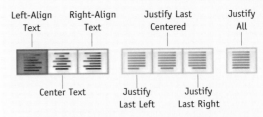

Left-Align Text Right-Align Text Justify Last Centered Justify All

Center Text Justify Last Left Justify Last Right

A These alignment and justification buttons are available on the Paragraph panel for horizontal type.

Left-Align Text

The reward for conformity was that everyone liked you except yourself.

Center Text

The reward for conformity was that everyone liked you except yourself.

Right-Align Text

The reward for conformity was that everyone liked you except yourself.

— *Rita Mae Brown*

B Three paragraph alignment options are shown above.

COMPOSING AND RESETTING PARAGRAPHS

There are a couple of commands on the Paragraph panel menu that you should be aware of:

➤ The Adobe Single-Line Composer and Adobe Every-Line Composer algorithms control how lines of type wrap within the bounding box, and affect the overall shape of the paragraph(s). Adobe Single-Line does this line by line, whereas Adobe Every-Line does it by evaluating the overall appearance of the paragraph. We prefer (love, actually) the latter method because when necessary, it will adjust word breaks at the beginning of a paragraph in order to create more visually appealing breaks toward the end of the paragraph. Both composers abide by the current Word Spacing and Letter Spacing values in the Justification dialog.

➤ Reset Paragraph resets all currently selected paragraphs to the factory-default settings.

Transforming type via its bounding box

Follow these instructions to scale, rotate, or move the bounding box that holds paragraph type without scaling or distorting the characters inside it. The characters will reflow into the new shape.

To transform type via its bounding box:

1. On the Layers panel, double-click the **T** icon for paragraph type.

2. Do one of the following:

   To change the **shape** of the bounding box, position the cursor over a handle, pause, then drag.  To preserve the proportions of the box as you scale it, start dragging, then Shift-drag. The type will reflow. **B**

   To **rotate** the box, position the cursor just outside one of the corners (you'll see a curved, double-arrow pointer), then drag.

   To **move** the whole type block, Ctrl-drag/Cmd-drag from inside the box (this is a temporary Move tool).

3. To accept the transformation, press Enter on the keypad or click the ✔ button on the Options bar. (To cancel it, press Esc or click the ⊘ button on the Options bar.)

➤ To align or distribute multiple type layers, follow the instructions on page 164.

A Drag a handle to make the bounding box larger or smaller.

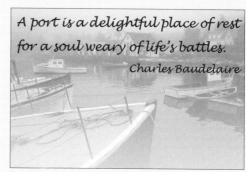

B When we made the bounding box wider, the type reflowed into the new shape.

TRANSFORMING TYPE

➤ When applied to type, the transform commands, such as Free Transform, affect both the bounding box and the type inside it (see pages 310–312).

➤ You can transform point type with the Move tool (check Show Transform Controls on the Options bar to make the bounding box and handles appear).

➤ You can move, scale, rotate, and skew both editable and rasterized type, and you can apply a distortion or perspective transformation to rasterized type.

➤ If you want to transform individual characters, put them on separate layers first.

Warping type

The Warp Text command transforms the bounding box that holds type and distorts the type accordingly. It offers numerous customizable style choices, such as arc, arch, shell, wave, and fish. Best of all, warped type remains fully editable.

To warp editable type:

1. Do either of the following:

   On the Layers panel, double-click a **T** icon, then click the **Warp Text** button ⌐ on the Options bar.

   Right-click/Control-click an editable type layer name and choose **Warp Text**.

2. The Warp Text dialog opens.**A** Move it to the side if it's in the way.

3. From the **Style** menu, choose a preset style.

4. Click **Horizontal** or **Vertical** as the overall orientation for the distortion.

5. *Optional:* Move any of the sliders—Bend, Horizontal Distortion, or Vertical Distortion— noting the changes in the document window.

6. Click OK.**B–E** The layer thumbnail will change to a Warp Text icon.⌐ To reopen the Warp Text dialog at any time, repeat step 1 above; you can choose a different style or

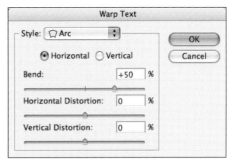

A When using the Warp Text dialog, you can either accept the default settings for a Style preset or customize it by using the sliders.

adjust the sliders; or to undo the warp, choose Style: None.

➤ Once you move the sliders in the Warp Text dialog, those settings are applied to any other Style you choose. To reset the sliders to their default settings, hold down Alt/Option and click Reset.

➤ To scale or reshape warped type to make it fit into a specific area of a composition, click the warped type layer, choose the Move tool (V), check Show Transform Controls on the Options bar, click a handle, then reshape the bounding box.

C Style: Shell Lower for "Greg's," Bulge for "Boat Yard"

D Style: Flag (layer effects are also applied)

B Style: Arc (layer effects are also applied)

E Style: Rise

Rasterizing type

To apply a filter or the Transform > Distort or Perspective command to type, or to draw strokes on type with a tool such as the Brush, you have to convert the type to pixels first via the Rasterize Type command. Unfortunately, you can't change the typographic attributes of type once it's been rasterized.

To rasterize type into pixels:

1. *Optional:* To preserve the editable type layer, duplicate it (Ctrl-J/Cmd-J), then hide it. Keep the duplicate layer selected.

2. Right-click/Control-click an editable type layer name and choose **Rasterize Type**. The layer thumbnail will update. Now be creative!

Filling type with imagery

Just to give you a few ideas, these are some of the ways that you can make it look as if editable type is filled with imagery (you don't need to rasterize it first):

➤ Use an editable type layer as the base layer in a **clipping mask** to clip the image layers above it. **A–B** You can edit (e.g., apply a filter) or reposition the image layers without affecting the type. To learn more about clipping masks, see page 308.

➤ Apply the **Pattern Overlay** effect to an editable type layer (see page 328). **C** While the Layer Style dialog is open, you can scale the pattern by using the Scale slider or move the pattern within the type by dragging in the document window. To create a custom pattern, with the Rectangular Marquee tool, select all or part of an image to use as a pattern tile, choose Edit > Define Pattern, click OK, then choose your new pattern from the Pattern Preset picker in the Pattern Overlay panel of the Layer Style dialog.

➤ Use a type selection in a **layer mask** (follow the instructions on the next page). **D** For an extra bit of fun, try warping some type first before using the type shapes as a layer mask.

A In this image, the type is the base layer in a clipping mask.

B This image was created in the same way as the previous one, except here we also rasterized the type layer (which is the clipping mask), then softened the edges via the Gaussian Blur filter to make it look more "snowy."

C We applied the Pattern Overlay layer effect to the type layer—plus the Drop Shadow, Inner Shadow, Outer Glow, and Emboss effects. The image layer below the type layer contains a subtle pattern.

D In this image, a type selection that we converted to a layer mask is masking a group of image layers. We also applied a gradient to the mask on each image layer to hide a side of each layer gradually (see pages 154–155).

To use type shapes as a layer mask:

1. Create an editable type layer.

2. Ctrl-click/Cmd-click the type layer thumbnail.**A** A selection will display in the document window.

3. Hide the type layer (click the visibility icon).**B** The selection marquee will remain visible. Don't deselect it.

4. Click the image layer to which you want to add the mask.

5. Do either of the following:

   To **reveal** layer pixels within the selection area, click the **Add Layer Mask** button ▣ on the Layers panel.**C–E**

To **hide** layer pixels within the selection area, Alt-click/Option-click the **Add Layer Mask** button on the Layers panel.

The type will display as white or black areas in the layer mask thumbnail.

➤ To reposition the type shapes within the layer mask, unlink the layer mask from the layer first by clicking the link icon,▯ then drag with the Move tool in the document window (restore the link when you're done).

➤ You can also add a layer mask by using the Masks panel. If you need to toggle the mask function between hiding and revealing pixels, click Invert.

A Ctrl-click/Cmd-click a type layer thumbnail to create a selection from type.

B Hide the type layer—but don't deselect!

C To reveal layer imagery within the selection, click the Add Layer Mask button (it's a "ski mask," ha-ha).

D To provide a solid backdrop for the type shapes, we added a layer below the image layer, which we filled with white.

E This is the Layers panel for the image shown at left.

Making type fade

In these instructions, you'll apply a gradient to a layer mask to make it seem as though the type is fading into thin air.

To make type fade: ★

1. Click an editable or rasterized type layer (for this exercise, make the type relatively large).

2. On the Masks panel, click the **Add Pixel Mask** button. A layer mask thumbnail will appear next to the layer name.

3. Choose the **Gradient** tool (G or Shift-G).

4. On the Options bar:

   Click the **Gradient Preset** picker arrowhead, then click the **Foreground to Background** preset in the picker (the first swatch in the default gradient library).

   Click the **Linear** gradient button.

   Choose **Mode**: Normal and 100% **Opacity**.

5. Make sure the layer mask thumbnail is still selected. In the document window, drag vertically or horizontally from the middle of the type to one of its edges. The type layer mask will fill with a white-to-black gradient **A** and the type will be hidden where black is present in the layer mask.**B**

6. On the Masks panel, lower the **Density** value to reveal more of the type.**C–D**

➤ To modify the type or the layer, click the type layer thumbnail; to modify the layer mask, click the layer mask thumbnail; or to toggle between the two thumbnails, click the layer, then click the Select Pixel Mask button on the Masks panel on or off. To learn more about layer masks, see pages 302–307.

C Via the Masks panel, you can adjust (and readjust) the Density of the layer mask to make the fading effect more or less gradual.

DON'T FORGET LAYER EFFECTS!

Layer effects can be applied to both editable and rasterized type layers. To open the Layer Style dialog, double-click next to a layer name. Browse through Chapter 20 and you'll see many examples of effects applied to type.

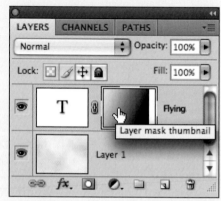

A With the layer mask selected, we dragged with the Gradient tool in the image from the middle of the type to the left edge of the layer.

B The type is fading, but too abruptly.

D To make the fade more gradual, we lowered the Density of the layer mask to 90%. Better.

Screening back type

In these instructions, you'll use a Levels adjustment layer to screen back type (we prefer this method to using the Type Mask tools). A lightened version of the image will be visible within the type shapes.

To screen back type:

1. Create a document that contains an image layer and an editable type layer (we suggest using a large point size in a bold or black style).**A**

2. On the Layers panel, Ctrl-click/Cmd-click the **T** icon, hide the type layer, then click the underlying image layer.

3. On the Adjustments panel, ⬤ click the **Levels** button. ⬛ ★ The Levels controls display and the type disappears from view temporarily.

4. Move the gray Input Levels (midtones) slider to the left to lighten the midtones in the type. You could also move the Input Levels highlights slider. Move the Output Levels shadows slider to the right to reduce the contrast in the type.**B–C**

➤ To screen back the imagery (instead of screening back the type), after the last step, above, click the Levels adjustment layer. On the Masks panel, click Invert. ★

➤ You can apply layer effects to the adjustment layer (try it!).

➤ To reposition the mask on the adjustment layer, unlink it from the layer thumbnail, then drag it with the Move tool.

A The original document contains an image layer and an editable type layer.

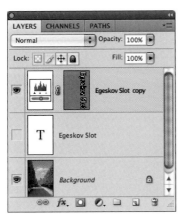

B The mask on the Levels adjustment layer is limiting the adjustment effect to just the type shapes.

C The type is now screened back. Only pixels within the character shapes are affected by the Levels adjustment layer.

Putting type in a spot color channel

To create type in a spot color channel:

1. Display the **Channels** panel, 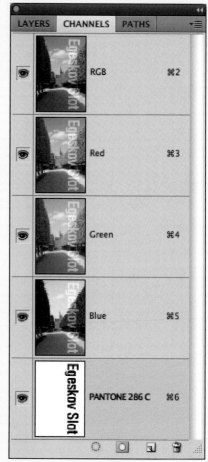 then from the panel menu, choose **New Spot Channel**.

2. In the New Spot Channel dialog, click the **Color** swatch, and if necessary, click **Color Libraries** to display the Color Libraries dialog.

3. From the **Book** menu, choose a spot color matching system, such as a nonprocess PANTONE system, then click the desired color or type a number from a swatch book.

4. Click OK (twice) to exit both dialogs.

5. Create editable type.

6. On the Layers panel, Ctrl-click/Cmd-click the T icon to select the type shapes, then hide the type layer.

7. On the Channels panel, click the new **spot color** channel.

8. Choose Edit > **Fill**. In the dialog, choose Use: Black; Mode: Normal; and an Opacity value that matches the tint (density) value of the spot color ink to be used on press. Click OK. The selection will fill with the color that you chose for the spot color channel.

9. Deselect (Ctrl-D/Cmd-D).**A** Note: The type shapes appear in the new spot channel on the Channels panel, but no layer is created on the Layers panel.

➤ Use the Move tool to reposition the type shapes in the spot color channel.

➤ You can't change the type characters in a spot color channel—you would have to start over. Fill the channel with White, 100% Opacity, edit the original type layer, then repeat steps 5–9 above.

A Now that our type shapes are in a spot color channel, our commercial printer will be able to create a special printing plate for them.

A gradient is a soft blend between two or more opaque or semitransparent colors. Gradients can be used to enhance the background behind imagery or type or to add color to objects. In this chapter, you will learn how to create gradients via the Gradient Editor and apply them via a Gradient Fill adjustment layer and the Gradient tool.

Creating a gradient fill layer

A gradient that you apply via a gradient fill layer appears in its own layer, complete with a layer mask that can be used to control how much of the gradient is visible. Like an adjustment layer, this type of gradient is editable, restackable, and removable—unlike a gradient that you apply directly to a layer. A good use for a gradient fill layer is to add color behind silhouetted imagery or type.

To apply a gradient as a fill layer:

1. To have the gradient fill display behind silhouetted imagery or type, click the layer directly below the image layer or type layer.

2. *Optional:* To confine the gradient to an area of the layer, create a selection.

3. From the **New Fill/Adjustment Layer** menu ⬤. on the Layers panel, choose **Gradient**. The Gradient Fill dialog opens.

4. Click the gradient arrowhead at the top of the dialog, click a gradient **preset** on the picker, **A** then click back in the dialog (keep it open). (If you want to load in other gradients, open the preset picker, then choose a library from the bottom of the picker menu; see also page 403.)

Continued on the following page

23

IN THIS CHAPTER

Creating a gradient fill layer. 369

Using the Gradient tool. 371

Creating and editing gradient
   presets 372

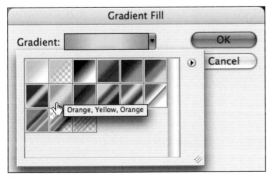

A In the Gradient Fill dialog, click the gradient arrowhead, then choose a gradient from the preset picker.

5. Do all of the following:

Choose a gradient **Style: Linear, Radial, Angular, Reflected,** or **Diamond.A**

Choose an **Angle** by moving the dial or by entering a value.

Use the **Scale** slider to scale the gradient relative to the layer. The higher the scale value, the more gradual the transition between colors in the gradient.

6. *Optional:* Drag in the document window (with the dialog still open) to reposition the gradient. Cool!

7. Do any of the following optional steps:

Check/uncheck **Reverse** to swap the order of colors in the gradient.

Check **Dither** to minimize banding (stripes) in the gradient on print output.

If you created a selection (step 2), check **Align with Layer** to have the complete gradient fit within the selection; or uncheck this option to have the gradient stretch across the whole layer (only a portion of the gradient will be visible within the selection).

8. Click OK.**B–C**

Note: If the gradient fill layer is above the image layers, it will obscure the entire image. Either lower the opacity of the gradient fill layer to reveal the underlying layer or move it below the image layer.

► You can double-click the gradient fill layer thumbnail at any time to reopen the Gradient Fill dialog and readjust the settings.

► Click the gradient fill layer, then change the layer blending mode.

► To apply a gradient as an editable Gradient Overlay layer effect, see page 327.

EDITING THE GRADIENT FILL LAYER MASK

If you create a selection before creating a gradient fill layer, the selection will be represented as a white area within the mask thumbnail for the gradient fill layer on the Layers panel. To reshape the mask, click the layer mask thumbnail, then paint with white to enlarge the white area or with black to enlarge the black area. Via the Masks panel, you can adjust the density of the black area in the mask or feather the edge of the mask.

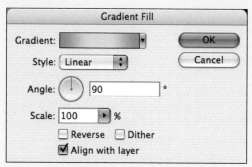

A In the Gradient Fill dialog, we chose the "Orange, Yellow, Orange" preset and also chose Style, Angle, and Scale settings.

B The original image contains a silhouetted image layer and a separate white Background.

C Below the silhouetted image layer, we added a gradient fill layer, which contains a linear gradient. The fill layer has an opacity of 65%.

Using the Gradient tool

With the Gradient tool, you create a gradient by dragging in the document window. Each time you drag, an additional gradient is applied. Although you can't edit the results in the same way that you would edit a gradient fill layer, if you use the tool on a separate layer, at least you will be able to change the layer blending mode or opacity.

To apply a gradient using the Gradient tool:

1. Create a new, blank layer for the gradient.
   Optional: To confine the gradient to an area of the layer, create a selection.

2. Choose the **Gradient** tool ▬ (G or Shift-G).

3. On the Options bar: **A**

   Click the **Gradient Preset** picker arrowhead, then click a preset on the picker.

   Click a **gradient style** button: **Linear, Radial, Angle, Reflected,** or **Diamond.**

   Choose **Mode: Normal** and **Opacity** 100%.

4. Do any of the following optional steps:

   Check **Reverse** to swap the order of colors in the gradient.

   Check **Dither** to minimize banding (stripes) in the gradient on print output.

> **OTHER USES FOR THE GRADIENT TOOL**
>
> To create a gradual masking effect, you can use the Gradient tool on an image layer mask, adjustment layer mask, fill layer mask, or Smart Filter mask.

   Check **Transparency** to enable any transparency that was edited into the gradient, or turn this option off for a fully opaque gradient.

5. For a Linear gradient, drag from one **side** or **corner** of the image or selection to the other.
   B–C For any other gradient style, drag from a **center** point outward (Shift-drag to constrain the gradient to a multiple of 45°). Drag a long distance to produce subtle transitions between colors or a short distance to produce abrupt transitions; this is equivalent to changing the Scale value in the Gradient Fill dialog.

6. Change the gradient layer mode or opacity. **D**

➤ To delete a fill that was applied to a layer via the Gradient tool, click the prior state on the History panel.

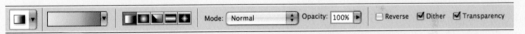

A On the Options bar for the Gradient tool, we chose the "Yellow, Green, Blue" preset (it's in the Pastels library) and clicked the Linear style button.

B This is the original image.

D Finally, for the layer that contains the gradient, we changed the Opacity to 85% and the blending mode to Overlay.

C We dragged with the Gradient tool diagonally from the middle of the image to the lower left on a new, blank layer (above the image layer).

Creating and editing gradient presets

You can edit any gradient preset in the picker
or create new, custom presets. When you edit
(or delete) a preset swatch, the original gradient
in the current gradient library doesn't change;
instead, Photoshop ensures that a copy of the preset is edited (or deleted). You can add or change
the colors in a preset, adjust the color transitions,
and make colors semi- or fully transparent.

A Click the Gradient thumbnail on the Options bar to
open the Gradient Editor.

To create or edit a gradient preset:

1. Do either of the following:

   Choose the **Gradient** tool ▓ (G or Shift-G),
   then click the Gradient thumbnail on the
   Options bar.**A**

   Double-click the thumbnail for an existing
   Gradient Fill layer, then click the gradient
   thumbnail at the top of the Gradient Fill
   dialog.

2. The Gradient Editor opens.**B** Do either of the
   following:

   Click the preset swatch that you want to
   create a variation of. (As you start to edit the
   gradient, the Name will change to Custom;
   this shows that you're editing a copy of the
   gradient.)

   To create a gradient that uses the Foreground
   and Background colors that are in effect when
   you apply the gradient, click the **Foreground
   to Background** preset (the first preset in the
   default gradient library).

3. For any gradient except Foreground to
   Background, click the starting (left) or ending
   (right) color stop under the gradient bar, then
   do either of the following:

   Click a color on the **Swatches** panel, or
   on the spectrum bar at the bottom of the
   Color panel, or in any open document window (the Eyedropper tool becomes selected
   automatically).

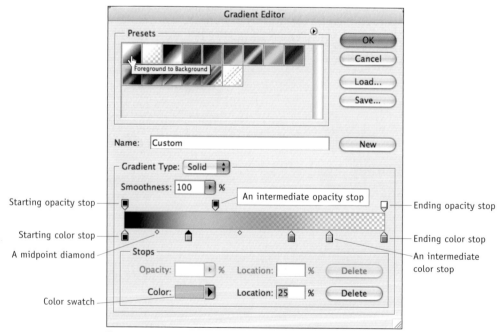

B Use the Gradient Editor to create or edit a gradient preset.

Click the Color swatch at the bottom of the **Gradient Editor**, choose a color from the Color Picker, then click OK.

Quirky note: If you opened the Gradient Editor from the Options bar, a color stop that uses the Foreground color will have this checkerboard pattern: 🔲 and a stop that uses the Background color will look like this: 🔲.

4. Do any of these optional steps:

To add an **intermediate** color to the gradient, click below the gradient bar to produce a new stop, then choose a color for the new stop, as described in the previous step. **A–B**

To add an **opacity stop**, click above the gradient bar, then use the scrubby slider to change the Opacity percentage (or click any existing opacity stop above the bar and change its Opacity percentage).

To change the location of a color or opacity **stop** in the gradient, drag it to the left or right.

To control the **abruptness** of a color transition, click a color or opacity stop, then drag the **midpoint diamond** on either side of it to the left or right. The diamond marks the point at which the two adjacent colors are 50% each. **C–E**

To **delete** an unwanted opacity or color stop, drag it upward or downward off the bar.

▶ Use Ctrl-Z/Cmd-Z when you need to undo the previous edit (some edits can't be undone).

5. Don't click OK yet! To create a preset of your custom gradient, type a name in the **Name** field, then click **New**.

6. Now you can click OK. Your new gradient is now available on the Gradient Preset picker (check the tool tip if you're skeptical).

▶ To save all the gradient presets currently on the picker as a library, load in other gradient preset libraries, or restore the default gradient library, see page 403.

▶ To delete a gradient preset, Alt-click/Option-click the preset thumbnail on the picker.

▶ To rename a gradient preset, double-click the swatch in the Gradient Editor (the Gradient Name dialog opens). Change the Name, then click OK.

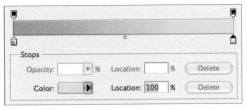

A In the Gradient Editor dialog, we created a two-color gradient.

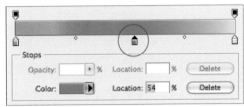

B We clicked below the gradient bar to add an intermediate color.

C We moved the midpoint diamond to make the transition between the middle and ending colors more abrupt.

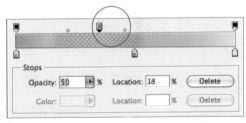

D We clicked above the bar to add an intermediate opacity stop, lowered the opacity of that stop to 50%, and moved the right midpoint diamond closer to it.

E This is our custom gradient, which we applied to a layer above the Background. The opacity stop created a semitransparent area in the gradient.

USING BLENDING MODES TO ENHANCE A GRADIENT

A This image contains a radial gradient on a separate layer below the silhouetted church tower. In the other figures on this page, a blending mode is applied to the image (tower) layer.

B Multiply blending mode

C Color Burn blending mode

D Screen blending mode

E Linear Light blending mode

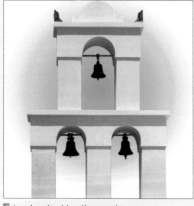

F Luminosity blending mode

In this chapter, you'll learn various ways to finish and present your photos to clients in print and onscreen. You'll learn how to frame your subject matter as a vignette; add a hand-painted border; embed a watermark; create a contact sheet or PDF presentation; and create and present layer comps (multiple versions of a document) manually and via a PDF slide show.

Creating a vignette

Aside from the fact that vignettes look beautiful, they also can be used as a cropping device to feature part of a composition.

To create a vignette: ★

1. Open an image, and press Ctrl-J/Cmd-J to duplicate the Background.

2. Click the Background, then press Shift-Backspace/Shift-Delete. In the Fill dialog, choose Use: White, Mode: Normal, and Opacity: 100%, then click OK.

3. Click the image duplicate layer. Choose the **Rectangular Marquee** tool □ or **Elliptical Marquee** tool ○ (or hold down M for a temporary marquee tool), then select the area of the image you want to keep visible.

4. Display the **Masks** panel. ◙ Click the **Add Pixel Mask** button, ▣ then adjust the **Feather** value to fade the edge of the mask. **A**

▶ To reposition the mask, on the Layers panel, click between the layer and mask thumbnails to unlink them, then hold down V (for a temporary Move tool) and drag in the document window.

PRESENTATION

24

IN THIS CHAPTER

Creating a vignette. 375

Adding a hand-painted border 376

Adding a watermark 378

Creating a contact sheet 380

Creating a PDF presentation. 382

Creating and using layer comps 384

Creating a PDF presentation of
   layer comps 386

A The oval, feathered mask gives this garden photo an old-fashioned look.

Adding a hand-painted border

To make an image look more distinctive, you can create a hand-painted frame or paint the image onto a white background.

To add a hand-painted border to an image:

1. *Optional:* To expand the canvas area to accommodate a frame, choose Image > **Canvas Size** (Ctrl-Alt-C/Cmd-Option-C), choose Percent from the Width menu, and enter 130 in both fields. Choose Canvas Extension Color: White, leave the white/gray Anchor square in the center of the grid, then click OK.

2. On the Layers panel, create a new, blank layer above an image layer, and keep it selected.

3. Choose the **Brush** tool 🖌 (B or Shift-B).

4. On the Options bar:

   Click the **Brush Preset** picker thumbnail, then choose Large List from the picker menu to display the presets by name. Locate and click the Oil Pastel Large preset or a similar rough-looking brush tip, then move the **Master Diameter** slider to a setting that's appropriate for your document (we chose a setting of 300 px for our document, which is 3,000 pixels wide).

   Choose **Mode:** Normal.

   Set the **Opacity** to 100% and the **Flow** to 60%.

5. Do either of the following:

   Press **D** to reset the Foreground and Background colors, then press **X** to reverse them.

   Alt-click/Option-click a color in the image (using a temporary Eyedropper tool).

6. Drag across the outer edge of the image, covering some of the image. Hold down Shift as you drag if you want to draw straight strokes.

7. *Optional:* Change the layer opacity for the layer that contains the brush strokes.**A-B**

To paint an image onto a white background:

1. Follow steps 2–4, above.

2. Choose Edit > **Fill**, choose **Use: White**; click OK.

3. On the Masks panel, 🔲 click the **Add Pixel Mask** button.🔲 ★

4. Draw strokes in the document window with **black** to reveal the image, releasing the mouse between strokes. To soften the edges of the mask, increase the Feather value on the Masks panel.**C**

A To the four edges of a new, blank layer, we applied white brush strokes, using the Oil Pastel Large brush preset. We also lowered the opacity of the layer slightly to blend it with the underlying image layer.

B To create this frame, we enlarged the canvas area, then applied strokes with the Brush tool (Hard Pastel on Canvas brush preset), using a color that we sampled from the image.

C Here, we painted with black on a layer mask to reveal the underlying image, then increased the Feather value via the Mask panel to soften the edges of the mask.

USING HAND-PAINTED FRAMES IN A MONTAGE

A To create this travel montage, first we applied a hand-painted border to each image separately in its own file, and merged the layer containing the brush strokes downward. Next, we dragged each image into a larger document that contains a textured background layer and moved — and rotated one of — the layers to finish the composition.

FAST FRAMES

Plug-ins that do the work of creating artistic frames for you are available from third-party suppliers, such as Photo/Graphic Edges from autofx.com and PhotoFrame from ononesoftware.com.

Adding a watermark

If you're planning to display any of your images online, you can help protect them from unauthorized use by embedding a copyright or other watermark into them, analogous to traditional watermarking on paper. In these instructions, you'll create a copyright shape with the Custom Shape tool, then save the shape as a tool preset for use in any document.

To embed a watermark into a file:

1. Choose the **Custom Shape** tool 🖌 (U or Shift-U).

2. On the Options bar, do the following:

    Click the **Shape Layers** button.⬚

    Click the **Custom Shape** picker thumbnail, then click the copyright symbol © (it's in the default custom shape preset library)**A** or click a custom shape that you've created for this purpose (see the instructions on the following page).

    Click the **Style** picker thumbnail, then click the **Default Style (None)**.⬚

    Click the **Color** swatch. In the Color Picker, choose white as the Foreground color, then click OK.

3. Shift-drag with the tool in the document window until the symbol is the desired size. A shape layer will appear on the Layers panel.

4. On the Layers panel, change the **Fill** value for the shape layer to 0%.

5. Double-click next to the shape layer name to open the Layer Style dialog, then click **Bevel and Emboss** (don't check Contour). Choose Style: Inner Bevel, Technique: Smooth, Depth around 60–90%, Size 5–25, and Soften 6–10, then click OK.**B**

6. You can use the **Move** tool to reposition the shape on the image. For a better view of the copyright symbol,**C** click another layer.

7. To save the layer settings and layer effects to the Styles panel to use again, click the shape layer for the copyright mark on the Layers panel. On the Styles panel,🔲 click the New Style button. 🔲 Type a name in the dialog, then click OK.

    To save the shape style as a tool preset, follow the second set of instructions on the next page.

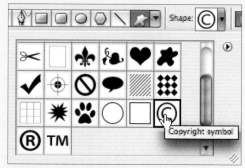

A Click the Copyright symbol (or a custom shape) on the Custom Shape picker.

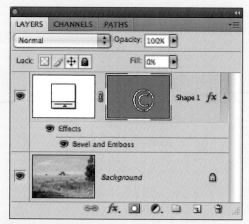

B The © symbol appears in the mask for the shape layer on the Layers panel.

C This is how the final watermark looks on the image.

You can also create a custom watermark by using the Type tool.

To create a custom watermark from text:

1. Choose the **Horizontal Type** tool, **T** create the desired text for the watermark, then scale and style it as desired. (To create the copyright symbol, we typed Alt+0169/Option-G.)

2. Choose Layer > Type > **Convert to Shape**.

3. Choose Edit > **Define Custom Shape**, enter a name (we entered the same name as in our watermark), then click OK.

4. Delete the shape layer.

5. Follow the steps on the previous page, except in step 2, choose your new custom shape from the Custom Shape picker. **A** Note: If you already saved a "watermark" style to the Styles panel, follow only steps 1–3. In step 2, click your custom shape on the Custom Shape picker and click your watermark style on the Style picker.

By saving your custom watermark as a Shape tool preset, you'll be able to add it quickly to any image with the Custom Shape tool.

To save a watermark shape and style as a tool preset:

1. Follow steps 1–7 on the previous page.

2. Choose the **Custom Shape** tool 🐾 (U or Shift-U).

3. On the Options bar, **B** make sure either the copyright symbol or your custom shape displays in the **Shape** thumbnail.

4. Click the **Style** thumbnail on the Options bar to open the Style picker, then click your custom style.

5. Click the **Tool Preset** picker thumbnail at the far left end of the Options bar, or display the **Tool Presets** panel. ✖

6. On the picker or panel, click the **New Tool Preset** button, 🔲 enter a name (we entered the text we used for our watermark), keep Include Color unchecked, and click OK. **C**

7. To place the watermark in any image, with the Custom Shape tool selected, click your tool preset on the Tool Preset picker or the Tool Presets panel, then Shift-drag in the document window. Note: If Current Tool Only is checked on the picker or panel, you'll have to choose the Custom Shape tool to make the preset appear as a listing.

A To create a custom watermark, we converted this text into a shape.

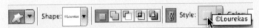

B On the Options bar for the Custom Shape tool, we chose Shape, Style, and Color settings, clicked our custom watermark on the Shape picker, and clicked our custom style on the Style picker.

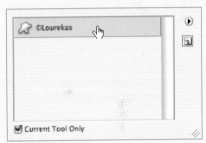

C Our new custom tool preset appears on the Tool Preset picker.

Next, we'll show you two vehicles for organizing images and displaying them to clients: contact sheets and PDF presentations. As a result of a major overhaul, you'll produce them by using an Output panel in Bridge, which replaces defunct Photoshop commands.

Creating a contact sheet

A contact sheet is an arrangement of image thumbnails in one document, comparable to the contact sheets that are traditionally used by film photographers. This is a good way to catalog your photos, for easy reference and identification. For example, you could generate contact sheets for photos that you've backed up onto DVDs.

To create a contact sheet: ★

1. In Bridge, put all the files you want to display on the contact sheet in the same folder, in the order in which you want them to appear on the sheet (they can be in a stack), and display the contents of that folder.

2. From the **Output** menu  on the Bridge toolbar, choose **Outout to Web or PDF.A** The middle and right panes of the Bridge window will reconfigure: a Preview panel displays above the Content panel and an Output panel with many options displays on the right side.

3. At the top of the Output panel, **B** click **PDF**, then from the **Template** menu, choose **4*5 Contact Sheet** or **5*8 Contact Sheet**.

   If you want to use the default settings for the chosen template, skip ahead to step 10; or if you prefer to customize the template instead, follow all the remaining steps.

4. In the **Document** category:

   For the sake of simplicity, choose a **Page Preset**, such as U.S. Paper, or a preset **Size**. Or for a custom size sheet, enter Width and Height values.

   For the **Quality**, choose High Quality or Low Quality, which in turn will determine the file size as well as the speed of transmission if the contact sheet is to be downloaded.

   From the **Background** menu, choose a background color for the contact sheet. For print output, we recommend choosing White.

   (For the Password options, see step 4 on page 382.)

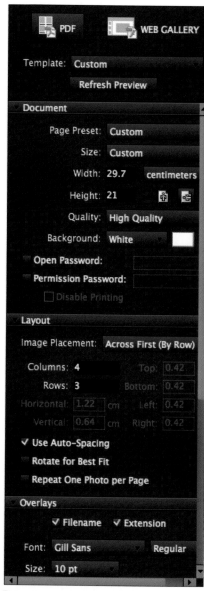

A Select multiple image thumbnails, then from the Output menu on the Bridge toolbar, choose Output to Web or PDF.

B We chose these Document and Layout settings for our PDF contact sheet in the Output panel in Bridge.

5. Select approximately 10–15 images, then click **Refresh Preview** to generate a preview of the contact sheet based on your settings.

6. In the **Layout** category, change any of the following settings:

Choose an **Image Placement** option for the order in which the images are to be arranged, based on the current order of thumbnails.

Enter the desired number of **Columns** and **Rows** for the contact sheet, depending on how many images you're using.

Check **Use Auto-Spacing** to let Photoshop calculate the spacing between thumbnails (the easy way); or uncheck this option, enter the desired spacing between thumbnails in the Vertical and Horizontal fields, and enter Top, Bottom, Left, and Right margin values.

Check **Rotate for Best Fit** to let Photoshop rotate thumbnails, if needed, for a better fit.

Check **Repeat One Photo per Page** to repeat a single image on a whole page rather than arranging all the selected images.

7. In the **Overlays** category (scroll downward if you don't see it), check whether you want the **Filename** and **Extension** to be listed below each image. If so, choose **Font, Size,** and **Color** options.

8. In the **Playback** category, uncheck **Open in Full Screen Mode.**

9. *Optional:* In the Watermark category, enter Watermark Text to appear in the center of each page, and for the text, choose Font, Size, and Color options and a low Opacity.

10. Select all the thumbnails to appear on the contact sheet, then click **Refresh Preview** to preview it. Adjust any settings, if needed, then click Refresh Preview once more. **A**

11. At the bottom of the panel, check **View PDF After Save,** then click **Save.** A Save As dialog opens. Enter a file name, choose a location, then click Save. A PDF file will be created; Adobe Acrobat, Adobe Acrobat Pro, or Adobe Reader will launch; and the PDF file will open onscreen. For multiple pages, use the arrow buttons to navigate.

A When Refresh Preview is clicked, the contact sheet previews in the Output Preview panel.

Creating a PDF presentation

Another way to package and send your files to a client or friend is via a PDF presentation, in which images play sequentially onscreen. Like contact sheets, PDF presentations are created via the Output panel in Bridge, but you'll need to make some different choices.

To create a PDF presentation: ★

1. In Bridge, put all the files you want to display in the presentation in the same folder, in the order in which you want them to appear (they can be in a stack). Display the contents of the folder, and select a few of the thumbnails.

2. From the **Output** menu ![icon] on the Bridge toolbar, choose **Output to Web or PDF.A** The middle and right panes of the Bridge window will reconfigure: a Preview panel displays above the Content panel and an Output panel with many options displays on the right side (**A**, next page).

3. At the top of the **Output** panel, click **PDF**, then from the **Template** menu, choose **Maximize Size**.

4. In the **Document** category (scroll downward to display it if you don't see it):

   For the **Quality**, choose **High Quality**. This will affect the file size, as well as speed of transmission if the file is to be downloaded.

   To have the color around the images match the black of full screen mode, from the **Background** menu, we recommend choosing **Black**.

   Optional: Check **Open Password** and enter a password. Your viewers will need to enter this password in order to open the PDF file.

   Optional: Check **Permission Password** and enter a password to restrict how the PDF file can be used (such as a restriction on print access). Your viewers will need to enter this password in order to print or edit the PDF file.

5. In the **Layout** category, uncheck **Rotate for Best Fit** to prevent any images from being rotated.

6. In the **Overlays** category, check whether you want the **Filename** and **Extension** to be listed below each image. If so, choose a **Font**, choose a **Size** of 18 pt, and set the **Color** to White (or if you prefer to choose a custom color, click the

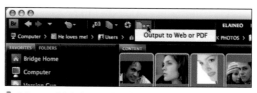

A Select multiple image thumbnails, then from the Output menu on the Bridge toolbar, choose Output to Web or PDF.

swatch and use the color picker, but remember that it must stand out against the black Background).

7. In the **Playback** category:

   Check **Open in Full Screen Mode** to display the presentation images at full screen size.

   To have the frames advance automatically, check **Advance Every**, then enter the number of **Seconds** each frame is to display.

   If you want the slide show to loop continuously, from the last frame back again to the first, check **Loop After Last Page**.

   If you want a transition effect to occur between frames, such as a Dissolve or a Fade, choose from the **Transition** menu, and also choose a **Direction** (this option is not available for all the Transition options) and a **Speed**.

8. In the **Watermark** category, enter the **Watermark Text** to appear in the center of each page, and for that text, choose Font, Size, and Color options and a low Opacity.

9. This time, select all the thumbnails to be included in the presentation, then click **Refresh Preview** to generate a preview of the first frame in the presentation, based on the chosen parameters.

10. Check **View PDF After Save** at the bottom of the dialog to have the presentation play automatically when you click Save.

11. Click **Save**. A Save As dialog opens. Enter a file name, choose a location, then click Save. A PDF file will be created, and Adobe Acrobat, Adobe Acrobat Pro, or Adobe Reader will launch. If an alert pertaining to Acrobat appears, click Yes. The PDF file will open onscreen, and then finally the slide show will commence. Press Esc at any time to halt it.

   To view the slideshow, all a viewer has to do is double-click the PDF file you send them!

A One frame of our PDF presentation is displaying in the Output Preview panel. (We dragged the vertical bar of the Folders panel to the left to hide the left pane, to make more room for the other panes.)

Creating and using layer comps

A layer comp (short for "composition") is a set of layer characteristics, which can include visibility, position, and layer effect settings. Via the Layer Comps panel, you can store multiple comps in one document. By displaying different comps, you can quickly present multiple design variations.

To create a layer comp:

1. Create all the layers to be used in your document, including any fill or adjustment layers, masks, Smart Object layers, or type layers, and edit them to create a document version (apply filters or adjustments, create type, choose a layer blending mode or opacity setting, etc.).

2. Choose visibility (hide and show), position (location in the image), and appearance (layer effects) settings for each layer.

3. Show the Layer Comps panel, **A** then click the **New Layer Comp** button at the bottom of the panel. The New Layer Comp dialog opens. **B**

4. Enter a **Name** for the comp, then check which layer settings you want it to store: **Visibility**, **Position**, and/or **Appearance (Layer Style)**.

    Note: Changes involving an unchecked attribute (e.g., repositioning layers if Position is unchecked) won't be saved in the new comp. When you click a different comp, then click back on the new comp, your unsaved changes will be lost.

5. *Optional:* Enter information in the Comment field to display on the panel when the list for that layer comp is expanded (such as explanatory notes for a client or coworker to read). **C**

6. Click OK. To create more layer comps, repeat steps 2–6 (e.g., hide or show different layers, change the layer settings, apply adjustments).

▶ To bypass the Layer Comp Options dialog as you create a comp, Alt-click/Option-click the New Layer Comp button.

▶ To change which layer settings a comp can store (and therefore display), double-click next to the comp name to open the Layer Comp Options dialog, then check or uncheck any of the Apply to Layers options.

▶ To rename a comp quickly, double-click the comp name on the panel.

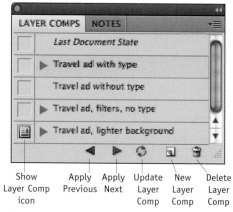

Show Layer Comp icon   Apply Previous   Apply Next   Update Layer Comp   New Layer Comp   Delete Layer Comp

A Use the Layer Comps panel to create, store, apply, edit, update, and delete your layer comps.

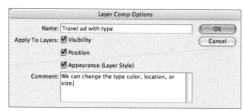

B In the New Layer Comp dialog, type a Name, decide which characteristics are to be saved in the comp, and enter optional comments.

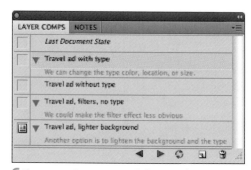

C These comp lists are expanded to reveal comments.

START FROM A DUPLICATE

If you don't want to create a new layer comp from scratch, start from a duplicate instead: Drag a layer comp name over the New Layer Comp button, then follow the third set of instructions on the next page to edit and update the duplicate.

To display a layer comp:

Do either of the following:

On the **Layer Comps** panel, click in the left column to make the Layer Comp icon ▦ appear.

To cycle through the comps on the panel, click the **Apply Next Selected Layer Comp** button ▶ or **Apply Previous Selected Layer Comp** ◀ button. **A**

Let's say you edit your document (e.g., create a new layer), then display a few different layer comps. If you need to get back to the last working state of the document, do as follows.

To restore the last document state:

On the **Layer Comps** panel, ▦ do either of the following:

Click in the left column next to the **Last Document State** listing.

Right-click/Control-click a layer comp and choose **Restore Last Document State**.

You can update any existing layer comp to incorporate new edits that you make to your document.

To update a layer comp:

1. On the **Layer Comps** panel, click the name of the layer comp that you want to update.

2. Edit or change the **visibility**, **position**, or **layer style** of any layers in the document.

3. Click the **Update Layer Comp** button ↻ at the bottom of the panel.

If you change the number of layers in a document that are recorded in a layer comp (e.g., delete or merge layers) or change the document color mode, an alert icon ⚠ indicating that the "Layer Comp Cannot Be Fully Restored" will appear next to the relevant comp name(s). You can ignore the alert icon, or you can clear it by doing the following.

To clear an alert icon:

Do one of the following:

Select the comp, click the alert icon, then click **Clear** in the alert dialog.

Select the comp, then click the **Update Layer Comp** button. ↻

Right-click/Control-click the alert icon and choose **Clear Layer Comp Warning** (or to clear all alert icons, choose Clear All Layer Comp Warnings).

A The layer comps shown above are all variations within the same image.

A PERMANENT SNAPSHOT

To preserve the original state of a document, create a layer comp when you first open your image (before making any edits). Yes, snapshots on the History panel serve a similar purpose, but they disappear when you close your document, whereas layer comps save with the file.

When you delete a layer comp, it doesn't affect how your document looks or delete any layers.

To delete a layer comp:

1. On the Layer Comps panel, click the layer comp to be deleted.

2. Click the **Delete Layer Comp** button 🗑 at the bottom of the panel.

Creating a PDF presentation of layer comps

The Layer Comps to Files automate command produces a flattened PDF file from each layer comp, from which you can produce a PDF presentation.

To create a PDF presentation of layer comps: ★

1. Open a Photoshop file that contains layer comps. *Optional:* To create the presentation from select layer comps rather than all the comps on the panel, select them now (Ctrl-click/Cmd-click to select nonsequential comps).

2. Choose File > Scripts > **Layer Comps to Files**. The Layer Comps to Files dialog opens.**A**

3. Click **Browse**, choose the location in which the PDF files are to be saved, then click Choose.

4. If you selected some layer comps in step 1, check **Selected Layer Comps Only**.

5. In the File Type area, do the following:

   From the **File Type** menu, choose **PDF**.

   Check **Include ICC Profile** to preserve any assigned or embedded profile.

   For the **PDF Options**, choose **Encoding: JPEG** as the compression method, then enter a **Quality** value (1–4 for low quality, 5–8 for medium quality, or 9–12 for high quality).

6. Click **Run**. The script will output each comp as a flattened PDF file in the designated folder. Click OK when the alert dialog appears.

7. To create a PDF presentation using the folder of images that you just created, follow the instructions on page 382.

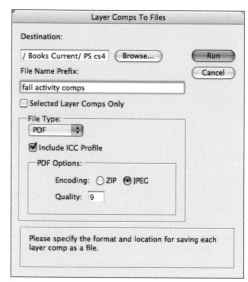

A In the Layer Comps to Files dialog, choose a destination folder and options for the files that Photoshop will generate from your layer comps.

Preferences are settings that apply to the application as a whole, such as the default ruler units, or whether tool tips display onscreen. Most preference changes take effect immediately; a few take effect when you relaunch Photoshop or Bridge (these exceptions are noted). In this chapter, in addition to learning about all the panels in the Preferences dialog, you'll also learn how to save and load brush, tool, and other presets.

Opening the Preferences dialogs

▶ To open the **Preferences** dialog for Photoshop, press **Ctrl-K/Cmd-K** or choose Edit (Photoshop, in the Mac OS) > **Preferences** > **General** or one of the other choices on the submenu. In the Preferences dialog, click one of the ten panel names on the left side,**A** or click Prev or Next, or press Ctrl-1/Cmd-1 through Ctrl-9/Cmd-9.

▶ To open the Preferences dialog for Bridge, press **Ctrl-K/Cmd-K** or choose Edit (Adobe Bridge CS4, in the Mac OS) > **Preferences**.

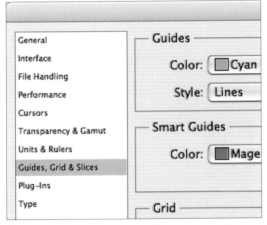

A The Preferences dialog in Photoshop has ten panels.

RESETTTING ALL THE PREFERENCES

To reset all the Photoshop or Bridge preferences to their default settings, hold down Ctrl-Alt-Shift/Cmd-Option-Shift as you launch that program. When the alert dialog appears onscreen for Photoshop, click Yes to delete the Photoshop Settings file. When the Reset Settings dialog appears for Bridge, check Reset Preferences, then click OK.

25

IN THIS CHAPTER

Opening the Preferences dialogs.... 387

General Preferences 388

Interface Preferences 390

File Handling Preferences 392

Performance Preferences........ 393

Cursors Preferences 394

Transparency & Gamut Preferences .. 394

Units & Rulers Preferences........ 395

Guides, Grid & Slices Preferences ... 396

Plug-ins Preferences........... 396

Type Preferences 397

The Bridge Preferences 398

Using the Preset Manager 400

Managing presets via pickers and panels................. 402

Creating tool presets 404

General Preferences (A, next page)

As the default **Color Picker**, choose Adobe (the default setting) or the system color picker.

Choose a default **Image Interpolation** option for commands, such as Image > Image Size, that involve resampling or transforming: Nearest Neighbor (preserve hard edges) is the fastest but least precise (use for hard-edged graphics); Bilinear is medium quality; Bicubic (best for smooth gradients) is higher quality but slower; Bicubic Smoother (best for enlargement); or Bicubic Sharper (best for reduction). The last two options also produce high-quality results.

Options

Check **Auto-Update Open Documents** to have open Photoshop documents that you edit in other applications update automatically when you return to Photoshop, such as when you enter metadata for a file in Bridge.

Check **Beep When Done** to have a beep sound after each command is completed. This is useful if you like to be notified when commands that take a while to process are completed (so you can grab a snack and not miss anything!).

Check **Dynamic Color Sliders** to have colors above the sliders on the Color panel update as you move the sliders.

Check **Export Clipboard** to retain the current Clipboard contents on the system's Clipboard when you switch between Photoshop and other applications.

With **Use Shift Key for Tool Switch** checked, in order to access a tool on a pop-out menu, you must press Shift plus the assigned letter (e.g., press Shift-B to select the Brush, Pencil, or Color Replacement tool). If you leave this option unchecked (as we do), you can press the letter without Shift to select a tool.

Check **Resize Image During Paste/Place** to have pixel or vector images from other applications scale to fit the current canvas area automatically when imported via the Edit > Paste or File > Place command.

Check **Animated Zoom** for smooth, continuous zooming when the Zoom tool or zoom shortcuts are used (OpenGL is required). ★

With **Zoom Resizes Windows** checked, a floating document window will resize when you change the zoom level via the Ctrl/Cmd- + (plus) or Ctrl/Cmd- – (minus) shortcut or the Zoom tool. This preference can be set either here or via the Resize Windows to Fit check box on the Options bar.

If your mouse has a scroll wheel and you check **Zoom with Scroll Wheel**, you can scroll the wheel to change the zoom level.

Check **Zoom Clicked Point to Center** to center the zoom view at the location you click. ★

Check **Enable Flick Panning** to move a magnified image across the screen by dragging with the Hand tool a short distance and then releasing the mouse (OpenGL is required). ★

History Log

Check **History Log** to have a log of your Photoshop activity be generated for every work session. For **Save Log Items To**, choose where the log will be saved: to the Metadata section of a file, to a separate Text File, or to Both (of the above). For the latter two options, click Choose and choose a location for the text file to be saved.

From the **Edit Log Items** menu, choose what you want saved in the log: Sessions Only to log only when you launch or exit/quit Photoshop and which files were opened; Concise to log Sessions information plus a list of edits (states on the History panel); or Detailed, which is like Concise but also logs actions and the options and parameters used in each editing step. These options may come in handy if you need to keep a tally of billable hours for clients.

Click **Reset All Warning Dialogs** to reenable any and all alert dialogs that you may have hidden by checking Don't Show Again.

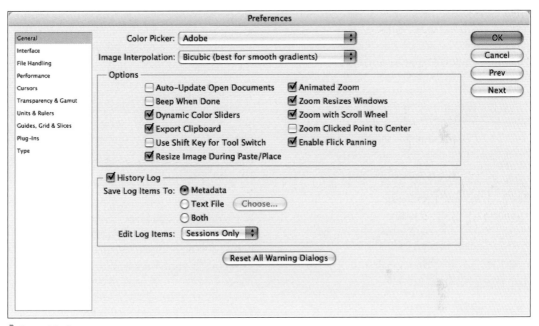

A General Preferences

Interface Preferences (A, next page)

General

You can customize all three of the Photoshop screen modes—**Standard Screen Mode**, **Full Screen with Menus**, and **Full Screen**—by choosing a background color from the first menu and a border style (or None) from the second menu. ★

Check **Use Grayscale Application Icon** to have the Photoshop icon at the top of the Application bar appear in grayscale Ps (if you're creating a fully grayscale interface for Photoshop); or uncheck this option for a color icon. Ps

Check **Show Channels in Color** to show RGB or CMYK channels in color on the Channels panel and in the document window when displayed individually. With this option off, channels display individually in grayscale, which you may find useful when you need to judge luminosity values.

Check **Show Menu Colors** to enable the display of any background colors that you assigned to menu commands via Edit > Menus or by choosing a workspace that contains them.

Check **Show Tool Tips** to permit the function and name of whichever tool, button, or panel feature the pointer is currently over (with the mouse button up) to appear briefly onscreen, for identification purposes.

Panels & Documents

If **Auto-Collapse Iconic Panels** is checked and you open a collapsed panel, it will collapse back to an icon when you click away from it. With this option unchecked, the panel stays expanded.

Check **Auto-Show Hidden Panels** to allow panel docks that you have hidden by the Tab or Shift-Tab shortcut to redisplay temporarily when you roll the mouse over the edge of the monitor or Application frame. ★ When the pointer is moved away from the panels, they disappear again.

With **Remember Panel Locations** checked, panels that are open when you exit/quit Photoshop will reopen in their last location upon relaunch, as opposed to the locations specified in the last displayed workspace.

Check **Open Documents as Tabs** to have documents dock automatically into a tabbed window when opened (whether the Application frame is displayed or not). ★

Enable Floating Document Window Docking to allow a floating document window to dock as a tabbed window when you drag its title bar below the title bar of another window or below the bar at the top of the Application frame. ★

UI Text Options

Choices made from the following two menus take effect upon relaunch.

If you own a multilingual version of Photoshop, from the **UI Language** menu, choose a language for the interface. ★

From the **UI Font Size** menu, choose Small (the default), Medium, or Large as the font size for the Photoshop user interface (menus, panels, tool tips, Options bar, etc.). (This option was formerly in the General Preferences panel.)

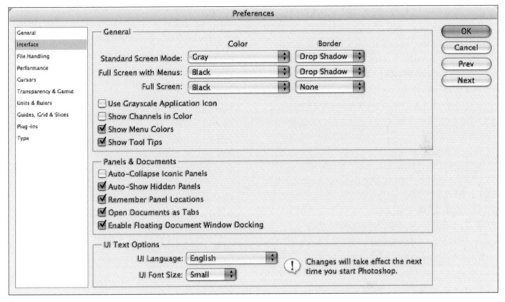

A Interface Preferences

File Handling Preferences A

File Saving Options

Choose **Image Previews**: Never Save to save files without a thumbnail preview for the desktop; or Always Save to have an updated preview save with your files each time they're saved; or Ask When Saving to decide which previews to include on a case-by-case basis via Image Previews check boxes in the Save or Save As dialog.

In the Mac OS, check Icon to have a thumbnail of an image display as its file icon on the Desktop and in the File > Open dialog. Check Full Size to include a 72-ppi PICT preview for applications that require this option. Check Macintosh Thumbnail and/or Windows Thumbnail to have a thumbnail of an image display when selected in File > Open.

In the Mac OS, choose **Append File Extension**: Always to always include a three-letter abbreviation of the file format (e.g., .tif, .psd) when saving files; or Ask When Saving to allow their inclusion via File Extension check boxes in the Save As dialog. This is helpful when converting files for Windows, and essential when saving files for the Web. Check Use Lower Case to have file extensions appear in lowercase characters instead of uppercase.

In Windows, choose **File Extension**: Use Lower Case or Use Upper Case.

File Compatibility

Check **Prefer Adobe Camera Raw for Supported Raw Files** to have raw files that you open via File >

Open open into Camera Raw, as opposed to other conversion software (we keep this checked).

Check **Ignore EXIF Profile Tag** to have Photoshop ignore a camera's EXIF metadata color space information when opening files.

Check **Ask Before Saving Layered TIFF Files** to have an alert appear when a layered file is saved in the TIFF format, giving you the option to proceed with the save or not.

The **Maximize PSD and PSB File Compatibility** option includes a flattened version of the file to make it compatible with programs that don't read Photoshop layers and with early versions of Photoshop. This option increases the file size but is often a necessity. Choose Ask to have the compatibility option be offered via an alert when files are saved, or choose Always to produce compatible files upon saving without an alert appearing.

Version Cue

Enable Version Cue enables the sharing and management of files among Adobe Creative Suite applications. For information about Version Cue, see Photoshop Help and adobe.com.

File list

In the **Recent File List Contains [ ] files** field, enter the maximum number of files that can be listed at a time on the File > Open Recent submenu (0–30).

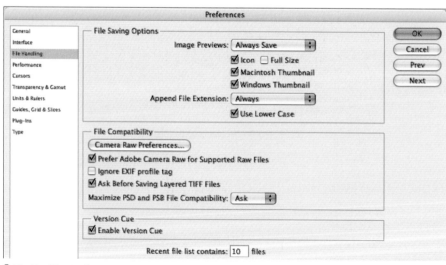

A File Handling Preferences

Performance Preferences A

Note: For changes made in this panel to take effect, you must relaunch Photoshop.

Use the **Description** window at the bottom of the dialog to learn about whichever feature your pointer is currently hovering over.

Memory Usage

Via the **Let Photoshop Use** field or slider, specify the maximum percentage of your machine's RAM that Photoshop can use, or leave it at the default setting of 70%.

History & Cache

Enter the maximum number of **History States** the History panel can list at a time (1–1000). Older states that exceed the maximum are deleted.

The image cache is designed to help speed up the screen redraw of high-resolution files. Low-resolution versions of the file are saved in individual cache buffers and are used for updating the document onscreen. The higher the **Cache Levels** value (1–8), the more buffers are used and the speedier the redraw but the more RAM is used. The Histogram panel also uses the current Cache Levels value to calculate pixel values based on cached data rather than actual data.

Scratch Disks

Check which hard drives you want to make available as **Scratch Disks** for Photoshop when available RAM is insufficient for processing or storing image data. To switch the order of the currently selected hard drive, click the up or down arrow.

➤ Hold down Ctrl-Alt/Cmd-Option as you launch Photoshop to open the Scratch Disk Preferences dialog.

GPU Settings

The **Detected Video Card** area lists which video cards, if any, the program detects in your system. Most video cards are designed to enhance the rendering and display of 3D graphics.

Check **Enable OpenGL Drawing** if your system has OpenGL graphics capability and you want to take advantage of OpenGL features in Photoshop, such as continuous zoom, flick panning, and the Rotate View tool.★

MONITORING SCRATCH DISK USAGE

Show the Info panel.ⓘ Choose Panel Options from the panel menu, and check Efficiency under Status Information. At the bottom of the panel, you'll see an Efficiency readout. When this value is below 100%, it means the scratch disk is being used.

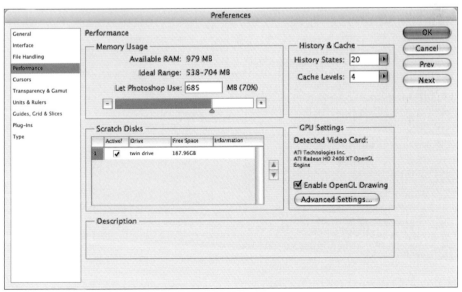

A Performance Preferences

Cursors Preferences A

Painting Cursors

For the **Painting Cursors** (the Art History Brush, Background Eraser, Blur, Brush, Burn, Clone Stamp, Color Replacement, Dodge, Eraser, Healing Brush, History Brush, Pattern Stamp, Pencil, Quick Selection, Sharpen, Smudge, Sponge, and Spot Healing Brush tools), click the type of cursor you want displayed onscreen as you use the tool: Standard for the tool icon; Precise for crosshairs; Normal Brush Tip for a half-size circle; or Full Size Brush Tip for a circle the full size of the current brush tip. For either of the latter two options, you can also check Show Crosshair in Brush Tip to have a crosshair appear in the center of the circle.

Other Cursors

For the **Other Cursors** (all those not listed in the previous paragraph) click Standard to have the tool icon display onscreen as you use the tool or Precise to have crosshairs display onscreen instead.

➤ Press Caps Lock to turn Standard cursors into Precise cursors (crosshairs) or, if Precise is the current Painting Cursors setting, to turn any Painting cursor into a Full Size Brush Tip.

Brush Preview

Click the **Color** swatch and choose a color from the Color Picker to display within the brush cursor when you Alt-right-click-drag/Control-Option-drag to scale the brush interactively (OpenGL only). ★

Transparency & Gamut Preferences B

Transparency Settings

Choose a **Grid Size** for the checkerboard that Photoshop uses to represent transparent areas on a layer. C

Change the **Grid Colors** for the transparency checkerboard by choosing Light, Medium, Dark, Red, Orange, Green, Blue, or Purple; or click each color swatch and choose a color from the color picker.

Gamut Warning

To change the color that Photoshop uses to mark out-of-gamut colors when the View > **Gamut Warning** command is on, click the Color swatch, then choose a color from the Color Picker. You can also lower the Opacity of the Gamut Warning color to make it easier to see the image behind it.

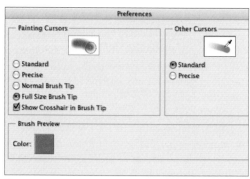

A Cursors Preferences

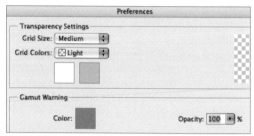

B Transparency Preferences

C The transparency checkerboard

Units & Rulers Preferences A

Units

Choose a unit of measure from the **Rulers** menu for the horizontal and vertical rulers that display in the document window. (To show or hide the rulers, press Ctrl-R/Cmd-R or choose Show Rulers from the View Extras menu 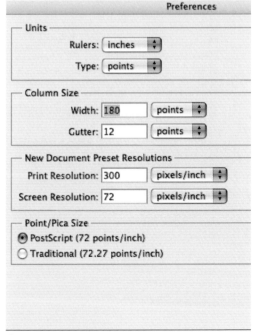 ▾ on the Application bar.★)

Choose a unit for **Type**: Pixels, Points, or Mm (to be used on the Character panel, Paragraph panel, and Options bar).

➤ To change ruler units quickly, right-click/Control-click either ruler in the document window and choose a unit from the context menu. Or to get directly to the Units & Rulers panel of the Preferences dialog, double-click either ruler.

➤ If you change the measurement units for the Info panel via the Info Panel Options dialog or for the rulers via the context menu (see the previous tip), the ruler units will also change in the Preferences dialog, and vice versa.

Column Size

Enter **Width** and **Gutter** values in any of the available units to allow the Image Size and Crop commands to fit images for a specific column width in a target layout program.

New Document Preset Resolutions

Enter **Print Resolution** and **Screen Resolution** values in either of the available units to display by default in the New dialog when you choose a preset print or screen size, respectively. The default settings are 300 ppi for print output and 72 ppi for onscreen display.

Point/Pica Size

Click **PostScript** (the default, and preferred setting) to have Photoshop use the standard PostScript value for calculating the points-to-inch ratio. Traditional uses the ancient, pre-desktop-publishing value.

Preferences

Units
- Rulers: inches
- Type: points

Column Size
- Width: 180   points
- Gutter: 12   points

New Document Preset Resolutions
- Print Resolution: 300   pixels/inch
- Screen Resolution: 72   pixels/inch

Point/Pica Size
- ● PostScript (72 points/inch)
- ○ Traditional (72.27 points/inch)

ABBREVIATIONS ALLOWED IN ENTRY FIELDS	
Pixels	px
Inches	in or "
Centimeters	cm
Millimeters	mm
Points	pt
Picas	p
Percent	%

A Units & Rulers Preferences

Guides, Grid & Slices Preferences A

Note: Changes in this dialog preview immediately in the document window.

Guides

Choose a **Color** for the moveable and removable ruler guides, and choose a **Style** for the guides.**B**

Smart Guides

Choose a **Color** for smart guides, the temporary lines that display onscreen as you move a layer or selection (turn on via View > Show > Smart Guides).

Grid

Choose a color for the nonprinting grid (View > Show > Grid) from the **Color** menu, and choose a grid **Style**.

To display gridlines at specific intervals, choose the desired unit from the menu, then enter a **Gridline Every** value. If you choose Percent from the menu, gridlines will appear at those percentage intervals of the overall document, starting from the left edge. For the thinner gridlines between the main gridlines, enter a **Subdivisions** value.

➤ For the Guides, Smart Guides, or Grid color, you can click the color swatch, then choose a color from the Color Picker or Color Libraries dialog.

Slices

Choose a **Line Color** for the lines that mark slices. Check **Show Slice Numbers** to have a slice number display in the upper left corner of each slice.

Plug-ins Preferences C

Note: For changes made in this dialog to take effect, you must relaunch Photoshop.

Plug-ins

In order to access third-party plug-ins that aren't in the Photoshop Plug-ins folder, you need to tell Photoshop where they're located. Check **Additional Plug-ins Folder**, locate the folder, then click Choose.

Extension Panels

Check **Allow Extensions to Connect to the Internet** to enable Photoshop extension panels to connect to the Internet.★ Adobe ConnectNow, an interactive Web conferencing application that offers screen sharing, chat, notes, audio, and video features, is one such extension (it is included with Photoshop CS4).

Check **Load Extension Panels** to have extension panels that are already installed load at startup automatically.★

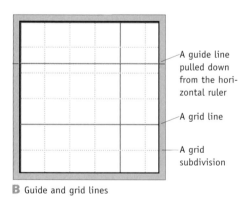

A guide line pulled down from the horizontal ruler

A grid line

A grid subdivision

B Guide and grid lines

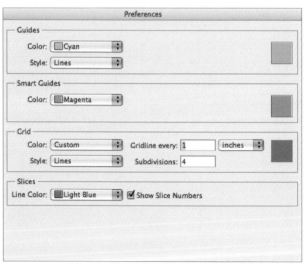

A Guides, Grid & Slices Preferences

C Plug-ins Preferences

Type Preferences A

Type Options

Be sure to check **Use Smart Quotes** to have Photoshop insert typographically correct (curly) apostrophes and quotation marks automatically when you create type, instead of the incorrect foot and inch marks.

Check **Show Asian Text Options** to display options for Chinese, Japanese, and Korean type on the Character and Paragraph panels.

Check **Enable Missing Glyph Protection** to permit Photoshop to substitute Roman characters for missing glyphs, such as Japanese or Chinese characters.

Check **Show Font Names in English** to have non-Roman font names on the Font menus display in English (e.g., "Adobe Ming Std" instead of the Chinese characters).

Check **Font Preview Size** to display font previews on the Font menu on the Options bar and the Character panel. For the preview size, choose Small, Medium, Large, Extra Large, or Huge.

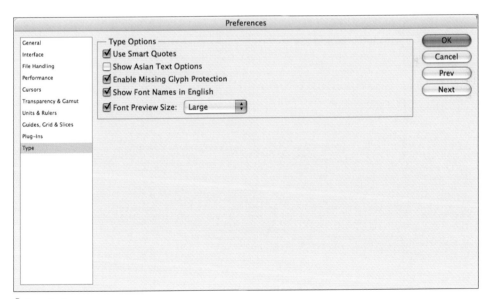

A Type Preferences

The Bridge Preferences

General Preferences A

Appearance

Choose a value between Black and White for the overall **User Interface Brightness** (for the side panels) and for the **Image Backdrop** (the area behind the Content and Preview panels).

Choose an **Accent Color** for highlighted items.

Behavior

Check **When a Camera is Connected, Launch Adobe Photo Downloader** to make the Downloader the default system utility for acquiring photos (this option is Mac OS only).

Check **Double-click Edits Camera Raw Settings in Bridge** to have raw files open into Camera Raw (hosted by Bridge) when double-clicked.

If **Ctrl-click/Cmd-click Opens the Loupe When Previewing or Reviewing** is checked, you have to Ctrl/Cmd-click an image preview to make a loupe display. With this option unchecked, you can make a loupe appear by clicking the preview without using the shortcut. ★

For **Number of Recent Items to Display**, enter the maximum number of folders (0–30) that can

be listed at a time on the Open Recent File menu � on the Path bar.

Favorite Items

Check which items and system-generated folders you want listed in the **Favorites** panel by default.

Thumbnails Preferences B

Performance and File Handling

Note: To implement Performance and File Handling changes, you must purge the folder cache (Tools > Cache submenu).

For **Do Not Process Files Larger Than**, enter the maximum file size that you will permit Bridge to display as a thumbnail (the default value is 1000 MB). Large files preview slowly.

Details

From the **Additional Lines of Thumbnail Metadata** menus, choose which categories of file information you want listed below or next to the image thumbnails in the Content panel.

Check **Show Tooltips** to allow tool tips to display when you rest the pointer on Bridge features, such as image thumbnails.

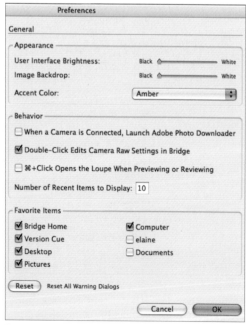

A General Preferences, in Bridge

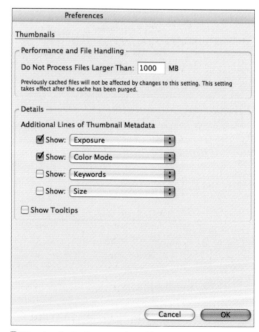

B Thumbnails Preferences, in Bridge

Playback Preferences ★

Choose options to control whether audio and video files will play and/or loop when previewed in the Preview panel. The **Stack Playback Frame Rate** controls the speed at which a group of ten or more thumbnails proceeds when the viewer clicks the Play button.

Metadata Preferences

Check which metadata categories you want displayed in the **Metadata** panel.

Check **Hide Empty Fields** to streamline the Metadata panel.

Check **Show Metadata Placard** to display camera data at the top of the Metadata panel.

Keywords Preferences ★

Check **Automatically Apply Parent Keywords** to have the parent keyword apply automatically when a subkeyword check box is clicked in the Keywords panel (we keep this option off). If this option is on and you want to override it (to apply just a subkeyword), Shift-click the keyword.

For **Write Hierarchical Keywords**, click a Delimiter option to tell Bridge how to separate keywords when exporting files. **Read Hierarchical Keywords** applies to keywords from imported files.

Labels Preferences

Check whether to **Require the Control/Command Key** [to be pressed] **to Apply Labels and Ratings** to selected file thumbnails. You can change the label names here, too, but not the colors.

File Type Associations Preferences

These settings tell Bridge which application to use when opening files of each type. Don't change these settings unless you know what you're doing!

Cache Preferences

Options

Check **Keep 100% Previews in Cache** to save a large JPEG preview to disk for faster previewing when using the loupe and when previewing in Slideshow mode at 100% view. This option uses significant disk space, so we keep it unchecked. ★

Check **Automatically Export Caches to Folders When Possible** to have Bridge export the cache that is created when thumbnails are generated to the same folders those images are stored in.

Location

Click **Choose** to specify a new location for the Bridge cache.

Manage

If you have a very large hard drive, you can use the **Cache Size** slider to raise the maximum number of items that can be stored in the cache. ★

Click **Compact Cache** to allow previously cached items that are no longer available to be removed from the cache for improved performance. ★

Click **Purge Cache** to purge all cached thumbnails and previews from the central database to free up space on your hard disk, or if you experience problems displaying thumbnails in Bridge.

Startup Scripts Preferences ★

Depending on your usual workflow, check which **Startup Scripts** you need to have running on a regular basis and, to improve performance, uncheck the ones you won't need. (Read the description below the script name.) Changes to these preferences take effect upon relaunch.

Advanced Preferences

Note: Most Advanced Preferences changes take effect upon relaunch.

Miscellaneous

Check **Use Software Rendering** to turn off hardware acceleration for the Preview panel and for Slideshow mode.

Check **Generate Monitor-Size Previews** to have Bridge generate previews in a dual-monitor setup based on the resolution of the larger monitor. ★

Check **Start Bridge at Login** to have Bridge launch automatically at startup, and into stealth mode. ★

International

Choose a **Language** for the Bridge interface and a language for the **Keyboard**.

Output Preferences ★

Check **Use Solo Mode for Output Panel Behavior** to show one category of Output settings at a time.

Check **Convert Multi-Byte Filenames to Full ASCII** to define Chinese and Japanese file names using the ASCII character system, to prevent problems when transferring files.

Check **Preserve Embedded Color Profile** to preserve any embedded profiles in files being output as PDF contacts sheets or presentations.

Using the Preset Manager

In the course of using Photoshop, you've probably become acquainted with many of the preset pickers, such as the Brush and Gradient Preset pickers. The Swatches and Brushes panels serve as preset pickers, too. Each item on a picker (e.g., swatch, brush, gradient, pattern, shape, contour, or style) is called a **preset**, and each collection of presets that you can load onto a picker is called a **library**. You can use the **Preset Manager** to organize, append, replace, and reset which items load onto the preset pickers at startup, or you can make those changes in the individual preset pickers. Changes you make to an individual preset picker are reflected in the Preset Manager, and vice versa.

To use the Preset Manager:

1. Do either of the following:

   Choose Edit > **Preset Manager**.

   From the menu on any panel or picker that contains presets, such as the Brush Preset picker or Brushes panel, choose **Preset Manager**.

   The Preset Manager dialog opens.**A**

2. Choose from the **Preset Type** menu (or use a shortcut, as shown in the figure below).

3. *Optional:* From the menu on the right,◉ choose a view option for the Preset Manager

(e.g., Text Only, Small Thumbnail, Large Thumbnail, Small List, or Large List). For Brushes, you can choose Stroke Thumbnail to see a sample of the brush stroke alongside each brush thumbnail.

4. Do any of the following:

   From the bottom of the menu on the right,◉ choose a library name. Click **Append** in the alert dialog to add that library to the current library, or click **OK** to replace the current library with the new one.

   Click **Load**, locate and click a library that's not currently on the menu to append its contents to the current presets, then click Load again.

   Respond to an alert prompt, if any, regarding saving changes to the current presets.

   Click a preset you want to delete (or Shift-click or Ctrl-click/Cmd-click multiple presets), then click **Delete**; this can't be undone. To load or reset presets, see the next page or page 403.

5. Click **Done**.

➤ Preset libraries can be shared among Photoshop users.

➤ Each type of preset library has its own file extension and default location (see the sidebar on page 402).

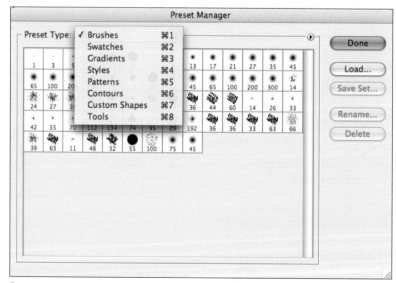

A Choose a category from the Preset Type menu in the Preset Manager dialog.

Via the Preset Manager, you can **save** a **selection** of presets into a **library**. Once saved, you can load the library onto the appropriate picker at any time—or share it with other Photoshop users. (If you prefer to save presets via an individual picker, follow the instructions on the next page instead.)

To save selected presets as a library:

1. Choose Edit > **Preset Manager** or choose **Preset Manager** from any picker or panel menu.

2. From the **Preset Type** menu, choose the category of presets that you want to create a library for.

3. Shift-click or Ctrl-click/Cmd-click the presets that you want to save as a library.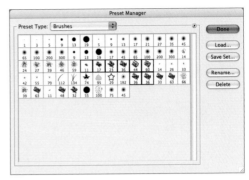

4. Click **Save Set**, keep the default extension and location as is, but enter a name for the new library.

5. Click **Save**, then click Done to close the Preset Manager.

Via the Preset Manager, you can **reset** any category of presets to the factory defaults or you can **replace** the current presets with a library of your choice. (To reset presets via an individual picker, see the instructions on page 403.)

To reset or replace presets:

1. Choose Edit > **Preset Manager** or choose **Preset Manager** from any preset picker or panel menu.

2. From the **Preset Type** menu, choose the category of presets that you want to reset or replace.

3. *Optional:* Any unsaved presets on the list will be deleted in the next step, so we recommend saving the current library before proceeding (see the previous set of instructions).

4. From the menu on the right,◐ choose either of the following. **B**

   Reset [preset type] to restore the default library for the chosen type, then click Append to append the default presets to the current library or click OK to replace the current library with the default presets (click Cancel if you change your mind).

   Replace [preset type]. A prompt may appear, allowing you to save the current presets. Next, locate the library that you want to replace the current library with, then click Load.

A Select the presets you want saved in a library.

B From the Preset Manager menu, choose Reset [preset type] or Replace [preset type].

A PRESET BY ANY OTHER NAME

► To rename a preset when the Preset Manager is in a Thumbnail view, double-click the thumbnail, then change the name in the dialog that opens.

► To rename a preset when the Preset Manager is in Text Only view or a List view, double-click the preset name.

► You can also select multiple presets and then click Rename. In this case, the naming dialogs will open one by one in succession.

Managing presets via pickers and panels

A new preset appears on the appropriate preset picker if you define a new pattern or custom shape via the Edit menu, add a new swatch to the Swatches panel, add a new style to the Styles panel, create a new gradient in the Gradient Editor dialog, create a new contour in any Contour Preset picker, or create a new brush or tool preset, among other tasks (see also the sidebar at right). The new preset will also display for that preset type in the Preset Manager.

New presets are saved in the Adobe Photoshop Preferences file temporarily and display in the appropriate preset picker even after you relaunch Photoshop—that is, provided you don't replace the preset with another library, reset that picker to the default library, or reset that preset type via the Preset Manager. If you do any of the above, your new presets will be discarded! Thankfully, there's a way to preserve all your hard work.

When you use the Preset Manager to create a library, you can select the presets you want to include. When you save presets as a new library via an individual preset picker, all the presets on the picker are included; you can't pick and choose. To outsmart this limitation, before creating the library, simply delete the presets you don't want to include.

Note: When you delete a preset from a picker or panel, no documents are altered and no presets are deleted from the library.

To delete a preset from a picker or panel:

Do either of the following:

On a preset picker or panel, Alt-click/Option-click a **preset** (you'll see a scissors pointer).

Right-click/Control-click a preset and choose **Delete [preset name]**. If an alert dialog appears, click OK.

HOW ARE PRESETS CREATED?

A new preset is created when you:

➤ Customize a brush via the Brushes panel or Brush Preset picker, then click the New Preset button ▣ on the panel or picker.

➤ Add a swatch to the Swatches panel.

➤ Create a gradient by clicking New in the Gradient Editor.

➤ Create a style by clicking the New Style button on the Styles panel or by clicking New Style in the Layer Style dialog.

➤ Create a pattern via Edit > Define Pattern.

➤ Create a contour by choosing New Contour from the Contour Preset picker in the Layer Style dialog.

➤ Create a custom shape via Edit > Define Custom Shape.

➤ Create a tool preset (see page 404) by clicking the New Tool Preset button ▣ in the Tool Preset picker or on the Tool Presets panel.

LOCATIONS FOR SAVING A LIBRARY

The default location for storing presets that are included with Photoshop in Windows is [drive]:\Program Files\Adobe\Adobe Photoshop CS4\Presets\[preset category]. In the Mac OS, it's Applications/Adobe Photoshop CS4/Presets/[preset category]. Libraries saved in this location will display in the lower part of the appropriate picker menu upon relaunch.

The default location for storing user-created presets in Windows is C:\Documents and Settings\[user]\Application Data\Adobe\Adobe Photoshop CS4\Presets\[preset category]. In the Mac OS, it's [user name]/Library/Application Support/Adobe/Adobe Photoshop CS4/Presets/[preset category]. Libraries saved in this location will display at the very bottom of the appropriate picker menu upon relaunch.

To save all the presets currently on a picker as a new library:

1. Make sure the preset picker or panel contains only the presets you want to save in a library. Delete any unwanted presets as per the previous set of instructions.

2. From the panel or picker menu, choose **Save** [preset type].

3. Enter a name, keep the default extension and location, then click **Save**.

   Note: In order for your new library to appear on the panel menu and the preset picker menu, and on the menu in the Preset Manager dialog, you must relaunch Photoshop.**A**

➤ To create document presets for use in the New dialog, see page 26.

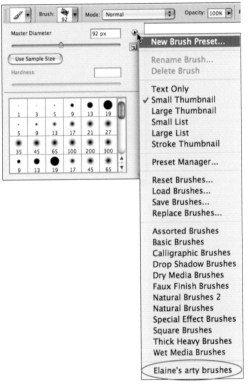

A The new library ("Elaine's arty brushes") appears on the preset picker menu.

In addition to the default presets and any custom libraries that you have created, Photoshop supplies an assortment of predefined preset libraries that you can load as needed. The libraries are available on the lower portion of the panel or picker menu when you select a tool that uses that panel or picker (for example, from the Brush Preset picker when you choose the Brush or Pencil tool).

To load a library of presets:

1. From the lower portion of the panel or the picker menu, choose the desired library name.

2. When the alert dialog appears, click **Append** to add the additional presets to the panel or picker, or click **OK** to replace the current presets on the panel or picker with those in the library.

   Note: If you made changes to the current presets, another alert dialog will appear. Click Save if you want to save your changes.

➤ To access a library that isn't listed on the menu because it isn't in the default folder, choose Load [preset name] from the panel or picker menu, locate the desired library, then click Load.

Any presets that are on a picker or panel when you exit/quit Photoshop will appear again when you relaunch the application. You can restore the factory default library to any individual picker or panel.

To restore the default presets to a picker or panel:

1. Choose **Reset** [preset name] from the picker or panel menu.

2. When the alert dialog appears, click **OK** to replace the existing presets on the panel or picker with the default presets.

   Note: If you made changes to the current presets, another alert dialog will appear. Click Save if you want to save your changes.

Creating tool presets

If you're looking for a worthwhile way to streamline your workflow, tool presets fit the bill. For any tool, you can choose a preset (such as a brush or gradient), choose custom Options bar settings, and choose a Foreground color (if applicable), then save that collection of settings as a tool preset. Thereafter, when you use that tool, you can choose your tool preset from the Tool Preset picker on the Options bar or from the Tool Presets panel. Creating tool presets saves time in the long run and is worth the effort even for small variations.

If you check Current Tool Only on the Tool Presets panel or on the Tool Preset picker, only those tool presets that were created for the current tool will display on the panel and picker. If you uncheck Current Tool Only, the tool presets for all tools will display. (When you click a tool preset, the tool that uses that preset becomes selected automatically.)

To create a tool preset:

1. Choose and customize any tool. For example, you could customize the Brush tool via the Brush Preset picker and Options bar, and also choose a Foreground color to save with the preset.

2. Do either of the following:

   On the Options bar, click the **Tool Preset** picker thumbnail or arrowhead.**A**

   Open the **Tool Presets** panel.✂ **B**

3. Click the **New Tool Preset** button ⬒ on the picker or panel. The New Tool Preset dialog opens.

4. *Optional:* Change the tool preset name, if desired. Also check Include Color, if available, if you want to save the current Foreground color with the preset.

5. Click OK. The new tool preset will appear on, and can be chosen from, the Tool Preset picker and the Tool Presets panel.

6. To preserve your tool presets for future use in any document, save them as a tool presets library by choosing **Save Tool Presets** from the picker or panel menu. You can also load any saved preset library via either menu.

➤ To restore the default presets for all tools, you should save any custom tool presets first, then choose Reset Tool Presets from the Tool Preset picker or the Tool Presets panel menu.

Click to open the Tool Preset picker

A Click the thumbnail or arrowhead to open the Tool Preset picker.

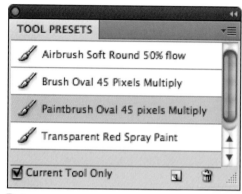

B The Tool Presets panel has the same function as the Tool Preset picker.

When your Photoshop image is done, you can output it on a laser printer, color printer (such as an inkjet), or imagesetter. In this chapter, you'll learn how to output a document to an inkjet printer, set up a file to be printed as a duotone, and prepare a file for commercial printing. (To export your file to another application or to optimize it for the Web, see the next chapter.)

To obtain a quality color print from an inkjet printer that closely matches your onscreen image, you will complete the color management setup that you started in Chapter 1. We also recommend that you refer to Photoshop Help, which contains a wealth of specialized technical information, and the documentation for your specific printer model.

When preparing files for an output service provider, be sure to consult those experts about which specific settings and formats to choose. In addition to following our basic instructions for printing from Photoshop, keep in mind that getting a good color print of an image requires a thorough understanding of the color management software that's built into your computer's operating system and the settings available on your printing device—as well as practice.

PRINT

26

IN THIS CHAPTER

Choosing Properties/Page Setup
   settings for inkjet printing 406

Choosing Print dialog settings for
   inkjet printing 407

Choosing output options 410

Printing the file in Windows. 411

Printing the file in the Mac OS 412

Creating a duotone. 413

Preparing a file for commercial
   printing 413

KEEP THE FILE IN RGB FOR AN INKJET

When printing to a desktop printer, keep your image in RGB Color mode. Although these printers print using CMYK inks (in fact, most use six or more process ink colors), their drivers are designed to receive RGB data and perform the conversion to printer ink colors internally. Be sure to use the installed profile that conforms to your printer model and paper (we'll show you how).

Choosing Properties/Page Setup settings for inkjet printing

Continuing the color management workflow that we started in Chapter 1, we'll show you how to print an image using a desktop inkjet color printer. The first step for any kind of print job is to tell Photoshop what type of printer and paper size you're using. Your printer driver and operating system determine which print options are available. A button in the Print dialog provides one-click access to the Page Setup dialog.

In Windows, the Page Setup command opens the confusingly named "[your printer] Properties" dialog. Here you'll find many printer-specific options beyond the basics of page size and paper type. In the Mac OS, you'll find equivalent options in the Print dialog for your system, which opens when you click the Print button in the Print dialog in Photoshop. Clear as mud?

To choose Properties/Page Setup settings for an inkjet printer:

1. Choose File > **Print** (Ctrl-P/Cmd-P). The Print dialog opens (**A**, next page).

2. From the **Printer** menu, choose the inkjet printer you want to use.

3. Click **Page Setup** to open the [**Printer**] Properties **A**/Page Setup dialog.**B**

4. In Windows, from the **Source** menu, choose the tray that holds the media you want to print on. From the **Type** menu, choose the specific kind of media you want to use. The actual names of these menus may be different for your printer.

   In the Mac OS, from the **Format For** menu, choose your inkjet printer (yes, again!). From the **Paper Size** menu, choose a paper size to print on. If your printer can print borderless pictures, you can choose a paper size that is listed as "(borderless)." Leave the Scale value at 100%. If you need to change the scale, it's better to do so in the Print dialog, where you can preview the results.

5. Click an **Orientation** button.

6. Click OK to close the Properties or Page Setup dialog. Now you're ready to choose options in the Print dialog (see the next page).

A This is the Properties dialog for an Epson printer, in Windows.

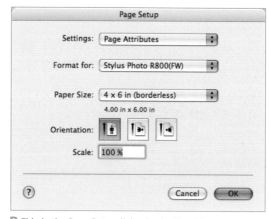

B This is the Page Setup dialog in the Mac OS.

Choosing Print dialog settings for inkjet printing

The Print dialog provides a preview of the image on your chosen paper size, along with position, print size, color management, and output options.

To print to an inkjet printer:

1. Choose File > **Print** (Ctrl-P/Cmd-P). The Print dialog opens, **A** complete with a preview.

2. Make sure the correct inkjet printer is chosen from the Printer menu.

3. If you haven't chosen page settings yet, follow steps 3–6 on the previous page.

4. Check **Center Image** to position the image in the center of the paper. Or to reposition the image on the paper, uncheck Center Image and enter new Top and Left values (note the preview); or check Bounding Box as well, then drag the bounding box in the preview.

5. *Optional:* To scale the print output slightly (not the actual image), do one of the following:

   Check **Scale to Fit Media** to have the image fit automatically to the paper size you chose in Properties/Page Setup.

   Change the **Scale** percentage or enter specific **Height** and **Width** values (choose from the Units menu). These three values are interdependent; changing any one option causes the other two to change.

   Check **Bounding Box** to display the image boundary in the preview, then drag a handle or the side of the box to scale the print slightly.

Continued on the following page

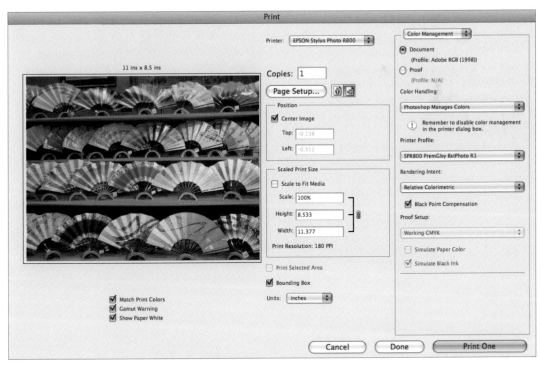

A The Color Management panel is showing in this Print dialog.

Note: Use the scaling features to scale the print by a small amount (i.e., fractions of an inch or a few percentage points). To scale more than that, cancel out of the dialog and use Image > Image Size to scale your image (see pages 98–100).

6. For the **Output** options, see page 410.

7. From the menu in the top right corner of the dialog, choose **Color Management** (**A**, next page). This is where you will tell Photoshop to use the profile for your specific printer and paper.

8. Click **Document** to use the color profile that's embedded in the image, which will be Adobe RGB (1998) if you're continuing with the color management workflow that you started in Chapter 1.

9. From the **Color Handling** menu, choose **Photoshop Manages Colors** to let Photoshop handle the color conversion. Assuming you downloaded and installed a profile for your specific printer, ink, and paper (see the instructions on pages 14–15), this option will ensure optimal color management.

10. Next, choose the installed printer, ink, and paper profile from the **Printer Profile** menu.

11. From the **Rendering Intent** menu, choose the same intent that you used when you created the soft-proof setting for your inkjet printer—most likely either Perceptual or Relative Colorimetric (see pages 17–18).

   ➤ You could run one test print for the Perceptual intent and one for the Relative Colorimetric intent, and see which one produces better results.

12. Check **Black Point Compensation**. This option, which preserves the darkest blacks and shadow details by mapping the full color range of the document profile to the full range of the printer profile, is recommended when printing an RGB image.

13. Below the preview, check **Match Print Colors** to display a color-managed soft proof of the image in the preview, based on the chosen printer and printer profile settings; check **Gamut Warning** to display out-of-gamut colors as gray in the preview, based on the current print profile; and check **Show Paper White** to set any white in the preview to the color of the paper, also based on the current print profile. ★

14. Click **Print** to access the systemwide Print dialog, then carefully follow the steps on page 411 for Windows or 412 for the Mac OS to turn off color management for your printer before sending the file to print.

   ➤ Click Done in the Print dialog to preserve most (but not all) of your settings and close the dialog.

OTHER COLOR HANDLING CHOICES

Other options that are available on the Color Handling menu in the Color Management panel of the Print dialog are as follows:

➤ Printer Manages Colors sends all of the file's color information to the printer along with the document profile, and the printer, not Photoshop, manages the color conversion. This isn't a good choice if you use either custom profiles or paper from a company other than the printer manufacturer, because (depending on the features and quality of the printer driver) the printer may not be aware of your custom choices. If you do use this option, be sure to enable color management options in the printer driver for the chosen printer.

➤ No Color Management prevents color values from being converted by Photoshop or the printer. Choose this option if you're planning to print a color target from which a color reading device will scan and generate a custom printer and paper profile. (Sorry for seeming cryptic, but to explain color targets fully would take a whole chapter in itself…)

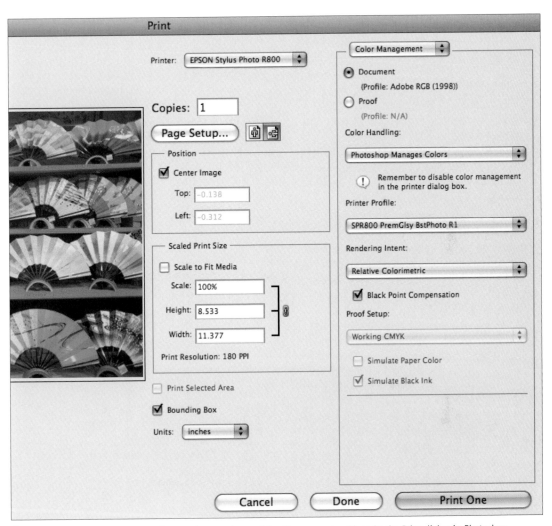

A To optimize the color accuracy of your printout, choose Color Management settings in the Print dialog in Photoshop.

Choosing Output options

This list of output options will be limited to the basic ones we think you need to be aware of. For other options, see Photoshop Help.

To access options for printouts, from the menu in the upper right corner of the File > Print dialog (in Photoshop), choose **Output**. In the **Printing Marks** area, you'll find these options: **A**

➤ **Calibration Bars** prints a grayscale and/or color calibration strip outside the image area.

➤ **Registration Marks** prints marks that a print shop uses to align color separations.

➤ **Corner Crop Marks** and **Center Crop Marks** print short little lines that a print shop uses as guidelines when trimming the printed pages.

➤ **Description** prints, outside the image area, whatever information is listed in the Description heading of File > File Info.

➤ **Labels** prints the file name, document color mode, and current channel name on each page (outside the image area).

The **Functions** area contains these options, among others:

➤ **Bleed** lets you specify the Width (distance) inward from the edge of the canvas area for the placement of crop marks (0–9.01 pt.).

➤ **Include Vector Data** causes the edges of any vector objects (such as type or shapes) to print at the printer resolution, not at the document resolution.

➤ In the Mac OS, **Send 16-Bit Data** enables color data from a 16-bits-per-channel file to be sent to the printer (the output device must be capable of handling 16-bit files). Because of the higher bit depth, the printouts will have finer details and smoother color gradations. ★

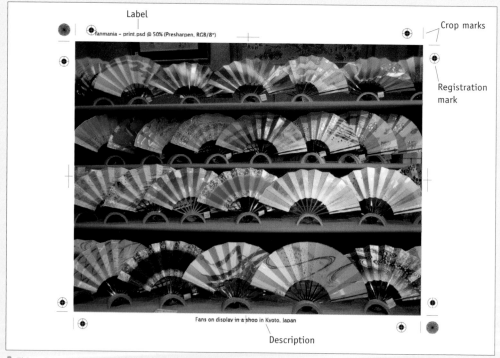

A This printout shows some of the Output options that can be produced from the Print dialog in Photoshop.

Printing the file in Windows

The last step before outputting your file from an inkjet printer is to turn off color management for that device to allow Photoshop to manage the color conversion. In Windows, the dialog that contains color management settings for printing is part of the printer driver software, not part of the system software. Therefore, the names and locations of the controls will vary from one manufacturer to another. In these instructions, printer color management will be turned off for an Epson printer driver. If you have a different printer model, research how to access print quality and color management settings for it, and use our steps as general guidelines.

To turn off color management for your printer in Windows, and print the file:

1. Open the File > **Print** dialog in Photoshop, then click **Print** to get to the Print dialog for your system.

2. In the **Select Printer** area of the **General** tab, choose the name of your inkjet printer.

3. Click **Preferences A** to open the Printing Preferences dialog for your printer, which is identical to the Properties dialog that you used to specify the size and media type.

4. In the **Main** tab of the Printing Preferences dialog, click **Advanced.B** A different set of options appears, including controls for color management.

5. In the **Color Management** area, click **ICM C** to switch color management from the Epson driver to the color management system that's built into Windows XP.

6. In the **ICC/ICM Profile** area, click **Off** (**No Color Adjustment**) to disable color management for the printer.

7. Click **OK** to close the Printing Preferences dialog and return to the Print dialog. Now you're ready to click **Print**. Phew! You made it.

➤ If you need to enable printer-based color management in Windows, follow the steps above, except in step 6, click Applied by Printer Software.

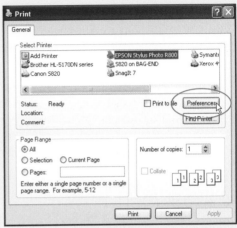

A In this Print dialog in Windows, an Epson printer is selected. We click Preferences to open the next dialog.

B In the Main tab of the Printing Preferences dialog for an Epson printer, click Advanced.

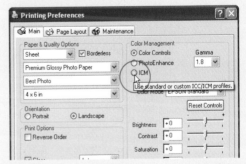

C These Color Management options are revealed when you click the Advanced button.

Printing the file in the Mac OS

In the Mac OS, the dialog that contains color management settings for the printer builds its list of options from both the system and the printer driver. Therefore, option names in the dialog will vary depending on the printer manufacturer. In these instructions, printer color management will be turned off for a Canon or Epson printer driver. If you have a different printer model, research how to access print quality and color management settings for it, and use our steps as general guidelines.

To turn off color management for your printer in the Mac OS, and print the file:

1. Open the File > **Print** dialog in Photoshop, then click **Print** to open the Print dialog for your system.

2. From the **Printer** menu, choose the name of your inkjet printer.

3. From the third menu, choose **Quality & Media** for a Canon printer **A** or **Print Settings** for an Epson printer.

4. Choose the **Media Type** (kind of paper); and for a Canon printer, choose the **Paper Source** (how the paper feeds into the printer).**B**

5. In the **Print Mode** area, click an option for the print quality.

6. Returning to the third menu from the top, choose **Color Options** for Canon **C** or **Color Management** for Epson. A new set of options displays in the dialog. Choose **None** from the **Color Correction** menu (Canon), or click **Off** (**No Color Adjustment**)(Epson).

7. Click **Print**. Congratulations!

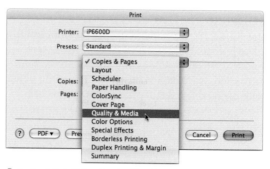

A In the Print dialog for the Mac OS, we chose the Canon Pixma iP6600D printer from the Printer menu and are now choosing Quality & Media from the third menu.

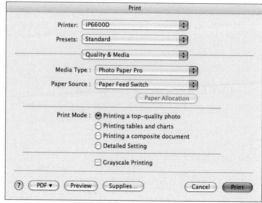

B For the Quality & Media settings, choose your paper type and source, and click the desired Print Mode.

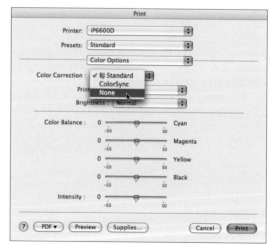

C From the third menu, choose Color Options, then choose Color Correction: None.

Creating a duotone

Here's a low-budget—but effective—way to print a grayscale image with a color tint. It will output as a monotone (from one plate).

To print a grayscale image using a spot color tint:

1. Either open a file that's in Grayscale mode or convert a copy of your file to Grayscale mode (you can use a Black & White adjustment layer to fine-tune the initial shift from color to grayscale before performing the actual conversion).

2. Choose Image > Mode > **Duotone**. The Duotone Options dialog opens.

3. Choose Type: **Monotone**.

4. Click the **Ink 1** (black) color square, click Color Libraries, if necessary, choose a spot (nonprocess) color, such as a PANTONE color, then click OK.

5. In the Duotone Options dialog, click the **Ink 1** curve (the square that contains a diagonal line).

6. In the **100%** field (for the darkest shadow value), enter the desired tint percentage value.**A** Leave the 0% field at 0 and all the other fields blank, then click OK.

7. Click OK to close the dialog. Use File > Save As to save the file in the Photoshop format; or if you're going to import the file into an Adobe Creative Suite version of InDesign, you could save the file in the Photoshop PDF format.

Preparing a file for commercial printing

Computer monitors display additive colors by projecting red, green, and blue (RGB) light, whereas commercial presses print subtractive colors using CMYK (cyan, magenta, yellow, and black) and/or spot color inks. Obtaining good CMYK color reproduction from a commercial press is an art.

Nowadays, with print shops creating their own profiles for their commercial presses, you don't need to concern yourself with creating a custom profile; you can leave this step to the pros. Do concern yourself with saving the custom profile from your print shop to the correct folder (as we showed you on page 14) so it can be accessed from the Color Settings dialog. The profile will control the CMYK conversion and can also be used to create a soft (onscreen) proof.

Continued on the following page

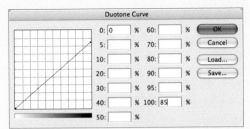

A This is the Duotone Curve dialog for a Monotone print. The 100% value has been lowered to the desired PANTONE tint percentage.

COLOR SEPARATIONS FROM PHOTOSHOP?

You're not likely to find yourself printing color separations directly from Photoshop, but if such a circumstance does arise, to print each channel as a separate page, do the following:

Convert the image to CMYK Color mode, then choose File > Print. Choose Color Management from the menu in the upper right corner of the dialog. Click Document (the CMYK Working Space profile you chose in the Color Settings dialog will be listed below that). Choose Separations from the Color Handling menu. Next, choose Output from the same menu in the upper right corner. Check any of the desired options in the Output panel, such as Calibration Bars, Registration Marks, Corner Crop Marks, Center Crop Marks, or Labels, if available for your device. When you're done choosing settings in the Print dialog, click Print, then click Print once more.

When you're ready to convert your file for commercial printing, the first step is to set the current CMYK working space to either the custom profile your print shop provided or to a predefined prepress profile. This CMYK profile will control the conversion of your images from RGB to CMYK color mode.

To choose a predefined CMYK profile:

1. Choose Edit > **Color Settings** (Ctrl-Shift-K/Cmd-Shift-K).

2. Do either of the following:

   From the **Settings** menu, choose the .csf profile that you received from your commercial printer.

   From the **CMYK** menu in the Working Spaces area, choose the .icc predefined prepress profile that your print shop sent you or choose a profile that matches your chosen press and paper type.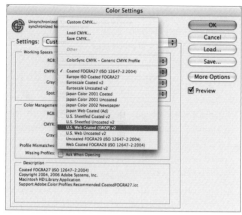

A In the Color Settings dialog, from the menu in the Workspace Spaces area, choose the correct CMYK profile.

A COLOR CORRECTION WORKFLOW

The color correction process is too complex to cover fully in this *QuickStart Guide*. The basic steps are summarized here.

▶ Calibrate your monitor (see pages 7–9).

▶ Ask your commercial printer what type of press your image will be printed on and what special requirements they have, if any. Most likely, your Photoshop files will be exported to and printed from another program, such as Adobe Illustrator or InDesign; ask your print shop if they can output from that program. Also ask what lines-per-inch setting will be used on the press for your job so you can choose the proper resolution for your Photoshop files, and in which file format they should be saved (save a copy of each file in the requested format).

▶ Ask your commercial printer to send you a printer profile for their press, ink, and paper. Load it into the Color Settings dialog (see page 14).

▶ Use the printer profile to create a custom proof condition, and view a soft (onscreen) proof of the image for that specific press (see pages 17–18).

▶ Make any necessary tonal adjustments, such as improving the contrast, and perform color adjustments, such as removing a color cast.

▶ Images that are to be color-separated for commercial printing should be edited in RGB Color mode and then converted to CMYK Color mode for printing. To control the conversion, use the printer profile from your print shop. (For desktop printing, keep the document in RGB Color mode.)

▶ Sharpen the image (see pages 274–278).

▶ Print a CMYK color proof and analyze it. Tweak the Photoshop image, if necessary, then print and analyze a second proof.

When you're ready to export your Photoshop image, you need to save it in the proper format for the drawing, layout, multimedia, Web page creation, or other program you're going to import it into. In this chapter, you'll learn how to save and prepare files for other programs for print output and for viewing online.

Preparing files for other applications

Photoshop to Adobe InDesign

InDesign can import PSD files directly, can separate Photoshop PDF files (RGB or CMYK), and can read ICC color profiles embedded in Photoshop files. In InDesign, you can turn Photoshop layer visibility on or off at any time and you can view Photoshop layer comps. Alpha channels, layer masks, and transparency are preserved, eliminating the need for clipping masks. And because it's in the Adobe Creative Suite, InDesign lets you use Bridge for file and color management.

If you need to place only a portion of a Photoshop image into InDesign CS4, do either of the following:

➤ Select an area of a layer, then create a new alpha channel. In InDesign, choose File > Place. In the Place dialog, check Show Import Options. In the Image Import Options dialog, choose the new **Alpha Channel**. The channel will mask parts of the image.

➤ Select an area of a layer, then create a layer mask. In InDesign, choose File > Place. In the Image Import Options dialog, show the layer that contains the **layer mask** and hide any other layers. The mask will hide parts of the image.

Photoshop to QuarkXPress

To color-separate a Photoshop image from Quark-XPress, you can convert it to CMYK Color mode before importing it into QuarkXPress, or you can let QuarkXPress read the embedded profiles and convert your RGB TIFF into a CMYK TIFF. Ask your output service provider which program to use for the conversion. With the PSD Import XTension installed, QuarkXPress 6.5 and later can also import a layered PSD file, but not layer effects. The program lets you make simple modifications to imported layers, channels, and paths.

Continued on the following page

EXPORT

27

IN THIS CHAPTER

Preparing files for other applications. .415

Saving files in the TIFF format 417

Saving files in the EPS format. 418

Saving files in the PDF format 420

Saving files for the Web. 421

Previewing optimized files. 422

Optimizing files in the GIF format . . .423

Optimizing files in the JPEG format . .425

If you need to place only a portion of a Photoshop image into QuarkXpress 7 or 8, select an area of a layer, then create a new alpha channel. In QuarkXPress, choose File > Import Picture. Choose Item > Modify, click the Picture tab, then choose the new alpha channel from the Channel menu.

Photoshop to Adobe Illustrator

Not surprisingly, files from Photoshop CS4 and Adobe Illustrator CS4 are compatible in many (but not all) respects.

► If you **drag and drop** a Photoshop selection or layer into Illustrator, the imagery will appear on the Layers panel in Illustrator as an image layer in Windows, or as a group with a generic clipping path and an image layer in the Mac OS. Opacity settings are reset to 100% but are preserved visually, the blending mode is reset to Normal, and layer and vector masks are applied to their respective layers. Transparent areas surrounding the imagery are ignored, whereas transparent areas within the imagery are filled with white.

► If you copy and **paste** a layer from Photoshop into Illustrator, layer masks are discarded.

► Via File > **Place**, you can place either a whole Photoshop image or just a single layer comp into Illustrator. If you place a Photoshop image with the Link option checked, the image will appear on the Layers panel on a single image layer, and any masks will be applied. If you embed the Photoshop image as you place it (uncheck the Link option), you'll have the option to convert layers into objects or flatten them into one layer; this choice is also available if you open a Photoshop image via File > **Open** in Illustrator.

Using the Place or Open command, if you decide to convert layers into objects, each layer will appear as an object on its own editable nested layer within a group. The Background (if any) will become a separate, opaque layer. All transparency values are preserved, and blending modes that are also available in Illustrator are preserved; both are listed as editable appearances in Illustrator. (To verify which blending modes are available in Illustrator, click the blending mode menu on the Transparency panel.) Layer masks become

opacity masks. We prefer this approach because it preserves layer transparency. In the Photoshop Import Options dialog, you can check Import Hidden Layers if you want to allow hidden layers to be imported.

► The presence of **adjustment layers** in a Photoshop image will prevent underlying Photoshop layers from becoming individual layers in Illustrator. To work around this limitation, merge any adjustment layers downward before opening or placing the file into Illustrator.

► If you decide to **flatten** Photoshop layers into one layer, all transparency, blending modes, and layer mask effects will be preserved visually, but they won't be editable as such in Illustrator.

► When you open or place a TIFF, EPS, or PSD file into Illustrator, the file resolution stays the same, but the Photoshop image adopts the **color mode** of the Illustrator file. Illustrator raster filters, raster effects, and some vector effects can be applied to imported images.

Saving files in the TIFF format

TIFF is a versatile format that most applications, including QuarkXPress and Adobe InDesign, can import. This format recognizes color profiles and works with color management options. QuarkXPress and InDesign can color-separate a CMYK TIFF.

To save a file in the TIFF format:

1. *Optional:* If your commercial printer requests it, convert the color mode of your file to Image > Mode > **CMYK Color**.

2. Choose File > **Save As**, enter a name or keep the current name, choose Format: **TIFF**, and choose a location for the file.

3. You can check **Layers** to preserve any layers in your file, but note that few image or layout programs can work with layered TIFFs, and those that don't will flatten layers upon import. You can also choose to save **Alpha Channels**, **Notes**, or **Spot Colors**.

4. *Optional:* Check ICC Profile/Embed Color Profile to include the currently embedded color profile with the file. For more about color management, see Chapter 1.

5. Click **Save**. The TIFF Options dialog opens.**A**

6. Choose an **Image Compression** method to reduce the storage size of the file. LZW and ZIP are non-lossy methods; some programs can't open TIFFs that are saved with ZIP or JPEG compression. For color separation, output service providers prefer noncompressed files (click None).

   Leave the **Pixel Order** on the default setting of **Interleaved (RGBRGB)**.

   Click **Byte Order: IBM PC** or **Macintosh**, depending on the platform the file will be used on.

   For a layered TIFF, click a **Layer Compression** method.

7. *Optional:* Check Save Image Pyramid to save multiple resolutions of the image in one file. Photoshop doesn't currently offer options for opening image pyramids, but Adobe InDesign does.

8. If your file contains transparency that you want to preserve, check **Save Transparency**. To access this option, the bottommost layer in the file must be a layer—not the Background.

9. Click OK.

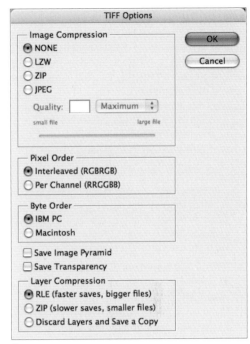

A This is the TIFF Options dialog in the Mac OS.

Saving files in the EPS format

If the drawing or page layout program you're planning to export your files to can't read Photoshop PSD or PDF files, the Photoshop EPS format is the next best option. Note that this format flattens layers and discards alpha channels and spot channels. To access it, your file can be in any color mode except Multichannel, but its color depth must be 8 bits per channel. Printing an EPS file requires a PostScript or PostScript-emulation printer.

To save a file in the EPS format:

1. *Optional:* If the file is going to be color-separated by another application and you want to see how it will be affected by the mode conversion, choose Image > Mode > CMYK Color, then choose Edit > Undo immediately.

2. Choose File > **Save As** (Ctrl-Shift-S/Cmd-Shift-S). The Save As dialog opens.

3. Enter a file name or keep the current name, choose Format: **Photoshop EPS**, and choose a location in which to save the file.

   Optional: Check ICC Profile/Embed Color Profile to have Photoshop embed the document color profile or current working color space into the file (see pages 10 and 16).

   Click Save. Note that any layers will be flattened. The EPS Options dialog opens. **A–B**

4. From the **Preview** menu, choose **TIFF** (**1 bit/pixel**) to save the file with a black-and-white preview or **TIFF** (**8 bits/pixel**) to save the file with a grayscale or color preview. Mac OS users, choose one of the "Macintosh" previews only if you're sure you won't be opening the file on another platform.

5. If the file is to be used in the Mac OS, choose **Encoding: Binary**, the default method used by PostScript printers; binary-encoded files are smaller and process more quickly than ASCII files. If the file is to be used in Windows, or for applications, PostScript printers, or printing utilities that can't handle binary files, you must choose **ASCII** or **ASCII85**. **JPEG** is the fastest encoding method, but it causes some data loss. A JPEG file can print only on a PostScript Level 2 or higher printer.

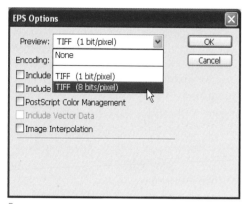

A In the EPS Options dialog in Windows, choose Preview and Encoding options.

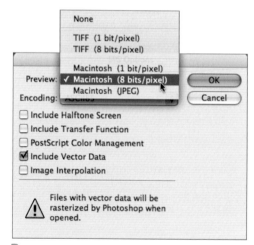

B In the EPS Options dialog in the Mac OS, choose Preview and Encoding options.

6. If you changed the frequency, angle, or dot shape settings in the Halftone Screen dialog in Photoshop, check **Include Halftone Screen**. (To get to the Halftone Screen dialog, choose File > Print, choose Output from the menu in the upper right corner of the dialog, then click Screen.)

7. The **PostScript Color Management Option** converts the file's color data to the printer's color space. Don't choose this option if you're going to import the file into another color-managed application (such as InDesign), as unpredictable color shifts may result.

8. If your document contains vector elements, such as shapes or type, check **Include Vector Data**. Although saved vector data in EPS files is available to other applications, as an alert will tell you when you reopen the file in Photoshop, the vector data will be rasterized.

9. Check **Image Interpolation** to allow other applications to resample pixels in an effort to reduce jagged edges on a low-resolution printout.

10. Click OK.

MAKING FILES COMPATIBLE

When you want to open a Photoshop (PSD) file in another application, ideally that target application should be able to read layers. To allow your PSD files to be readable by those that don't, go to Preferences > File Handling and choose Always from the Maximize PSD and PSB File Compatibility menu. A composite preview will be saved with the layered version for applications that don't support layers, and a rasterized copy of any vector art will be saved for applications that don't support vector data. Although this option produces larger files that take longer to save, it's an acceptable trade-off for the needed compatibility.

COMPRESSING FILES

To reduce the storage size of a file without discarding image data, you can use the ZIP compression command that's built into your system:

➤ To create a ZIP file in Windows, select a folder, then right-click it and choose New > Compressed (Zipped) Folder from the context menu. A new folder (with a ZIP icon) will be created. Drag the files to be compressed into the folder.

➤ To create a ZIP file in the Mac OS, Control-click a file name in the Finder and choose Create Archive of [file name] from the context menu.

Saving files in the PDF format

PDF (Portable Document Format) files can be opened in many Windows and Mac applications, as well as in Adobe Reader, Acrobat Standard, and Acrobat Professional. 8-bit and 16-bit files (not 32-bit files) in any color mode except Multichannel can be saved as a PDF. Photoshop will create one of two kinds of PDF files, depending on which preset you choose in the Save Adobe PDF dialog.

The default PDF format, Photoshop PDF, preserves image, font, layer, and vector data, but it can contain only one image per file. To create a Photoshop PDF file, Preserve Photoshop Editing Capabilities must be checked in the Save Adobe PDF dialog.

Photoshop can also create generic PDF files, which are similar in format to PDFs from graphics and page layout applications and, unlike Photoshop PDFs, can contain multiple images or pages. To save a Photoshop image as a generic PDF file, uncheck Preserve Photoshop Editing Capabilities in the Save Adobe PDF dialog. This will flatten and rasterize the image, though, so your ability to reedit it in Photoshop will be very limited.

To save a file in the PDF format:

1. Choose File > **Save As**, enter a file name or keep the current name in the File Name/Save As field, choose a location in which to save the file, choose Format: **Photoshop PDF**, then click Save. If an alert dialog appears, click OK. The Save Adobe PDF Options dialog opens.**A**

2. From the **Adobe PDF Preset** menu, choose one of the predefined settings, depending on how the file will be reproduced (press, Internet, etc.). The first two presets listed below create a large Photoshop PDF file that is compatible with Adobe Acrobat 5 and later, compress the file using JPEG at Maximum quality, and embed all fonts automatically. The above-mentioned Preserve Photoshop Editing Capabilities option is selected for both presets by default:

High Quality Print (the default preset) creates PDF files for desktop printers and color proofing devices. The color conversion is handled by the printer driver.

Press Quality is designed for high-quality pre-press output. Colors are converted to CMYK.

For these presets, Preserve Photoshop Editing Capabilities is unchecked, so they produce generic PDF files:

PDF/X-1a:2001, **PDF/X-3:2002**, and **PDF/X-4: 2008** create PDF files that will be checked for compliance with specific printing standards, to help prevent printing problems. The resulting files are compatible with Acrobat 4 and later or, in the case of PDF/X-4, compatible with Acrobat 5 and later.

Smallest File Size uses high levels of JPEG compression to produce very compact PDF files for output to the Web, e-mail, etc.

➤ Read about the currently selected preset in the Description field.

3. Click **Save PDF**, then click Yes in the alert box.

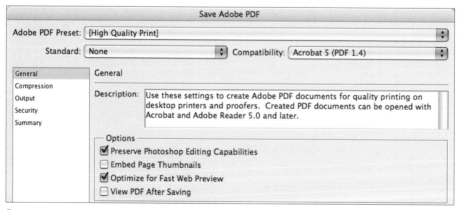

A In the Save Adobe PDF dialog, choose a preset from the Adobe PDF Preset menu.

Saving files for the Web

Issues of file size and the transmission of data come into play when preparing graphics for viewing online as opposed to for print. When you optimize your files for online viewing (resave your files within format, storage size, and color parameters), your goal is to compress your images enough that they download quickly on the Web while preserving as much of their quality as possible. The two main parameters you'll need to focus on as you optimize your files are the file size and the file format (GIF or JPEG).

File size

The length of time it takes for an image to load into a Web page is related directly to its file size. The file size, in turn, is governed by the dimensions of the image in pixels and the amount and kind of compression applied.

When choosing dimensions for your image, keep in mind that most people view the Web in a browser window that's about 1,024 pixels wide by 768 pixels high; that provides you with an upper limit. Remember also that Web browsers always display images at 100% magnification, so use the Image > Image Size command to set your image resolution to 72 ppi, and be sure to choose View > Actual Pixels to judge the image size when choosing final dimensions.

Although the GIF and JPEG formats cause a small reduction in image quality as they apply compression, the resulting smaller file sizes download more quickly on the Web, so the reduction is worthwhile. Bear in mind that some types of images are more compressible than others. For example, a document with a solid background color and a few solid-color shapes will compress a lot, whereas a large document with many color areas, textures, or patterns won't compress nearly as much. The JPEG format has greater compression power than GIF.

File format

GIF and JPEG, the two file formats most commonly used for Web graphics, are suitable for different types of images:

➤ **GIF** preserves flat colors and sharp edges (such as type) better than JPEG, but it's an 8-bit format, meaning it can save only up to 256 colors. The color restriction makes GIF more suitable for flat graphics than for continuous-tone (photographic) images, which contain more colors. For images containing transparency, GIF is your only choice, because it supports transparency whereas JPEG does not.

You don't have to use the full complement of 256 colors when saving a file in the GIF format. If you lower the color depth of a GIF file, you reduce its size and the number of colors it contains, which in turn enables it to download more quickly. (The set of colors in a GIF is called the "color table.") The color reduction may produce dithered or grainy-looking edges and duller colors, but you'll achieve the desired reduction in file size.

➤ Because it retains the full 24-bit color depth, the **JPEG** format does a better job of preserving color fidelity for continuous-tone images (such as photographs) than GIF does. Another advantage of JPEG is its compression power; it can shrink an image significantly without lowering its quality. When saving an image in JPEG format, you can choose a quality setting. Higher-quality settings produce larger files, and lower settings produce smaller ones. Unfortunately, unlike the GIF format, JPEG doesn't preserve transparency.

Each time an image is optimized in the JPEG format, some image data is lost; the greater the compression, the greater the loss. Always remember to optimize a copy of your file—not the original!

Don't panic! We'll break down the optimization steps for you next.

Previewing optimized files

In the Save for Web & Devices dialog, you'll find everything you need to optimize your graphics for the Web, including multiple previews that let you test the effects of different optimization settings.

To use the previews in the Save for Web & Devices dialog:

1. Choose File > **Save for Web & Devices** (Ctrl-Alt-Shift-S/Cmd-Opt-Shift-S). The dialog opens.**A**

2. Click the **4-Up** tab to see the original image and three previews simultaneously. Photoshop will use the current optimization options to generate the first preview (to the right of the original), then automatically generate the two other previews as variations on the current optimization settings. You can click any preview and change the optimization settings for

just that preview or choose a download speed from the **Download Speed** menu.★

3. From the **Preview** menu, choose a gamma value to be simulated onscreen (see the sidebar on page 426).★

4. After choosing settings for a GIF (see pages 423–424) or JPEG (see pages 425–426), for a more definitive test of those settings for the currently selected tab, click the **Preview** button (browser icon) at the bottom of the dialog. This will open your optimized image in the default Web browser application that's installed on your computer. Or to choose another browser that's installed in your system, from the menu next to the button, choose a browser name or choose Other and locate a browser application.

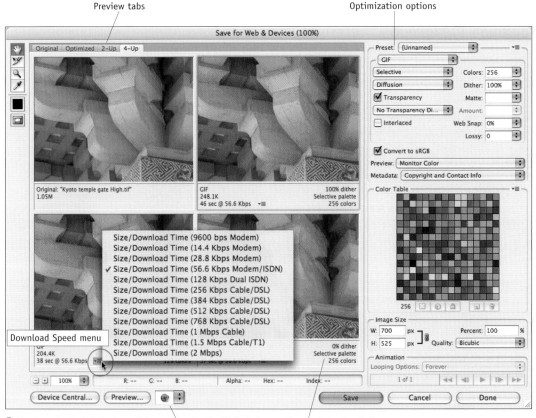

A The Save for Web & Devices dialog   Preview in [default browser] button and menu   Optimization info

Optimizing files in the GIF format

To optimize a file in the GIF format:

1. Change the resolution of your file to 72 ppi (screen resolution), resize it to the desired dimensions, and save it.

2. Choose File > **Save for Web & Devices** (Ctrl-Alt-Shift-S/Cmd-Opt-Shift-S) to open the Save for Web & Devices dialog.

3. Click the **2-Up** tab at the top of the dialog box so you can compare the original and optimized previews of the image.

4. Do either of the following:

   To optimize the file using a preset, from the **Preset** menu, choose one of the **GIF** options. Leave the preset settings as is, then click Save. The Save Optimized As dialog opens. Leave the name as is, choose a location, then click Save.

   To choose **custom** optimization settings instead, follow the remaining steps.

5. From the **Optimized File Format** menu, choose **GIF**.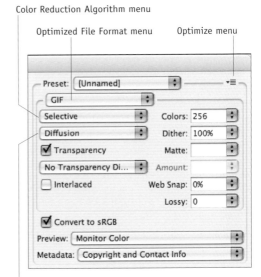

6. From the **Color Reduction Algorithm** menu, choose a method for reducing the number of colors in the image (see the sidebar at right) (**A**, next page).

7. Choose the maximum number of **Colors** for the color table by choosing a preset from the menu or by entering an exact number in the field. The fewer colors, the smaller the file size.

8. Choose a method from the **Dither Algorithm** menu. Dithering is a process by which Photoshop mixes dots of a few different colors to simulate more colors. Although the Diffusion option produces a larger file, it also yields the best compromise between quality and file size. With the No Dither option chosen, gradients may exhibit banding.

   Also choose a **Dither** percentage. A high dither value will produce more color simulation and a larger file size (**B**, next page).

9. Check **Transparency** to preserve any fully transparent pixels in the image. The Transparency option allows for the creation of nonrectangular image borders. With Transparency unchecked, transparent pixels will be filled with the current color chosen on the Matte menu. Regardless of

Continued on the following page

Color Reduction Algorithm menu

Optimized File Format menu   Optimize menu

Dither Algorithm menu

A Choose optimization options for the GIF file format in the Save for Web & Devices dialog.

THE COLOR REDUCTION ALGORITHMS

► **Perceptual** generates a color table based on the colors currently in the document, with a bias toward how people actually perceive colors.

► **Selective**, the default option, generates a color table based on the colors currently in the image, with a bias toward preserving flat colors, Web-safe colors, and overall color integrity.

► **Adaptive** generates a color table based on the part of the color spectrum that represents the most colors in the document. This choice produces a slightly larger optimized file.

► **Restrictive (Web)** generates a color table by changing the image colors to those that are available on the standard Web-safe palette. (This palette contains only the 216 colors that the Windows and Macintosh browser palettes have in common.) This choice produces the least number of colors and the smallest file size but not necessarily the best-looking image.

the Transparency setting, the GIF format can't preserve semitransparent pixels.

Keep the **Interlaced** option unchecked.

10. To control how semitransparent pixels along the edge of an image blend with the background of a Web page (such as on the edges of anti-aliased elements), choose a **Matte** option. Set the Matte color to the color of the Web page background—if you happen to know what that color is. Any soft-edged effect (such as a Drop Shadow) on top of transparent areas will fill with the current Matte color. If the background color is unknown, set Matte to None; this will create a hard, jagged edge.**D**

Another option is to choose **Matte: None**, then check Transparency and choose one of three options from the **Transparency Dither Algorithm** menu. These effects will look the same on any background. **Diffusion** applies a random pattern to semitransparent pixels and diffuses it across adjacent pixels. This method usually produces the most subtle results and allows you to set the dithering amount. **Pattern** applies a halftone pattern to the semitransparent pixels. **Noise** applies a pattern similar to Diffusion without affecting neighboring pixels.

11. *Optional:* You can adjust the **Lossy** value to further reduce the file size. As the name "Lossy" implies, this option discards some image data, but the savings in file size may justify the slightly reduced image quality.

12. Check **Convert to sRGB** to convert the optimized color to sRGB, the standard profile for Web browsers. ★

13. From the **Preview** menu, choose a gamma value for the preview to simulate (see the sidebar on page 426). ★

14. From the **Metadata** menu, choose which metadata is to be saved with the optimized file, such as Copyright and Contact Info. This data was assigned to your image via Bridge or your camera or in File Info. ★

15. Follow steps 2–4 on page 422 to preview your settings, make any adjustments, then click Save. The Save Optimized As dialog opens. Leave the name as is, choose a location, then click Save.

A This image was optimized as a GIF with 32 colors using the Selective algorithm but no dither.

B This the same image optimized with 100% dither.

C This image was optimized as a GIF with Transparency checked and Matte set to black (a thin black line appears along the edge of each shape).

D This image was optimized as a GIF with Transparency checked and Matte set to None (the shapes have hard edges).

Optimizing files in the JPEG format

JPEG is the best format for optimizing continuous-tone imagery (photographs, paintings, gradients, blends, and the like) because it saves a file's 24-bit color—and those colors can be seen and enjoyed by any viewer whose display is set to thousands or millions of colors. Two drawbacks to JPEG are that its compression methods discard image data and that it doesn't preserve transparency.

To optimize an image in the JPEG format:

1. Change the resolution of your file to 72 ppi (screen resolution), resize it to the desired dimensions, and save it.

2. Choose File > **Save for Web & Devices** (Ctrl-Alt-Shift-S/Cmd-Opt-Shift-S) to open the Save for Web & Devices dialog (**A**, page 422).

3. Click the **2-Up** tab at the top of the dialog so you can compare the original and optimized previews of the image.

4. Do either of the following:

   To optimize the file using a preset, from the **Preset** menu, **A** choose one of the **JPEG** options. Leave the preset settings as is, then click Save. The Save Optimized As dialog opens. Leave the name as is, choose a location, then click Save.

   To choose **custom** optimization settings instead, follow the remaining steps.

5. From the **Optimized File Format** menu, choose **JPEG**.

6. Do either of the following:

   From the **Compression Quality** menu, choose a quality level for the optimized image **B–C** (and **A**, next page).

   Choose a **Quality** value for the desired level of compression.

   ► The higher the compression quality, the better the image quality—and the larger the file size.

7. Increase the **Blur** value to lessen the visibility of JPEG artifacts that arise from the JPEG compression method, and to reduce the file size. Be careful not to overblur the image, though, or the details will become too soft. The Blur setting can be lowered later to reclaim some diminished sharpness.

Continued on the following page

Compression Quality menu

Optimized File Format menu   Optimize menu

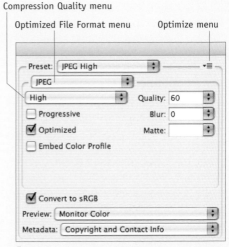

A Choose optimization options for a JPEG file in the Save for Web & Devices dialog.

B This image was optimized as a JPEG with High Quality.

C This is the image optimized as a JPEG with Medium Quality.

8. Choose a **Matte** color to be substituted for areas of transparency in the original image. If you choose None, transparent areas will become white in the optimized image.

   Note: The JPEG format doesn't support transparency. To have the Matte color simulate transparency, make it the same solid color as the background of the Web page (you need to know what that color is). Click the Matte color swatch, and mix the color via the Color Picker.

9. Leave the **Progressive** and **Embed Color Profile** ★ options unchecked.

10. Check **Convert to sRGB** to convert the optimized color to sRGB, the standard profile for Web browsers. ★

11. From the **Preview** menu, choose a gamma value for the preview to simulate (see the sidebar at right). ★

12. From the **Metadata** menu, choose which metadata is to be saved with the optimized file, such as Copyright and Contact Info. This data was assigned to your image via Bridge or your camera or in File Info. ★

13. *Optional:* Check Optimized to produce a smaller file size.

14. Follow steps 2–4 on page 422 to preview your settings, make any adjustments, then click **Save**. The Save Optimized As dialog opens. Keep the current name, choose a location, then click Save.

A And this is the image optimized as a JPEG with Low Quality.

CHOOSING A PREVIEW OPTION ★

Monitor Color	No gamma change
Macintosh (No Color Management)	Mac 1.8 gamma
Windows (No Color Management)	Windows 2.2 gamma (the most common gamma)
Use Document Profile	Matches the gamma in an assigned document profile, if any

CREATING AN OPTIMIZATION PRESET

To save a current (Unnamed) set of optimization settings, choose Save Settings from the Optimize menu ▼≡ in the Save for Web & Devices dialog. In the Save Optimization Settings dialog, enter a name (in Windows, include the .irs extension), locate and open the Adobe Photoshop CS4 > Presets > Optimized Settings folder, then click Save. Your saved set is now available on the Preset menu in the Save for Web & Devices dialog for all files.

INDEX

The entries in this index pertain to Photoshop, except when Camera Raw or Bridge are listed.

8 Bits/Channel mode, 21
16 Bits/Channel mode
    advantages of, 21
    producing with Camera Raw, 234
    sending to printer, 410

A

Adjustment Brush (Camera Raw), 252
adjustment layers, 175–179
    applying to multiple documents, 222
    Black & White, 206–207
    Brightness/Contrast, 189
    clipping, 178
    Color Balance, 211–212
    color correction using, 203–221
    creating, 175–176
    Curves, 218–221
    deleting, 179
    dodging and burning with
        neutral, 190
    editing layer mask for, 180, 181
    editing settings for, 177
    hiding and showing effect of, 177,
        178, 180
    Hue/Saturation, 213
    Levels, 186–188, 214–217, 271, 367
    merging, 179, 416
    Photo Filter, 260
    Posterize, 183
    resetting, 178
    saving presets for, 178–179
    screening back image with, 188
    techniques for working with, 180
    Threshold, 182
    Vibrance, 208–210
    viewing previous state of, 177
Adjustments panel, 83, 175–179
Adobe Creative Suite programs. *See
        also* Bridge; Illustrator; Photoshop
    Bridge and, 33
    Illustrator, 58–59, 416
    InDesign, 415
    managing files among, 392
    saving color settings for, 14
    synchronizing color with other, 12
Adobe Every-line Composer, 361
Adobe RGB color space, 5–6, 10

Adobe Single-line Composer, 361
alert dialogs
    current swatches not saved, 196
    Embedded Profile Mismatch, 60
    missing font, 60
    resetting, 388
    saving unsaved changes to
        document, 32
    Smart Filter, 336
    unsynchronized color settings, 12, 13
    when editing Smart Object layer, 314
algorithms
    auto color correction, 215
    color reduction, 423
aligning
    gradients, 370
    layers, 117, 164
    paragraphs, 361
    Pattern Overlay effect, 328
    type, 352, 353
alignment buttons
    for layers, 164
    for type, 352, 353, 361
alpha channel
    combining with selection, 140
    deleting, 141
    displaying, 140
    duplicating, 140
    effect of EPS format on, 418
    exporting partial image to InDesign
        using, 415
    file size of, 139
    illustrated, 3
    loading onto image as selection, 140
    reshaping masks for, 141
animated zoom function, 67
anti-aliasing, 129, 352
appending swatches library, 196
Apple RGB color space, 10
Application bar
    Arrange Documents menu on, 64,
        153
    illustrated, 76
    launching Bridge from, 33
    screen mode menu on, 68
    using, 76
Application frame, 61–62

Arrange Documents menu, 64, 153
Artistic filters, 341–342
aspect ratios
    constraining marquee, 106
    preserving when cropping, 107
Assign Profile dialog, 16
Auto Color Correction Options dialog,
    214–215

B

Background (on Layers panel)
    about, 109
    choosing color for, 191, 195, 197
    converting from layer into, 112
    converting into layer, 112
    enlarged canvas area filled with color
        of, 105
    for new document, 24
    transforming, 311
    turning selected pixels into layer
        from, 111
Batch Rename dialog, 52
Bevel layer effect, 324–325, 329
bit depth, 333, 336
Bitmap color mode, 4
bitmap images, 2
black point data, 7, 17
blemishes
    retouching, 290–294
    retouching (Camera Raw), 241
blending
    imagery with layer masks, 154–155
    layers, 298–301
    seams on layer masks, 160
    Smart Filters, 337
blending modes, 198–202
    about, 198
    Basic, 198
    changing for adjustment layer, 180
    changing for layer, 118
    Comparative, 202
    Component, 202
    Contrast, 201–202
    Darken, 199
    enhancing gradients with, 374
    HSL, 202
    illustrated, 198–202

blending modes *(continued)*
Lighten, 200
selecting for layers, 298
shortcuts for changing, 198
Blending Options (Layer Style dialog),
300–301, 323
blurring
capturing motion with, 268–269
replicating depth of field by, 265–267
borders, hand-painted, 376–377
bounding box for type, 362
Bridge, 33–60
batch renaming files via, 52
collections of thumbnails in, 54–55
comparing image previews in, 42–43
contact sheets via, 380–381
Content panel in, 36–37, 40–42, 45,
50–51
copying files via, 47
creating folders in, 51
deleting files via, 51
displaying and selecting images
in, 40
downloading images via, 34–35
exporting cache for, 56
Favorites panel, 36, 37
filtering thumbnails in, 49
Filter panel, 36, 37, 49
finding files via, 53
Folders panel, 40
full screen previews in, 42
hosting Camera Raw, 236
illustrated, 37
JPEGs opened in Camera Raw
dialog, 98
Keywords panel, 57
labeling thumbnails in, 48
launching, 33
loupe for examining thumbnails in,
42–43, 398
metadata displayed in, 36, 40, 45
moving files via, 47
opening files into Photoshop from, 44
opening PDF and Adobe Illustrator
files via, 58–59
Open Recent Files menu, 44
panels and panes in, 36–39, 46
PDF presentations via, 382–383
preference for launching, 33, 399
preference settings for, 397–399
previewing thumbnails in, 40–43

purging cache files for, 56
quality for previews in, 41
rating thumbnails in, 48
renaming files via, 51–52
resetting workspace in, 47
Review Mode, 43, 48
saving custom workspaces for, 47
sorting thumbnails in, 49
synchronizing color settings via, 12
Thumbnail Size slider, 37, 39, 46
thumbnail stacks in, 50–51
View Content buttons, 45
window for, 36–37
workspaces, choosing, 38–39
workspaces, customizing, 44–47
brightness
adjusting layer, 189
calibrating display, 7
defined, 194
modifying for raw file, 244, 245
**Brightness/Contrast adjustment
layer,** 189
brushes, 223–229
customizing presets for, 226–229
editing layer masks with, 181
methods for selecting, 84
options for, on Brushes panel, 225
preference for color in cursor when
scaling, 394
Brushes panel
about, 84
basic instructions for using, 225
customizing presets for, 226–229
brush presets
customizing, 226–229
previewing, 226
restoring saved settings to, 229
saving, 228
selecting from Brush Preset picker,
84, 223
brush strokes
adding texture to, 228
adjusting placement of pigment
in, 227
controlling opacity of, 227
customizing tip for, 226–228
Brush Strokes filters, 343
Brush tool
blending layer mask seams with, 160
choosing settings for, 223–224
creating Quick Mask with, 142–143

cursors for, 394
dodging or burning with, 190
painting with, 223–224
burning and dodging, 190
buying a digital camera, 20

C
cache (Bridge)
preferences for, 399
purging files from, 56, 399
calibrating displays, 7–9
Camera Raw, 233–256
Adjustment Brush tool, 252–253
Basic tab, 238, 242–245
Crop tool, 240
Detail tab, 238, 250
extensions for raw files, 236
function of buttons in, 239
HSL/Grayscale tab, 238, 248–249
JPEG files in, 98, 235
key features of, 233–235
opening files from, 255
opening photos as Smart Objects
from, 256
opening photos into, 237
preferences for opening photos
into, 236
producing 16-bit images from, 234
raw vs. JPEG files in, 235
resetting settings in, 242
retouching photos in, 241
saving and applying settings in, 251
saving files via, 255
selecting host for, 236
setting preferences for, 392
Settings menu, 242
Spot Removal tool, 241
Straighten tool, 240
synchronizing settings for multiple
photos in, 254
tab icons, 238
TIFF files in, 235
tonal adjustments in, 244
Tone Curve tab, 246–247
tools, 239
updating raw formats, 15
Workflow Options in, 241
zooming in, 239
Camera Raw badge, 236
Camera Raw dialog, 237–238
cameras. *See* digital cameras

canvas
changing size of, 102, 105
enlarging or reducing when
cropping, 105–106
pixels outside live area of, 149
rotating and resetting, 67
Canvas Size command, 102
card readers, 34–35
channels. See also alpha channel
adjusting in RGB image, 216–217
defaults per image mode, 3
defined, 2–3
displaying channel selection, 140
duplicating alpha, 140
enhancing contrast in, 215
loading alpha channel as
selection, 140
on Histogram panel, 184
preferences for, 390
saving selection to, 139
type in spot color, 368
Channels panel, 85, 139
Character panel
about, 86
font controls on, 356
illustrated, 86, 351
kerning and tracking controls on, 357
leading control on, 358
opening, 357
shifting character baseline, 359
type style control on, 359
units of measure for, 359
characters. See also type, Character
panel, Paragraph panel
selecting, 354
shifting baseline of, 359
transforming individual, 362
Clipboard
about, 148
copying selections via, 148–150
dimensions in New dialog and, 25
pasting into selection, 150
clipping adjustment layers, 178
clipping masks, 308, 364
clipping shadows and highlights, 244
Clone Source panel
about, 86
using, 156–157
Clone Stamp tool, 156–157, 282–283
closing
documents, 32

panels, 70
CMYK color mode. See also CMYK
images
about, 3, 4
choosing prepress profile for,
413–414
simulating for soft proofs, 18
CMYK images
Curves adjustments layer in, 220
importing Illustrator file
containing, 59
Levels adjustment layer in, 217
collapsing/expanding
dock into icons/icon names, 70
Tools panel, 80
collections (Bridge), 54–55
Collections panel (Bridge)
about, 36, 37
displaying and creating collections
in, 54–55
color adjustments, 203–222
applying to multiple images, 222
Color Balance adjustment layer for,
211–212
converting layers to grayscale,
206–209
correcting color automatically,
214–215
Curves adjustment layers for,
218–221
Hue/Saturation adjustment layers
for, 213
Levels adjustment layer for, 216–217
Match Color command for, 281
Photo Filter adjustment layer
for, 260
Solid Color fill layers for, 205
Standard Screen Mode for, 203
Vibrance adjustment layer for,
208–210
Color Balance adjustment layer,
211–212
color blindness, 18
color casts. See color adjustments
color labels. See labels
color management, 1–18
accounting for color blindness, 18
calibrating displays, 7–9
changing color profiles, 16
channels and, 2–3
choosing Photoshop color space,
10–11

color correction workflow, 414
customizing policies for, 13
displaying color images on screen, 2
downloading printer profiles, 14–15
Photoshop color modes for, 3–4
proofing colors onscreen, 17–18
setting camera's color space, 5–6
synchronizing color settings, 12
turning off for printer in Mac OS, 412
turning off for printer in Windows, 411
Color Management panel (Print
dialog), 407–409
color models
for Color panel, 87, 194
for Web output, 196
selecting for Info panel readouts, 89
color modes. See document color
modes and specific color modes
Color Overlay effect, 327
Color panel
about, 87
features of, 191
out-of-gamut indicator on, 2
using, 194
Color Picker, 191, 192
color profiles
changing, 16
commercial printing and, 413–414
controlling color with, 11
current profile listed on Status bar, 6
defined, 5
embedding in file, 16, 28, 399
missing, 60
Color Range command
make selections using, 130–131
selections with Magic Wand tool
vs., 128
Color Replacement tool, 288–289
colors. See also color adjustments,
color management
adding with gradient fill layer,
369–370
choosing before selecting filter, 334
choosing Foreground and
Background, 191–195, 197
color libraries, 193
Color panel, 191, 194
Color Picker, 192
Color Replacement tool, 288–289
copying as hexidecimals, 197
correcting color casts, 211–212

colors *(continued)*

editing for gradient preset, 373

Eyedropper tool for sampling, 197

matching between documents, 280–281

PANTONE, 193

replacing in image, 284–286

restoring to layer selectively, 209

selecting via Color Range, 130–131

smudging, 230

Solid Color fill layer, 205

surrounding the image, 69

Swatches panel, 195–196

Color Sampler tool (Camera Raw), 239

color separations, 413–414

Color Settings dialog, 414

alerts to unsynchronized color settings in, 12, 13

choosing color setting presets, 10–11

illustrated, 11

saving custom color settings, 14

setting policies for, 13

color space

changing for Camera Raw images, 241

choosing for Photoshop, 10–11

setting camera's, 5–6, 20

ColorMatch RGB color space, 10

Color Replacement tool, 288

ColorSync RGB color space, about, 10

combining images, 145–164

aligning and distributing layers, 164

blending seams on layer masks, 160

cloning, 156–157

copying and pasting selections in documents, 148–149

copying layers between files, 152–153

dragging and dropping selections between documents, 147

duplicating selections, 146

matching image dimensions, 151

moving selection contents, 145

pasting into selections, 150

rulers, guides, and grids for, 161–164

stitching photos, 158–159

transferring selections via Clipboard, 148

commands

Canvas Size, 102

Color Range, 128, 130–131

Crop, 106

Crop and Straighten Photos, 108

Extras, 161

Flatten Image, 122

Free Transform, 312, 362

hiding and showing menu, 72–73

Image > Adjustments submenu, 175

Layer Via Copy or Cut, 111, 149

Match Color, 280–281

merging layer, 120–121

Photo Filter, 260

Photomerge, 158–159

Refine Edge, 132–134

Replace Color, 284–286

Replace Contents, 315

Select > Modify submenu, 134

Shadows/Highlights, 257–259

Undo, 88

used for selections, 144

commercial printing

selecting color profiles for, 413–414

softproofs for, 18

workflow for, 414

compatibility

between Photoshop and Adobe Illustrator files, 416

Camera Raw formats and, 233

preferences, 392

PSD and PSB files, 419

compressing files,

for Web output, 421

GIF, 423–424

in Windows and Mac OS, 419

JPEG, 425–426

TIFF, 417

contact sheets, 380–381

context menus

for Layers panel, 115

using, 78

Contour preset picker, 329

contrast. *See* tonal adjustments

Convert to Profile dialog, 16

copying

alpha channels, 140

color as hexidecimals, 197

files in Bridge, 47

filter effects between Smart Object layers, 337

layer effects, 330

layer mask to another layer, 306

layers, 111, 121

layers between files, 152–153

matching dimensions of two files when, 151

selections, 146–149

Creative Suite. *See* Adobe Creative Suite programs

Crop and Straighten Photos command, 108

Crop command, 106

crop marks, 410

cropping, 103–107

Crop and Trim commands for, 106

enlarging canvas when, 105

image to specific size, 104

image with Crop tool, 103–105, 107

in Camera Raw, 240

matching image dimensions by, 151

preserving aspect ratio when, 107

scanned images, 23

CRT displays, 7

Cursors preferences, 394

Curves adjustment layer, 218–221

Curves Display Options dialog, 218

Customize Proof Condition dialog

CMYK simulation for soft proofs, 18

rendering intents for, 18

simulating inkjet printer, 17

Custom Shape tool, 378–379

D

Delete Workspace dialog, 75

deleting

adjustment layers, 179

alpha channels, 141

color profiles, 16

custom workspaces, 75

files, 51

filter masks, 337

history states, 168

layer comps, 386

layer effects, 330

layer masks, 307

layers and layer groups, 116

layer styles, 332

Photoshop Settings file, 387

presets from picker or panel, 402

ruler guides, 163

selected pixels, 135

Smart Filters, 337, 339

snapshots, 171

swatches from Swatches panel, 195

workspaces, 75

density of layer mask, 304, 366

depth of field, replicating blurring of, 265–267

desaturate layer, 206–210

deselecting/reselecting selections, 135

dialogs. *See* alert dialogs *and specific dialogs*

digital cameras
buying and using, 20
downloading photos via Bridge from, 34–35
extensions for raw file names, 236
noise and, 250
pixel count of images from, 97–98
raw files from, 233–235
setting color space for, 5–6, 20
shooting photos for panoramas, 158
tonal values captured by, 234
use of white balance in, 243

displays
calibrating, 7–9, 203
representing color on screen, 2
types of, 7

distorting
layers and layer groups, 310–312
using Distort filters, 346

distortion, lens, correcting for, 272–273

distributing layers, 164

DNG files, 255

docking document windows, 63

docks, panel
adjusting, 71
collapsing, 70
displaying panels on, 69

document color modes
about, 3–4
adopted by file exported to Illustrator, 416
applying filters and, 333
preserving layers when switching, 110, 336
setting for new document, 24
Smart Filters and, 336

documents
closing, 32
creating from history state or snapshot, 171
creating Photoshop, 24–25
data in Status bar about, 31

dragging and dropping layers between, 152–153
dragging and dropping selections between, 147
duplicating selections within, 146
exporting, 415–426
grids, displaying in, 162
matching zoom or location for multiple, 66
moving linked layers in, 309
new versions of, 30
opening PDF and Illustrator files as new, 58–59
placing vector art in, 27
presets for new, 26
printing, 405–414
reverting to last version of, 29
rulers in, 161, 163
saving, 28–30
Snap feature for, 162
transferring selections between, 147–148

document windows
arranging, 64
docking as tabs, 63
drag-copying layers between floating and tabbed, 152–153
floating all open, 63
restoring to tabs, 64
zooming in and out in, 65
zooming in multiple, 67

dodging and burning, 190

downloading
images with Photo Downloader, 34–35
printer profiles, 14–15
updates for Camera Raw, 238

Drop Shadow layer effect, 320–321

Duotone color mode, 4, 413

duotones, 413

duplicating. *See* copying

Dust & Scratches filter, 295

E

edges
anti-aliasing and, 129, 352
contouring Bevel and Emboss layer effect, 325
feathering, 124, 146
modifying for layer mask, 304
refining, 132–134

removing pixels from, 148
sharpening for raw images, 250

editable type. *See* type

editing
adjustment layer masks, 181
adjustment layer settings, 177
gradient mask, 370
layer effects, 318
layer masks, 303–305
selecting type for, 354
Smart Collections, 54
Smart Filter settings, 336
Smart Object layers, 256, 314–315
type layer, 352–353, 354
unavailable for rasterized type, 351, 364

effects. *See* layer effects

Elliptical Marquee tool, 124, 138, 375

Embedded Profile Mismatch alert dialog, 60

embedding
color profile in file, 16, 28, 399
files as Smart Objects, 27, 256, 314–315
watermarks in file, 378–379

Emboss layer effect, 323, 324–325, 329

EPS files
opening in Photoshop, 59
saving files as, 418

Eraser tool, 231

erasing pixels, 231–232

EXIF metadata, 392

exiting Photoshop, 32

exporting, 415–426
Bridge cache to current folder, 56, 399
content to Web, 421–426
document to TIFF format, 417
file in EPS format, 418–419
files to other applications, 415–416
layers to separate files, 122
PDFs, 420

exposure, 257–264
adjusting for raw files, 244, 245
correcting via Layers panel, 261
evaluating image's, 257
histograms, reading for, 185
Lighting Effects filter to change, 262–264
shadow and highlight corrections for, 257–259
verifying with histograms, 20

extensions. *See also* files
  appending file, 392
  Internet connections for specific, 396
Extras command, 161
Eyedropper tool, 197
eyes
  correcting red-eye in, 296
  removing wrinkles around, 293
  retouching bags under, 294
  whitening, 286

F

fading
  edge of image layers, 154–155
  effects, 340
  type, 366
feathering
  layer masks, 304, 305
  selection edges, 124
File Handling preferences, 392, 419
files. *See also* raw file *and specific file types*
  alpha channels and size of, 139
  assigning keywords to (Bridge), 57
  changing color profile of, 16
  compatible formats for Camera Raw, 233
  copying layers between, 152–153
  creating new version of, 30
  deleting, via Bridge, 51
  DNG, 255
  embedding color profile in, 16, 28
  EPS, 29, 418–419
  exporting document layers as separate, 122
  exporting to other applications, 415–416
  flattening and saving, 122
  formats for, 19, 21, 29
  GIF, 421, 423–424
  JPEG, 19, 29, 421
  locating in Explorer/Finder, 47
  matching image dimensions of, 151
  methods for opening, 56
  missing fonts, profiles, or plug-ins, 60
  moving and copying via Bridge, 47
  opening directly into Camera Raw, 236–238
  opening from Bridge into Photoshop, 44

packaging as PDF presentations, 382–383
PDF, 420
Photoshop Settings, 387
PICT, 29
previewing optimized, 422
printing, 406–412
proprietary camera extensions for raw, 236
PSB format for large, 19, 25, 29
PSD, 19, 29
purging cache, 56
raw, 20, 233–235
reducing size of layered, 110, 120–122
renaming via Bridge, 51–52
reopening recent via Bridge, 44
saving, 28–30
saving and compatibility preferences for, 392
searching for via Bridge, 53
sidecar (raw files), 233
storage size of, 31
TIFF, 29, 417
watermarks in, 378–379, 381, 382
Fill dialog, 174, 316
fill layers
  applying tint with, 205
  gradient, 369–370
  pattern, 204
  solid color, 205
Filter Gallery, 334–335
filter masks. *See* Smart Filters
filters, 333–350. *See also* Filter Gallery; Smart Filters
  applying, 333–340
  Artistic, 341–342
  availability for color mode or bit depth, 333, 336
  Brush Strokes, 343
  choosing colors before selecting, 334
  creating mask for, 337
  creating watercolor with, 350
  Cutout, 183
  Distort, 346
  Dust & Scratches, 295
  fading effect gradually, 340
  Find Edges, 349
  Gaussian Blur, 270, 335
  Lens Blur, 265–267

  Lens Correction, 272–273
  Lighting Effects, 262–264
  mastering techniques for, 338–340
  Median, 350
  Minimum, 350
  Motion Blur, 268–269
  Pixelate, 344
  reducing effect with History Brush tool, 339
  Render, 344
  sharpening, 274–278
  shortcuts for reapplying, 334
  Sketch, 345–346
  Smart Filters, 336–337
  Smart Sharpen, 274–276
  Stylize, 347
  Surface Blur, 287
  Texture, 348
  turning photos into tinted drawing using, 349
  Unsharp Mask, 274, 277–278
Find dialog (Bridge)**,** 53
Flatten Image command, 122
flattening layers
  EPS format and, 418
  file size and, 110
  saving flattened copy of file, 28, 122
  steps for, 122
  using Smart Object layers vs., 315
  when exporting file to Illustrator, 416
flipping
  clone source overlay, 157
  images, 107
  layers, 117
floating
  document windows, 63, 152–153
  panels and groups, 71
focusing techniques, 265–278
  about, 265
  correcting lens distortion, 272–273
  Lens Blur filter, 265–267
  Motion Blur filter, 268–269
  sharpening filters as, 274–278
  vignettes as, 270–271
folders
  creating (Bridge), 51
  exporting Bridge cache to current, 56, 399
  location of plug-in, 396
  moving files to other (Bridge), 47
  swatch library locations, 196

fonts, changing, 356
fonts, missing, 60
Foreground color, 191–195, 197
frames for images, 377
frame-shaped selections, 138
free-form selections, 125
Free Transform command, 312, 362
Full Screen mode, 68, 390
fx icon, 317, 319, 320

G

gamma settings, 7
Gamut Warning command, 394
Gamut Warning on Colors panel, 192
Gaussian Blur filter, 270, 335
General preferences
  Bridge, 398
  Photoshop, 388–389
GIF files, 421, 423–424
Gradient Editor dialog, 372–373
Gradient Fill dialog, 369, 370
Gradient Overlay layer effect, 323,
    327, 329
gradients, 369–374
  creating and editing presets for,
    372–373
  defined, 369
  enhancing with blending modes, 374
  fill layers, 369–370
  Gradient tool, 371
  moving on layer mask, 160
  on filter mask, 340
  on layer masks, 154–155
  on type layer masks, 366
Gradient tool, 371
Grayscale color mode, 4
grid, document, 162, 396
Grow command, 134
guides, 163, 396
Guides, Grid & Slices preferences, 396

H

hand-painted image borders, 376–377
Hand tool, 66
Healing Brush tool, 290–292
hiding/showing
  adjustment layers, 178
  all panels, 69
  Application frame, 61, 62
  effect of adjustment layers, 178, 180
  filter effects, 334

grids, 162
layer comps, 385
layer effects, 318, 319
layer masks, 307
layers, 116, 121
menu commands, 72–73
panel as icon, 70
selection marquees, 137
Smart Filter effects, 337
Tool Tips, 82
Histogram panel, 184–185
  8- vs. 16-bit images and, 21
  about, 87
  displaying shadows and highlights
    on, 257–258
  interpreting, 185
  monitoring tonal ranges with, 82,
    184–185, 244
  updating, 184
histograms
  for Levels adjustment layer, 186–187
  in Camera Raw dialog, 242, 244
  interpreting, 185
  on digital cameras, 20
  viewing tonal range, 82, 184–185, 244
history, 165–174
  changing history states, 167
  creating documents from history
    state, 171
  deleting and clearing history
    states, 168
  filling selection or layer with history
    state, 174
  History Brush tool, 172–173, 339
  history log, 388
  linear and nonlinear modes for,
    165–166
  making snapshot current state, 171
  maximum number of states, 166, 393
  snapshots, 169–171, 173
History Brush tool
  reducing filter effect with, 339
  using, 172–173
History panel, 165–174
  about, 88, 165
  changing states on, 167
  clearing, 168
  layer visibility as states on, 166
  linear mode/nonlinear mode,
    165–166
  options on, 165–166

history states. *See* history
Horizontal Type tool
  creating presets for, 358
  selecting characters, 354
  using, 351, 352, 353
hue
  adjusting in Camera Raw, 248
  adjusting via Hue/Saturation, 213
  adjusting via Replace Color, 284
  blending mode, 202
  defined, 194
Hue/Saturation adjustment layer, 213

I

ICC printer/paper profiles, 14
icons
  fx, 317, 319, 320
  hiding and showing panels as, 70
  non-Web-safe, 192
  out-of-gamut, 2, 192
  panel, illustrated, 78
  reconfiguring panels that are, 70–71
Illustrator, Adobe
  exporting files to, 416
  importing type from, 355
  opening files in Photoshop, 58–59
  pasting AI art into Photoshop, 59
  placing AI art into Photoshop, 27
images. *See also* combining images;
    thumbnails; tonal adjustments
  16-bit, 21
  adding motion blur to, 268–269
  adjusting color for multiple, 222
  canvas size for, 102
  capturing with scanners, 23
  changing zoom levels in, 66
  comparing previews of (Bridge), 42
  contact sheet of, 380–381
  converting to tinted drawing, 349
  correcting lens distortion for, 272–273
  cropping in Camera Raw, 240
  cropping in Photoshop, 103–107
  downloading, 34–35
  editing Smart Object, 256
  embedding watermarks in, 378–379
  erasing pixels on, 231–232
  file resolution of, 22–23
  filters applied to, 333
  flattening layers of completed, 28, 122
  flipping, 107
  histogram views of, 184–185

images *(continued)*
layer comps for, 384–386
layer effects recommended for types of, 319
light adjustments for, 262–264
masking, 305
matching dimensions of files when copying, 151
moving magnified, in document window, 66
moving separately from layer masks, 306
opening into Camera Raw, 236
packaging as PDF presentations, 382–383
pasting Illustrator art into, 59
placing PDF or Illustrator file in, 27
preserving aspect ratio for cropped, 107
previewing in Bridge, 40–41
quality of JPEG vs. raw, 235
Review Mode for (Bridge), 43
rotating precisely, 108
saving for Web, 421
screening back, 188
size and resolution vs. pixel count, 101
sorting thumbnails of (Bridge), 49
stitching together, 158–159
straightening, 108
viewing without current adjustments, 177
vignettes for, 270–271, 375
Image Size dialog, 98–100
Import PDF dialog, 58
InDesign, 415
Indexed Color mode, 4
Info panel
about, 89
out-of-gamut indicator on, 2
tool information found in, 79, 82
Info Panel Options dialog, 89
inkjet printers
document color mode for, 405
finding profiles for, 15
Print dialog settings for, 407–409
properties and page setup for, 406
rendering intents favored by, 18
simulating color output onscreen, 17
Inner Glow layer effect, 322
Inner Shadow layer effect, 320–321

Interface preferences, 390–391
inverting
alpha channel, 140
layer mask, 304
selection, 137

J
JPEG files
about, 19, 29, 421
in Camera Raw, 98, 235, 236–238
optimizing images as, 425–426
raw files vs., 235
justification of type, 361

K
kerning type, 357
keyboard shortcuts
assigning custom, 73
for Brush tool, 224
for Camera Raw tools, 239
for changing blending modes, 198
for filling a selection or layer, 316
for layer masks, 181
for Photoshop tools, 80–82
for reapplying filters, 334
for Refine Edge dialog, 132
for selecting type, 354
for zooming in and out, 65
Keyboard Shortcuts and Menus dialog, 72–73
keystoning, 272
keywords (Bridge)
creating and assigning to files, 57
setting preferences for, 399
Keywords panel (Bridge), 36, 37, 57

L
Lab color, 2, 4
labels
assigning menu colors as, 72–73
color behind visibility icon on Layers panel, 112, 119
preferences (Bridge), 399
thumbnail (Bridge), 48
Lasso tools
compared, 144
Quick Selection tool vs., 126
selections using, 125
launching
Bridge, 33, 399
Photo Downloader, 398
Photoshop, 1

layer comps, 384–386
Layer Comps Options dialog, 384
Layer Comps panel, 90, 384–385
Layer Comps to Files dialog, 386
layer effects. *See also* layer styles
Bevel and Emboss, 324–325, 329
Color Overlay, 327
copying and moving, 330
Drop Shadow and Inner Shadow, 320–321, 323
generic instructions for applying, 317–319
Gradient Overlay, 323, 327, 329
hiding and showing, 318, 319
imagery suitable for, 319
Layers panel features for, 319
linking to layer, 315
mastering, 323
Outer or Inner Glow, 322
Pattern Overlay, 328, 364
removing, 330
Satin, 326
storing as layer style, 331
Stroke, 329
layer groups
changing blending mode or opacity for, 118
creating, 114–115
deleting or disbanding, 116
duplicating, 111
flipping, 117
hiding and showing, 121
locking, 119
moving layers out of or between, 115
moving manually, 117
renaming, 115
selecting with Move tool, 113
transforming, 310–311
Layer Mask Display Options dialog, 303
layer masks
adjusting density of, 304–305, 366
applying or deleting, 307
blending with, 154–155, 160
creating, 302
deactivating temporarily, 307
display options for, 303
duplicating, 306
editing, 303–305
editing adjustment, 181
feathering, 304–305

inverting black and white areas of, 304

keyboard shortcuts for, 181

limiting effect of tonal adjustments with, 180

loading as selections, 306

modifying edges of, 304

moving separately from layer, 150, 160, 306

reshaping, 303

type selections in, 364, 365

using with Lens Blur filter, 265–266, 267

layers, 109–122, 297–316. *See also* adjustment layers; Background; fill layers; layer groups

adding to layer group, 115

aligning, 117, 164

assigning color labels to, 119

choosing blending modes for, 118, 198–202, 298–301

blending duplicate with original, 299

clipping adjustment effect to, 178

clipping masks and, 308, 364

compositing via layer masks, 154–155

converting Background into, and vice versa, 112

converting to grayscale, 206–207

copying and merging, 121

copying between files, 151–153

creating, 109–111

creating from Background, 112,

defined, 91, 109

deleting, 116

desaturating, 206–210

distributing, 164

dragging/dropping between windows, 152–153

duplicating, 111

erasing on, 231–232

file formats that preserve, 29

filling with history state or snapshot, 174

flattening, 122

flipping, 117

forming groups from existing, 114

hiding and showing, 116, 121

history of visibility changes for, 166

layer comps and, 384–386

linking, 309, 325

locking, 119

merging, 120–121

modifying blending options for, 300–301

moving, 117, 162

opacity, fill settings for, 118, 297

preserving or flattening, 110

renaming, 115

restacking, 114

restoring detail after blurring, 287

sampling all, 282, 283

screening back, 188

selecting, 113, 123

Smart Object, 121, 314–316

TIFF files with preserved, 110, 417

transforming, 310–313

turning selected pixels into, 111

type, 351, 352–353

using layer masks, 302

warping, 313

working with from Layers panel, 91

Layers panel. *See also* layers

about, 91

changing blending mode and opacity, 118

choosing blending mode from, 118, 298–299

context menus on, 115

editing adjustment layer settings on, 177

exposure adjustments using, 261

flipping layers from, 117

illustrated, 91, 109

kerning and tracking from, 357

locking layers and layer groups, 119

locking transparent pixels via, 118

selecting layers from, 113

showing Motion Blur filter and Smart Object layer in, 269

thumbnail options for, 119

versatile options of context menu for, 115

Layer Style dialog

applying layer effects from, 317

illustrated, 318

modifying blending options in, 300–301

layer styles

applying, 331

creating and saving, 332

defined, 331

removing, from layer, 332

Layer Via Copy, Cut commands, 111, 149

LCD displays, 7

leading for type, 358

Lens Blur filter, 265–267

Lens Correction filter, 272–273

Levels adjustment layer

for a darkening vignette, 271

for Auto Color Correction, 214–215

for color adjustments, 216–217

for screening back type, 367

for tonal adjustments, 186–188,

libraries

loading preset, 403

location for user-created presets, 402

saving all presets on picker as, 403

swatches, 196

lighten blending modes, 198, 200

Lighting Effects filter, 262–264

linear mode

defined, 166

history states and, 167

illustrated, 165

linking

layer effects to layer, 315

layers, 309

Liquify filter, 336

loading

pattern libraries, 204

preset libraries, 403

swatch libraries, 196

location

matching for multiple documents, 66

plug-in folder, 396

presets, 402

locking/unlocking

layers and layer groups, 119

ruler guides, 163

transparent pixels, 118

M

Mac OS computers

calibration utility for, 7

compatible Photoshop file formats for, 19

file extension preferences for, 392

hiding Application frame in, 61

launching Photoshop in, 1

printing file from, 412

showing Application frame in, 62

ZIP compression from, 419

Magic Eraser tool, 232

Magic Wand tool, 128–129

marquees
  constraining proportions of, 106
  crop, 103–107
  hiding and showing selection, 137
  moving and transforming
    selection, 136
  Rectangular and Elliptical
    selection, 124
masks. *See also* layer masks; Quick Mask
  adjustment layer, 180–181
  clipping, 308, 364
  creating in Quick Mask mode, 143
  creating via Adjustment Brush in
    Camera Raw, 252–253
  creating via Masks panel, 302
  filter, 337, 338
  gradient, 370, 371
  layer, 302–307
  reshaping alpha channel, 141
  Smart Filter, 270
Masks panel
  about, 92
  applying or deleting mask using, 307
  creating layer mask using, 302
  deactivating mask using, 307
  illustrated, 92, 302
  loading mask as selection using, 307
  measure with Ruler tool, 164
  modifying masks using, 304–305, 366
Match Color command, 280–281
Match Zoom, Match Location, 66
measure with Ruler tool, 164
megapixels
  cameras and, 20
  resolution and, 25
memory usage preferences, 393
Menu bar, 61
menus. *See also* submenus
  context, 78, 115
  customizing, 72–73
merging layers
  adjustment layers, 179
  grouping layers into Smart Object
    layer vs., 121
  options for, 120–121
  using Smart Object layers vs., 315
merging photos, 158–159
metadata
  listed in Status bar, 31
  selecting for display (Bridge), 45
  setting Bridge preferences for, 399

Metadata panel (Bridge)
  displaying, 36, 37
  information in, 31, 399
  placard on, 40
minimizing/maximizing
  Application frame, 62
  panels, 70
Mode submenu, 3
Monitor RGB color space, 10
monitors. *See* displays
Motion Blur filter, 268–269
Move tool
  copying layers using, 151–153
  copying selections using, 146–147
  moving layer or layer mask
    using, 306
  moving selection content using, 145
  scaling type using, 356
  selecting layer or layer group
    using, 113
  transforming layers and layer groups
    using, 152, 312
  transforming point type using, 362
moving
  files via Bridge, 47
  layer content, 117, 162
  layer content separate from
    mask, 306
  layer effects, 330
  layer masks, 150, 306
  linked layers in documents, 309
  magnified image in document
    window, 66
  selection contents, 145
  selection marquees, 136
  thumbnail stacks (Bridge), 50–51

N
navigation controls in Bridge, 40
Navigator panel
  about, 93
  changing zoom level using, 66
  moving image using, 66
New dialog, 24–26
New Document Preset dialog, 26
New Layer Comp dialog, 90
New Layer dialog, 112
New Snapshot dialog, 170
New Workspace dialog, 47
noise, reducing (Camera Raw), 250
non-Web-safe icon, 192

O
On-Image Adjustment tool, 206, 213,
  219, 220
opacity
  brush stroke, 227
  changing for layer, 118, 297
  changing for Quick Mask, 143
  changing via Layer Style dialog, 300
  editing for gradient preset, 373
  Fill command, 316
  Layers panel Fill setting vs., 297, 319
  making tonal adjustments with, 180
  shortcuts for changing, 224
Open command, 56
OpenGL features, 67, 393
opening
  Camera Raw images as Smart
    Objects, 256
  Character panel, 357
  files from Bridge into Photoshop, 44
  images into Camera Raw, 236–237,
    255
  JPEG files into Camera Raw, 236
  multiple photos simultaneously into
    Camera Raw, 254
  PDF or Illustrator file as new
    document, 58–59
  recent files, 44
optimizing files. *See* Web Output
Options bar
  Alignment buttons on, 352, 353
  Brush tool, 223–224
  Custom Shape tool, 378
  Gradient tool, 371
  illustrated, 61
  scaling type from, 356
  Transform command features on, 312
  type features on, 352
  using, 76, 352–353
Options for Thumbnail Quality
  (Bridge), 41
orientation
  for printing, 406
  of type, 360
Outer Glow layer effect, 322
out-of-gamut icon, 2, 192
output. *See* inkjet printers; printing;
  Web output
Output Preview panel (Bridge),
  380–381, 383
overexposure. *See* exposure

P

Page Setup dialog, 406

painting
borders, 376–377
cursor preferences, 394
image on white background, 376
on adjustment layer mask, 181
on layer mask, 303
Quick Mask, 143
with Brush tool, 223–224

panels. *See also* Bridge *and specific panels*
changing values in, 77
closing, 70
configuring, 69–71
deleting presets from, 402
groups, 70–71
hiding and showing, 69–70
icons for, 78
illustrated, 80–96
making free floating, 71
preferences for, 390
resizing, 71
restoring default presets to, 403

panes in Bridge, 36, 37, 46

panoramas
layout options in Photomerge for, 159
shooting photos for, 158

PANTONE color matching system, 193

Paragraph panel
about, 93
units of measure for, 359
using, 361

paragraph type
about, 352
choosing paragraph settings for, 361
converting to point type, and vice versa, 355
creating, 352

pasting
copied selections, 148–149
Illustrator art into Photoshop, 59
into selections, 150

Patch tool, 290, 294

Paths panel, 94

Pattern Fill dialog, 204

Pattern Overlay layer effect, 328, 364

PDF files
creating presentation from layer comps, 386

opening as new Photoshop documents, 58–59
packaging as PDF presentation, 382–383
placing into Photoshop image, 27
preserving layers with, 110
saving documents as, 420

PDF presentation, 382–383, 386

Performance preferences, 393

perspective transformations
using for layers and layer groups, 311
vertical and horizontal, 273

Photo Downloader
downloading photos with, 34–35
preference for launching, 398

Photo Filter adjustment layer, 260

Photomerge command, 158–159

photos. *See* images

Photoshop
color models available in, 2
creating documents for, 24–25
enabling OpenGL features for, 67
exiting/quitting, 32
host for Camera Raw, 236
launching, 1
opening files from Bridge into, 44
preparing files for export, 415–416
Preset Manager for, 400–401
resetting all preferences for, 387
selecting color space for, 10–11
syncing color with other programs, 12

Photoshop Raw format, 233

Photoshop Settings file, 387

picker
Brush Preset, 84, 223
Contour Preset, 329
Custom Shape Preset, 378–379
deleting preset from, 402
Gradient Preset, 369, 371
Pattern Preset, 204
restoring default presets to, 403
saving all presets as library, 403

Pixelate filters, 344

pixel count
changing in Image Size dialog, 99–100
defined, 97
effect of image size and resolution on, 101

resampling image to increase, 99, 100

pixels. *See also* pixel count
cropping, 103–107
defined, 2, 97
deleting selected, 135
erasing, 231–232
histograms of clipped, 185
locking transparent, 118
outside live canvas area, 103, 149
rasterizing type into, 364
replacing color for contiguous/discontiguous, 288, 289
turning selection of into layer, 111

pixels per inch (ppi), 22

Place command
creating Smart Object via, 256, 314
for EPS files, 59
importing Illustrator files via, 27, 355
importing PDF files via, 27
importing Photoshop files into Illustrator via, 416

Place PDF dialog, 27

plug-ins. *See also* Camera Raw
for creating frames, 377
missing, 60
setting location for, 396

Plug-ins preferences, 396

point type
about, 352
converting to paragraph type, and vice versa, 355
creating, 352
transforming with Move tool, 362

Polygonal Lasso tool, 125

pop-up sliders, 77

Posterize adjustment layer, 183

ppi (pixels per inch), 22

Preferences (Bridge), 398–399
Appearance, 44
opening, 387
resetting all preferences, 387

Preferences (Photoshop)
Cursors, 394
File Handling, 392, 419
General, 388–389
Guides, Grid & Slices, 396
Interface, 390–391
maximum number of history states, 166
opening, 387

Preferences *(continued)*
opening photos into Camera Raw, 236
Performance, 393
Plug-ins, 396
resetting all preferences, 387
setting document resolution, 26
Tool Tips, 82
Transparency & Gamut, 394
Type options, 397
Units & Rulers, 395
prepress preparation, 413–414
Preset Manager, 400–401
presets. *See also* brush presets, picker
Camera Raw, 251
color setting, 12
creating, 402
default location for storing, 402
deleting, 400, 402
document, 26
gradient, 372–373
loading library of, 403
optimization, 426
Preset Manager, 400–401
renaming, 401
replacing, 401
restoring default, 401, 403
saving adjustment settings as, 178–179
saving, resetting, or replacing, 401
saving to library, 401, 403
tool, 379, 404
Type tool, 358
using multiple adjustment, 180
watermarks saved as, 379
previewing
brush presets, 226
filter effects, 335
images in Bridge, 40–43
optimized files, 422
raw photos (Camera Raw), 237
Print dialog
Mac OS, 412
Photoshop, 407–409
Windows, 411
printer profiles, 14–15, 408
printing, 405–414. *See also* inkjet printers
16-bit images, 410
choosing color library for, 193
duotone, 413

file preparation for commercial, 413–414
files from Mac OS, 412
files from Windows, 411
output options for, 410
pixel count needed for, 97–101
preparing a file for inkjet, 406–409
resolution for, 22
process colors, 192–193
proofing colors onscreen, 17–18
Properties/Page Setup dialog, 406
PSB files, 19, 25, 29
PSD files, 19, 28–29, 419
purging cache files (Bridge), 56, 399

Q
QuarkXPress, exporting to, 415–416
Quick Mask, 142–145
options for, 143
painting a, 143
previewing selections with, 132
reshaping selection with, 142
switching color of, 143
Quick Selection tool, 126–127
Quitting Photoshop, 32

R
Rasterize EPS Format dialog, 59
rasterizing
Smart Object layer, 316
type, 351, 364
ratings (Bridge)
applying to thumbnails, 48
sorting images by, 49
raw files. *See also* Camera Raw
advantages of, 233–235
defined, 20, 233
JPEG vs., 235
opening as Smart Objects, 256
opening into Camera Raw, 237
opening into Photoshop, 255
saving, 255
sidecar files, 233
synchronizing settings for multiple, 254
Rectangular Marquee tool, 124, 138, 375
rectangular selections, 124
Red Eye tool, 296
Refine Edge dialog
Feather option in, 146

keyboard shortcuts for, 132
refine selection edges using, 132–134
Refine Mask dialog, 304
registration marks, 410
rejected thumbnails (Bridge), 48–49
removing
Adjustment Brush edits (Camera Raw), 253
filter effects, 334
layer effects, 330
ruler guides, 163
thumbnails from stacks (Bridge), 51
renaming
color swatches, 195
files, 51–52
gradient presets, 373
layers and layer groups, 115
presets, 401
Render filters, 344
rendering intents for soft proofs, 18
repairing photos, 279, 294–295
repeating last transformation, 311
Replace Color command, 284–286
Replace Contents command, 315
replacing
layer effects, 330
layer styles, 331
presets, 401
Smart Object content, 315
swatches library, 196
resampling
adjusting resolution and, 98, 99
defined, 97
during multiple transformations, 313
images, 98–100
scanned images for printing, 100
reselecting last selection, 135
resetting
adjustment layers, 178
all preferences for Photoshop and Bridge, 387
Bridge workspaces, 47
canvas, 67
paragraphs, 361
presets, 401
tools, 79
reshaping
alpha channel masks, 141
layer masks, 150, 303
type bounding box, 362

resizing
  Camera Raw images, 241
  canvas area, 102, 105
  dock and panels, 71
  image by cropping, 104
  images, 98–100
  scanned images, 99, 100
resolution
  changing for file in Photoshop,
    98–100
  changing for photo in Camera
    Raw, 241
  defined, 22, 97
  document preset, 26
  effect on selections transferred
    between documents, 148
  image size and, 97–101
  print, 22
  resampling and adjustments
    to, 98, 99
  scanning, 23
  screen and print default, 26
  setting for new documents, 24
  Web output, 23, 100, 421
restacking
  filter effects, 337
  layers, 114
restoring
  Bridge workspaces, 47
  canvas angle, 67
  default Camera Raw settings, 242
  default presets to picker or
    panel, 403
  detail after using Surface Blur
    filter, 287
  layer comps, 385
  Photoshop workspace, 75
  saved brush preset settings, 229
retouching, 279–296
  cloning imagery for, 282–283
  color matching between documents,
    280–281
  color with brush, 288
  Healing Brush tool for, 290–292
  Patch tool for, 279, 294–295
  photos in Camera Raw, 241
  red eye, 296
  replacing colors, 284–286
  smoothing skin and surfaces, 287
  Spot Healing Brush tool for, 293
  Surface Blur filter for, 287

  tools for, 279
  whitening teeth or eyes, 286
Revert command, 29
Review Mode (Bridge), 43
RGB color mode
  about, 2–4
  for inkjet printing, 405
  for new document, 24
  for Web graphics, 196
RGB color model, 194
RGB color space, 5, 10–11
Rotate View tool, 67
rotating
  canvas view temporarily, 67
  clone source overlay, 157
  image, 108
  layers and layer groups, 310
rubylith. *See* masks
ruler guides, 163
ruler origin, 161
rulers
  setting units for, 161, 395
  showing and hiding, 161
Ruler tool,
  measuring distance or angle with,164
  straightening images with, 108

S

Samples folder, 1
sampling
  all layers, 282, 283
  colors with Eyedropper tool, 197
  options for Color Replacement
    tool, 288
Satin layer effect, 326
saturation
  blending mode, 202
  defined, 194
  HSL/Grayscale tab (Camera Raw),
    248–249
  Hue/Saturation adjustment layer, 213
  Replace Color command, 284
  Vibrance adjustment layer, 208–210
Save As dialog. *See* saving
Save for Web & Devices dialog,
  422–426
  creating GIF file via 423–424
  creating JPEG file via, 425–426
  previewing optimization settings
    in, 422
Save Settings dialog, 251

Save Workspaces dialog, 75
saving
  adjustment presets, 178–179
  brush presets, 228
  Camera Raw settings, 251
  color settings, 14
  custom shape preset, 379
  EPS files, 418–419
  flattened version of file, 28, 122
  GIF files, 423–424
  images via Camera Raw, 255
  JPEG files, 425–426
  new version of file, 30
  PDF files, 420
  preferences for, 392
  presets, 401, 403
  presets as library, 401, 403
  previously saved file, 29
  reverting to last version, 29
  selections as alpha channels, 139
  swatches as library, 196
  TIFF files, 417
  unsaved documents, 28
  workspaces, 74–75
scaling
  clone source overlay, 157
  layers and layer groups, 310
  scanned images, 23
  type, 356, 360
  type bounding box, 362
scanned images
  producing, 23
  resizing, 99, 100
scratch disk preferences, 393
scratched photos, repairing, 295
screen modes
  changing, 68
  preferences for, 390
screening back images, 188, 367
scrolling in multiple windows, 67
scrubby sliders, 77
searching for files (Bridge), 53
selections, 123–144
  anti-aliasing option for, 129
  Clipboard for transferring, 148
  Color Range command to create,
    130–131
  combining alpha channel with, 140
  creating layer from, 111
  creating on layer before applying
    filter, 338

selections *(continued)*

deleting selected pixels from, 135

deselecting and reselecting, 135

dragging and dropping between documents, 147

duplicating, 146

expanding, 134

feathering edges of, 124, 146

filling history state or snapshot with, 174

filling with solid color, 316

frame-shaped, 138

Grow command, 134

hiding/showing marquees for, 137

ignored by layer effects, 319

intersection of two, 138

inverting, 137

lasso tools, 125

layer-based, 123

limiting with localized color clusters option, 131

loading alpha channels as, 140

loading masks as, 306

Magic Wand tool, 128–129

methods compared, 144

Modify submenu commands vs. Refine Edge for, 134

moving contents of, 145

moving marquees for, 136

pasting into, 150

Quick Selection tool, 126–127

Rectangular and Elliptical Marquee tools, 124

Refine Edge dialog for, 132–134, 146

removing pixels from edges of, 148

reshaping via Quick Mask, 142

saving, 139

selecting type for editing, 354

Similar command, 134

transforming marquees for, 136

turning into silhouette, 129

Shadows/Highlights command, 258–259

sharpening

Detail tab in Camera Raw for, 250

filters for, 274–278

Smart Sharpen command, 275–276

Smart Sharpen vs. Unsharp Mask, 274

Unsharp Mask command, 277–278

shifting type from baseline, 359

shortcuts. *See* Keyboard shortcuts

showing. *See* hiding/showing

sidecar files, 233

silhouettes, 129

Similar command, 134

Sketch filters, 345–346

skewing layers and layer groups, 310

Smart Collections, 54–55

Smart Filters. *See also* Smart Objects

applying Motion Blur filter as, 268

blending options for, 337

creating, 336

creating selection before appying, 338

deleting, 337, 339

editing settings for, 336

hiding and showing, 337

masks for, 337

smart guides

aligning layers with, 117

moving layer using, 162

preferences for, 396

Smart Objects

about Smart Object layers, 91

applying filter to, 333, 336

creating and editing layers as, 314–315

grouping layers into Smart Object layer, 121

importing type from Illustrator as, 355

opening and placing Camera Raw files as, 256

rasterizing, 316

reclaiming Photoshop layers from, 315

replacing content with another file, 315

warping, 313

Smart Sharpen filter, 274, 275, 276

Smudge tool, 230

Snap feature

aligning Pattern Overlay effect with, 328

Document Bounds and, 105

using, 162

snapshots on History panel

creating, 170, 171

defined, 169

filling selection or layer with, 174

making documents from, 171

options for, 169

preserving layer comp vs., 385

source for History Brush tool, 173

soft proofing

color simulation for CMYK output, 18

simulating inkjet printer, 17

Solid Color fill layer, 205

sorting thumbnails (Bridge), 49

spectrophotometer, 7

spot color channels, type in, 368

spot colors, using, 193

Spot Healing Brush tool

blemish removal with, 293

compared with Healing Brush and Patch tools, 290

Spot Removal tool (Camera Raw), 241

spring-loading tools, 79

Spyder3Pro calibrator, 8–9

Standard Screen Mode, 68, 203, 390

Status bar

current document profile listed on, 16

file data on, 31

stitching photos together, 158–159

straight-edged selections, 125

straightening

images in Photoshop, 108

photos in Camera Raw, 240

Stroke layer effect, 329

Surface Blur filter, 287

styles

selecting type for changes in, 354

type, 359

Styles panel. *See also* layer styles

about, 94

applying layer styles using, 331

creating layer styles, 332

illustrated, 94, 331

Stylize filters, 347

Suite Color Settings dialog, 12

Surface Blur filter, 287

swatches, color

adding, deleting, and renaming, 195

auto color correction, 214

choosing, 195

loading library of, 196

restoring default, 196

saving library of, 196

Swatches panel, 95, 195–196

synchronizing

Camera Raw settings for multiple photos, 254

color settings, 12

T

tabs
  Camera Raw dialog, 237, 238
  docking document windows as, 63
  restoring document windows as, 64
teeth whitening, 286
temperature
  correction via Color Balance
    adjustment layer, 211–212
  correction via Photo Filter
    adjustment layer, 260
  values for white balance, 242–243
text. *See* type
texture
  adding to Bevel and Emboss layer
    effects, 325
  adding to brush strokes, 220, 228
  pattern fill layers for applying, 204
  preserving with Healing Brush tool,
    290–292
Texture filters, 348
Threshold adjustment layer, 182
Threshold mode, 187
thumbnails (Bridge)
  choosing preview quality for, 41
  comparing, 42
  examining with loupe, 42–43, 398
  filtering, 49
  full screen preview of, 42
  labeling and rating, 48
  metadata display with, 45
  preferences for, 398
  previewing, 40–43
  previewing in Review mode, 43
  sorting, 49
  stacks, 50–51
  Thumbnail Size slider, 37, 39, 46
TIFF files
  asking before saving layered, 392
  opening directly into Camera
    Raw, 236
  Photoshop features preserved
    with, 29
  preserving layers with, 110, 417
  saving documents as, 417
  working with in Camera Raw, 235
TIFF Options dialog, 417
tonal adjustments, 175–190. *See also*
  adjustment layers; histograms
  adjustment layers for, 175–176, 180
  Basic tab (Camera Raw), 238, 242–245

  Black & White, 206–207
  Brightness/Contrast, 189
  Camera Raw for, 244
  commands for applying, 175
  correcting light-to-dark balance, 186–187
  dodging and burning, 190
  HSL/Grayscale tab (Camera Raw),
    248–249
  Levels, 186–188, 216
  monitoring on Histogram panel,
    184–185
  Posterize, 183
  Shadows/Highlights, 257–259
  Smart Sharpen filter and, 274–275
  Threshold, 182
  Vibrance, 208–210
Tool Preset picker thumbnail, 79, 379
Tool Presets panel, 96, 379, 404
Tool Tips
  displaying, 82
  setting preference for, 390
  showing metadata via (Bridge), 45
tools. *See also* Options bar, Tools panel,
  and specific tools
  Camera Raw, 239
  choosing, 79
  choosing settings for, 76, 79, 96
  keyboard shortcuts for choosing, 79–82
  keyboard shortcuts to change
    settings for, 224
  on Tools panel, 80–82
  presets for, 404
  resetting, 79
  saving and reusing customized, 96
  showing Tool Tips for, 82
  spring-loading, 79
  used for selections, 144
Tools panel
  changing between single and
    double column, 80
  choosing tools from, 79
  illustrated, 80–82
  showing Tool Tips for, 82
tracking type, 357
transforming
  Drop Shadow layer effect, 321
  layers, 310–313
  multiple layers, 313
  selection marquees, 136
  tips for, 311
  type, 362

  using Free Transform command, 312
  vertical and horizontal
    perspective, 273
  warping layers, 313
  warping type, 363
transparency
  preserving for GIF files, 423–424
  saving for TIFF files, 417
  when exporting files to Adobe
    Illustrator, 416
Transparency & Gamut preferences, 394
transparent pixels
  checkerboard for, 118, 394
  locking, 118
Trim command, 106
type, 351–368. *See also* Character panel,
  layer effects, Paragraph panel
  applying paragraph settings to, 361
  converting point to paragraph, and
    vice versa, 355
  creating editable, 352–353
  editable versus rasterized, 351
  fading, 366
  fonts, 356
  filling with imagery, 364–365
  importing from Illustrator as Smart
    Object, 355
  kerning and tracking, 357
  leading, 358
  making wider or narrower, 360
  Options bar for, 352
  orientation of, 360
  Paragraph panel settings for, 361
  point vs. paragraph, 352
  preference settings for, 397
  rasterizing, 351, 364
  scaling, 356, 360
  screening back, 367
  selecting, 354
  shifting from baseline, 359
  spot color channels for, 368
  styles, 356, 359
  tool presets for, 358, 404
  transforming, 362
  units of measure for, 395
  using type shapes in layer mask, 365
  warping, 363
  watermarks, creating from, 379
Type preferences, 397
Type tools. *See* Horizontal Type tool;
  Vertical Type tool

U

underexposure. *See* exposure
Undo commands, 88
Units & Rulers preferences, 395
units of measure
  accepted by Character and
    Paragraph panels, 359
  choosing for Info panel, 89
  for document width and height, 24
  preferences and abbreviations
    for, 395
Unsharp Mask filter, 274, 277–278
updating
  Histogram panel, 184
  layer comps, 385
  open documents preference, 388

V

vector art in Photoshop, 27
Version Cue, 392
Vertical Type tool
  creating presets for, 358
  selecting characters, 354
  using, 351, 352, 353
Vibrance
  adjusting for raw files (Camera Raw),
    244, 245
  adjustment layer, 208–210
vignettes
  creating via Levels, 270–271
  creating via Masks panel, 375
  focusing interest with, 270
visibility. *See* hiding/showing

W

warning icons. *See also* alert dialogs
  Cached Data (Histogram panel), 184
  Clipping, 244
  color for Gamut Warning, 394
  layer comp, 385
  on Color Picker, 192
warping
  layers, 313
  type, 363
Warp Text dialog, 363
watercolor, 350
watermarks, 378–379
Web output, 421–426
  contact sheets for, 380
  copying colors as hexidecimals
    for, 197
  creating optimization preset for, 426

GIF files, 421, 423–424
image resolution for, 23, 421
JPEG files, 421, 425–426
non-Web-safe color, 192
optimizing files for, 421–426
previewing optimized files for, 422
RGB color model for, 195, 196
saving files for, 421–426
saving PDF presentation for, 382
white balance (Camera Raw), 242–243
white point data, 7
windows. *See* document windows
Windows computers
  file extension preferences for, 392
  launching Photoshop in, 1
  Photoshop file formats for, 19
  printing files from, 411
  ZIP compression on, 419
Workflow Options (Camera Raw), 241
workspace, 61–76. *See also* Bridge
  Application bar, 76
  arranging document windows in, 64
  changing color surrounding
    image, 69
  configuring panels, 69–71
  customizing menus for, 72–73
  deleting custom, 75
  hiding Application frame for, 61
  Options bar, 76
  preferences for, 390
  restoring default, 75
  saving custom, 74–75
  screen modes for, 68
  tabbed document windows, 63
  zooming in and out in, 65–67

Z

zooming
  animated, 67
  in Camera Raw, 239
  methods for, 65–67
  Navigator panel for, 66
  preferences for, 388
  shortcuts for, 65

Photography credits

Shutterstock.com
Photographs on the following pages © ShutterStock.com

pp. 1, 32, 93, 131, 149, 304, 305, Ultimathule

pp. 63, 68, 69, Sarit Saliman

p. 67, Marc Goff

p. 99, Pichugin Dmitry

pp. 101, 109, 177, 178, Igor Dutina

pp. 102, 107, Ajt

pp. 103–106, Jason Stitt

pp. 109, 153, 178, 252, 253, Laurin Rinder

pp. 123, 313, 394, Nicole Waring

pp. 124, 135, 205, 365, Galina Barskaya

p. 125, Elke Dennis

pp. 125, 210, 341–348, Magdalena Bujak

pp. 126, 127, 133, 136 , Karin Lau

pp. 128, 129, Robert Sarosiek

pp. 130, 131, 138, Steve Maehl

p. 134, Chen Heng Kong

pp. 134, 137, 139, 140, 302, 303, 306, Dhoxax

pp. 135, 199, 200, 315, 369, 374, Radovan

p. 139, Lars Madsen

pp. 141, 142, 269, Lario Tus

p. 143, 154, Taolmor

pp. 145, 154, 160, 162, Alexander Gitlits

pp. 145, 156, 163, 186, 187, 246
247, 371, 376, 377, Styve Reineck

p. 146, Bobby Deal/RealDealPhoto

pp. 146, 282, 283, Miranda Zeegers

p. 147, Raymond Kasprzak

pp. 150, 151, Lois M. Kosch

p. 152, Kristian Peetz

pp. 154, 155, 156, Faberfoto

p. 154, Doug Stacey

pp. 154, 162, Jarno Gonzalez Zarraonandia

pp. 154, 377, Kheng Guan Toh

p. 154, Zdorov Kirill Vladimirovich

pp. 161, 162, 204, 377, Vera Bogaerts

p. 180, Dario Diament

p. 189, Suzanne Tucker

pp. 191, 198–202, 209, 213, 265, 270, 271,
Liv Friis-larsen

p. 197, Andrew F. Kazmierski

p. 208, Tootles

pp. 211, 212, Laura Frenkel

p. 230, Afaizal

p. 231, Rohit Seth

p. 243, Robert Kyllo

p. 260, Keith Levit

pp. 262, 264, 298, Brian Stewart-Coxon

pp. 266, 267, Maria Weidner

pp. 275, 276, 286, 292, Zina Seletskaya

pp. 279, 287, Nick Stubbs

pp. 279, 294, Photobank.ch

pp. 290–293, Franck Camhi

p. 299, Linda Bucklin

pp. 299, 301, Gina Smith

pp. 320, 321, Timothy Large

pp. 322, 323, Samsonov Juri

pp. 358, 360, Beat Glauser

p. 370, Gilmanshin

p. 371, Alfio Ferlito

p. 383, Adrian Moisei

Photos.com
Photographs on the following pages
© 2007 JupiterImages.com

pp. 165, 172, 173, 174, 183, 203, 206, 207, 214,
215, 232, 277, 278, 280, 284, 285, 289, 310,
312, 333, 335, 338, 339, 340, 362

PhotoDisc (Getty Images) Gettyimages.com
Photographs on the following pages © PhotoDisc

pp. 22, 279, 295

Other photographs
pp. 407, 410, 422, 424, 425, 426 © Victor Gavenda

All other photographs © Elaine Weinmann and
Peter Lourekas

pp. 77, 349 © Elaine Weinmann, access to garden
courtesy firstbornmultimedia.com

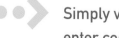